Gabriele Dietze, Julia Roth (eds.)
Right-Wing Populism and Gender

Gender Studies

In memory of Toni Morrison (1931-2019)

Gabriele Dietze (PD Dr.) has taught Cultural, Media and Gender Studies at Humboldt University, Berlin, as well as in Austria, Switzerland and the US. Currently she is Harris Guest Professor at Dartmouth 2020. Her research focuses on race, migration, and populism.

Julia Roth (Prof. Dr.) is a professor for American Studies with a focus on Gender Studies at Bielefeld University. She was post-doc of the BMBF-sponsored research networks »desi-guALdades.net« at Freie Universität Berlin and »The Americas as Space of Entanglements« at Bielefeld University, lecturer at Humboldt University Berlin, Potsdam University and the Universidad de Guadalajara, Mexico. Her research focuses on intersectionality, citizenship, gender and global inequalities, right-wing populism, as well as gender and social movements in transnational contexts with focus on the Americas.

Gabriele Dietze, Julia Roth (eds.)
Right-Wing Populism and Gender
European Perspectives and Beyond

[transcript]

Bibliographic information published by the Deutsche Nationalbibliothek
The Deutsche Nationalbibliothek lists this publication in the Deutsche Nationalbibliografie; detailed bibliographic data are available in the Internet at http://dnb.d-nb.de

© 2020 transcript Verlag, Bielefeld

All rights reserved. No part of this book may be reprinted or reproduced or utilized in any form or by any electronic, mechanical, or other means, now known or hereafter invented, including photocopying and recording, or in any information storage or retrieval system, without permission in writing from the publisher.

Cover layout: Maria Arndt, Bielefeld
Proofread by Mirjam Galley, Bielefeld; Sophie Hanisch, Bielefeld

Print-ISBN 978-3-8376-4980-2
PDF-ISBN 978-3-8394-4980-6

Contents

Right-Wing Populism and Gender: A Preliminary Cartography of an Emergent Field of Research
Gabriele Dietze and Julia Roth 7

Authoritarian Right-Wing Populism as Masculinist Identity Politics. The Role of Affects
Birgit Sauer 23

Why Gender and Sexuality are both Trivial and Pivotal in Populist Radical Right Politics
Niels Spierings 41

Sexual Politics from the Right. Attacks on Gender, Sexual Diversity, and Sex Education
Imke Schmincke 59

Post-Socialist Conditions and the Orbán Government's Gender Politics between 2010 and 2019 in Hungary
Eszter Kováts 75

Man, Woman, Family. Gender and the Limited Modernization of Right-Wing Extremism in Austria
Stefanie Mayer, Edma Ajanović, Birgit Sauer 101

Sexual Politics as a Tool to "Un-Demonize" Right-Wing Discourses in France
Cornelia Möser 117

Identitarian Gays and Threatening Queers, Or: How the Far Right Constructs New Chains of Equivalence
Patrick Wielowiejski 135

Why Are Women Attracted to Right-Wing Populism?
Sexual Exceptionalism, Emancipation Fatigue, and New Maternalism
Gabriele Dietze 147

Populist Mobilizations in Re-Traditionalized Society:
Anti-Gender Campaigning in Slovenia
Roman Kuhar, Mojca Pajnik 167

'You're Fired!' Retrotopian Desire and Right-Wing Class Politics
Simon Schleusener 185

The *Alternative Right*, Masculinities, and Ordinary Affect
Simon Strick 207

Angry Women: Poland's *Black Protests* as 'Populist Feminism'
Agnieszka Graff 231

Intersectionality Strikes Back: Right-Wing Patterns of En-Gendering and Feminist Contestations in the Americas
Julia Roth 251

Acknowledgements 273

List of image sources 275

Authors 279

Right-Wing Populism and Gender: A Preliminary Cartography of an Emergent Field of Research

Gabriele Dietze and Julia Roth

Borrowing from Marx, we start our introductory remarks with the first words of the Communist Manifesto, 'A specter is haunting Europe': the specter of right-wing populism. This specter looks different everywhere, and it is also at home in other parts of the world, for example in the Americas, in India, in the Philippines. Some features appear in almost all places that are haunted by it: nativist ethnonationalism (Betz 2001), hostility towards elites (Canovan 1999), anti-pluralism (Müller 2017), or the opposition to immigration (Rydgren 2008). Other spectral attributes are context-specific: in Hungary, the government has closed down universities and abolished gender studies programs to impede 'foreign' influences; in Brazil, indigenous communities are expelled from their reclaimed land and excluded from political power; and the current US president wants to build a wall at the country's southern border as a protection against 'Mexican rapists.' Due to this oscillation of content and the lack of a consistent program, populism has been conceptualized as a 'thin centered ideology' (Mudde/Kaltwasser 2017: 6), to which diverse projects, convictions, and attitudes can cling and connect.

In any case, a common feature can be observed in all current versions of right-wing populism: an 'obsession with gender' and sexuality in different arenas. Populist actors conjure up the heteronormative nuclear family as the model of social organization, attack reproductive rights, question sex education, criticize a so-called 'gender ideology,' reject same-sex marriage and seek to re-install biologically understood binary gender differences. Although this 'obsession with gender' has become an omnipresent mark in right-wing discourse, canonical research has rarely addressed this aspect, nor has gender been considered as one of the major attributes for the attractiveness of populism. Rather, the success of right-wing populism is usually attributed and reduced to economic, nationalistic, or culturalist reasons and motivations (Brubaker 2017; Gidron/Hall 2017; Norris/Inglehart 2019) and seen as unrelated to gender. The Oxford Handbook of Populism's entry on Gender still argues that gender is not central to right-wing populism; however, the connection between the two is described as, admittedly, 'largely understudied' (Abi-Hassan 2017: 1).

By contrast, the authors of this collection assume that analyzing the increase and persuasiveness of right-wing populist tendencies is not possible without a gender perspective. Furthermore, we claim that an approach that encompasses gender as a social construction, as a social practice, as an axis of inequality, and as a link to the economic developments of neo-liberal globalization, poverty, and structural racism, is indispensable for understanding the political shift to the right. Consequently, an important dimension of right-wing populism research, for us, is the observation that populism is not only concerned with gender as an issue itself but also with gender as a meta-language for negotiating different conditions of inequality and power in the context of current struggles over hegemony, and over resources forged by neoliberalism.

Given that in the meantime numerous different modes of political objectives and utterances have by now been assembled under the umbrella term 'right-wing populism,' it seems productive to expand and elaborate on the concept. The essays assembled in this volume thus relate right-wing populism not only to parties, movements, or organizations, but also to media discourses, narratives, and forms of action. Therefore, the editors of this volume suggest to speak of a right-wing populist complex. Our notion of a 'complex' contains the older – but in many ways similar – phenomenon of right-wing extremism, as the chapter by Edma Ajanović, Stefanie Mayer, and Birgit Sauer shows. Furthermore, speaking of a right-wing populist complex also enables us to include religious fundamentalisms and formations of Catholicism as demonstrated by the contributions by Agnieszka Graff, Imke Schmincke, Cornelia Möser, and Roman Kuhar and Mojca Pajnik. Neither do we want to leave out certain fractions of mainstream feminism called 'Femonationalism' that partake in the stigmatization of male Muslim migrants – see the article by Niels Spierings – and refugees as a sexual threat to 'autochthonous' women (Hark/Villa 2017), discussed in the contributions by Julia Roth and Gabriele Dietze. And finally, it would be impossible to omit parts of the liberal bourgeois camp that have shifted from the middle ground to the right (Zick et. al. 2019) via their polemics against 'genderism' or and an alleged 'censorship.'

A strong anti-gender sentiment is also pervasive in populist regimes in Latin America and parts of Eastern Europe, where a 'gender ideology' is perceived as a form of 'ideological colonization' pushed by Western decadent liberal voices from the EU and NGOs, who impose their thus-perceived ill-advised emancipation programs on poorer countries (Korolczuk/Graff 2018). The latter strand of politics is addressed in the essays by Roman Kuhar and Mojca Pajnik, Agnieszka Graff, and Eva Kováts. Additionally, we observe an appropriation of identity politics and some sort of 'reverse anti-colonialism' (see Roth's contribution), according to which the victim's perspective is reclaimed by structurally hegemonic speakers. The latter is particularly obvious in the case of extreme right-wing masculinist actors on the internet (such as online networks and producers), who are intensely hostile to gender issues, as Simon Strick's contribution illustrates.

The notion of a right-wing populist 'complex' allows us to connect different narratives relating to gender to various fields of inquiry. Thus, the chapters not only focus on actors or formations of the right-wing populist complex but also on the intersections of gender with other categories of social stratification such as race, ethnicity, class and religion. Hence, gender issues are structurally connected to globalization and the effects of gendered neoliberal transformations and encompass the question of pay and breadwinning as well as the international division of labor. The ways in which right-wing agents orchestrate the current shift to the right by the evocation of strong feelings provide a further important field of inquiry. Ruth Wodak, for instance, calls such affective strategies a Politics of Fear (Wodak 2015). Congruously, we add the crucial arenas of affect and emotion to the categories of gender, race, and class as the usual aspects of intersectional investigation. Because we think that sexuality is of major importance and plays a central role for mobilizing affects, we address this dimension separately (especially in the contributions by Patrick Wielowiejski, Möser, Schmincke, and Dietze).

Fields of Inquiry – Emergent Research

Although the field of inquiry 'right-wing populism and gender' is only just now beginning to emerge, we can draw on a number of pioneer publications: the special issue "Gender and the Populist Radical Right Politics" of the journal Patterns of Prejudice (Spierings et al. 2015) and the groundbreaking anthology Gender and Far Right Politics in Europe (Bitzan/Kötting 2017) as well as Birgit Sauer's fundamental essay "Gesellschaftstheoretische Überlegungen zum europäischen Rechtspopulismus. Zum Erklärungspotenzial der Kategorie Geschlecht" (Social-theoretical Thoughts on European Right-Wing Populism: On the Explanatory Potential of the Category Gender , in English) promotes a gender perspective for research on right-wing populism (Sauer 2017); Sauer pursues this perspective also in her contribution to this volume. In addition, special issues of gender-theoretical journals have lately been published on specific topics of right-wing populism.[1]

Feminist research has been dealing with women in the extreme right since early on, e.g. with women from the far-right in the KuKluxKlan (Blee 2008) or in

---

1   Internationally, special issues appeared in Signs (Spring 2019, vol. 44 no. 3, on 'Gender and the Rise of the Global Right') and Women's Studies International Forum (May-June 2018, vol. 68, on 'Feminisms in Times of Anti-Genderism, Racism and Austerity'), and Feministische Studien (Nov. 2018, vol. 36, no. 2, on the normalization of neo-reactionary policies).

a global perspective (Bacchetta/Power 2013), as well as in extremist parties (Amesberger/Halbmayr 2002; Birsl 2013; Bitzan 2017). We can further draw on a number of regional studies of particular national contexts on right-wing populism and gender,[2] as well as on the Pan-European study on right-wing women, Triumph of the Women (Gutsche 2018a), by the German Friedrich Ebert Foundation.[3] Recent research indicates that 'anti-genderism' is not only a major issue for right-wing populism (Hark/Villa 2015; Brandini-Aissis/Ogando 2018), but that it can be seen as a wide-spread phenomenon (Kuhar/Paternotte 2017; Gunnarsson Payne 2019), and that the fight against 'gender-ideology' is a potential tool to construct the totalitarian idea of 'people-as-one' (Salcel 2004: 96).

The emergent field of research on right-wing populism and gender has a strong affinity with the already established research on masculinity related to the subject (Norocel 2010; Erzeel/Rashkova 2017; Kimmel 2017; Mudde/Kaltwasser 2015). The chapters by Simon Schleusener, Sauer, and Strick pursue this dimension. Here, the relationship of patriarchal gender relations and capitalist socialization and subjectivization is central, as it had formerly been discussed in feminist research as 'capitalist patriarchy' (Eisenstein 1979), 'neopatriarchy,' (Campbell 2014) and in reflections on 'colonial patriarchy' (Lugones 2012).

The recent victory of capitalist market mechanisms in almost all areas of daily life has also resulted in a 'neoliberal equality' of well-educated women (see the articles by Schleusener and Dietze), which is one of the economic premises of 'femonationalisms' (Farris 2017) and neoliberal feminisms (Rottenberg 2014; Fraser 2016; Banet-Weiser et al. 2019). In contrast to such 'toxic feminisms' (Thelandersson 2014; Hark/Villa 2017), intersectional constellations of feminisms – that is, feminisms dedicated to the structural and inseparable entanglements of different axes of oppression and inequalities such as race, class, and gender – which practice a variety of forms of resistance against White mainstream feminisms, who often side with right-wingers in their anti-immigration stance. Intersectional feminists provide platforms against right-wing populism in the U.S. (Hess 2017; Draper/Mason-Deese 2018), in Latin America (Bidaseca/Loi 2017), and Europe (Wizorek 2014; Hark/Villa 2017), as the article by Roth illustrates.

Additionally, we want to emphasize the neoliberal revolution as a central backdrop of the right-wing populist complex and thus as one relevant field of research.

---

2   See for example from the Netherlands: de Lange; Mügge, 2015, 61-80; Scandinavia: Akkerman; Hagelund, 2007, 197-214; Meret; Siim, 2013, 78-96; Norocel, 2010, 170-183; Italy: Farris, 2017, and for France: Mayer, 2015, 391-414; Morgan, 2017, 887-906; Scrinzi, 2017, 87-101.

3   The study is also published in German: Gutsche, 2018b, Both, the English and the German version can be found online as pdf files: library.fes.de/pdf-files/dialog/14636.pdf; https://library.fes.de/pdf-files/dialog/14630.pdf. For an overview of German-language research on right-wing populism and gender, see Lang, 2018b, 147-161; Lang, 2018a; Fritzsche, 2018, 335-346 and FE.IN, 2019.

Related critical gender-sensitive research (Brown 2015; Duggan 2003, Fraser 2012) is therefore of great importance for any consideration of right-wing populism and gender. The economization and commodification of many areas of life, the erosion of the welfare state, the shift from solidarity to individual responsibility for oneself (the referral back to the family as agency of care, i.e. mostly to women), the associated global financial crises and the redistribution of social wealth, have an immense impact on the gender order (Lombardo et al. 2009), as the contributions of Schleusener and Sauer emphasize.

In particular, the gendered (or sexual) division of labor is gaining new importance – locally within families, and globally in the form of global care chains through which the care work of women in wealthier countries (who are integrated into the labor market) is 'outsourced' to women from mostly poorer regions. Meanwhile, the unequal division of labor between men and women at home remains largely untouched (Ehrenreich/Hochschild 2003). So far, approaches critical of neoliberalism with a gender focus (Dörre et al. 2006; Beier et al. 2018; Pühl/Sauer 2018) have hardly been combined with or applied to the right-wing populist complex (with the exception of Sauer). Conversely, existing studies of the right-wing populist complex that emphasize economic aspects mostly operate without a gender perspective (Schwander/Manow 2017; Rodrik 2018). We think that a gender perspective will shift the focus to one of the central fields of mobilization for the right and thus allow us to analyze the different effects that precarization has on male and female employment, on the gendered division of labor in families and on care work (Wichterich 2000).

Instead of addressing economic or political structures to explain current wrongs, right-wing populists claim that injustices and inequalities result from the success of liberal accomplishments that allegedly led to the rise of an undeserving elite whilst de-privileging the thus-perceived more deserving members of the White middle and lower classes, as the contributions by Spierings, Eszter Kováts, and Simon Strick show. Right-wing populists use this strategy to blame the achievements of emancipatory movements such as feminism or gay liberation for their followers' feeling of social insecurity.

Finally, a central dimension for the analysis of how the right-wing populist complex works is the examination of affects and emotions (Ahmed 2004; Wodak 2015; Rico/Guinjoan 2017). The fields of gender, family, and sexual politics are heavily loaded with emotions – fears, passions, impulses to protect – which right-wing populist actors trigger and transfer into affective patterns: in the 'crusades' against homosexual educators and the adoption of children by gay couples (see the contribution by Wielowiejski), for instance, the need to contain sexuality in the safe space of the heteronormative family is particularly evident. Likewise, early sex education is attacked with the same arguments, as Möser and Schmincke explain for the French and German campaigns, such as Manif pour tous or Demo für alle, respectively. As Sauer's contribution shows, emotional patterns beyond sexuality lead to new forms of 'affective citizenship.' Patterns such as 'concern' – think of the many 'concerned citizens' (besorgte Bürger, in German) in right-wing populist propaganda – or anger, counting as male virtues that are cultivated as legitimate 'political feelings' in right-wing populism. Kovát's contribution illustrates how such patterns work in the Hungarian context, where feelings of hatred towards allegedly dangerous foreigners and feminists are kindled and supported by the government.

Right-wing populists often manage to mobilize particular features of shared affects. The anthropologist Arlie Hochschild has recently described the attractiveness of Trumpism for women at Trump's election rallies as the chance for 'feeling politically together' (Hochschild 2016). In his contribution, Strick examines the workings of masculinist 'affective communities' on the Internet. These observations seemingly feed Chantal Mouffe's claim, made at the turn of the millennium, of the right dominating the affective realm at the time, since the left did not seem to have alternative imaginaries to offer (Mouffe 2000). Fifteen to twenty years later there are indicators of a change. By uniting precarious and diverse bodies in the streets, new feminist movements such as the 'Black Protest' in Poland, NiUnaMenos in Argentina, the international Women's Strike of March 8, or the Women's Marches in the U.S. seemingly provide a powerful emotional counterforce to the right-wing populist trend (Butler 2016; Roth 2020a). By evoking shared feelings of 'embodied intersectionality,' these movements promote and perform an inclusive form of solidarity as opposed to the exclusive notion that is grounded in the imaginary of the national supremacy predominating the right-wing populist complex (see the contributions by Graff and Roth).

Racialized Sexual Politics – Old and New Modernities

Right-wing 'obsession with gender' is most closely linked to a promotion of the 'ethno-sexist' (Dietze 2016) exclusion of racialized Others who are constructed as dangerous to the reproduction of the White national body. The narrative of migrants as a sexual threat, as was brought forward by the 'cultural panic' surrounding the harassments at New Year's Eve 2015/16 in Cologne, Germany, and through Trump's dictum of the 'Mexican rapist intruder,' provides striking examples. Another narrative constructs the fear of 'autochthonous' citizens being 'outnumbered' by the fertility of non-autochthonous 'invaders,' through which right-wing actors launch a selective pro-natalism (Schultz 2015) targeting particularly White women. Feminists, especially activists in pro-choice campaigns, are regarded as enemies in this respect. Recent transnational efforts to abolish or limit reproductive rights are closely related to this narrative (Gökarıksel et al. 2019), as Graff's contribution on the struggle of the feminist 'Black Protest' in Poland shows. Beyond the obvious control of women's bodies, the cut into reproductive rights is aimed particularly at demographic policies (Schultz 2015; Fixmer-Oraiz 2019) in order to promote a 'New Maternalism' (Mezey/Pillard 2011), as Dietze argues in her contribution.

In consequence, right-wing populists question, oppose, and ambitiously fight feminists, non-traditional ways of life, and gender studies, perceiving them as obstacles to demographic goals. They represent emancipatory projects as a version of an 'old modernity' that terrorizes the 'people' with their sexualized ideas and models of the 'normalcy' of homosexuality and the alleged existence of more than two genders. Conversely, almost all formations of the right-wing populist complex claim to stand for a 'new' and 'other' modernity. Accordingly, in their contribution, Ajanović, Mayer and Sauer speak of a 'limited modernity' and Spierings of neo-traditionalization. This modern window dressing re-arranges traditional 'values' in a new narrative. Elaborating on Bauman's concept of 'Retrotopia' (Bauman 2017), for such visions of the future based on an idealized past, Schleusener coins the notion 'retrotopian desire' in his contribution. Related right-wing populist or conservative new/old brands of politics encase traditional forms of social life such as the church, the homeland (Heimat, in German), the 'people,' and the heteronormative family with an aura of a counterrevolution aiming at reoccupying lost territory. As a consequence, they fight an elite perceived as sexually licentious, unprincipled (secular), cosmopolitan (without homeland) and narcissistic-individualistic (singles, promoters of homosexuality). Right-wing populist logics are built on the construction of an inner enemy (the 'corrupt' elite, feminists, LGBTQI activists, political correctness etc.) and an outer enemy (immigrants as competitors for jobs and welfare and as threat to the national culture and sexual liberty of White women, 'gender ideology' as transnational menace to families, children, and the reproduction of the nation). These peculiarities stage gender as a central arena for polarizations, and thus for the working of right-wing populism in general.

Simultaneously, but not contradictorily, a kind of 'strategic progressivism' in sexual matters can be observed in right-wing populism in Europe and the United States. This pattern is expressed in the form of a 'sexual nationalism' (Mepschen/Duyvendak 2012) or 'sexual exceptionalism' (Bracke 2011; Puar 2011; Dietze 2019), which projects sexism onto racialized Others constructed as intruders and sexual threats to the nation and the national culture. Following this pattern, right-wing populists can claim to defend the sexual freedom of women (and sometimes of gays and LGBT persons) against the sexism and homophobia of Others. In Germany, gay activists within the AfD defend (non-queer) homosexuality as a stronghold against gender-ambivalence, due to the assumed implied preference for one clear-cut gender (see Wielowiejski's contribution). Following this pattern, women from the Global North need to be protected from sexual harassment by racialized or ethnicized men – in the European context that means mostly young Muslim migrants. Western women can thereby draw an 'occidental dividend' (Dietze 2010: 100) based on the supposed superiority of occidental sexual and gender regimes in contrast to backwards 'oriental' gender regimes. Thereby they can simultaneously be presented as already 'fully emancipated' and as having achieved sexual self-determination. Equality politics and gender mainstreaming thus appear as not only unnecessary but also as harmful, because they undermine the self-confidence and agency of 'autochthonous' women and condemn them to an eternal victim position. The underlying contradictions – such as pro traditional family and for the defense of the sexual liberty of women and gays – a phenomenon Gutsche (2018) calls "pro women, against feminists," are foundational for the gendered logics of right-wing populists and represent "calculated ambivalences" aimed to reach different fractions of a possible electorate (Reisigl 2020).

Gender as Meta-Language for Political Maneuvering

Right-wing populists not only raise questions of gender because they touch deep inner beliefs about what is considered appropriate by considerable parts of the population who feel overrun by 'progressively contaminated' public discourse, but also because it is a tool with which alliances can be forged. A study by the Friedrich Ebert Foundation on European anti-gender mobilization in 2015 is aptly titled Gender as Symbolic Glue (Kováts/Põim 2015). In France, a campaign against gender-sensitive sex education and adoption rights for homosexuals united conservative Catholics, right-wing populists, and supporters of a private school system. There was a large turn-out by these groups to protests, and the campaign was able to recruit voters in favor of the Front National for the next election. Gender could be instrumentalized as a tool of coalition building, not only on national grounds but in international realms as well: Brazil's newly elected President Jair Bolsonaro bonded with US President Donald Trump during his inaugural visit in March 2019 over being united in their 'fight against gender ideology' and 'political correctness' (Wempel 2018). In Hungary, gender mainstreaming introduced by the EU was perceived as 'Western imperialism' aimed at destroying the cultural identity of a small country. In a similar vein, Pope Francis described 'gender ideology' as "ideological colonization" used by international institutions to push pressure on poorer countries by forcing their dangerous concepts on them, thus uniting a broad spectrum of actors ranging from conservative Catholics to Evangelicals, Muslims, and orthodox Jews who consider themselves to be victims of this 'ideology' (Case 2019). After several priests in Poland had been accused of molesting children over a long period of time – incidents which the clerical authorities had known about but decided not to persecute –, the Catholic Church chose to decry the harmfulness of the gender category in December 2013 with a pastoral letter against the "gender ideology" instead of responding to the allegations against their priests.

Each of these examples shows that gender issues are suitable to fuel the struggle over 'cultural hegemony' in a Gramscian sense. Following Gramsci, launching certain ideas can bring about a slight shift in public discourse (senso communo), which is structurally capable of leading to a change in the entire perception of 'reality'. The French right-wing intellectual Alain de Benoist took up this concept in order to develop strategies to push the senso communo more into the political camp of the right-wingers. In order to set this in motion, following Benoist, so-called meta-politics is needed, i.e. the political propaganda should not be oriented towards parties, elections, and parliaments, but should work with everyday topics that are strongly interconnected with feelings. In this context, art forms like music, such as right-wing rock and folk festivals, are strategic fields through which cultural hegemony can be promoted meta-politically. The right-wing extremist campaign '1 % for Germany' is based on the conviction that if small minorities can be seduced and convinced by right-wing extremist ideas, the concept can be transferred to society as a whole and thereby create cultural hegemony via meta-politics.

All these political maneuverings considered, one question is still in need of explanation: Why of all things is the category 'gender' so useful for meta-politics? The editors of this volume agree with Sauer's analysis (2017) that gender relations, or more precisely the relation of two sexes as an imagined binary, are still regarded as immutable natural facts – regardless of the emancipation movements of recent decades. Populists do not tire of invoking the allegedly inescapable 'biological' difference of the sexes, which are understood as antagonistic and complementary. This assertion naturalizes heteronormative couplings and reifies the related hierarchy between men and women. Assuming two (and only two) sexes as binary and hierarchically arranged is the essential category of order per se. The right-wing struggle against gender is thus always also a struggle against the dissolution of 'natural' orders, indeed a challenge of order in general (see the contribution of Spierings on 'order society'). In this respect, the sexes cannot be socially constructed in any case, because they would then be malleable and would thereby not only lose their function to describe and guarantee a hierarchical order, but would also question male domination, which is still one of the major motivations for problematizing 'gender' in the first place.

**

By bringing different actors and fields of investigation together, this collected volume seeks to combine case studies and theoretical considerations on a right-wing populist complex and gender with an intersectional perspective that integrates 'race'/ethnicity/religion, class/neoliberalism/milieu, and affect/emotion/feelings into its analysis, thereby identifying sexual politics as one of the main arenas of contention. Moreover, the collection of contributions seeks to demonstrate that the category of gender is not only crucial not just for analyzing the shift to the right, analyzing its programmatic contents and objectives, and understanding its attractiveness. Employing gender in right-wing rhetoric can also mean using the category as a tool for coalition building, a right-wing critique of globalization and for ethnonationalism, and as a vehicle for gaining cultural hegemony. Taken together, all these elements are constitutive for the success and impact of the right-wing populist complex in different and context-related forms and they cannot be understood without implementing a systematic gender lens.

As we have seen, right-wing populist actors have moved the struggle over hegemony center stage, and gender serves them as a meta-language, as an "affective bridge" (Dietze 2019) and as a central arena for that matter. Judith Butler recently described the right-wing obsession with gender as a replacement, condensation and abbreviation of cultural anxiety (Butler 2020). However, this struggle is far from being decided. Because of the strong entanglements of the right-wing populist complex with other forces of inequality and injustice and its spectral presence in so many areas, the disruption of these articulations requires many different paths. The numerous feminist protests emerging recently – that are the focus of the last part of this volume (see chapters of Roth and Graff) – have indicated that the fight concerning the contestations and withdrawals of rights takes place on the streets. These movements demonstrate that it continues to be worthwhile to intervene in public discourse at the discursive level in order to ward off the right-wing grasp for cultural hegemony, albeit without zeal and anger but with patience and emphasis. The current protests also show that the manipulations via exclusionary affects such as fear and wrath can be countered with inclusive affects like solidarity and empathy. The right-wing populist offer part of 'the people-as-one' can be denied on grounds of a preference for a 'people-as-multiple' (Gunnarsson-Payne 2019: 7) and nonconformist notions of diversity. In this current state of affairs, to quote Toni Morrison, who passed away while these last lines were in the making, "All necks are on the line." (Morrison 1989).

Bibliography

Abi-Hassan, Sahar (2017): "Populism and Gender." In: Cristóbal Rovira Kaltwasser/Paul A. Taggart/Paulina Ochoa Espejo et al. (eds.), The Oxford Handbook of Populism. Oxford: Oxford University Press, pp. 2-22.

Ahmed, Sara (2004): "Collective Feelings." In: Theory, Culture, and Society 21 (2), pp. 25-42.

Amesberger, Helga/Halbmayr, Brigitte (eds.) (2002): Rechtsextreme Parteien, eine Mögliche Heimat für Frauen?. Opladen: Leske & Budrich.

Akkerman, Tjitske/Hagelund, Anniken (2007): "'Women and Children First!' Anti-Immigration Parties and Gender in Norway and the Netherlands." In: Patterns of Prejudice 41 (2), pp. 197-214.

Bacchetta, Paola/Power, Margaret (2013): Right-Wing Women: From Conservatives to Extremists Around the World. New York: Routledge.

Banet-Weiser, Sarah/Gill, Rosalind/Rottenberg, Catherine (2019): Postfeminism, Popular Feminism and Neoliberal Feminism? Sarah Banet-Weiser, Rosalind Gill and Catherine Rottenberg in Conversation. Online: journals.sagepub.com/doi/full/10.1177/1464700119842555, 03.10.2019.

Bauman, Zygmunt (2017): Retrotopia. Cambridge: Polity Press.

Beier, Friederike/Haller, Lisa Yashodhara/Haneberg, Lea (eds.) (2018): Materializing Feminism. Positionierung zur Ökonomie, Staat und Identität. Münster: Unrast.

Betz, Hans-Georg (2001): "Rechtspopulismus und Ethnonationalismus. Erfolgsbedingungen und Zukunftschancen." In: Klaus Leggewie/Richard Münch (eds.), Politik im 21. Jahrhundert. Frankfurt a. M.: Suhrkamp, pp. 122-138.

Bidaseca, Karina/Loi, Yanina (2017): "8M: Ni una Menos: Paro Internacional de Mujeres." In: Milena Caserola (ed.), 8M: Ni una Menos: Vivos nos Queremos. Buenos Aires:, pp. 9-14.

Birsl, Ursula (2013): Rechtsextremismus: Weiblich - Männlich? Eine Fallstudie zu Geschlechtsspezifischen Lebensverläufen, Handlungsspielräumen und Orientierungsweisen. Wiesbaden: VSA.

Bitzan, Renate/Köttig, Michaela/Petö, Andrea (2017): Gender and Far Right Politics in Europe. London: Palgrave.

Blee, Kathleen M. (2008): Women of the Klan: Racism and Gender in the 1920s. Berkeley: University of California Press.

Bracke, Sarah (2011): "Subjects of Debate. Secular and Sexual Exceptionalism and Muslim Women in the Netherlands." In: Feminist Review 98 (1), pp. 28-46.

Brandini-Aissis, Mariana/Ogando, Ana C. (2018): Gender Ideology and the Brazilian Elections. Online: www.publicseminar.org/2018/11/gender-ideology-and-the-brazilian-elections/, 21.06.2019.

Brubaker, Roger (2017): "Between Nationalism and Civilizationism: The European Populist Moment in Comparative Perspective." In: Ethnic and Racial Studies 40 (8), pp. 1191-1226.

Butler, Judith (2020): "Gender, whose Fantasy." Keynote at the 10th anniversary of the Fachgruppe Gender-Studies at the Technische Universität, Berlin 31.01.2020.

Campbell, Beatrix (2014): Neoliberal Neopatriarchy: The Case for Gender Revolution. Online: www.opendemocracy.net/en/5050/neoliberal-neopatriarchy-case-for-gender-revolution/, 27.07.2019.

Canovan, Margaret (1999): "Trust the People! Populism and the Two Faces of Democracy." In: Political Studies 47 (1), pp. 2-16.
Case, Mary Ann (2019): "Trans Formations in the Vatican's War on 'Gender Ideology'." In: Signs: Journal of Women in Culture and Society 44 (3), pp. 639-664.
de Lange, Sarah L./Mügge, Liza M. (2015): "Gender and Right-Wing Populism in the Low Countries. Ideological Variations across Parties and Time." In: Patterns of Prejudice 49 (1-2), pp. 61-80.
Dietze, Gabriele (2010): "Occidentalism, European Identity, and Sexual Politics." In: Hauke Brunkhorst/Gerd Groezinger (eds.), The Study of Europe. Baden Baden: Nomos, pp. 87-116.
Dietze, Gabriele (2016): "Ethnosexismus." In: Movements 2, pp. 157-165.
Dietze, Gabriele (2019): Sexueller Exzeptionalismus. Überlegenheitsnarrative in Immigrationsabwehr und Rechtspopulismus. Bielefeld: transcript.
Dörre, Klaus/Kraemer, Klaus/Speidel, Frederic (2006): "The Increasing Precariousness of the Employment Society: Driving Force for a New Right Wing Populism?" In: International Journal of Action Research 2 (1), pp. 98-128.
Draper, Susana/Mason-Deese, Liz (2018): "Strike as Process: Building the Poetics of a New Feminism." In: South Atlantic Quarterly 117 (3), pp. 682-691.
Ehrenreich, Barbara/Hochschild, Arlie Russell/Kay, Shara (2003): Global Woman: Nannies, Maids, and Sex Workers in the New Economy. London: McMillan.
Eisenstein, Zillah R. (ed.) (1979): Capitalist Patriarchy and the Case for Socialist Feminism. New York: Monthly Review Press.
Erzeel, Silvia/Rashkova, Ekaterina R. (2017): "Still Men's Parties? Gender and the Radical Right in Comparative Perspective." In: West European Politics 40 (4), pp. 812-820.
Farris, Sara R. (2017): In the Name of Women's Rights: The Rise of Femonationalism. Durham: Duke University Press.
FE.IN, Autor*innen Kollektiv (2019): Frauen*rechte und Frauen*hass. Antifeminismus und die Ethnisierung von Gewalt. Berlin: Verbrecher Verlag.
Fixmer-Oraiz, Natalie (2019): Homeland Maternity. Chicago: Illinois University Press.
Fraser, Nancy (2016): "Progressive Neoliberalism versus Reactionary Populism: A Choice that Feminists Should Refuse." In: NORA-Nordic Journal of Feminist and Gender Research 24 (4), pp. 281-284.
Gidron, Noam/Hall, Peter A. (2017): "The Politics of Social Status: Economic and Cultural Roots of the Populist Right." In: The British Journal of Sociology 68, pp. 57-84.
Gunnarson-Payne, Jenny (2019): "Challenging 'Gender-Ideology' (Anti)Gender Politics in Europe's Populist Moment." In: The New Pretender (February 10), pp. 1-10.

Gutsche, Elisa (ed.) (2018a): Triumph of Women. The Female Face of the Populist and Far Right in Europe. Berlin: Friedrich Ebert Stiftung.

Gutsche, Elisa (ed.) (2018b): Triumph der Frauen. Das Weibliche Gesicht der der Populistischen und Extremen Rechten in Europa. Berlin: Friedrich Ebert Stiftung.

Hark, Sabine/Villa, Paula-Irene (eds.) (2015): Anti-Genderismus. Sexualität und Geschlecht als Schauplätze Aktueller Politischer Auseinandersetzungen. Bielefeld: transcript.

Hark, Sabine/Villa, Paula-Irene (2017): Unterscheiden und Herrschen. Ein Essay zu den Ambivalenten Verflechtungen von Rassismus, Sexismus und Feminismus in der Gegenwart. Bielefeld: transcript.

Hess, Amanda (2017): How a Fractious Women's Movement Came to Lead the Left. Online: www.nytimes.com/2017/02/07/magazine/how-a-fractious-womens-movement-came-to-lead-the-left.html, 05.05.2019.

Hochschild, Arlie Russell (2016): Strangers in Their Own Land: Anger and Mourning on the American Right. New York: The New Press.

Kimmel, Michael (2017): Angry White Men: American Masculinity at the End of an Era. London: Hachette.

Korolczuk, Elżbieta/Graff, Agnieszka (2018): "Gender as 'Ebola from Brussels': The Anticolonial Frame and the Rise of Illiberal Populism." In: Signs: Journal of Women in Culture and Society 43 (4), pp. 797-821.

Kovàts, Eszter/Põim, Maari (eds.): Parties in the Anti-Gender Mobilizations in Europe. Berlin: Friedrich Ebert Stiftung.

Kuhar, Roman/Paternotte, David (2017): Anti-Gender Campaigns in Europe: Mobilizing against Equality. London: Rowman & Littlefield.

Lang, Juliane (2018a): Feminismus von Rechts. Neue Rechte Politiken zwischen Forderung nach Frauenrechten und Offenem Antifeminismus. Online: dekonstrukt.org/impulse-3-feminismus-von-rechts-erschienen, 10.03.2019.

Lang, Juliane (2018b): "Alles beim Alten?! Überlegungen zu Anhaltenden Relevanz von Geschlechterpolitik in der Extremen Rechten." In: Alexander Häusler/Helmut Kellershohn (eds.), Das Gesicht des Völkischen Populismus. Neue Herausforderungen für eine Kritische Rechtsextremismusforschung. Münster: Unrast, pp. 147-161.

Lang, Juliane/Fritzsche, Christopher (2018): "Backlash, Neoreaktionäre Politiken oder Antifeminismus. Forschende Perspektiven auf Aktuelle Debatten um Geschlecht." In: Feministische Studien (2), pp. 335-346.

Lombardo, Emanuela/Meier, Petra/Verloo, Mieke (2009): The Discursive Politics of Gender Equality: Stretching, Bending and Policy-Making. New York: Routledge.

Lugones, Maria (2012): "The Coloniality of Gender." In: Walter Mignolo/Arturo Escobar (eds.), Globalization and the Decolonial Option. New York: Routledge, pp. 369-391.

Mayer, Nonna (2015): "The Closing of the Radical Right Gender Gap in France?" In: French Politics 13 (4), pp. 391-414.

Mepschen, Paul/Duyvendak, Jan Willem (2012): "European Sexual Nationalisms. The Culturalization of Citizenship and the Sexual Politics of Belonging and Exclusion." In: Perspectives on Europe 42 (1), pp. 70-76.

Meret, Susi/Siim, Birte (2013): "Gender, Populism and Politics of Belonging. Discourses of Right-Wing Populist Parties in Denmark, Norway and Austria." In: Birte Siim/Monica Mokre (eds.), Negotiating Gender and Diversity in an Emergent European Public Sphere. London: Palgrave, pp. 78-96.

Mezey, Naomi/Pillard, Cornelia T. (2012): Against the New Maternalism. In: Michigan Journal of Gender & Law (18), pp. 229-296.

Morgan, Kimberly J. (2017): "Gender, Right-Wing Populism, and Immigrant Integration Policies in France, 1989–2012." In: West European Politics 40 (4), pp. 887-906.

Morrison, Toni (1989): "Unspeakable Things Unspoken: The Afro-American Presence in American Literature." In: Michigan Quarterly Review 28, pp. 1-34.

Mouffe, Chantal (2000): "Politics and Passions: The Stakes of Democracy." In: Ethical Perspectives 7 (2-3), pp. 146-150.

Mudde, Cas/Kaltwasser, Cristóbal Rovira (2015): "Vox Populi or Vox Masculini? Populism and Gender in Northern Europe and South America." In: Patterns of Prejudice 49 (1-2), pp. 16-36.

Mudde, Cas/Kaltwasser, Cristóbal Rovira (2017): Populism: A Very Short Introduction. Oxford: Oxford University Press.

Müller, Jan-Werner (2017): What Is Populism? London: Penguin.

Norocel, Ov Cristian (2010): "Constructing Radical Right Populist Resistance: Metaphors of Heterosexist Masculinities and the Family Question in Sweden." In: Norma 5 (2), pp. 170-183.

Norris, Pippa/Inglehart, Ronald (2019): Cultural Backlash. Trump, Brexit and the Rise of Authoritarian Populism. Online: www.un.org/development/desa/dspd/wp-content/uploads/sites/, 05.04.2019.

Puar, Jasbir (2011): "Abu Ghraib and U.S. Sexual Exceptionalism." In: Works and Days 29, pp. 115-142.

Pühl, Katharina/Sauer, Birgit (2018): Kapitalismuskritische Gesellschaftsanalyse: Queerfeministische Positionen. Münster: Unrast.

Reisigl, Martin (2020): "Mit zweierlei Maß gemessen, kalkulierte Ambivalenz in rechtspopulistischen Repräsentationen von Geschlechterverhältnissen." Forthcoming in: Zeitschrift für Literatur und Linguistik, spring.

Rodrik, Dani (2018): "Populism and the Economics of Globalization." In: Journal of International Business Policy 1 (1-2), pp. 12-33.

Roth, Julia (2020a): Can Feminism Trump Populism? Right-Wing Trends and Intersectional Contestations in the Americas. Trier WVT/Bilingual Press (in print).

Roth, Julia (2020b): ¿Puede el Feminismo Vencer al Populismo? Tendencias de Derecha y Disputas Interseccionales en las Américas. Bielefeld: Kipu Verlag.

Rottenberg, Catherine (2014): "The Rise of Neoliberal Feminism." In: Cultural Studies 28 (3), pp. 418-437.

Rydgren, Jens (2008): "Immigration Sceptics, Xenophobes or Racists? Radical Right-Wing Voting in Six West European Countries." In: European Journal of Political Research 47 (6), pp. 737-765.

Salecl, Renata (2004) [1994]: The Spoils of Freedom: Psychoanalysis, Feminism and Ideology after the Fall of Socialism. London: Routledge.

Sauer, Birgit (2017): "Gesellschaftstheoretische Überlegungen zum Europäischen Rechtspopulismus. Zum Erklärungspotenzial der Kategorie Geschlecht." In: PVS Politische Vierteljahresschrift 58 (1), pp. 3-22.

Schultz, Susanne (2015): "Reproducing the Nation: The New German Population Policy and the Concept of Demographization." In: Distinktion: Scandinavian Journal of Social Theory 16 (3), pp. 337-361.

Schwander, Hanna/Manow, Philip (2017): "It's Not the Economy, Stupid! Explaining the Electoral Success of the German Right-Wing Populist AfD." In: CIS Working Paper (94).

Scrinzi, Francesca (2017): "Gender and Women in the Front National Discourse and Policy: From 'Mothers of the Nation' to 'Working Mothers'?" In: New Formations 91 (91), pp. 87-101.

Spierings, Niels/Zaslove, Andrej/Mügge, Liza M. et al. (2015): "Gender and Populist Radical-Right Politics. An Introduction." In: Patterns of Prejudice 49 (1-2), pp. 3-15.

Thelandersson, Fredrika (2014): "A Less Toxic Feminism: Can the Internet Solve the ageold Question of How to Put Intersectional Theory into Practice?" In: Feminist Media Studies 14 (3), pp. 527-530.

Wemple, Erica (2019): President Trump. Our Fakenews Ambassador. Online: www.washingtonpost.com/opinions/2019/03/19/alongside-brazilian-president-trump-hails-fake-news-bond/, 03.10.2019.

Wichterich, Christa (2000): The Globalized Woman: Reports from a Future of Inequality. North Geelong: Spinifex Press.

Wizorek, Anne (2014): Weil ein Aufschrei nicht reicht. Für einen Feminismus von Heute. Frankfurt a. M.: Fischer.

Wodak, Ruth (2015): The Politics of Fear. What Right-Wing Populist Discourses Mean. London: Sage.

Zick, Andreas/Küpper, Beate/Berghan, Wilhelm (2019): Verlorene Mitte – Feindselige Zustände. Rechtsextreme Einstellungen in Deutschland 2018/19. Berlin: Dietz.

Authoritarian Right-Wing Populism as Masculinist Identity Politics. The Role of Affects

Birgit Sauer

1. Introduction

Since the turn of the century, Europe, but also other regions in the world, have been confronted with the growth and emergence of right-wing populist, nationalist, and authoritarian parties and organizations. In Hungary and Poland, nationalist right-wing parties in government have started to transform their countries into so-called 'illiberal democracies.' The Austrian Freedom Party FPÖ (Freiheitliche Partei Österreich) pushed its partner in the government coalition, the conservative Austrian People's Party (ÖVP), towards racist anti-immigration policies, towards further dismantling the Austrian welfare state and social partnership, attacking the state radio and TV stations as well as feminist civil society organizations. The French Front National (now Rassemblement National) has developed into a major force in France's political landscape as have the Sweden Democrats. For a long time, Germany seemed to be immune to right-wing political strategies; however, the recent electoral successes of the "Alternative for Germany" (AfD, Alternative für Deutschland) proved that this is no longer the case. Moreover, rightwing social movements like the German PEGIDA (Patrotische Europäer gegen die Islamisierung des Abendlandes, Patriotic Europeans against the Islamization of the Occident) and the Identitarian movements across Europe challenge liberal democracies.

In this article, I want to argue that recent right-wing populist mobilization is a gendered movement, which fosters masculinist identity politics at the intersection of gender, class, religion, ethnicity, and sexuality. Antagonistic strategies of the nationalist, authoritarian, and populist right have to be located in simultaneous transformations of capitalist market societies, of European gender regimes, especially in strong male bread-winner-oriented countries and, thus, ongoing social struggles over class, gender, sexuality, and ethnicity. Or, in other words: intersecting structures of difference and domination, which have shaped welfare states since their emergence in the 19th century, have been put into question by neoliberal transformations over the last 30 years and are politicized by right-wing actors.

Already at first glance the importance of gender relations seems to be indicated by the right-wingers' obsession with gender, i.e. their mobilization against the concept of gender for the last ten years, their construction of an endangered masculinity, and their framing of a 'crisis of masculinity.' The so-called manifesto by the Norwegian nativist white-supremacist mass murderer Anders Breivik was based on such sexist assumptions. His fear of a "feminisation of European culture" (Breivik 2011: 36) has become an important dimension of today's radical right-wing populist discourse.

This alleged endangerment of masculinity points to another dimension of masculinist identity politics – the use of affects in right-wing populist political mobilization – be it *fear* of 'the Other,' i.e. migrants, feminists or gender equality politicians, be it *anger* towards the elite, *love* of one's country, the 'Heimat,' as well as new feelings of belonging to a 'we,' of solidarity within this group. Masculinity and affect meet in debates about *thymos* by Marc Jongen (2016), one of the *AfD*'s intellectuals.[1] This affective politicization by the radical right is also rooted in other fundamental social and political transformations of the last 30 years, namely the mobilization of affect for neoliberal economic instrumentalization and subjectivization. Thus, the overall aim of my article is to theorize the populist radical right with a gender and affect perspective.

In the following, I will *first* discuss right-wing populism as a male phenomenon in order to demonstrate the importance of a gendered focus on its causes. *Second*, I will explain the success of right-wing populism with reference to changing gender relations and gender regimes. I will argue that right-wing populist mobilization is a project of masculinist identity politics. In a *third* step, I will highlight the affective entanglements of right-wing populist masculinist identity politics, to *finally* reflect on the right-wing gendered project as a new affective anti-democratic political hegemony.

2. Right-Wing Populist Parties as "Männerparteien": Description of the Gendered Phenomenon

While right-wing groups and parties were re-established in several European countries right after the Second World War, the emergence and growth of the 'new' right is a relatively recent phenomenon of the last two decades (Birsl 2011: 11; Müller

---

[1] In Platon's work 'thymos' denotes one of the three basic human motivations, the passionate and angry affect. The German philosopher Peter Sloterdijk (2006) applied the meaning of 'thymos' to the contemporary situation, and his academic student Marc Jongen introduced the concept into right-wing discourse.

2016: 18). Hans-Jürgen Bieling (2017: 557) identifies three waves of right-wing parties and movements since the 1970s. The third wave is characterized by a sort of 'modernization' of 'old' right-wing parties into 'new' *populist* parties which at the same time became more nationalist, nativist, and authoritarian. Cas Mudde (2004: 543) considers populism to be a "thin-centred ideology," a communicative strategy of appealing to and creating *first* a 'we,' 'the' people, versus 'them,' the elite or the establishment. Other ideologies can be attached to this thin ideology – such as nationalism, nativism, and racism on the right. Right-wing populist parties and movements are characterized by a *second* antagonism, despite their different national and historic backgrounds – the opposition of the 'we' to the 'Others,' be it immigrants, asylum seekers, Muslims, LGBTIQ-people, or feminists. These 'Others' are supposedly posing a threat to the assumed autochthonous people, the 'we.' The 'we,' emerging in these right-wing antagonisms, is a homogeneous, morally pure, and ethnicized people. Mudde (ibid.) eventually mentions a *third* feature of right-wing populism, namely an authoritarian element. Hence, Stuart Hall's (1985) term "authoritarian populism," coined for the Thatcher government in the UK, also fits for recent radical right-wing populist strategies across Europe.

Notwithstanding national differences across Europe, gender and sexuality have been important pillars of radical right-wing ideologies for a long time – such as a gender binary which is perceived as natural, or a traditional gendered division of labor in the heterosexual model of the male bread-winner and the woman as mother (Sauer et al. 2016: 113; Mayer/Sori/Sauer 2016). Moreover, hegemonic masculinity (Connell/Messerschmidt 2005) in the right-wing narrative and imaginary is constructed as heroic masculinity, able to protect the weak and vulnerable woman, who is regarded as important for the reproduction of heterosexual families, the nation, and the state (Rommelspacher 2011: 54). Thus, the extreme right's ideology has always been based on sexist assumptions. However, heroic masculinity is not only attractive for men but also for women.

While the role of gender and sexuality in the new populist right has only recently received some scholarly attention (Spierings/Zaslove 2015; special volume of West European Politics, Vol. 40/4, 2017), the most common gendered assumption is that right-wing populist parties are "men's parties," *Männerparteien*, as Cas Mud (2007, chapter 4) called them, referring to the German expression. The label *Männerpartei* includes five contested changing and paradoxical dimensions. *First*, right-wing parties are "drawing especially from the support of male voters" (Erzeel/Rashkova 2017: 813). Nevertheless, this radical right gender gap in voting varies in different national contexts (Spierings/Zaslove 2017: 839; Harteveld et al. 2015). Nonna Mayer's (2013) research shows that Marine Le Pen appeals much more to women than her father Jean-Marie Le Pen did and that hence, the gender gap in voting decreased in the latest French elections. I suggest that the gender gap in voting cannot be fully explained by gender alone, but that dimensions of class, education, race, and ethnicity also need to be taken into account. In most European countries, the intersection of education, social status or class, and gender explains the growth of the radical right, as mainly young, poorly educated, or unemployed men vote for the populist right (ibid.: 162). In the last US presidential elections, 52 percent of white women drew their vote for Trump, while he only received 4 percent of the female African-American votes (Bump 2018). Hence, in the US, race and gender intersect in explanations of the rise of right-wing populism.

Second, gender differences in political opinions and motivations make right-wing parties "*Männerparteien*" and lead to the gender gap in voting: men, for instance, "have stronger populist (i.e. antagonistic, B.S.) attitudes than women" (Spierings/Zaslove 2017: 840). This means that the framing of a 'we' against 'Others' regarding the issue of migration appeals more to men than to women. Also, men seem to be more attracted to masculinist-heroic leadership than women (Birsl 2011: 12; Schellenberg 2012: 2).

The *third* characteristic of maleness refers to parliamentary representatives of right-wing parties. Traditionally, these parties attract a male constituency and this translates into a large proportion of male representatives in parliament, not least due to the rejection of quota regulations. However, this 'male' picture of parliament gets blurred in different contexts: in the last European Parliament, for instance, the 'Europe of Nations and Freedom' (ENF) group, which includes the Austrian *FPÖ*, the Belgian *Vlaams Belang*, the French *Front National*, the Italian *Lega Nord*, and the Dutch *Partje for the Vrijheid*,[2] counted on 34 percent women representatives, while overall the EP had 36 percent women representatives (Erzeel/Rashkova 2017: 814).

Fourth: traditionally, right-wing parties were headed by "male charismatic leaders" (ibid.: 813) – as for instance Jörg Haider in Austria or Pim Fortuyn in the Netherlands. However, today, women also take over leadership positions in these parties. These women do not fit the right-wing image of motherhood – such as Marine Le Pen, Pia Kjærsgaard from the *Danish People's Party*, Siv Jensen from *Norway's Progress Party* or Alice Weidel, an openly lesbian mother, from the *AfD* (Meret 2015; Meret/Siim/Pingaud 2016; Blee/McGee Deutsch 2012; Bitzan 2000). This 'feminization' strategy or strategy of "de-demonization" (Mayer 2013: 161) allows right-wing parties to counter or relativize the image of being men's parties and to attract female voters. Nevertheless, these female leaders struggle with a masculinist party structure and thus have to perform their own form of political masculinity (for a definition of political masculinity see Starck/Sauer 2014).

Fifth, substantive representation of women, i.e. acting *for* women and fighting *for* women's policies in parliament, is lower in right-wing parties than in others parties. Especially, right-wingers in parliament do not support women's issues

---

2   www.enfgroup-ep.eu

such as abortion, reproductive rights, quota regulations, or equal opportunity policies. Nevertheless, right-wing parties modernized their male-oriented programs and their conservative gender ideology in order to "remain electorally successful" (Erzeel/Rashkova 2017: 816). Amesberger and Halbmayr (2002: 308), for instance, addressed the "modernized traditional gender images" of the Austrian *FPÖ*.

These five features demonstrate the importance of a gendered perspective on the radical populist right. The genderedness of the radical populist right is also mirrored in the recent development of its new "gender ideology" (Mudde 2007: 92), which is supposed to enrich the populists' "thin-centred ideology." This new 'gender ideology' of the right refers explicitly to the scientific and political concept of gender in order to fight what they call "genderism" – be it gender studies, gender mainstreaming, gender equality policies and the recognition of sexual diversity (Kuhar/Paternotte 2017; Hark/Villa 2015; for Austria Mayer/Sauer 2017). This anti-gender discourse matches the antagonistic politics of the authoritarian right across Europe. For instance, anti-gender framing modulates resentments against the EU by presenting gender mainstreaming as imposed 'from above,' from Brussels. The anti-gender discourse also frames gender equality and gender studies as projects concocted by a cosmopolitan feminist establishment or a feminist "metropolitan elite" (Cain 2016), who only pursue their own interests, while neglecting the interests of the 'women in the streets.' Finally, the recognition of sexual diversity is framed as a threat for children, especially for boys who are presented as endangered of being harassed by homosexual teachers (Mayer/Sauer 2017; Schmincke 2015).

This 'anti-genderist' mobilization, however, seems to be ambivalent when "it comes to the rights of Muslim women" (de Lange/Mügge 2015: 65): right-wing populist parties condemn the alleged backwardness, the pre-modern, patriarchal, and misogynist barbarism and the violence of migrant, especially of Muslim, men. The aim is to stigmatize Muslim 'Others' as incompatible with the presumed gender equality of Western societies. This "femonationalist" argument, as Sara Farris (2017) calls it, or these ethno-sexist struggles (Dietze 2016) have been activated especially after the sexual assaults in Cologne on New Year's Eve 2015.

Thus, the so-called 'anti-genderism' became an element of a politics of *Othering*, referring to gender, sexuality, ethnicity, religion, and migration. Radical right-wing parties "couch their anti-immigrant proposals in gendered terms" (Morgan 2017: 888). But it would be too easy to consider gender as being merely instrumentalized by the radical right for their anti-migrant policies. Right-wingers' focus on gender points to a broader political picture: the radical right actively engages in ongoing gender struggles, in transformations of gender relations, in order to transform liberal democracies and to push towards a new hegemonic project.

3. Gendered Explanations of the Rise of the Radical Populist Right

The growth of the radical right is perceived as a breakdown of trust in the liberal democratic order, and especially in the political elites that represent this order. But why this decline of trust? Why the decline of a belief in liberal-democratic institutions and politicians? Why the 'crisis of representation'? According to Mudde (2004), a "populist Zeitgeist" emerged in the 1980s, which has since characterized most parties in Western liberal democracies that moved towards post-democratic (Crouch 2004) or – as Chantal Mouffe (2000) writes – post-political conditions. The move to the center of the catch-all-parties and their search for consensus, Mouffe claims, opened a window of opportunity for the radical populist right to politicize new antagonisms.

Scholars following the theory of materialism tend to trace back the success of today's right-wing populist extremism to the fundamental economic and social transformations since the 1990s, which are widely labelled as neoliberal restructuring and the financialization of capitalism. These transformations have strengthened the interests of capital at the expense of the working class and parts of the middle class (Jessop 2016: 134). The deregulation of labor, austerity policies, the dismantling of public provisions, and cuts in social welfare resulted in rising unemployment, the precarization of labor, social insecurity and uncertainty, in an unequal distribution of wealth that is visible in growing poverty and in the emergence of the super-rich (Piketty 2014). At the same time, neoliberal subjectivization fostered individualization, responsibilization and competitiveness as well as the decline of solidarity and care for others as a social value. These transformations eroded the liberal democratic compromise – the consensus of welfare, equality, and regulated political participation – of the 1970s.

Hence, right-wing populist parties and organizations can be seen, in the words of Klaus Dörre (2016: 2), as "movements against the impositions and compulsion of the capitalist market," movements against the disappointment over cuts in welfare and the fear of losing wealth.[3] Thus, the emergence of the radical populist right is understood as a class-specific reaction, a movement against the deprivation of neoliberal economic globalization, job loss and cuts in social welfare. Philip Manow (2018) developed the concept of a "political economy of populism." He claims that right-wing populism emerges and grows in countries with high immigration levels and with open and generous welfare states that include migrants and refugees into their welfare schemes (ibid.: 65ff.).

However, the success of right-wing populism is not only a result of the precarization of labor and the fear of losing economic and social security, i.e. it is not

---

3 Translation by the author.

only a working-class issue, not least due to the fact that parts of the middle-class are also afraid of losing wealth, recognition, power, and prestige (Koppetsch 2017). Therefore, right-wing populism is also a gendered issue, a movement against the transformation of gender regimes, fueled by affective politics.

The emergence and growth of a new kind of right-wing populism in the last two decades is rooted in fundamental neoliberal transformations of gender regimes, especially in Western bread-winner-oriented societies. Until the late 1970s, the welfare consensus and gender regimes in most European countries had been based on the *in*equality between men and women, on the division between (male) paid labor and (female) unpaid care work, which made women dependent on a male breadwinner. The inclusion of women into higher education, the expansion of the so-called Keynesian welfare state, and the struggle of women's movements since the late 1960s have led to more gender equality in European societies, as women successively entered the labor market. Since the late 1980s, neoliberal restructuring has resulted – with different paces in different European countries – in an acceleration of the inclusion of women into labor markets, in the intensified commodification of female labor, and thus in an ambivalent "neoliberal gender equality," in the words of Christa Wichterich (2007).[4] Hence, neoliberal arrangements allowed for a further – albeit ambivalent – emancipation of women, especially of well-educated women who became the target of affirmative action policies.

At the same time, male labor became more precarious and the 'family income' declined as a consequence of neoliberal restructuring. Overall, the systematic erosion of wealth among the working- and middle-class population through labor deregulation and cuts in welfare from the 1990s was accompanied by the erosion of hierarchical gender regimes and of male dominance in the private sphere as well as in the public sphere, i.e. of wage labor, politics, and the state (Wimbauer/Motakef/Teschlade 2015). These developments created a considerable challenge to masculine hegemony and fostered the discourse about "failed patriarchs," i.e. men who are supposed to take over dominant or bread-winner-positions but at the same time are confronted with their declining significance on the labor market (Radhakrishnan/Solari 2015). Men are confronted with a loss of "hegemony and power of interpretation" (Koppetsch 2017).[5]

Against this background, the radical right claims to compensate these losses. In this vein, Björn Höcke (*AfD*) mobilized fear of a loss of forceful masculinity at the 2015 party congress: "We have to rediscover our masculinity. Only if we rediscover our masculinity we will be manful. And only if we are manful we will be able

---

4   Translation by the author.
5   Translation by the author.

to become fortified; and we have to be able to become fortified, dear friends!"[6] The populist right frames the marginalization of working- and middle-class men as a 'crisis of masculinity' and blames this crisis on female labor market integration, gender equality and, of course, migration policies. Instead of arguing for a new distribution of labor and time between men and women, the populist right channels the feelings caused by the deprived class status of "subordinated men" (Connell/Messerschmidt 2005) into *hatred* against well-educated women and against migrants. Hence, the right-wing anti-gender discourse and the evocation of a 'crisis of masculinity' is another facet of the re-signification process of neoliberal social inequality, strategically confounding causes and consequences by interpellating "wounded white men" (Brown 2010).

In this discourse of drawing boundaries, of exclusion and 'Othering,' right-wing populism contributes to the self-affirmation of masculinity by offering points of reference for the re-establishment of traditional gender constellations and thus for the abolishment of gender equality policies. The right-wing interpellation of the 'little man in the streets' is part of a masculinist identity politics, which includes the promise that a charismatic leader might increase the self-confidence of subordinated masculinities. However, masculinist identity politics can also attract women: those who are exhausted by the double burden of neoliberal emancipation and who long for a 'male hero or savior,' or those who find new forms of agency in masculinist gender constellations. Moreover, the masculinist setting also includes subordinated women who are afraid of losing 'secure' gender relations in their daily lives.

This explicit focus on gender relations helps to understand that the right-wing populist mobilization of a (traditional) masculinist identity is part of a discourse against the commodification of everyday life and of securing the everyday life – however, at the expense of gender equality. In the following I want to illustrate the role of affect in this masculinist identity politics.

4. "Politics of Fear." Affective Mobilization of the Nationalist Populist Right

Emotions and affects have been recognized as important elements of right-wing populist mobilization in the past years. Betz (2002) perceives populist rhetoric as "designed to tap feelings of *ressentiment* and exploit them politically" (ibid.: 198). Ruth Wodak (2015) coined the term "politics of fear," which underpins right-wing populist strategies.

---

6   Speech at the party convention of the AfD, November 2015 at Erfurt, (translation B.S.), www.youtube.com/watch?v=yBvyoMR3KBE, 30.11.2016.

However, from a political science perspective, the link between "populism and emotions remains undertheorized" (Rico/Guinjoan/Anduiza 2017: 3). Recent political science research under the paradigm of rational choice includes emotions as variables in its analysis of right-wing populism (Vasilopoulou/Wagner 2017: 384). This research aims to explain the influence of emotions on citizens' political preferences, political judgement, and voting behavior. Thus, emotions are conceptualized as individual experiences or preferences, as variables that shape political behavior: such studies show that "anger boosts political participation" and protest (Rico/Guinjoan/Anduiza 2016: 6; also Wagner 2013: 684), while fear leads to "increased vigilance" and sadness supports "compassionate politics" (Rico/Guinjoan/Anduiza 2016: 7). Hence, they conclude that the radical right needs to mobilize and foster anxiety, fear, and insecurity and has to transform these feelings into anger against somebody who can be made accountable.

While mainstream political parties have been neglecting the issue of rising social inequality as well as "feelings of dispossession" (Müller 2016: 21), right-wing parties actively caught up with the fears of deprivation and disempowerment: "Right-wing populism gains support where fear of economic and social decline meets anger over social inequality." (Saxer 2017: 16)

While I agree with some of these findings, I think that in order to fully understand the role of affects in recent transformations of democracy we need a critical, social-theoretical approach, which perceives affects not only as a political variable or as an individual feature but as a social "structure of feeling" (Williams 1977), as a power structure between people and thus as a mode of governing people.[7] In this perspective, bodily affects are always part of discursive or representational constellations. Therefore, settings of power and domination as well as processes of subjectivization rest not only on material conditions, on symbolic and discursive identifications but also on affective and bodily practices.

An affect perspective highlights that in the last 30 years, affects have moved to the center of new neoliberal forms of governance. In our recent work, Otto Penz and I labelled these new technologies of governing as "neoliberal affective governmentality" in a Foucauldian sense (Sauer/Penz 2017). Affective governmentality aims at affective subjectivization in a double sense – of *creating* subjects as affective and cognitive rational beings but also of *dominating* citizens in neoliberal conditions. The neoliberal 'will to feel' and the tradition of affective governmentality mobilize affects' aim towards engaging the 'whole person,' her cognitive and affective competencies in the work place but also in the public and private spheres. Neoliberalism has mobilized the affects of people to instrumentalize them for capitalist production, while at the same time devaluating care and solidarity. Neoliberalism

---

[7] I prefer the concept of affect over the concept of emotion as affect points to the interconnectedness of body, mind, and cognition.

mobilized affects in the sphere of wage labor for the transformation into service economies and new forms of exploiting of the workforce by transgressing boundaries between work and private lives.

This led to what Papadopoulos and Tsianos (2006) labelled "embodied capitalism." The *homo oeconomicus* shall be accompanied by the *homo affectus* (Sauer/Penz 2017). In addition, governments use affective means to govern citizens. The call for creativity and permanent availability at the work place, activation paradigms of social policies and community engagement are new affective strategies to interpellate 'active and affective citizens' in times of rising unemployment, cuts in welfare provisions, and a less protective and redistributive state. These affective citizens, however, have only limited opportunities to political participation. New forms of "affective citizenship" have replaced citizenship as rights (Fortier 2010). Another dimension of neoliberal affective governmentality are politics of responsibilization, of insecurity and securitization. The "entrepreneurial self" needs to take risks, to be competitive and successful. Failure produces shame.

Neoliberal affective governmentality thus produces insecurity and fear, while unleashing passions against those deemed unsuccessful and in need. In right-wing discourse, especially men but also women are given the right to be furious and passionate, they are freed from caring about others (as they have always been), from feelings of solidarity; and men are encouraged to modulate fear into anger and direct this anger towards 'Others.' Thus, blaming the elite, which is presented as ignoring people's needs and feelings, or blaming refugees and feminists for being responsible for their losses of wealth and security, i.e. turning fear into anger against these groups, are right-wing affective strategies to mobilize anger, to compensate for the loss of men's position of supremacy and to give agency back to lost voters (Hochschild 2016; Cramer 2016). Blaming the elite can be seen as relief, as a way of de-responsibilizing men and re-sovereignizing masculinity by re-establishing dominance through anger and aggression. The transformation of anxiety and fear, which originate in neoliberal affective demands at the workplace, for instance, towards anger against 'Others' is a way of reclaiming agency and control over one's life, over men's and women's lives – which were sacrificed to neoliberal competition and risk-taking.

Moreover, a feminist perspective points to the intersection of affective structures of domination and gender structures. These intersecting structures of domination point to constellations which are engrained in capitalist-patriarchal structures and bourgeois society, such as relations of production, division of labor, the separation between public and private as well as between national and international. The emergence of the radical right can therefore be explained by affective masculinist identity politics and the right-wing canalization of affect, especially aggression, towards an exclusive form of belonging that Marc Jongen (2017), the *AfD*'s ideologist, fosters with his notion of *thymos*, of (male) aggressiveness. The fear of a crisis of masculinity and the affective wish for a better future based on traditional gender roles, the heterosexual family and its promise of love, is constructed and politicized by right-wing populists. Affective masculinist identity politics promises to compensate the loss of traditional masculinist power positions and gender relations (Strick 2018).

At the same time, right-wing affective mobilization entails the promise of new forms of solidarity in times when 'traditional' forms of solidarity, for instance of the welfare state and the family, are eroding, an exclusive solidarity based on welfare chauvinism and nationalism, promising hope and empathy only within a group of 'similar people.' A case in point are the *Sweden Democrats*, who re-defined the notion of the "folkhem" in such an exclusive direction (Norocel 2013: 12) by creating a right-wing exclusive, affective atmosphere and "attunements" (Stewart 2011).

Hence, masculinist identity politics has been accompanied on the one hand by affective constructions of nationhood – of Austrianness, Germanness or Frenchness – whilst affectively excluding those constructed as 'Others.' On the other hand, right-wing populism includes an affective claim for recognition and citizenship. However, this "affective citizenship" (Fortier 2010) has to be related to 'appropriate' national and gendered feelings. Affective citizenship thus excludes and disrespects those who are marked as not belonging, those who should not belong to the national affective community and who should therefore be deprived of rights. Affective citizenship creates a specific form of affiliation to a community, an identity at the intersection of all genders who identify as natural.

Moreover, neoliberal citizenship is linked to processes of affective individualization, in which citizens are seen as customers, not endowed with rights but forced to develop an entrepreneurial spirit. Thus, the affective mobilization by the populist right includes the promise of affective agency in a time in which people have been deprived of agency and rights.

My overall argument is that it is not only right-wing populist strategies that draw on the triple register of cognition, body, and affect. The success of the radical right's affective strategy rests on an affective governmentality which became a general mode of governing people in times of neoliberalism. While right-wing populist parties across Europe seem to have one single issue – the mobilization against migration –, they still try to capture the fears of insecurity in the relations between men and women, the shame of 'failed patriarchs,' in order to safeguard against commodification of labor and life, by restoring the inequality of gender relations. Moreover, neoliberal affective strategies of self-entrepreneurship, of competition and insecurity have created masculinist affective subjectivities – entitled to compensate for fear and shame by anger and irresponsibility for others. Hence, the affective strategy of the radical right is successful because affect mobilization has been part of neoliberal subjectivization for a long time.

In the following, I want to reflect why gender is so important for right-wing mobilization and what the affective perspective tells us about the struggle over cultural and political hegemony and the new hegemonic project of the radical right.

5. Gendered Struggles for Hegemony and the Role of Affects

A gender perspective reveals that the radical right's project pushes towards the fundamental transformation of liberal democracies and welfare states. Right-wing so-called 'anti-genderist' mobilization must be seen as a 'cultural war' which turns the critique of neoliberal global restructuring *against* emancipatory movements of the 1960s and 1970s and *against* the Keynesian welfare state with its aims of (albeit limited) social equality and democratization. In these cultural and political struggles, gender works as an "empty signifier" (Laclau 1996) which is able to combine populist right-wing visions of society and the state, – such as natural inequality, exclusion, and authoritarianism – in order to modulate new hegemonic constellations. Hence, the empty signifier 'gender' becomes a catalyst in the movement of a masculinist identity politics to restore traditional gender regimes but also to push forward an anti-democratic project.

Referring to gender constructs a specific notion of 'the people' in three discursive modes: as a binary concept, gender *first* builds the paradigm for dividing societies into two distinct groups and eventually legitimizes the fundamental inequality of people and thus of social hierarchies (Lewandowsky/Giebler/Wagner 2016: 252ff.; Birsl 2011: 17). *Second*, gender evokes a natural, homogeneous, and pure people (Diehl 2016: 17) and thus represents an ethnopluralist idea of a people and an aversion towards a mix of different ethnicities. This nationalist-populist politics rejects plurality and legitimizes securitization, walling off the nation and walling out migrants and refugees (Brown 2010).

Third, in the antagonistic gender frame, the people is constructed as weak and passive, without agency – a deceived victim of elites. This people needs to be saved from the seduction of corrupt political and intellectual elites – such as gender politicians or the media. The savior is, of course, a right-wing populist leader. Hence, the interpellation of the people in right-wing populist political communication is part of the quest for more political leadership and thus for more authoritarianism.

In the populist right's struggle, gender works as a discourse that fundamentally challenges social equality, non-discrimination, and democratic sovereignty by evoking the natural inequality of human beings and the nativist people in need of leadership. In this argument, democracy as sovereignty of the people seems impossible due to the inequality of people and due to the need of protection, hierarchy, and leadership. The paternalistic and patriarchal image of the people results in an anti-democratic move.

Moreover, the transformation of gender relations and the right-wing mobilization of gender have been accompanied and spurred by a neoliberal mobilization and modulation of affects. Self-reliant people have to govern themselves; they have to be responsible for their own affects; they have to produce affects but at the same time moderate and manage their affects in order to be successful either on the job or in the private sphere. Affective citizenship is a masculinist notion of the sovereign subject.

Moreover, neoliberal affective governmentality has produced an excess of affects – especially of fear and insecurity. Right-wing antagonistic mobilization is able to draw on the modes of neoliberal affective governmentality. The political radical right is able to channel these affects in their gender ideology as the masculinist right to be aggressive without caring for others.

Against this background, I suggest to further engage in studying (right-wing) politics as an intersectional struggle over social relations – class, gender, sexuality, religion, and ethnicity, which have been embedded in Western liberal democracies and welfare states since the 19th century. Such an intersectional approach requires new coalitions in the struggle for democracy and democratization as well as against the radical populist right. It requires cooperation between social justice movements, such as the women's movements, migrant movements, leftist parties, and trade unions. These struggles are and have to be – in a Weberian sense – passionate struggles. However, we need more conceptual work to elaborate on the perspectives of affective emancipatory politics – of an affective democracy. In order to reclaim emancipatory ways of affective politics, it is not enough to mobilize passions and antagonisms "towards democratic designs" as Chantal Mouffe (2013) claims in "Politics and Passions." Affects are not per se democratic, they are always modulating power relations and are, thus, a dimension of *ongoing* struggles for – and against – equality and solidarity.

Bibliography

Amesberger, Helga/Halbmayr, Brigitte (eds.) (2002): Rechtsextreme Parteien – Eine mögliche Heimat für Frauen? Opladen: Leske und Budrich.

Bieling, Hans-Jürgen (2017): "Aufstieg des Rechtspopulismus im heutigen Europa – Umrisse einer gesellschaftstheoretischen Erklärung." In: WSI Mitteilungen 8, pp. 557-565.

Birsl, Ursula (2011): "Rechtsextremismus und Gender." In: Ursula Birsl (ed.): Rechtsextremismus und Gender. Opladen/Farmington Hills: Barbara Budrich, pp. 11-26.

Bitzan, Renate (2000): Selbstbilder Rechter Frauen. Zwischen Antisexismus und völkischem Denken. Tübingen: Edition Diskord.

Blee, Kathleen/McGee Deutsch, Sandra (eds.) (2012): Women of the Right: Comparisons and Interplay across Borders. University Park: Penn State Press.

Breivik, Anders (2011): 2083. A European Declaration of Independence. London.

Brown, Wendy (2010): Walled States, Waning Sovereignty. New York: Zone Books.

Bump, Philip (2016): "Trump Celebrates Winning 52 Percent of Women in 2016 – Which is only how he did among Whites." In: Washington Post (March 10, 2018), (www.washingtonpost.com/gdpr-consent/?destination=%2fnews%2-fpolitics%2fwp%2f2018%2f03%2f10%2ftrump-celebrates-winning-52-percent-of-women-in-2016-which-is-only-how-he-did-among-whites%2f%3f, 02.05.2019).

Cain, Ruth (2016): "Post-Truth and the 'Metropolitan Elite' Feminist: Lessons from Brexit." In: Feminist@law 6 (1), (journals.kent.ac.uk/index.php/feministsatlaw/article/view/259, 02.05.2019).

Connell, Raewyn/Messerschmidt, James W. (2005): "Hegemonic Masculinity. Rethinking the Concept." In: Gender & Society 6, pp. 829-859.

Cramer, Katherine J. (2016): The Politics of Resentment. Rural Consciousness in Wisconsin and the Rise of Scott Walker. Chicago: Chicago University Press.

Crouch, Colin (2004): Post-Democracy. London: Polity Press.

Diehl, Paula (2016): "Demokratische Repräsentation und ihre Krise." In: Aus Politik und Zeitgeschichte 40-42, pp. 12-17.

Dietze, Gabriele (2016): "Ethnosexismus. Sex-Mob-Narrative um die Kölner Sylvesternacht." In: Movements 1, (www.movements-journal.org, 02.05.2019).

Dörre, Klaus (2016): "Die National-Soziale Gefahr. Pegida, Neue Rechte und der Verteilungskonflikt – Sechs Thesen." In: Karl-Siegbert Rehberg/Franziska Kunz/Tino Schlinzig (eds.): PEGIDA – Rechtspopulismus zwischen Fremdenangst und "Wende"-Enttäuschung? Bielefeld: transcript.

Erzeel, Silvia/Rashkova, Ekaterina R. (2017): "Still Men's Parties? Gender and the Radical Right in Comparative Perspective." In: West European Politics 40 (4), pp. 812-20.

Farris, Sara (2017): In the Name of Women's Rights. The Rise of Femonationalism. Durham, London: Duke University Press.

Fortier, Anne-Marie (2010): "Proximity by Design? Affective Citizenship and the Management of Unease." In: Citizenship Studies 14 (1), pp. 17-30.

Hall, Stuart (1985): "Authoritarian Populism: A Reply to Jessop et al." In: New Left Review I/151 (May-June), pp. 115-124.

Hark, Sabine/Villa, Paula-Irene (eds.) (2015): Anti-Genderismus. Sexualität und Geschlecht als Schauplätze aktueller politischer Auseinandersetzungen. Bielefeld: transcript.

Harteveld, Eelvo et al. (2015): "The Gender Gap in Populist Radical-Right Voting: Examining the Demand Side in Western and Eastern Europe." In: Patterns of Prejudice 49 (1), pp. 103-134.

Hochschild, Arlie R. (2016): Strangers in Their Own Land: Anger and Mourning on the American Right. New York/London: New Press.

Jessop, Bob (2016): "The Organic Crisis of the British State: Putting Brexit in its Place." In: Globalizations 14 (1), pp. 133-141.

Jongen, Marc (2017): Migration und Thymostraining. (Lecture at the Winter Academy of the "Institut Für Staatspolitik") Online: www.youtube.com/watch?-v=cg_KuESI7rY, 12.06.2019.

Koppetsch, Cornelia (2017): "Aufstand der Etablierten? Rechtspopulismus und die Gefährdete Mitte." In: Soziopolis. Gesellschaft Beobachten, (soziopolis.de/beobachten/kultur/artikel/aufstand-der-etablierten/, 02.05.2019).

Kuhar, Roman/Paternotte, David (eds.) (2017): Anti-Gender Campaigns in Europe. Mobilizing against Equality. London: Roman and Littlefield.

Laclau, Ernesto (1996): Emancipation(s). London/New York: Verso.

Lange, Sarah de/Mügge, Liza M. (2015): "Gender and Right-Wing Populism in the Low Countries: Ideological Variations across Parties and Time." In: Patterns of Prejudice 49 (1), pp. 61-80.

Lewandowsky, Marcel/Giebler, Heiko/Wagner, Aiko (2016): "Rechtspopulismus in Deutschland. eine empirische Einordnung der Parteien zur Bundestagswahl 2013 unter besonderer Berücksichtigung der AfD." In: Politische Vierteljahresschrift 57 (2), pp. 247-275.

Mayer, Nonna (2013): "From Jean-Marie to Marine Le Pen: Electoral Change on the Far Right." In: Parliamentary Affairs 66 (1), pp. 160-178.

Mayer, Stefanie/Sauer, Birgit (2017): "'Gender Ideology' in Austria: Coalitions around an Empty Signifier." In: Roman Kuhar/David Paternotte (eds.): Anti-Gender Campaigns in Europe. Mobilizing against Equality. Lanham: Rowman and Littlefield, pp. 19-30.

Mayer, Stefanie/Sori, Iztok/Sauer, Birgit (2016): "Gendering 'the People': Heteronormativity and 'Ethno-Masochism' in Populist Imaginery." In: Maria Ranieri (ed.): Populism, Media and Education. Challenging Discrimination in Contemporary Digital Societies. London/New York: Routledge, pp. 84-104.

Meret, Susi (2015): "Female Charismatic Leadership and Gender: Pia Kjaesgaard and the Danish People's Party." In: Patterns of Prejudice 49 (1), pp. 81-102.

Meret, Susi/Siim, Birte/Pingaud, Etienne (2016): "Men's Parties with Women Leaders: A Comparative Study of the Right-Wing Populist Leaders Pia Kjærsgaard, Siv Jensen and Marine Le Pen." In: Gabriella Lazaridis/Giovanna Campani (eds.): Understanding the Populist Shift. Othering in a Europe in Crisis. London/New York: Routledge, pp. 122-149.

Morgan, Kimberly J. (2017): "Gender, Right-Wing Populism, and Immigrant Integration Policies in France, 1989-2012." In: West European Politics 40 (4), pp. 887-906.
Mouffe, Chantal (2000): The Democratic Paradox. London/New York: Verso.
Mouffe, Chantal (2013): Hegemony, Radical Democracy, and the Political, edited by James Martin. London: Routledge.
Mudde, Cas (2004): "The Populist Zeitgeist." In: Government and Opposition 39 (4), pp. 541-563.
Mudde, Cas (2007): Populist Radical Right Parties in Europe. Cambridge: Cambridge University Press.
Müller, Jan-Werner (2016): Was ist Populismus? ein Essay. Berlin: Suhrkamp.
Norocel, Ov Cristian (2013): "'Give us back Sweden!' A Feminist Reading of the (Re)Interpretations of the Folkhem Conceptual Metaphor in Swedish Radical Right Populist Discourse." In: NORA. Nordic Journal of Feminist and Gender Research 21 (1), pp. 4-20.
Piketty, Thomas (2014): Capital in the Twenty-First Century. Cambridge: Harvard University Press.
Papadopoulos, Dimitris/Tsianos, Vassilis (2006): Precarity: A Savage Journey to the Heart of Embodied Capitalism. Online: eipcp.net/transversal/1106/tsianospapadopoulos/en, 02.05.2019.
Radhakrishnan, Smitha/Solari, Cinzia (2015): "Empowered Women, Failed Patriarchs: Neoliberalism and Global Gender Anxieties." In: Sociology Compass 9 (9), pp. 784-802.
Rashkova, Ekaterina R./Zankina, Emilia (2017): "Are (Populist) Radical Right Parties Männerparteien? Evidence from Bulgaria." In: West European Politics 40 (4), pp. 848-68.
Rico, Guillem/Guinjoan, Marc/Anduiza, Eva (2017): "The Emotional Underpinning of Citizens' Populism: How Anger, Fear, and Sadness Affect Populist Attitudes and Vote Choice." In: Research Gate.
Rommelspacher, Birgit (2011): "Frauen und Männer im Rechtsextremismus – Motive, Konzepte und Rollenverständnisse." In: Ursula Birsl (ed.): Rechtsextremismus und Gender. Opladen/Farmington Hills: Barbara Budrich, pp. 43-68.
Sauer, Birgit et al. (2016): "Exclusive Intersections: Constructions of Gender and Sexuality." In: Gabriella Lazaridis/Giovanna Campani (eds.): Understanding the Populist Shift. Othering in a Europe in Crisis. London/New York: Routledge, pp. 104-121.
Sauer, Birgit/Penz, Otto (2017): "Affective Governmentality: A Feminist Perspective." In: Christine Hudson/Malin Rönnblom, Katherine Teghtsoonian (eds.): Gender, Governance and Feminist Analysis. London/New York: Routledge, pp. 39-58.

Saxer, Marc (2017): "Ten Theses for the Fight Against Right-Wing Populism." In: Social Europe, (www.socialeurope.eu/ten-theses-fight-right-wing-populism, 02.05.2019).

Schellenberg, Britta (2009): "Aktuelle Entwicklungen im europäischen Rechtsextremismus." In: Bundeszentrale für Politische Bildung, (www.bpb.de, 02.05.2019).

Sloterdijk, Peter (2012): Zorn und Zeit, politisch-psychologischer Versuch. Berlin: Suhrkamp.

Spierings, Niels/Zaslove, Andrje (2015): "Gendering the Vote for Populist Radical-Right Parties." In: Patterns of Prejudice 49 (1), pp. 135-162.

Spierings, Niels/Zaslove, Andrje (2017): "Gender, Populist Attitudes, and Voting: Explaining the Gender Gap in Voting for Populist Radical Right and Populist Radical Left Parties." In: West European Politics 40 (4), pp. 821-847.

Starck, Kathleen/Sauer, Birgit (2014): A Man's World? Political Masculinities in Literature and Culture. Cambridge: Cambridge Scholar.

Stewart, Kathleen (2011): "Atmospheric Attunements." In: Environment and Planning 29 (3), pp. 445-453.

Strick, Simon (2018): "Alt-Right-Affekte. Provokationen und Online-Taktiken." In: zfm (Zeitschrift für Medienwissenschaft) 19 (2), pp. 113-125.

Vasilopoulou, Sofia/Wagner, Markus (2017): "Fear, Anger and Enthusiasm about the European Union: Effects of Emotional Reactions on Public Preferences towards European Integration." In: European Union Politics 18 (3), pp. 382-405.

Wagner, Markus (2013): "Fear and Anger in Great Britain: Blame Assignment and Emotional Reactions in the Financial Crisis." In: Political Behavior 36 (3), pp. 683-703.

Wichterich, Christa (2007): "Globalisierung und Geschlecht. Über Neoliberale Strategien zur Gleichstellung." In: Blätter für Deutsche und Internationale Politik 6, pp. 686-695.

Wimbauer, Christine/Motakef, Mona/Teschlade, Julia (2015): "Prekäre Selbstverständlichkeiten. Neun Prekarisierungstheoretische Thesen zu Diskursen gegen Gleichstellungspolitik und Geschlechterforschung." In: Sabine Hark/Paula-Irene Villa (eds.): Anti-Genderismus. Sexualität und Geschlecht als Schauplätze Aktueller Politischer Auseinandersetzungen. Bielefeld: transcript.

Williams, Raymond (1977): "Structures of Feeling." In: Raymond Williams: Marxism and Literature. Oxford: Oxford University Press, pp. 128-135.

Why Gender and Sexuality are both Trivial and Pivotal in Populist Radical Right Politics

Niels Spierings

Introduction: Similar But Different

The role of women and gender in the political far and extreme right has long been studied in the social sciences and humanities. Most recently, considerable attention has been paid to the rise of the Populist Radical Right (PRR), including three special issues in a matter of years (Spierings/Zaslove 2015b; Erzeel/Rashkova 2017; Miller-Idress/Pilkingon 2017). These and other studies have provided a great deal of insight into the existing but relatively secondary role of women leaders, cadre and voters (Givens 2004; Hartevelt et al. 2015; Immerzeel/Jaspers/Lubbers 2013; Meret 2015; Mayer 2013; Stasulane 2017; Spierings/Lubbers/Zaslove 2017; Spierings/Zaslove 2015), and the ways in which gender and sexual hierarchies and images prevail in the policies and discourses of the PRR (Akkerman 2015; De Lange/Mügge 2015; Norocel 2009, 2010; Meret/Siim/Pingaud 2016; Spierings/Lubbers/Zaslove 2017), particularly when it comes to its nativist and anti-Islam agenda across the European region (De Lange/Mügge 2015; Spierings/Zaslove 2015b).

At the same time, this wide array of studies has laid bare a puzzling set of observations: All PRR parties are conservative in one way or another when it comes to the topic of gender (i.e. social relations and institutions shaped by gender and sexuality); there are clear differences in their positions on gender equality; and the party family is quite divided on issues related to sexuality specifically. Still, gender and sexuality seem to be recurring themes across parties, and yet they are not considered defining characteristics of PRR ideology (see Mudde 2007: 96). Put simply: gender is omnipresent but in context-dependent ways. However, this truism is a rather unsatisfying assessment from comparative and theoretical perspectives.

Comparatively, it leaves us with a mixed bag of comparable but distinctly different cases, and without a clear understanding of what distinguishes one from the other. A common (and insightful but post-hoc) classification draws on references to national and political culture. This may help to understand individual cases, but it does not produce comparative demarcations as are needed to understand the movement's impact and success patterns across Europe. Simply put, we need a more systematic understanding of how PRR parties differ from one another in terms of gender. Theoretically, such a comparative approach should be guided by a clear and testable logic. Nonetheless, there have been very few attempts "to explain such variations [...] related to gender across the ideology of right-wing populist parties" (De Lange/Mügge 2015: 66). As the focus here is on the PRR, I propose that for understanding the role of gender in PRR politics in a coherent and parsimonious way, our theoretical frame needs to connect to the conceptual definition of PRR parties' ideology: populism, nativism, and authoritarianism (Mudde 2007; Mudde/Kaltwasser 2017). This chapter thus works to extend beyond the question of how parties in a specific country position themselves in terms of gender equality and sexuality (for excellent case studies with that approach, see Dudink 2017; Norocel 2010). Building on the existing literature, I will instead present an explanation for both the omnipresence of, and differences concerning gender and sexuality in the politics of PRR parties.

This argument relies on the observation that our societies are highly gendered, whereby gender and sexuality are core markers of our social identities (see Buikema/Plate/Van der Tuin 2009; Sandfort et al. 2000; Walby 2009) and central to ongoing political struggles (see Paternotte/Kuhar 2018; Verloo 20018; Walby 2011) and to significant demographic and economic shifts (e.g. Inglehart 1997; Inglehart/Norris 2003). Importantly, these latter developments contest the entitlements and privileges as captured in existing gender and sexuality norms and structures. Given this context, gender may not be a defining quality of PRR ideology (Mudde 2007; Mudde/Kaltwasser 2015), but it is nonetheless near to the PRR core as it brings together and highlights every element of PRR ideology, tapping into fundamental parts of people's identity. In this sense, gender is 'trivotal' – i.e. a combination of trivial, meaning that it is not at the PRR's ideological core, and pivotal, meaning a core social relation that is instrumentalized to center and emphasize the PRR ideology.

To elaborate, I argue that it is precisely the populist element that helps to explain differences in the party family. Firstly, the PRR appeals to common sense by supporting the general will of those thought to be morally good. This leads to an effective "feel-good" politics entailing an implicit praise for the 'common man' and his moral superiority. The positions of the PRR are thereby mere translations of the current common sense, the dominant opinion of 'the people.' From where the people come is irrelevant to the PRR, and so it can vary significantly. Secondly, the anti-elitist quality of populist ideology sets this 'common sense good' against the intentions of the political elite. If those aims include the advancement of women's rights or LGBT emancipation so as to actually hurt the entitlements of the common people (e.g. obligate a change in behaviors or additional sensitivities), they can be used to demonstrate how the political elite goes 'too far' in protecting the rights of minorities (e.g. LGBT people, feminists).

Additionally, it is unsurprising that gender and sexuality are central to the populist right and not the populist left: the authoritarian dimensions of the radical right appeal to natural orders; and gender and sexual relations under nativism are ideal markers for distinguishing the good from the threat, which is thought to emerge through allegedly non-native groups such as Muslims and other migrants.

In what follows, I will first set the empirical scene from which this argument has been developed. The focus will be on Western Europe, and on the Dutch case in particular, which is a rather exceptional and therefore illuminating case when it comes to sexuality and traditionalism. Next, I will unfold the theoretical argument by taking the dominant definition of the PRR and systematically theorizing the connections of populism (i.e. the general will, the people, the elite) and the radical right (i.e. authoritarianism, nativism) with gender and sexuality. The arguments presented in this chapter are of course limited by the scope of my empirical knowledge, which is largely restricted to the Dutch and Flemish cases in a comparative perspective to Western Europe. Nonetheless, I anticipate that the arguments presented here resemble the situation of other contexts. Hence, the closing section of this chapter will summarize the main arguments and challenges, and suggest avenues for future research, including the formulation of testable implications of the *trivotality of gender in the PRR*.

Gender and the PRR in Contemporary Western Europe

In his seminal 2007 book, *Populist radical right parties in Europe*, Cas Mudde labeled the PRR parties 'Männerparteien' (2007: 90-118), thereby accounting for the predominance of men and masculinity in the PRR party family. However, as Mudde also notes, this must be considered in relation to the fact that politics are male dominated overall (2007: 91). It could thus be argued that masculinity in the PRR is at one extreme of the spectrum, but it is not an outlier that is fully off of the political charts (see also Erzeel/Rahskova 2017; Spierings/Zaslove 2015a, 2015b).

Indeed, if PRR parties are regarded on a masculinity spectrum, where on the spectrum are they located? Understanding the gender and sexual politics of the PRR party family is dependent on a response to this question. I thus discuss below several dimensions of the gendered PRR politics and party diversity: (a) their positions on family and social relations and on gender and immigration, and (b) the demographics of PRR actors, including its leaders, activists and voters.

Platforms and Policies

Family and Societal Relations

The complex positions of the PRR, as party family, on gender equality becomes clear when one zooms in on the topics of family and social relations. As summarized by Kofman (1998) and echoed by others (Mudde 2007; Akkerman 2015; De Lange/Mügge 2015), PRR parties do not have a common position on these issues. While they can each be considered traditionalist, also compared with conservative right-wing parties (Akkerman 2015), their views vary considerably between parties and over time.

In general, the parties can be divided into two large blocks: conservative, traditionalist or neo-traditionalist parties on the one hand, and modern conservative or modern traditional ones on the other (Amesberger/Halbmayr 2002; Mudde 2007; Akkerman 2015; De Lange/Mügge 2015). The former grouping positions the family as the cornerstone of society, they are starkly opposed to abortion, and they have tried to make divorce more difficult, such as among the *Dutch Centrum Demokraten (CD)* and *Centrumspartij/Centrumspartij 86 (CP/CP'86)*, or the *Flemish Vlaams Belang (VB)* in the eighties and nineties (Akkerman 2015; De Lange/Mügge 2015; Mudde 2007). These parties echo or directly refer to the alleged "natural roles" of men and women. But even some of these groups have mixed their positions on the family with more modern conservative stances, which, such as with the *VB*, include support for childcare and women's participation in the labor market (Akkerman 2015). It should also be noted that the *PVV* of Geert Wilders did not show any interest in family issues in their party documents (2007-2012); they actually voted against a revision of childcare regulations in parliament (Akkerman 2015: 44-45). Moreover, the *PVV* is viewed to be far less traditional in expert survey-based comparative studies (Campbell/Erzeel 2018). At the same time, almost all PRR parties are against, if not hostile to, gender quotas and other affirmative action policies (but see Mudde 2007: 94).

LGBT issues, about which the party family might once have been united, increasingly provoke divisions (Spierings/Lubbers/Zaslove 2017; Spierings/Zaslove 2015b). While most parties remain conservative on the topic – opposing marriage equality and adoption by same-sex couples (Akkerman 2015) –, there are important deviations. Most notably, the *Dutch Partij voor de Vrijheid (PVV)* has argued for equal rights on several fronts, a politic that began with its more liberal populist predecessor, the *Lijst Pim Fortuyn (LPF)* (De Lange/Mügge 2015; Dudink 2017). This is more than window dressing. For instance, they actually voted in support of a bill that denied civil servants the right to refuse marrying same-sex couples. This was all the more remarkable given that the minority government they supported (and with whom they had a minority agreement) was depending on support from the ultraorthodox Christian *Staatkundig Gereformeerde Partij* (*SGP*) in the upper house (Akkerman 2015; Spierings/Lubbers/Zaslove 2017). Other PRR parties take relatively moderate positions as well. For instance, the *Danish Dansk Folkeparti* (*DF*) supports civil unions for same-sex couples (Akkerman 2015; Meret 2015), and the Flemish VB, not wanting to propagate discrimination, is said to prefer conciliation over opposing same-sex marriage (Akkerman 2015: 47), which at least indicates that they do not want to be seen as anti-gay.

However, there are clear limits to these pro-LGBT positions, even for the Dutch PVV, and particularly when it comes to the 'T'. In the Netherlands, transgender rights have become part of general public debates. For instance, in 2017, the national railways made public that their general announcements would soon address railway users with 'Dear travelers', thereby replacing 'Dear Ladies and Gentlemen.' The *PVV* responded by stating that the "Dutch Railways clearly lost any sense of direction," and they formally asked the transport minister what would happen with railway employees who would refuse to use the new gender-less greeting (Spierings 2017). As one might expect, attitudes among the Dutch are more ambivalent towards transgender people than towards LGB people. For instance, more people agree than disagree that gender confirming surgeries should be funded by the pursuers of care rather than the state, and only a very small majority disagrees with the statement that they would rather not socialize with people who have an unclear sex (Kuyper 2016: 25).

Overall, we could draw the provisional conclusion that the most traditional parties are found in the most traditional times and countries. Several Western European PRR parties have become increasingly modern conservative, while others have been moving even further towards the modern end of the spectrum (see also De Lange/Mügge 2015:73). For instance, Belgian PRR parties are more conservative than the Dutch, which reflects differences in public opinion: more Belgian than Dutch citizens oppose gender equality (see Spierings 2018).

Gender and Anti-Immigrant Politics

Another major policy area when it comes to gender and the PRR concerns immigration and Islam. All parties stress the perceived misogynist nature of immigrants' or Islamic cultures, which are thought to threaten the native culture, alleged to have already achieved emancipation (Akkerman 2015; De Lange/Mügge 2015; Mudde 2007). Related policies of interest to the parties have been the veil, Female Genital Mutilation (FGM), honor killings, segregated activities like swimming, and forced marriages; policy plans for empowering immigrant women via self-organization, support and education are hardly mentioned (see Akkerman 2015; De

Lange/Mugge 2015). It thus seems that the parties are not so much concerned with the position of Muslim women but with a fight against Islam(ization) in general.[1]

The entanglements of gender in critiques of immigration or Islam are strong and clear across parties, but there are also notable differences. Three elements stand out (see Akkerman 2015; De Lange/Mügge 2015; Kofman 1998; Mudde 2007; Spierings/Zaslove 2015b). First, parties differ in their evocation of a nature-based logic, which can include elements such as a racist ideology or procreation policies. Second, the focus has shifted from immigrants in general to a framing around Islam, with 9/11 (2001) as a critical turning point. Third, parties differ with regards to the importance of this issue: For example, parties in Scandinavia and the Netherlands focus more on migration and Islam than parties in the Alpine countries and France; PRR parties in France, for instance, have shown explicit respect for French Muslim combatants in the Algerian colonial war (Akkerman 2015: 53).

In sum, gender and sexuality importantly demarcate nativist policies across the PRR. Nonetheless, common to all parties has been concerns about the perceived risks posed by migrants to gender relations in the so-called native society has been common to all parties; the entanglements of gender and immigration are not connected with a concern for non-native Muslim or immigrant women per se.[2] Gender relations thus seem to be secondary to the PRR (Mudde 2007; Spierings/Zaslove 2015b).

Gender and PRR Actors

Leadership and Activists

The general lack of female leaders is one reason why PRR parties have been considered Männerparteien. However, Mudde has noted that the leaders of other parties tend to be men as well (2007). Indeed, debates from the last two Dutch national elections are more likely to include no female leaders than more than one. When it comes to sexuality, the picture is actually very similar across political parties, though the number of openly gay PRR leaders is remarkably low.[3] Nonetheless, leadership is not just about descriptive representation: the ways in which parties and their leaders evoke masculinities and femininities matter too (see Meret 2015; Norocol 2009, 2010). They tell us about how gender is trivotal to PRR politics.

---

1 This is a topic about which Geert Wilders and Ayaan Hirsi Ali disagree although they are often named in the same breath (Hirsi Ali 2006).
2 The PRR parties' positions on development aid are illustrative here.
3 Jörg Haider was not openly gay as party leader. Pim Fortuyn was open about his sexuality, but the *LPF* is often considered neo-liberal right-wing populist more than PRR (De Lange/Mügge 2015; Spierings/Lubbers/Zaslove 2017).

Motherhood and care are recurring themes that reveal how female leaders of the PRR present themselves. This holds true for mothers among PRR leaders but also for Siv Jensen of the *Norwegian Progress Party* (SD), who regularly calls herself a caring person, and the Dutch Rita Verdonk of *Trots op Nederland* (TON), who is known for her stories about household work, such as cooking, and is the only female PRR leader in recent Dutch politics (Meret 2015; Meret/Siim/Pinguad 2016; Vossen 2010). Of note is that male leaders also use care and family metaphors in PRR discourses sometimes (Norocel 2010).

Several female leaders balance traditional gender role images by presenting themselves as strong leaders and self-made women who go against the social or political grain. Sometimes, this also ties back into a framing around motherhood, such as when they emphasize being a single mother as proof of strength (Meret 2015; Mudde 2007). These women often build on or defend women's accomplishments and the rights won by the first two waves of feminism. However, the relationship between the female leaders and today's feminism is more complex. For instance, Nordic Pia Kjærsgaard in Denmark and Siv Jensen might acknowledge the progresses that have been made for women, but they see no further need for feminism in that native women can now make their own choices. Still, Le Pen does not shy away from the label "feminist," regularly connecting it to her own life course and struggles (Meret/Siim/Pinguad 2016).

What can be said of those increasingly active, oft-analyzed female party members (Erzeel/Rashkova 2017; see also Dietze's contribution to this volume)? As noted before, such studies are limited (Mudde 2007; but see Scrinzi 2014), but there are some important parallels with several of the afore-presented observations. The PRR parties permitting ordinary membership[4] may appear skewed in terms of gender, but, again, the degree of difference does not put them far outside of the political charts. In the Dutch case, the numbers are close to those of the Christian Democrats and, in fact, the PRR generally outperforms the orthodox Christian parties (Mudde 2007). Moreover, many women are active in the PRR even if they do not fit the ideal picture of women as promoted by the parties. For instance, the Dutch CD has been opposed to divorce, but divorced women were noticeably active in the party (Mudde 2007). Moreover, not all party activists agree with all of the parties' gender policies. Similarly, LGBT party members have at times joined forces to attempt to create LGBT party bodies, such as the failed effort in the SVP (Akkerman 2015; see also the contribution by Wielowiejski to this volume).

Overall the position towards women in PRR parties is dualistic. Gendered images in the PRR parties appeal to notions of traditional families and empowered women; there is room for divergence from official party policies on gender issues.

---

4 The Dutch *PVV* does not.

It may appear that the PRR parties embrace first and second wave feminism, but it remains taboo to address the specific needs of women or sexual minorities.

The Voter Base

There is a gender gap in public support for the PRR (Evans/Ivaldi 2002; Immerzeel/Jaspers/Lubbers 2013; Hartevelt et al. 2015; Mayer 2013, 2015; Lubbers 2001; Spierings/Zaslove 2015a, 2017). Nonetheless, nuance is needed when analyzing and describing this gap and its causes; the label Männerparteien presents a grave oversimplification. In recent elections, women accounted for 40% or more of PRR voters (Spierings/Zaslove 2015a). In earlier elections, by contrast, around one third of voters were women (Evans/Ivaldi 2002; Lubbers 2001; Mudde 2007). This declining difference suggests that the gap is not only limited, but it may also be closing (Mayer 2015).

While different theories have been put forth to explain this gap, we can say with some certainty that women are not less anti-migrant than men, and although they show more support for gender equality on average, additional factors must be considered (Hartevelt et al. 2015; Mayer 2002; Spierings/Zaslove 2015a). Moreover, attitudes towards homosexuality do not generally explain voting patterns in support of PRR parties, and the combination of pro-LGBT and anti-immigrant attitudes has not clearly determined voting behaviors – in part due to competition with the conservative liberals (Spierings/Zaslove 2015a; Spierings/Lubbers/Zaslove 2017).

In addition to several convincing arguments on gendered structural differences (see Hartevelt et al. 2015; Spierings/Zaslove 2017), an important explanation for different voting patterns across genders has been the fact that women are 'less political' in terms of knowledge, interest, and efficacy. Women tend to vote for established parties even if they are ideologically close to the new PRR parties (Gidengil et al. 2005; Mayer 2002; Mudde 2007; Spierings/Zaslove 2015b). In short, programmatic ideology matters, but so does being depicted as radical outsiders.

Gender: Trivial to PRR Ideology but Pivotal to PRR Politics

Populist Radical Right

While the PRR parties may have thus 'normalized' their political platforms (Erzeel/Rashkova 2017), they are still at the conservative end of the political spectrum (see also Mudde 2007; Spierings/Zaslove 2015a). Moreover, their perspective on social relations when it comes to gender and sexuality clearly differ by time and space. Blaming national culture is hardly satisfying, not least because it does not explain why gender is so omnipresent and yet not central to PRR ideology. If gender and sexuality were fundamental parts of the PRR ideology, their positions should not differ so much.

In this paragraph, I thus follow an ideational approach to populism, defining it as "a thin-centered ideology that considers society to be ultimately separated into two homogeneous and antagonistic camps, 'the pure people' versus 'the corrupt elite,' and which argues that politics should be an expression of the *volonté générale* (general will) of the people." (Mudde/Kaltwasser 2017: 6) The advantages of an ideational approach align precisely with the goals of this chapter: it helps to understand why populism creates malleability, and accounts for the interaction between supply and demand (ibid: 19-20). Next to populism, the focus here is on the Radical Right as the second most programmatically substantive ideology to which populism is attached, with nativism and authoritarianism at its core (Mudde 2007).

I argue below that a focus on the core elements of PRR ideology is needed to demonstrate how gender relations resonate with its core structures. As we will see, such a focus can help to explain why gender is so present in PRR politics today, and to understand its internal variation when it comes to gender politics.

Populism: the General Will of the People

A simplified construction of reality, 'the people' alludes to a vague but shared notion of the common and "native" man. As a community, common people know what is morally good, whereby this knowledge is often rooted in common sense (Mudde/Kaltwasser 2017: 9-19). There are no such things as a Marxist false conscience, ignorance or uncertainty; the people know what is right – i.e. what is in their common interest.

This connection to common sense and morality resonates strongly with the gender policies and discourse of PRR parties. Their gender politics are not just products of the national culture; they (unconsciously or consciously) instrumentalize existing gender and sexual relations. It is believed that these relations are optimal among the common people. And while the current situation is thought to be better than ever before (i.e. when women had no rights and homosexuals were prosecuted), supranational politics or (national) social movements that push for change are alleged to be enforcing something against the will of the people. Correspondingly, women or LGBT interest groups demanding too much might actually jeopardize that unity.

The PRR parties' positions thus differ between countries simply because the gender regimes across Europe differ due to the variations in structural conditions and successes of social movements. For instance, same-sex marriage was normalized in the Netherlands well before the *PVV* existed, so it is simply a given and even defended by them, but not in other European countries. At the same time, transgender rights and unisex toilets (that is "toilets") are perceived as infringing on the entitlements of the common man in the Netherlands, and the PRR can defend these entitlements based simply on common sense, references to natural differences,[5] or accusations of exaggerated claims (i.e. 'we have given them equality, they should not force their will upon us').

Importantly, in our gendered societies, everyone is subject to gender norms, and gender is highly fundamental to one's self-identification and identifying with others. In current debates, however, gender norms are being questioned in a wide range of contexts, and many 'common people' feel as though they are being accused of sexism and homophobia by being told that they are and have been doing things wrong for as long as they remember (all fallacies of our memory included). Instead of seeking change to include other experiences into societal norms and practices as other parties do, the PRR insists that things are perfectly fine as they are. The PRR thus takes positions that allow for people to feel good about the ways in which they have been behaving rather than suggesting that their behaviors have been wrong or exclusionary and should be changed accordingly. And they can do this while defending gender equality simply because this politic is not at the heart of their ideology, making an absolute position on this unnecessary. Gender and sexuality are thus ideal arenas through which they can display an agenda in line with the will of the general people – i.e. the status quo.

Populism: the Elite

At the other end of the Manichean divide of society are the elite, who are considered corrupt and thought to not represent the interests of the common people. Established political actors are part of this elite, but it can also include the media and social movements (Mudde/Kaltwasser 2017: 11-14). In other words, while the elite-people distinction is moral (Mudde/Kaltwasser 2017), drawing the dividing lines separating them is situational.

In drawing these lines, public opinion can be crucial; but public opinion does not simply shape policies, it also adapts to politics. For instance, policies designed to enhance gender equality are often proposed by political actors to support women in leadership positions or, generally, in the labor market, which in turn are intended to influence public perceptions and opinions regarding the role of women in society. However, these policies often do not initially align with public opinions among large parts of societies. In other words, existing regimes matter in determining what demarcates the elite.

---

5 Nature serves as an anchor for common sense, but the interpretation of what nature is or does varies considerably. This might also explain why nature plays far less of a prominent role in the official PRR discourse than it has in previous non-mainstream right ideologies.

Support for gender equality and affirmative action in particular differs considerably across countries. In the Nordic countries, which are known for their state feminism, feminism is firmly anchored among the elite, an observation that was reflected in the fact that the PRR party leader regularly emphasized family and care. This politics clearly sets them apart from the elite. Similarly, the European Union is a main proponent of gender equality, which then becomes part of the elitist agenda. And yet in other cases, like we saw for Marine Le Pen, leaders can co-opt the label "feminist," evidencing that it is not or is no longer elitist.

Thus, if people are morally in agreement with the current local situation with regards to gender and sexual relations, any political efforts to further gender and sexual equality and rights are vulnerable to being framed or experienced as an elitist attempt to go against the general will of the common people. Given that gender as a frame or reference is so deeply engrained in societies, and given the active (and successful) social and political movements around these issues, gender and sexual politics are very much well-suited as grounds for populism to mobilize against an elite, although such a framing does not define their ideology.

Radical Right

In addition to its populist core, the current PRR ideology centers on authoritarianism and nativism – as the Radical Right (Mudde 2007). Focusing on these elements makes clear, why PRR parties are generally so keen to politicize gender relations.

First, authoritarianism does not refer to non-democratic, authoritarian regimes but to "the belief in a strictly ordered society, in which infringements of authority are to be punished severely [...] [including] [...] law and order and punitive conventional moralism" (Mudde 2007: 23). I would argue that this part of the PRR is currently somewhat less dominant in European politics, particularly when it comes to the discussions presented here. However, the notion of an ordered society does resonate well with contemporary constructs of sex and the ways in which all kinds of practices and objects are gendered. While not formally segregated, European societies are gendered in many ways: from toys to toothpaste, and from childcare to cheese spread.[6] The focus of PRR parties on keeping gender relations as they are echoes this part of their ideology.

Second, nativism links to the idea of a homogenous people, whereby "the people" are demarcated as native (like the elite) but threatened by outsiders in their common way of life. This threat can take many shapes and can be thought to target the economic underpinnings of the common way of life, or to directly threaten a way of life culturally. The fact that gender equality and LGBT empowerment are

---

6   Yes, the toothpaste and cheese spread are real examples. The leading-brand advertisements presenting tooth paste and cheese spread for men can be obtained from the author.

relatively strong in Europe, particularly compared to the imagined average overall status of these issues in the origin countries from where immigrants come, makes them ideal points of demarcation: it makes the native common man feel good, it frames the Islamic or immigrant outsider as a threat, and it allows for blaming the elite for not closing the borders.

Blaming the elite for not protecting the people against misogynic, homophobic and sexist outsiders and for pushing the emancipation agenda too far with proposals like affirmative action and transgender rights, has been called anything from window-dressing to hypocritical and ironic (see Akkerman 2015; Mudde 2007: 96). From the perspectives presented here, however, these initiatives do have an ideological logic, and that logic is applied rather consistently. In other words, these positions might be more than opportunistic or strategic choices; they may actually be rooted in the ideology of the PRR.

And it is no surprise that the populist right in particular has had few problems with incorporating gender into its program and discourse, especially because the framing of 'the West' versus 'Islam'/'migrant cultures' along gender lines has had a long history that extends as far back as the Orientalist colonial 'mission civilatrice' (Said 1978; Spierings 2015). Still, as stressed above, gender relations are secondary to the PRR, and they service nativist and populist ideologies. For example, while PRR voters might be distinguished from other voters on account of their anti-immigrant and populist attitudes, this difference is not or is only slightly moderated by strong support for gender equality or LGBT rights.

Re-Understanding Gender & PRR Politics

In short, because gender (i.e. social relations and institutions shaped by gender and sexuality) is so fundamental to our societies' organization, it has been an ideal frame through which PRR parties can showcase the core elements of their ideology: it allows for them to compliment people on being morally just about an area of life that is so deeply engraved in their identity, allude to a notion of order that normalizes differences, and at the same time use gender* to showcase how the elite, who is pushing emancipation beyond the interests of the common man, is not effectively protecting emancipation from the threats posed by (immigrant or Muslim) outsiders.

Gender thus uniquely brings together all elements of PRR politics around an identity marker that is so fundamental to people's perceptions of themselves and of society, rendering it pivotal in PRR politics. At the same time, it is not intrinsically part of their ideological core, which ultimately makes it trivial to the PRR. This 'trivolaty' is important as it helps us to understand why PRR parties across Western Europe tend to focus on the issue of gender, thereby showing very similar patterns, even as they vary considerably between countries and times (e.g. Mudde 2007; Spierings/Zaslove 2015b). It is thus not just about context (e.g. Akkerman 2015; Dudink 2017; Mudde/Kaltwasser 2015); it is a very specific pattern, whereby current gender and sexual relations are understood to be morally just.

The shifts from hardcore gender traditionalism towards modern-traditionalism within countries and within parties (see De Lange/Mügge 2015; Mayer 2013) fit this argument that parties adjust to the norms of today, and reflect the growing importance of the populist dimension in this segment of the European party systems. Connections between the nativist (and related nationalist, fascist, and extreme-right) agenda to the thin-centered populist ideology have facilitated the normalization of nativism (cf. Mudde 2007); the degrees to which PRR parties have embraced populism have also shaped their relationship with gender.

Analyzing the different degrees of populism and their electoral successes also touches on an issue I have ignored for the sake of argument until now: not all parties and examples from Western European PRR gender politics fit my assessment seamlessly. For instance, the *True Finns* are somewhat more conservative than the country's context suggests, and the positions of some Nordic parties on homosexuality are leaning towards the more conservative side than one would expect based on public opinion (see Akkerman 2015; Norocel 2009 2010; Spierings 2018). Here, it is crucial to realize that political parties, the PRR included, do not always act in accordance with their ideological core. If the arguments I make in this chapter are correct, the parties should continue to shift towards the positions on gender as considered normal in their context. More specifically, a testable implication of my argument is that the new parties fit the populist take on gender more strongly than those parties that have been around much longer, the latter of which stem from fascist, far-right or agrarian parties that have had a fixed gender traditionalism at the core of their ideologies (e.g. *FPÖ*, *Front National*, and *True Finns*). These new parties should thus still be relatively conservative even as they have moved towards a more populist take on gender.

More testable implications can be derived from the idea of alignment with public opinion, or, more precisely, that PRR parties are expected to follow the publics' shifting attitudes on gender issues. For instance, transgender equality and rights currently run counter to what is experienced as "common sense" (Kuyper 2016), and, accordingly, no PRR parties have supported the transgender community. However, in the Netherlands, debates on these issues have become much more commonplace in the mainstream (e.g. several television programs focus on it, there is a strong transgender rights social movement, and the parliament has given the issue attention). Moreover, actual societal change is taking place. This includes the examples presented above (on the national railways using 'Dear passengers' instead of gendered pronouns and gender-free toilets), and, at the time of writing this chapter, the senate voted to change the anti-discrimination law to explicitly include protection for transgender people (as "transgenderism").[7] Such efforts in progressive lawmaking and emancipation generally lead to further attitudinal changes, hence the normalization of transgender rights in Dutch society. If so, it could be expected that the PVV will not abruptly embrace queerness and gender fluidity, but that it might start to defend the use of neutral pronouns not to exclude anyone. This may be unlikely to happen tomorrow, in the coming months, or even in the next few years, but this example demonstrates that the arguments made above can be translated to testable hypotheses on between and within party differences.

One last testable suggestion, derived from the broader arguments presented herein, relates to the realization that populist politics are feel-good politics. It does not simply play into emotions like fear and anger (e.g. Rico/Guinjoan/Anduiza 2017); implicitly and consistently it also provides people with an impression that they are doing something good. This extends beyond claims made about people knowing what is right. As with gender, it stresses that people are doing the right thing, and that they do so regularly in their daily lives. I would argue that the better a PRR party incorporates this framing, the more successful the party will be (ceteris paribus).

Overall, this chapter set out to offer a better understanding of the trivial but pivotal role of gender in PRR politics, particularly its place in PRR ideology. The perspective presented here provides a rather parsimonious understanding as it works from the core definition of populism (Mudde 2007; Mudde/Kaltwasser 2017) in explaining gender differences between parties. Moreover, it responds to calls for enhanced theorizing on the origins of these differences and their roles in explaining (the effects of) electoral successes (Erzeel/Rashkova 2017; Spierings/Zaslove 2015). At the same time, this chapter is an intervention into a growing field of literature and ongoing debate.[8] A major limitation in this respect is that the chapter is evidently grounded in the empirical work most familiar to its author. Based on that knowledge, I have formulated an understanding that is generally applicable, but it requires further refining and consideration in contexts such as the PRR in CEE countries, or in settings where the elite may not be pushing emancipation policies. In the latter settings, gender becomes less clearly a demarcation for the elite-people divide, which makes it less relevant to the PRR, and hence more trivial. For now, gender remains fundamental to our understanding of society, and thus also remains trivotal to PRR politics in Europe.

---

7   www.eerstekamer.nl/nieuws/20190312/wetsvoorstel_rechtspositie, 06.03.2019.
8   In which my own understanding is constantly developing too; see for instance this address: www.youtube.com/watch?v=Bdp6Cryo4Cg&list=UUpU-23_OHPdJrQVgQoB-kBQ&index=9&t=0s, 06.03.2019

Bibliography

Akkerman, Tjitske (2015): "Gender and the Radical Right in Western Europe: A Comparative Analysis of Policy Agendas." In: Patterns of Prejudice 49 (1-2), pp. 37-60.

Amesberger, Helga/Halbmayr, Brigitte (2002): "Einleitung." In: Helga Amesberger/Brigitte Halbmayr (eds.): Rechtsextreme Parteien – eine Mögliche Heimat für Frauen? Opladen: Leske und Budrich, pp. 17–26.

Buikema, Rosemarie/Plate, Liedeke/van der Tuin, Iris/Thiele, Kathrin (eds.) (2009): Doing Gender in Media, Art and Culture. London: Routledge.

Campbell, Rosie/Erzeel, Silvia (2018): "Exploring Gender Differences in Support for Rightist Parties: The Role of Party and Gender Ideology." In: Politics & Gender 14 (1), pp. 80-105.

De Lange, Sarah/Mügge, Liza (2015): "Gender and Right-Wing Populism in the Low Countries: Ideological Variations Across Parties and Time." In: Patterns of Prejudice 49 (1-2), pp. 61-80.

Dudink, Stefan (2017): "A Queer Nodal Point: Homosexuality in Dutch Debates on Islam and Multiculturalism." In: Sexualities 20 (1-2), pp. 3-23.

Erzeel, Silvia/Rashkova, Ekaterina (2017): "Still Men's Parties? Gender and the Radical Right in Comparative Perspective." In: West European Politics 40 (4), pp. 812-820.

Evans, Jocelyn/Ivaldi, Gilles (2002): "Les Dynamiques Électorales de L'extrême Droite Européenne." In: Revue Politique et Parlementaire, Nr. 1019, pp. 67-83.

Gidengil, Elisabeth/Hennigar, Matthew/Blais, André/Nevitte, Neil (2005): "Explaining the Gender Gap in Support for the New Right: The Case of Canada." In: Comparative Political Studies 38 (10), pp. 1171-1195.

Givens, Terri (2004): "The Radical Right Gender Gap." In: Comparative Political Studies 37 (1), pp. 30-54.

Harteveld, Eelco/van der Brug, Wouter/Dahlberg, Stefan/Kokkonen, Andrej (2015): "The Gender Gap in Populist Radical-Right Voting: Examining the Demand Side in Western and Eastern Europe." In: Patterns of Prejudice 49 (1-2), pp. 103-134.

Hirsi Ali, Ayaan (2006): The Caged Virgin: An Emancipation Proclamation for Women and Islam. New York: Simon and Schuster.

Immerzeel, Tim/Jaspers, Eva/Lubbers, Marcel (2013): "Religion as Catalyst or Restraint of Radical Right Voting?" In: West European Politics 36 (5), pp. 946-968.

Inglehart, Ronald (1997): Modernization and Postmodernization: Cultural, Economic, and Political Change in 43 Societies. Princeton: Princeton University Press.

Inglehart, Ronald/Norris, Pippa (2003): Rising Tide: Gender Equality and Cultural Change Around the World. Cambridge: Cambridge University Press.

Kofman, Eleonore (1998): "When Society Was Simple: Gender and Ethnic Division and the Far and New Right in France." In: Nickie Charles/Helen Hintjes (eds.): Gender, Ethnicity and Political Ideologies. London: Routledge, pp. 91–106.

Kuyper, Lisette (2016): "LHBT-Monitor 2016." Den Haag: Sociaal Cultuur Planbureau, (www.scp.nl/Publicaties/Alle_publicaties/Publicaties_2016/LHBT_monitor_2016, 12.05.2016).

Lubbers, Marcel (2001): Exclusionistic Electorates: Extreme Right-Wing Voting in Western Europe, Amsterdam/Utrecht: Thesis/ICS [ICS dissertation series 79].

Mayer, Nonna (2002): Ces Français Qui Votent Le Pen. Paris: Flammarion-Pere Castor.

Mayer, Nonna (2013): "From Jean-Marie to Marine Le Pen: Electoral Change on the Far Right." In: Parliamentary Affairs 66 (1), pp. 160-178.

Mayer, Nonna (2015): "The Closing of the Radical Right Gender Gap in France?" In: French Politics 13 (4), pp. 391-414.

Meret, Susi (2015): "Charismatic Female Leadership and Gender: Pia Kjærsgaard and the Danish People's Party." In: Patterns of Prejudice 49 (1-2), pp. 81-102.

Meret, Susi/Siim, Birte/Pingaud, Etienne (2016): "Men's Parties with Women Leaders: A Comparative Study of the Right-Wing Populist Leaders Pia Kjærsgaard, Marine Le Pen and Siv Jensen; Komparativ Analyse af Højrepopulistiske Ledere Pia Kjærsgaard, Siv Jensen og Marine Le Pen." In: Gabriella Lazaridis/Giovanna Campani (eds.): Understanding the Populist Shift. London: Routledge, pp. 122-149.

Miller-Idriss, Cynthia/Pilkington, Hilary (2017): "In Search of the Missing Link: Gender, Education and the Radical Right." In: Gender & Education 29 (2), pp. 133-146.

Mudde, Cas (2007): Populist Radical Right Parties in Europe. Cambridge: Cambridge University Press.

Mudde, Cas/Kaltwasser, Cristobal Rovira (2015): "Vox Populi or Vox Masculini? Populism and Gender in Northern Europe and South America." In: Patterns of Prejudice 49 (1-2), pp. 16-36.

Mudde, Cas/Kaltwasser, Cristobal Rovira (2017): Populism: A Very Short Introduction. Oxford: Oxford University Press.

Norocel, Ov Cristian (2009): "Globalisation and Its Male Contenders? The Question of Conservative Masculinities Within the Radical Right Populist Discourses Across the EU." In: Jukka Kultalahti/Ilari Karppi/Olli Kultalahti/Enrico Todisco (red.): Globalisation – Challenges to Research and Governance. Helsinki: East–West Books Helsinki, pp. 237-250.

Norocel, Ov Cristian (2010): "Constructing Radical Right Populist Resistance: Metaphors of Heterosexist Masculinities and the Family Question in Sweden." In: Norma 5 (2), pp. 170-183.

Paternotte, David/Kuhar, Roman (2018): "Disentangling and Locating the 'Global Right': Anti-Gender Campaigns in Europe." In: Politics and Governance 6 (3), pp. 6-19.

Rico, Guillem/Guinjoan, Marc/Anduiza, Eva (2017): "The Emotional Underpinnings of Populism: How Anger and Fear Affect Populist Attitudes." In: Swiss Political Science Review 23 (4), pp. 444-461.

Said, Edward (1979): Orientalism. New York: Vintage.

Sandfort, Theo/Schuys, Judith/Duyvendak, Jan-Willem/Weeks, Jeffrey (eds.) (2000): Lesbian and Gay Studies: An Introductory, Interdisciplinary Approach. London: Sage.

Scrinzi, Francesca (2014): "Gendering Activism in Populist Radical Right Parties. A Comparative Study of Women's and Men's Participation in the Northern League (Italy) and the National Front (France)." In: Preliminary Analysis Report, March 15, n.p..

Spierings, Niels (2017): "Eén Angst, Één Volk? De Emancipatieparadox Van Populistisch Radicaal-Rechts." In: Res Publica 59 (4), pp. 507-512.

Spierings, Niels (2018): "Popular Opposition to Economic Gender Equality and Homosexual Lifestyles." In: Mieke Verloo (ed.): Varieties of Opposition to Gender Equality in Europe. London: Routledge, pp. 172-194.

Spierings, Niels/Lubbers, Marcel/Zaslove, Andrej (2017): "'Sexually Modern Nativist Voters': Do They Exist and Do They Vote for the Populist Radical Right?" In: Gender and Education 29 (2), pp. 216-237.

Spierings, Niels/Zaslove, Andrej (2015): "Gendering the Vote for Populist Radical-Right Parties." In: Patterns of Prejudice 49 (1-2), pp. 135-162.

Spierings, Niels/Zaslove, Andrej (2015): "Conclusion: Dividing the Populist Radical Right Between 'Liberal Nativism' and Traditional Conceptions of Gender." In: Patterns of Prejudice 49 (1-2), pp. 163-173.

Spierings, Niels/Zaslove, Andrej (2017): "Gender, Populist Attitudes, and Voting: Explaining the Gender Gap in Voting for Populist Radical Right and Populist Radical Left Parties." In: West European Politics 40 (4), pp. 821-847.

Spierings, Niels/Zaslove, Andrej/Mügge, Liza/De Lange, Sarah (2015): "Gender and Populist Radical-Right Politics: An Introduction." In: Patterns of Prejudice 49 (1-2), pp. 3-15.

Stasulane, Anita (2017): "Female Leaders in a Radical Right Movement: the Latvian National Front." In: Gender & Education 29 (2), pp. 182-198.

Verloo, Mieke (ed.) (2018): Varieties of Opposition to Gender Equality in Europe. London: Routledge.

Vossen, Koen (2010): "Populism in the Netherlands after Fortuyn: Rita Verdonk and Geert Wilders Compared." In: Perspectives on European Politics and Society 11 (1), pp. 22-38.

Walby, Sylvia (2009): Globalization and Inequalities: Complexity and Contested Modernities. London: Sage.
Walby, Sylvia (2011): The Future of Feminism. Cambridge: Polity Press.

Sexual Politics from the Right. Attacks on Gender, Sexual Diversity, and Sex Education

Imke Schmincke

Sexual Politics

In her famous 1984 essay, *Thinking Sex*, Gayle Rubin argued that sexuality is often the battleground for other social conflicts. Rubin maintained, "Disputes over sexual behavior often become the vehicles for displacing social anxieties and discharging their attendant emotional intensity. Consequently, sexuality should be treated with special respect in times of great social stress." (1984: 267) The term "sexual politics" first gained prominence in a study by Kate Millett on the role of (heterosexual) sexuality in sustaining patriarchy (Millett 1970). Rubin then used the term in reference to conservative forces and the ways in which they create what Chris Weeks later described as "sexual moral panics"[1] to reverse liberal achievements (which, in the 1980s, included moral crusades against homosexuality, pornography, abortion, and sex education). However, her main argument was that sexuality is political in its own right, and should not be reduced to gender. She wrote, "Like gender, sexuality is political. It is organized into systems of power, which reward and encourage some individuals and activities, while punishing and suppressing others." (Rubin 1984: 309) Feminism should therefore not be the privileged site for analyzing sexuality (ibid.: 307).

In this paper, I want to stress the role of sexuality, or sexual politics, in recent right-wing populism. Unlike Rubin, my aim here is to show how gender *and* sexual politics *intersect* and constitute core elements of right-wing populisms' discourses

---

1   With reference to Stanley Cohen's (1982 [1972]) concept "moral panics," Weeks wrote, "The moral panic crystallises widespread fears and anxieties, and often deals with them not by seeking the real causes of the problems and conditions which they demonstrate but by displacing them on to 'Folk Devils' in an identified social group (often the 'immoral' or 'degenerate'). Sexuality has had a peculiar centrality in such panics, and sexual 'deviants' have been omnipresent scapegoats." (1989: 14)

and strategies. I would argue that we have to consider their connections with sexual politics to grasp the significance of the anti-gender campaigns of right-wing populism.

In her investigation into the history of the term 'sexual politics,' Gabriele Dietze noted that it always includes intersections with race and not just sexuality and gender (Dietze 2017: 17). She observed that sexual politics include two aspects: discrimination via sexualization *and* sexual politics as a strategy of power (as in biopolitics). In this paper, I will use the term sexual politics to grasp how right-wing populist discourses *problematize* sexuality (sexual practices, sexual identities and bodies) and make it a battlefield for cultural hegemony. I aim at enhancing the understanding of how gender, sexuality and race intersect within right-wing populist discourses, and how these intersections are used to propagate an authoritarian and exclusive social order.

While studying the 'new' targets of conservative or right-wing protest movements, which are linked to a specific stance on gender, family and sexuality, I discovered that they always target at least one of three objects: *gender* (via a strong antifeminism aimed, especially, at gender studies and gender mainstreaming), *sexual diversity* (via a strong stance against same sex marriages and adoption rights); and *sex education* (targeting, especially, curricula sensitizing to gender and sexual diversity). More striking, even if campaigns targeted only one of these three objects, sooner or later the arguments were extended to the others.

Before I look at how this holy trinity ('gender,' 'sexual diversity,' 'sex education') functions in the texts of right-wing discourses, and try to disentangle the implicated arguments, I want to very briefly describe the field of right-wing populist sexual, gender and family politics in Europe and beyond. I will then narrow my focus by concentrating on a case study from Germany. To this end, I will examine the texts of two groups: the campaign network *Demo für alle*, and the right-wing populist party *Alternative für Deutschland*. I will conclude with a discussion about why right-wing populist sexual politics appear to be so successful at the current moment.

Attacks on Gender, Sexual Diversity, Sex Education – Discursive Weapons in Transnational Alliances

In recent years, we have been observing a new form of antifeminism that does not attack feminism or emancipation per se, but rather 'gender,' and, more specifically, gender mainstreaming or gender studies.[2] The key concept here is 'gender

---

2   Several anthologies provide helpful analyzes of anti-gender campaigns and case studies from different European countries. See, for example, Kováts/Põim (2015); Köttig/Bitzan/Petö

ideology,' a term coined to denigrate everything related to 'gender' and the idea that gender differences are not determined by nature. 'Gender' is misconceived by these anti-gender campaigners who view it as something that one can always choose anew. Nonetheless, as Hark and Villa have argued, these opponents have rightly understood the non-essentialist aspect of 'gender' – i.e. that it is very much formed by social norms (Hark/Villa 2015b: 19). 'Gender' is something negative and frightening, yet deliberately fuzzy, in the campaigners' misleading and defaming statements. Above all, it functions as an umbrella term, which allows for attacking different things, such as gender studies, quotas, abortion, or LGBTIQ rights. As Paternotte/Kuhar have written, 'gender ideology,' as a discourse, "regards gender as the ideological matrix of a set of abhorred ethical and social reforms, namely sexual and reproductive rights, same-sex marriage and adoption, new reproductive technologies, sex education, gender mainstreaming, protection against gender violence and others" (2018b: 5). As many scholars have pointed out, the terms 'gender' and 'gender ideology' function as *discursive weapons* that merge different topics and allude to different (negative) emotions. Paternotte/Kuhar have described it is an 'interpretative frame' (2018: 5) that "is not only regarded as an anthropological and epistemological threat but also as a covert political strategy, a sort of conspiracy aimed at seizing power and imposing deviant and minority values to average people" (ibid.: 6). Describing this specific function as 'symbolic glue,' Kováts/Põim (2015) have claimed that "'gender' serves as 'symbolic glue' for agenda setting for conservatives and the far-right political forces" (2015: 148).

Especially in Eastern Europe, 'gender' is interpreted and attacked as an expression and representation of neoliberalism and Western colonialism. Mayer/Sauer have argued that, in anti-gender campaigns, the term 'gender' functions as an 'empty signifier' (2018; see also Mayer/Ajanovic/Sauer 2018). Referencing Laclau/Mouffe, they argued that it is typical for right-wing populism to use empty signifiers, which allows for constructing chains of equivalences that sustain antagonisms. Thus, 'gender' allows the construction of alliances between different groups and fractions. Mayer/Ajanovic/Sauer concluded that the anti-gender discourse thus functions as a vehicle by which the idea of the 'natural inequality' of human beings becomes normalized and part of public discourse (2018: 56).

As many scholars have pointed out, the discourse around 'gender ideology' must be understood as a tool in a fight for cultural hegemony. Conservative, right-wing populist forces have tried to reject liberal achievements concerning gender and sexuality (ibid.; Paternotte/Kuhar 2018: 10). The project to (re)gain cultural hegemony has not been restricted to a specific region, but instead must be seen as a *transnational project*. Several analyzes have shown how the discourse of 'gender

---

(2017); Kuhar/Paternotte (2018); Verloo (2018), and, with a focus on Germany, Hark/Villa (2015a) or Lang/Peters (2018).

ideology' is constructed and disseminated by transnational groups and alliances in Europe and beyond[3] (Paternotte/Kuhar (2018: 9ff.) and Miskolci (2017) have traced the origins of the introduction and use of 'gender ideology' as a discursive strategy and, in fact, 'counter-strategy,' back to the Vatican's reaction to the UN conferences in Cairo in 1994, and in Beijing in 1995, from which it was then proliferated by different regional and transnational catholic intellectuals.) The significance of catholic or other fundamentalist religious groups has varied across countries. The rise of anti-gender campaigns is not only a genuine catholic project, but it must also be understood against the background of the recent rise of right-wing populist parties and authoritarian leaders. Campaigners can be divided into fundamentalist Christian groups; conservative journalists, scientists and politicians; masculinists; and right-wing extremist parties and fractions. These groups and strands overlap and build campaign networks.

Although anti-gender campaigns are not grassroots movements per se, they sometimes attract much support. This became apparent in mass demonstrations that occurred in France from 2012 until 2013. The alliance *Manif pour tous* ("Demonstrations for all") was founded by the Catholic Church and other conservative groups in the autumn of 2012 to protest an initiative to legalize same-sex marriages, which was widely known as the *Marriage pour tous* ("Marriage for all") (Stambolis-Ruhstorfer/Tricou 2018). Over the subsequent months, the group organized demonstrations and gained massive support, including many young people who opposed adoption and reproductive rights for homosexual couples. After the same-sex marriage law passed parliament in 2013, the protest movement faded. But some groups found another object of protest: school curricula sensitizing to gender stereotypes and gender quality. The prime enemy became 'gender theory' or 'gender ideology.'

In Germany, two expressions of right-wing populist sexual politics gained nationwide media attention some months later: the defamation of a handbook on sex education and sexual diversity, and a petition against sexual diversity as a topic of school curricula in the region of Baden-Württemberg. The petition's initiator (an evangelical teacher and his network) warned that the curricula would propagate homosexuality and thus harm students. The petition gained much media attention, many votes and strong support through demonstrations that were organized by a new initiative, the *Demo für alle* ("Demonstration for all"). This German campaign network thus borrowed the French protest movements' name, logo and political agenda.

---

3   For case studies in Europe, see footnote 2; for Argentina and Latin America, see Miskolci 2017.

Case Studies from Germany: *Demo für alle* and *Alternative für Deutschland* (AfD)

The following section examines the sexual politics of two German right-wing populist players: the campaign network *Demo für alle* (*DfA*) and the right-wing populist party *Alternative für Deutschland* (*AfD*).

Demo für alle

At the start of 2014, the *Demo für alle* was strongly connected to the *AfD* party. Indeed, a prominent party member organized the protest in the name of the initiative. The initiative is best characterized by its slogan, "Marriage and Family first! Against Gender Ideology and the Sexualization of our Children!"[4] Since 2014, initative members have organized demonstrations, petitions and symposia against same-sex marriage, the inclusion of gender and sexual diversity in sex education curricula, children's rights, and sex education projects organized by LGBTIQ people. On their website, they claim that they fight for the notions of marriage and family upon which society – in their eyes – has been built for "thousands of years." They reject the "indoctrination" organized by "lobby groups and ideologists," which they then identify as 'gender mainstreaming' and 'gender ideology.' Both are held responsible for abolishing the "natural gender (identity)" and the family. They thus invite people to join the fight for parents' rights, marriage and the family, and against "gender ideology" and the sexualization of children in kindergartens and schools.

Instead of arguments, one only finds key concepts (i.e. discursive weapons) on their website, which are repeated and framed within a rhetoric of fear, loss and destruction. Marriage and the family are in danger; "gender ideology" is abolishing "natural" gender identities (male/female); parents' rights are in danger and must be defended; sexualization takes place in schools (via sex education), threatens children by violating their sense of shame; and indoctrination is underway (through sex education, "gender ideology," gender mainstreaming, "lobby groups" or LGBTIQ people).

The key concepts "gender ideology" and "sexualization (too) early in childhood" are not clarified in the texts, and thus remain deliberately opaque. To understand the argument that links gender and sexuality, I have analyzed two texts on sex education: one is a petition against "Sexual Pedagogy of Diversity," and the other is a leaflet on sex education in schools and kindergartens.

---

4   This slogan and all subsequent related quotations can be found on the website of the initiative: demofueralle.blog/eine-seite/, 12.03.2019; translations by the author.

The core message of both texts is that children must be protected from "The Sexual Pedagogy of Diversity."[5] Children are in danger because the pedagogy of sexual diversity is taught in schools, sometimes even taught by external LGBTIQ groups. Arguments against this form of sex education are varying: it is not age appropriate for children and hurts their "natural sense of shame"; it propagates lust and diversity; it is indoctrinating children; and it is linked to gender mainstreaming, which is polemically equated with "identity confusion"; its founding father was a pedophile, which discredits the whole tradition of liberal emancipatory sexual pedagogy.[6] In the typical antagonizing rhetoric, parents and their children are presented as potential victims of the advocates of sexual and gender diversity and their institutional allies. Here, we find, as a common right-wing populist feature, two antagonisms: us (parents and children) against them (institutions/state/EU/"lobby groups") and against the alien others (LGBTIQ groups, pedophilic sexual experts and, occasionally, gender theorists).

These arguments are not supported by research. In everyday life, the primary context in which children are confronted with sexually explicit content is through media, especially the internet, and not in the classroom. Similarly, the majority of sexual abuse does not occur in schools, but rather in families or other proximal relationships, or, as has been discussed in recent years, within closed institutions, some of which are run by the Catholic Church. So what does this fear of sexual and gender diversity actually reveal? How can we understand and explain its obviously irrational elements? As these texts emphasize, one core topic are borders. The authors claim that a problem of "The Sexual Pedagogy of Diversity" is that it aims to destroy the child's shame, which is seen as a "natural protection shield." In this

---

5   "The Sexual Pedagogy of Diversity" ("Sexualpädagogik der Vielfalt") is the title of a handbook, whose authors have been the target of a 2014 shitstorm. Its core intention is to sensitize children to sexual and gender diversity. Diversity with respect to gender and sexuality has been increasingly introduced as an important goal of sex education curricula. In this context, diversity is mainly connected to gender and sexuality, though sometimes it also includes other forms of diversity. This trend has mobilized right-wing and right-populist activists. For them, "The Sexual Pedagogy of Diversity" has become the general name for liberal and progressive sex education, which, it is believed, must be kept away from 'innocent' children.

6   In their arguments, opponents of sexual diversity and sex education often refer to protagonists of a very problematic strand within post '68 anti-authoritarian pedagogy, which supported sexual autonomy for children, but also sexual contacts between adults and children. These pedophile individuals and groups, which exist in certain parts of the alternative left, including in several progressive education initiatives and liberal parties, such as the green party, have been severely criticized in recent years from different sides. Studies that have exposed these and other problems of certain progressive sexual liberty and children's rights initiatives have only just begun to appear (see, for example, Baader/Jansen/König/Sager 2017).

context, the authors speak about the "dismantling of borders and shelters."[7] (The rhetoric here is very similar to the anti-migration rhetoric of right-wing populist groups in general.) Unlike the authors of these texts, I understand shame as an effect of the internalization of social norms; it is not naturally given from birth, but rather socially produced.[8] If shame functions as a protective shield, what must be protected, and from whom? Responses to these questions yield a very repressive conservative conception of sexuality: Sexuality and sexual desire are imagined as dangers that must be contained, and are permitted in matrimonial contexts only with the aim of reproduction. We can also detect a great fear of blurring boundaries that separate (and constitute) hierarchical binaries: parents – children; men – women; heterosexuals – homosexuals. "Diversity" is interpreted as a name for blurring these boundaries; "diversity," in their eyes, means disintegration.

This fear is dependent on an authoritative notion of society as social order constituted by 'natural' hierarchies. In the campaigns against sex education and sexual diversity, we can see the extent to which the idea of sexual and gender diversity is experienced as a threat. This corresponds to right-wing populist politics against diversity in a racialized context and how much the idea of diversity is charged with fear. The campaigns, as an expression of sexual politics from the right, demonstrate paradigmatically what Judith Butler described in *Gender Trouble* (2008 [1990]): Because gender/sex differences are regulated within a heterosexual matrix, gender and sexuality are deeply interwoven. This is why the campaigners themselves regularly merge sexual and gender politics. Thus, heterosexuality can be understood as a hegemonic, albeit precarious, norm because it only exists in relation to the excluded Other. As Butler states: "under the conditions of normative heterosexuality, policing gender is sometimes used as a way of securing heterosexuality" (2008 [1990]: xii).

While we can clearly see the intersections of gender and sexuality in these campaigns against sex education, intersections with race are not as obvious. When campaigners talk of 'the children' and 'the family' that must be protected, it is quite obvious that they mean a particular form of the family: the heterosexual married couple with children. Enemies are non-heterosexuals and gender mainstreaming advocates, and they become associated with pedophiles. In the campaigns against same-sex marriage, we find traces of connections with racism. The problems that might follow same-sex marriages are "polygamy" and "surrogate motherhood." The

---

7   According to the authors of the brochure, the argument for sexual autonomy of children follows a typical pedophile strategy, namely to break the child's natural protection shield ("Zuerst wird die Schamgrenze des Kindes überschritten und damit sein Schutzraum angetastet"). Progressive emancipatory sex education aims at breaking personal borders ("Aufbrechen der natürlichen Schutzvorrichtungen").

8   There is a wide debate on the character and function of shame, see for example Fanon (1967).

gateway for racism in sexual politics is the idea of family relations as reproductive units. This becomes more explicit in the party program of the *AfD*.

Alternative for Germany (AfD)

The *AfD* originated in 2013 as a right-wing conservative party with a strong stance against the EU. In subsequent years, the party became more radical, which led to a shift in its agenda and a more overtly racist political program. Together with this shift, right-wing populist family, gender and sexual politics became core elements. Having received 10 percent of votes on average (in some regions significantly more, in others less), the party is now represented in national and all regional parliaments.

To best reconstruct the *AfD*'s gender and sexual politics, I will now present an analysis of two texts: the 2017 national election and 2019 EU election programs.[9] More specifically, I will focus on the chapters covering family policies, which include problematizations of 'gender' and 'sexual diversity.'

The party's racist/'völkisch' attitude becomes obvious in the general claim that the state must guarantee the reproduction of the people, which is understood in racial terms ("Staatsvolk"). Hence, family policies are translated as population policies, and must ensure that a particular sub-group of the German population reproduces itself (i.e. heterosexual, bio Germans). The state provokes reproduction through laws that regulate the number of children one can have, decrease the number of divorces, and reduce or eliminate abortions. Not only concerning reproduction, the notion of the family is defined as the reproductive unit of father, mother and children, and so it is also defined by norms. The last paragraphs make this clear: "Gender ideology is against constitutional law"; "Gender ideology must leave schools – (premature) sexualization has to stop"; "no waste of tax money for gender research." "Gender ideology" is portrayed as the enemy because it questions gender identities and thus (affectively) aims to abolish the traditional family. The indoctrination and re-education program of the pedagogy of sexual diversity, propagating homosexuality, thus confuses sexual identities of children and also contributes to abolishing the traditional family. Since "gender studies" are an ideology and not science, it should no longer be funded.

The *AfD*'s sexual and gender politics are more explicitly linked to the rest of their political program, which is opposed to migration and the presence of Muslims in the country (reflecting, in short, a racist and nationalist ideology), thus

---

9   The party's programs can be found online: www.afd.de/wp-content/uploads/sites/111/2017/-06/2017-06-01_AfD-Bundestagswahlprogramm_Onlinefassung.pdf, 12.03.19, and www.afd.de/wp-content/uploads/sites/111/2019/03/afd_europawahlprogramm_A5-hoch_web.pdf, 12.03.19.

feeding into their nationalist and racist agenda to reproduce an imagined pure and homogenous group of Germans.

The party's agenda for the EU parliament is slightly more moderate in terms of spelling out the ideas for an active population policy. The main argument here is that Europe has a demographic problem that is not to be solved through migration, and that the EU should not interfere with national family policies. The first paragraph also makes clear that the notion of the family should only include married heterosexual couples with children. The 'demographic crisis' is then mentioned as one of Europe's most dramatic current problems. People must be made more aware of this fact, it is claimed, and of the potential decline of European civilization. As a conclusion, the *AfD* suggests to cancel funding for gender studies research on the European level. Interestingly, the reader is not provided with an argument that would logically combine the 'demographic crisis' with gender studies, but one is encouraged to assume that gender studies do play a role in the crisis, and that they are somehow responsible either for the people's ignorance of the problem, or for the problem itself. Do gender studies stop Europeans from reproducing? The next paragraphs more explicitly discuss reasons for the 'demographic crisis' that merge different topics: poverty is a problem for families with many children (later in the agenda, they propose to deny child benefits to those families that are entitled but live outside of Germany); abortion is a problem; and homosexual couples should be denied reproductive rights.

Although the whole text tries to avoid explicit racial claims, the message seems quite obvious: Certain groups of the population should reproduce and others should not (migrants, homosexuals). The underlying idea of a pure homogeneous social body is central to the whole argument. This idea is at the heart of a right-wing extremist ideology of natural inequalities. At the core of the party's sexual and gender politics, and at its point of intersection with race, lies the notion of the social as an order of 'natural' hierarchies. The social is embedded in antagonisms: on a vertical line between 'them above' and 'us below' (EU/lobby groups etc. versus 'us'), between 'us above' and 'them below' (so-called bio Germans versus migrants/Muslims) and on a horizontal line between 'us' and 'the deviant others' (LGBTIQ; pedophiles). Gender, sex and race are linked together by the idea of a regime that secures the reproduction of an imagined pure and superior collective (understood in racial terms).

'Family' is the term that connects the individual with this collective. But family here refers to a very specific understanding of social relations (as has been mentioned earlier: non-migrant, heterosexual, married couples with children). Ruth Wodak has noted that we find a nativist definition of the family in right-wing populist discourses:

> "The investigation of gendered body politics, both in Europe and the US, substantiates the assumption that the conceptual metaphor of the 'family' has taken on a nativist dimension, related to the 'authoritarian syndrome' as well as to post-modern bio-politics and the threat, experienced by many in our globalizing societies, of changing gender roles." (Wodak 2015: 174)

On a more explicit level, the figure of the child serves as an emotional trigger in right-wing populist mobilizations (Schmincke 2015). However, as Butler has argued, the child is also centered in this imagined nativist collective. With reference to debates around same-sex marriage and the ban on adoption for homosexuals, she concludes: "[O]ne can see that the child figures in the debate as a dense site for the transfer and reproduction of culture, where 'culture' carries with it implicit norms of racial purity and domination." (Butler 2004: 110)

Why Sexuality?

As in Rubin's quote from the beginning of this text, one can see that "disputes over sexual behavior often become the vehicles for displacing social anxieties" (1984: 267). In the arguments of right-wing sexual politics, we see quite a few interesting displacements at work: The claim that sex education in schools is the place where children are sexualized and threatened sits uncomfortably with the empirical fact that sexual violence in most cases takes place in the family and in (closed) institutions such as the church. In addition, the fear of homosexuality is full of bizarre displacements. However, from a broader perspective, we see the displacement of anxieties – concerning identity, social order, and cultural values – to the field of sexuality, anxieties that have their origins somewhere else. In a similar vein, Judith Butler has remarked, with respect to a debate on gay marriage in France more than 15 years earlier:

> "Indeed, the debates on gay marriage and gay kinship, two issues that are often conflated, have become sites of intense displacement for other political fears, fears about technology, about new demographics, and also about the very unity and transmissibility of the nation, and fears that feminism, in the insistence on childcare, has effectively opened up kinship outside the family, opened it to strangers." (Butler 2004: 110)

But why does sexuality seem to provide such a popular field for the displacement of anxieties and fears?

Concluding Remarks

One might identify four explanatory dimensions regarding the emergence and success of right-wing populist discourses and sexual politics.

Reaction to Liberal Achievements – Counter-Movements and the Fight for Cultural Hegemony

The emergence of right-wing discourses around sexual and gender politics can also be understood as a counter-movement responding to liberal achievements such as gay marriage, enhanced gender equality, equal rights for minority groups, laws against sexual violence, child abuse and changes in sexual morals. Although the right to live in heterosexual marriages persists (and a majority still prefers to do so), the hegemony of conservative norms has been challenged through these changes. Right-wing sexual politics can thus be understood as a response to this change of values, and as an attempt to regain hegemony.

Strategic Tool

As has been mentioned earlier in this paper, several researchers have proposed that right-wing populist sexual and gender politics should be understood as strategy. It is strategic on two levels: it allows for mobilizing people who do not identify with radical right-wing ideology (including, for example, overt anti-semitism or racism) and thus enables the forging of broader alliances (Mayer/Sauer 2018). In addition, as I have shown with respect to the *AfD*, it serves as a link to the core topics of right-wing populism – i.e. racism and an authoritarian idea of society. Right-wing populist sexual and gender politics communicate the idea of a 'natural' hierarchical order of the social, which is structured by hierarchical binaries (us vs. them, White vs. Black, Christian vs. Non-Christian or Muslim, strong vs. weak, parents vs. children). The ideology of this form of imagined community includes the fear of reproduction, of not being able to reproduce the homogenous entity.

Neoliberal Side Effects and a General Feeling of Precarity

Kováts (2017) and others use the concept of "symbolic glue" to propose yet another explanation: In their eyes, especially in Eastern Europe, a very conservative stance on gender and sexuality constitutes a response to neoliberalism. By rejecting gender and sexual diversity, people deliberately oppose liberal values, which they perceive as having been imposed on them and as entwined with neoliberal capitalism and western colonialism. Other scholars use a similar argument with respect to Western societies. They claim that people feel attracted to right-wing populist discourses due to a general feeling of precarity resulting from either neoliberalism and globalisation, the erosion of democratic institutions, a change in cultural values, or, not least, a change in gender relations (Wimbauer/Motakef/Teschlade 2015; Mayer/Ajanovic/Sauer 2018: 48; Chmilewski/Hajek 2017). Therefore, one can interpret the vote for right-wing populist parties in Eastern and Western Europe as a reaction to recent economic and social shifts, and to the crisis of representative democracy.

Sexuality and Affect

All of these theories and explanations are very useful, yet I think that the role of sexuality needs to be analyzed more thoroughly. The obsession with sex that we can see in right-wing sexual politics should also be understood in relation to the role of sexuality in contemporary society - i.e. its function for both neoliberal capitalism and individual lives. I think that a theoretical framework for this has yet to be elaborated. I just want to briefly delineate some of its elements. Sexual morals have changed massively during the last 40 years. These changes are most often framed as liberalization, but they also follow from the commodification and marketization of sexuality. To grasp these changes, it might be useful to look at Foucault's *sexuality dispositive*, and to consider how this dispositive translates into the 21st century. With his idea of biopolitics, Foucault analyzed how sexuality became the hinge by which the state would regulate individual sexual practices and the reproduction of the population. At the same time, looking at the role of sexuality and desire, their connections to gender and violence, their affective forces and potentials, and how these are instrumentalized, stimulated and displaced, it might be useful to integrate a psychoanalytical perspective. For right-wing populism, the mobilizing of affects is one of its core strategies. Affects play an important role in authoritarian conceptions of social order. As Adorno et al. (1950) have shown in their study on the authoritarian personality, the repression of needs and desires and the identification with very rigid sexual norms is part of the personality structure of authoritarian groups. The oppression of inner desires is compensated by the oppression of others who are identified with the oppressed inner objects.

In right-wing sexual politics, sexuality has at least two functions with respect to the two different aspects associated with sexuality: desire and reproduction. The notion that desire is a danger that must be contained fuels the imagination of people. The attraction to right-wing politics is in part due to its mobilizing affective force (and less due to rational arguments). Or, as Chmilewski/Hajek (2017) have argued, right-wing sexual and gender politics provide an emotional pedagogy that helps to canalize affective states (by which they mean general feelings of precariousness). With respect to the reproductive dimension of sexuality, these politics also serve to sustain the imagination of a racially pure collective by referring to the generative aspect of the people. As has been mentioned in the beginning of this text, sexual politics also have a racialist dimension. Not only do ideas of a white homogenous collective sustain racist phantasies, but racist phantasies are fueled by sexual phantasies. As Dietze (2017) has pointed out with the concept of ethnosexism, the interrelation of sexuality, gender and race can serve different political aims. Especially in right-wing discourses in Germany, Muslim men and refugees are generally imagined as sexually aggressing native White women.

Understanding the function of sexuality in right-wing populist sexual and gender politics might help to see why these illiberal ideologies are so appealing to some. And it might also help to find ways to intervene and fight against them.

Bibliography

Adorno, Theodor W. (1950): The Authoritarian Personality (Studies in Prejudice). New York: Harper & Row.
Baader, Meike Sophia/Jansen, Christian/König, Julia/Sager, Christin (eds.) (2017): Tabubruch und Entgrenzung. Kindheit und Sexualität nach 1968. Köln/Weimar/Wien: Böhlau Verlag.
Butler, Judith (2004): Undoing Gender. New York: Routledge.
Butler, Judith (2008 [1990]): Gender Trouble. Feminism and the Subversion of Identity. New York/London: Routledge.
Chmilewski, Katja/Hajek, Katharina (2017): "Mit Gefühl von rechts zur Verteidigung der 'Lufthoheit über Kinderbetten'." In: Brigitte Bargetz/Eva Kreisky/Gundula Ludwig (eds.): Dauerkämpfe: Feministische Zeitdiagnosen und Strategien. Frankfurt a. M./New York: Campus, pp. 175-184.
Cohen, Stanley (1982 [1972]): Folk Devils and Moral Panics. The Creation of the Mods and Rockers. Oxford: Robertson.
Dietze, Gabriele (2017): Sexualpolitik. Verflechtungen von Race und Gender. Frankfurt a.M./New York: Campus.
Fanon, Frantz (1967): Black Skin, White Masks. New York: Grove Press.
Hark, Sabine/Villa, Paula-Irene (eds.) (2015a): (Anti-)Genderismus. Sexualität und Geschlecht als Schauplätze Aktueller Politischer Auseinandersetzungen. Bielefeld: transcript.
Hark, Sabine/Villa, Paula-Irene (2015b): "'Eine Frage an und für unsere Zeit': Verstörende Gender Studies und Symptomatische Missverständnisse." In: Sabine Hark/Paula-Irene Villa (eds.): (Anti-)Genderismus: Sexualität und Geschlecht als Schauplätze Aktueller Politischer Auseinandersetzungen. Bielefeld: transcript, pp. 15-39.
Köttig, Michaela/Bitzan, Renate/Petö, Andrea (eds.) (2017): Gender and Far Right Politics in Europe. Cham: Palgrave Macmillan.

Kováts, Eszter (2017): "Das Schlachtfeld Gender in Europa: Die Krise der Neoliberalen Demokratie." In: Ariadne. Forum für Frauen- und Geschlechtergeschichte 71, pp. 62-69.

Kováts, Eszter/Põim, Maari (eds.) (2015): Gender as Symbolic Glue. The Position and Role of Conservative and Far Right Parties in the Anti-Gender Mobilizations in Europe. FES, Berlin

Kuhar, Roman/Paternotte, David (eds.) (2018): Anti-Gender Campaigns in Europe. Mobilizing against Equality. London/New York: Rowman & Littlefield.

Lang, Juliane/Peters, Ulrich (eds.) (2018): Antifeminismus in Bewegung. Hamburg: Marta Press.

Mayer, Stefanie/Ajanovic, Edma/Sauer, Birgit (2018): "Geschlecht als Natur und das Ende der Gleichheit. Rechte Angriffe auf Gender als Element Autoritärer Politischer Konzepte." In: Femina Politica 1 (18), pp. 47-60.

Mayer, Stefanie/Sauer, Birgit (2018): "'Gender Ideology' in Austria: Coalitions around an Empty Signifier." In: Roman Kuhar/David Paternotte (eds.): Anti-Gender Campaigns in Europe: Mobilizing against Equality. London/New York: Rowman & Littlefield, pp. 23-40.

Millett, Kate (1970): Sexual Politics. Garden City/New York: Doubleday.

Miskolci, Richard (2017): "'Gender Ideology': Notes for the Genealogy of a Contemporary Moral Panic." In: Revista Sociedade e Estado 32 (3), pp. 722-742.

Paternotte, David/Kuhar, Roman (2018): "'Gender Ideology' in Movement: Introduction." In: Roman Kuhar/David Paternotte (eds.): Anti-Gender Campaigns in Europe: Mobilizing against Equality. London/New York: Rowman & Littlefield, pp. 1-22.

Rubin, Gayle (1984): "Thinking Sex: Notes for a Radical Theory of the Politics of Sexuality." In: Carole S. Vance (ed.): Pleasure and Danger: Exploring Female Sexuality. Boston: Routledge & Paul, pp. 267-319.

Schmincke, Imke (2015): "Das Kind als Chiffre politischer Auseinandersetzung am Beispiel Neuer Konservativer Protestbewegungen in Frankreich und Deutschland." In: Sabine Hark/Paula-Irene Villa (eds.): (Anti-)Genderismus: Sexualität und Geschlecht als Schauplätze Aktueller Politischer Auseinandersetzungen. Bielefeld: transcript, pp. 93-107.

Stambolis-Ruhstorfer, Michael/Tricou, Josselin (2018): "Resisting 'Gender Theory' in France: A Fulcrum for Religious Action in a Secular Society." In: Roman Kuhar/David Paternotte (eds.): Anti-Gender Campaigns in Europe: Mobilizing against Equality. London/New York: Rowman & Littlefield, pp. 79-98.

Verloo, Mieke (ed.) (2018): Varieties of Opposition to Gender Equality in Europe. New York/London: Routledge.

Weeks, Jeffrey (1989): Sex, Politics and Society. The Regulation of Sexuality since 1800. London: Longman.

Wimbauer, Christine/Motakef, Mona/Teschlade, Julia (2015): "Neun Prekarisierungstheoretische Thesen zu Diskursen gegen Gleichstellungspolitik und Geschlechterforschung." In: Sabine Hark/Paula-Irene Villa (eds.): (Anti-) Genderismus: Sexualität und Geschlecht als Schauplätze Aktueller Politischer Auseinandersetzungen. Bielefeld: transcript, pp. 41-57.

Wodak, Ruth (2015): The Politics of Fear. Analyzing Right-Wing Popular Discourse. London: Sage.

Post-Socialist Conditions and the Orbán Government's Gender Politics between 2010 and 2019 in Hungary

Eszter Kováts

In 2010, the party alliance of *Fidesz (Alliance of Young Democrats)* and *KDNP (Christian Democratic People's Party)* gained a two-third majority in the Hungarian Parliament, and, with that, the mandate and legal authority to enact deep changes in the country's legal and constitutional architecture. As a result, they introduced a series of changes that aimed both at fundamentally reshaping the political system of the country and cementing their own power. They changed the Constitution without involving the opposition in the process; curtailed the rights of the Constitutional Court; filled the ranks of institutions representing checks and balances, like the office of the Chief Prosecutor, with loyal party members; changed the electoral system to benefit the most popular party; and took over the vast majority of media outlets, which now serve as channels of propaganda for the ruling coalition.[1] In 2014, the government was re-elected with another two-third majority;[2] and in 2018, a historically large turnout yielded the same result again. The electoral system clearly made it easier to attain such a repeated supermajority. However, if we grant that the –undoubtedly relevant– media dominance and years of fear-mongering hate-propaganda are not the sole explanatory factors, the fact that 49% of votes went to the *Fidesz-KDNP* in 2018 offers a clear sign of the huge support of the governing parties.

A defining feature of this system is the use of ongoing campaigns, based on hate-filled propaganda, targeting alleged enemies (among others George Soros, a Hungarian-American financier and investor) and paid for by public funds. It is in this context that the image of the threat of 'gender ideology' has been mobilized.

This antagonizing politicization in Hungary is part of a transnational phenomenon, often called 'anti-gender movements'[3] (Kuhar/Paternotte 2017) in the

---

1   For a brief summary of these deep changes see, for instance: Enyedi/Krekó 2018, Körösényi/Patkós 2017.
2   Following a by-election in 2014, *Fidesz-KDNP* lost its second two-third majority.
3   Despite the fact that it seems to have been established in relevant scholarship, it is problematic to describe the movements attacking 'gender ideology' as 'anti-gender movements' (cf. Scheele 2016, Wimbauer et al. 2016, Kováts 2018a). Those using the terms 'genderism' or 'gen-

literature, which only partly overlaps with populist or far-right parties and their agendas (Kuhar/Paternotte 2018). The Hungarian case is one of few in Europe in which 'gender' is politicized by the government itself as 'gender ideology,' which supposedly threatens 'traditional families,' children's identity, and, overall, the future of Europe.

The expression 'gender ideology' appears daily in Hungary in publicly-funded hate propaganda designed to polarize society and maintain a wartime narrative. The government referenced 'gender ideology' in its refusal to ratify the Istanbul Convention and in its 2018 decision to remove accreditation from gender studies MA programs in Hungarian universities, hereby fulfilling a demand of many right-wing opponents of 'gender ideology' in Europe and presenting a worrying precedent case of interference into academic freedom.

At the same time, the attacks on gender studies fit into a broader hegemonic project in which Fidesz also targets the autonomy of science and intellectuals (potentially) critical of the government. Besides these cases used in the war rhetoric, gender policy was reformulated by the government as family policy, and family policy was reformulated as demographic policy, which was then presented as an alternative to migration, the alleged liberal solution to the "demographic crisis" of Europe.

As I argue below, these developments cannot be interpreted as the mere resurrection of 1930's Europe (as is routinely invoked in journalistic articles and political speeches), nor can they be grasped as a kind of conservative cultural backlash that assigns women the sole role of a mother confined to the family. Instead of treating it as old wine (i.e. antifeminism and homophobia, or social conservatism more broadly) in a new bottle (i.e. attacks on the abstract concept of 'gender'), and without playing down the gravity of the changes leading to more authoritarian forms of governance, I will argue for an approach that aims to address the societal support of the system, and the developments of the emancipatory movements and progressive parties that provided fertile soil for the kind of political alternative that Fidesz represents. Obviously, a thorough analysis of the political situation in Hungary exceeds the boundaries of this study. Nonetheless, a discussion of several aspects of this situation will help me to situate and contextualize the gender debates.

---

der ideology' do not only or always reject the arguments of feminist and gender scholars who use gender as a structural analytical category; instead, one finds contradictory contents and ideologies under these labels. If these movements were indeed all anti-gender, it would suggest a symmetry across terms and camps – i.e. one would be for gender as analytical category and the other would be against it (Scheele 2016: 3–4). While the term 'anti-gender' rightly expresses the novelty of the phenomenon – which is to say that it is distinct from the antifeminism and homophobia of previous times – it also plays into the hands of actors defending a dichotomous understanding of gender politics – both on the liberal and conservative sides of the argument.

The necessity of a transdisciplinary approach presents itself as a further challenge for the analysis. Gender studies scholars, often from the field of cultural studies, frequently ignore knowledge produced in political science,[4] or they attempt to understand these complex political systems through the prism of sexism and racism *only*.[5] This also results in them importing and applying ready-made conceptual tools to various contexts (e.g. describing Orbán through 'white male privilege'). On the other hand, political science scholars tend to ignore relevant concepts and studies of gender and political economy, and specifically the economic underpinnings that come with power relations (including gender relations) and that lead to and sustain (semi-)authoritarian regimes. And those preoccupied with describing 'anti-gender movements' or right-wing politics often ignore the knowledge produced by sociology that can further index structural understandings of societal processes and, therefore, best address the demand side. By virtue of describing *them*, they also sometimes, wittingly or unwittingly, reproduce false binaries of 'them vs us,' 'good vs evil,' 'conservative-fundamentalists vs progressives,' 'actors for vs against equality,' or 'essentialists vs post-essentialists' (Kováts 2018a).

The latter distinction points to the biggest challenges for such an analysis, namely that it comes with political stakes. The ways in which we understand these developments lead to different political strategies. If we, for instance, are inclined to think that democracy is threatened by what is happening to gender, if it is a conservative backlash, or if it is a new form of a gender regime that cannot be described by the available conceptual tools – our conclusions will differ accordingly about the necessary political strategies that we must mobilize to respond.

Underlying my analysis is a normative aspiration that needs to be uncovered: It often seems that progressive forces confuse right-wing parties with their voters. However, those who actually strive to understand why feminism and gender can serve as negative projection screens within society must ask critical questions of

---

4   This can be best illustrated by Agnieszka Graff attributing one of the most prominent concepts for describing Hungary's and Poland's political regimes, "competitive authoritarianism" (Way-Levinsky 2004, applied e.g. by Bozóki/Hegedűs 2017, see below), to a New York Times commentator (Graff et al. 2019: 550).

5   For example, in the above-quoted text, which was intended to provide an overview of the gendered aspects of the rise of the Global Right, Susanna Danuta Walters uses arrogant and outright ignorant descriptors: "If you can't see that the rise of Trump is all about racism and sexism and that these aren't some narrow 'cultural' issues that are somehow trumped by rising income inequality (as if that weren't raced and gendered) […] well, then maybe you are part of the problem." (Graff et. al. 2019: 557)

themselves and should not shy away from conflicts[6] with an argument along the lines of, "we cannot afford internal debates now."

We should not limit our current scrutiny of equality policies to a mere power struggle and believe that the demand for such political parties and movements within society is wholly derived from medieval essentialist attitudes or from 'fake news brainwashing.'

Having said this, attempts at understanding the social demand for right-wing policies beyond references to attitudes and 'manipulation' obviously do not mean sympathy for anti-democratic forces. On the contrary, this is exactly why we urgently need an alternative that goes beyond the customary dichotomy of regress versus progress, a picture alien to large sections of society that merely serves to mobilize elites.

This chapter attempts to analyze ideological cornerstones of the gender politics of the Orbán government since 2010. First, I will classify the regime; then I will describe the regime's gender policy, which must be understood within the context of post-socialism. Following that, I will offer an analysis of the 'gender as an enemy' discourse, concentrating on two major battlefields: gender studies and the Istanbul Convention. In the conclusion, I will formulate the most important conceptual and political challenges presented by the case study of Hungary.

1. The Orbán regime since 2010[7]

To best situate gender politics in Hungary since 2010, I would like to insist on the following three proposals.

---

6   Here I subscribe to Gudrun Axeli-Knapp's call for "courage to controversy" within feminist theorizing, as some of the feminist strands are mutually exclusive (Knapp 2018: 28). Since these theories inform feminist politics, this controversy has not only theoretical but also political significance.

7   In focusing on the governing coalition, my description omits an analysis of the party Jobbik, which gained 17% in the elections of 2010 and has since become the largest opposition party represented in the Parliament. They gained 19,8% in the 2018 Parliamentary elections, since then, for various reasons, they are on constant decline, in the 2019 May EP elections they scored 6.3%. To date it is uncertain if they will recover. Their orientation used to be far-right, gaining prominence largely based on their anti-Roma messages. Since 2013, the party leadership has attempted to rebrand the party as center-right. As Zsolt Enyedi has pointed out, Fidesz has implemented plenty of Jobbik's early ideas. In a recent interview, the founder and recently resigned leader of Jobbik, Gábor Vona, claimed that they had seen several of their propositions in practice under the governing coalition, which terrified their party officials and ultimately turned them against their own ideological roots. For more on Jobbik, see Enyedi 2016. For Jobbik's gender politics, see Félix 2015 and Félix 2018.

1. The Orbán regime is neither a liberal democracy nor authoritarianism. Since the 1990s, it has been a recurrent rhetorical device for Hungarian right-wing parties to write off leftists and liberals as not being members of the nation. At the same time, leftists and liberals were constantly accusing conservatives of not being democrats or of being outright fascists, who strive for nothing less than dictatorship (Gagyi 2016). The moralizing inflation of these serious concepts has led to a wariness of their usage in broad segments of the Hungarian electorate and makes it difficult to address anti-democratic developments to this day (Szűcs 2018). In political science literature, however, despite the heated debates about how to describe the present political system, there is a relative consensus around the statement that the Orbán regime is neither a liberal democracy nor an openly authoritarian system.

One of the most influential concepts to describe regimes of this hybrid type has been coined by Steven Levitsky and Lucan A. Way (2004, 2010): 'competitive authoritarianism.' In recent years, this term has been adopted by scholars describing Orbán's regime (e.g. Bozóki/Hegedűs 2018). Such regimes combine competitive elections with a serious violation of democratic procedures, which "drastically decreases the chances of the opposition, and thus a democratic change of government" (ibid.: 1174).

In the era of proliferating but conceptually shallow references to 1930s Germany, both in Hungarian and international media, this is a very important distinction from a political point of view: References to 'fascism' tend to shatter the credibility of any criticism from the outset.[8] Smear campaigns are not outright violence and a culture war is not an actual civil war (Szűcs 2018: 51). However, this distinction also makes clear that the regime is still not a liberal democracy.

Competition is made uneven via the concentration of power, the elimination of the independence of government bodies to provide checks and balances, the occupation of public media and the constant obstruction of the normal functioning of independent media, financial blackmailing, and the threatening and smearing of oppositional politicians and civil organization representatives. All of these partly explain the political and intellectual counter-selection of the opposition.

2. The role of the European Union must be considered. The country's external exposure and embeddedness also influences the political system. Not only is Hungary a hybrid regime, but it is a hybrid regime within the European Union; as

---

8   This has been described as such by the political scientist Gábor Filippov in the most influential journalistic article of 2018 in Hungary. Discussing the nature of the regime, Filippov applies Way's and Levitsky's concept to influence the Hungarian discourse captured between dictatorship-fascism accusations and belittlements of the gravity of the developments. Online: 24.hu/belfold/2018/07/31/filippov-gabor-a-hibrid-ellenforradalom-kora/, accessed 13.12.2019.

such, it is an "externally constrained hybrid regime" (Bozóki/Hegedűs 2018). However, the EU is not only constraining, but it also functions as a system of support and legitimation for the Hungarian regime (ibid.). The ruling elite's appropriation of public resources is a crucial element of the system, which is further supported by the inflow of investment money made available by the EU cohesion fund. Not less intriguing is the legitimizing function of the EU: "[...] [a] lack of sanctions and open criticism of the political developments in Hungary indirectly legitimize the Orbán regime, and strengthen the self-legitimizing discourse of its leaders who argue for the illiberal but democratic nature of their regime" (ibid.: 1181-1182). Paradoxically, even penalties and admonitions from Brussels strengthen its legitimacy, as the government can "present itself as the shield of the Hungarian national sovereignty while rallying citizens around the flag" (Enyedi/Krekó 2018: 45). EU leaders are thus consequently portrayed as foreign, hostile agents, who must be confronted (ibid.): "Orbán has successfully redirected traditional Hungarian ressentiment towards the great powers and the West against the European Union." (Körösényi/Patkós 2017: 329)

Being a member state of the European Union would thus necessarily mean that Hungary can only be a liberal democracy, and the mere fact that this is not the case is a tell-tale sign of serious deficiencies in EU polity. Furthermore, the hesitating approach of the European People's Party towards its member, Fidesz, despite the widely known changes of the past ten years, since the September 2018 EP-adoption of the Sargentini report,[9] a document that offers a set of proofs on the breach of the rule of law in Hungary, showcases the fragility of core values of the European Union that seems to be vulnerable to political or economic interests. As Enyedi and Krekó put it, the EU is "trapped in a form of 'authoritarian equilibrium' where the political and economic advantages of keeping an increasingly authoritarian regime within the EU still exceed its disadvantages" (2018: 45).

3. Populism has limited explanatory power in describing the system. As argued by many, populism has become an over-stretched and over-used concept and is thus unable to capture the nature of current political developments. Sometimes it is used as a euphemistic description for the far-right, and other times it is a means of tabooizing topics and passions unpopular among the liberal elite.[10] For the Hungarian political system, both of these usages are relevant: calling it populism down-

---

9 European Parliament resolution of 12 September 2018 on a proposal calling on the Council to determine, pursuant to Article 7(1) of the Treaty on European Union, the existence of a clear risk of a serious breach of the values, on which the Union is founded, by Hungary: www.europarl.europa.eu/sides/getDoc.do?type=TA&reference=P8-TA-2018-0340&language=EN&ring=A8-2018-0250, 13.12.2019.
10 Chantal Mouffe calls this "anti-populist hysteria," suggesting that it delegitimizes anything outside of the neoliberal consensus: www.opendemocracy.net/en/democraciaabierta/populist-challenge/, 13.12.2019.

plays the significance and extent of changes while also blurring its popular support, thereby assisting in its escape from scrutiny.

What can be described as the populist elements of Fidesz's discourse and ideology, are its anti-elitism (while depicting itself as not part of the elite), anti-pluralism (in its construction of a homogeneous "them vs us" narrative, and a distinct preference for a majoritarian rule), and ferocious anti-liberalism. In light of the political uses of the term, however, it must be noted here that it is not inherently anti-democratic to criticize the elites – who may indeed be disconnected from the problems or language of much of the population – nor is it anti-democratic to criticize liberal economic and cultural views. However, it is anti-democratic to use these claims to justify undermining the institutions of liberal democracy that guarantee an even playing field through the rule of law and the checks and balances.

2. Gender Politics in Hungary 2010-2019

As Weronika Grzebalska and Andrea Pető have described, gender politics is a crucial – rather than mere additional – element of the illiberal[11] restructuring of the Hungarian state (Grzebalska/Pető 2018). Gender here stands not only for itself, but it also symbolizes many of the problems within the current order (Grzebelska et al. 2017).

To understand why gender and feminism can function as enemies in the Hungarian public discourse, we must take a historical approach, and go back at least to 1989 and to what Anikó Gregor and Weronika Grzebalska call the "original sins" of the regime changes in the region from a feminist point of view (Gregor/Grzebalska 2016). One such sin was that the post-1989 feminist movements in East-Central Europe were largely founded on the negation of the previous, dictatorial socio-economic systems. Distancing themselves from communism helped feminists in East-Central Europe to legitimize their movement among the liberal elites, but it also made them more compliant with emergent neoliberal reforms, and more

---

11 The term illiberal democracy was coined by Fareed Zakaria (1997) and became the dominant description of the Hungarian regime after Prime Minister Viktor Orbán declared, in his annual programmatic speech in 2014, that "the new state that we are constructing in Hungary is an illiberal state, a non-liberal state. It does not reject the fundamental principles of liberalism such as freedom, and I could list a few more, but it does not make this ideology the central element of state organization, but instead includes a different, special, national approach." Deliberately conflating liberal values with institutions of liberal democracy, this rhetorical move proved to be decisive in the building up support for the system: www.kormany.hu/en/the-prime-minister/the-prime-minister-s-speeches/prime-minister-viktor-orban-s-speech-at-the-25th-balvanyos-summer-free-university-and-student-camp, 13.12.2019.

likely to draw from Western theories and solutions rather than look to their own recent histories for models of empowerment and justice. The second original sin is that human rights came hand-in-hand with the region's re-integration into global capitalism, from a semi-peripheral, inferior position, and often the same actors promoted both austerity and human rights (e.g. IMF, World Bank).

To secure a place within the globalist elites of the West, Hungarian liberal elites in the 1990s and 2000s reformulated the structural inequalities between West and East in terms of civilization. This went hand-in-hand with the taboo-ization of class struggles by branding any critique of economic inequalities 'anti-semitic': 'exploitation within capitalism = accusation of Jewish people' (Gagyi 2016). As a consequence, emancipatory movements of today, including feminist and LGBT movements, either treat capitalism and the region's economically inferior position as irrelevant for their struggles – which have been reformulated as a struggle exclusively in terms of recognition, or as an economic system that is beneficial for furthering women's and LGBT rights, or, at most, that it is in no contradiction with emancipatory claims, and that these were two separate and separable struggles. There is a still-prevailing discourse about the necessity of 'catching up with the developed West,' even claiming that 'the Hungarian women's movement is lagging 40 years behind the West.'[12]

This is the context that we must consider when we analyze the claims of actors antagonizing the imported concept of gender as 'ideological colonization.' Existing analyzes describing this rhetorical tool used by the Right (Graff/Korolczuk 2018) must be complemented by an accurate analysis of the North-South, West-East power relationships that shape gender debates. We can build on the insights of many scholars in this field. For instance, Susan Zimmermann has described how implementing gender studies in the countries of the former Eastern bloc in the 1990s was less a commitment to gender equality and to gaining more knowledge in the field than to the values of liberal democracy and the ensuing social-economic order as enacted in Anglo-Saxon countries (2007). Andrea Pető has emphasized the importance of the fact that "[g]ender as a category of analysis reached Central Europe together with the neoliberal market economy and Anglo-Saxon dominance in science after 1989" (2018: 2). She also stated, "[t]he fact that gender studies was mostly embedded in the humanities and less in the social sciences contributed to the 'cultural turn' in Eastern European gender studies" (ibid.: 3), and that this "epistemic community is connected to post-structuralism and the English language" (ibid.: 7).

What the Right calls colonization, therefore, can also be reformulated and understood through an analysis of the geopolitical power relations in which eman-

---

12 https://hvg.hu/itthon/20170618_Magyarorszag_jobban_teljesit_szexizmusban_es_ez_komoly_karokat_okoz, 13.12.2019.

cipatory struggles and gender studies are embedded (Bajusz/Feró 2018; Mészáros 2017; Grzebalska/Kováts 2018; Nyklová/Fárová 2018). Indeed, this may be all the more true as liberal elites actively contributed to the maintenance of this narrative of dominance by buying in or constructing themselves through the civilisatory formulation of 'lagging behind.' This is what Alexander Kiossev has called the 'self-colonizing' discourse of the Eastern European elites (1999), and what Ivan Krastev and Stephen Holmes identify as one of the major driving forces behind the popularity of the Right (2018).

Given the lack of state funding and a donation-ready middle-class, another element to consider is the dependency of feminist and LGBT activism on donors, which Ghodsee has described as a major source of vulnerability and lack of legitimacy: "This dependence on external funders redirects accountability upward toward the aid giver and away from the aid recipients of the NGOs' so-called constituency." (2004: 238) As many have determined: When social movements become professionalized and donor-dependent NGOs and service providers of the state, they lose societal support for their causes and their potential to criticize both the state and the market processes on which they then come to depend.

The role of what is called Europeanization in the field of women's and LGBT rights is also part of this phenomenon (Valkovičová 2017). Gender equality in Western terms became a condition for 'joining Europe' (this seemingly benign, yet not-so-innocent equation drawn between the terms 'European Union' and 'Europe' already expresses a relationship of dominance), and it made any progress contingent on this relationship.

While there is a huge scholarly interest in postcolonialism, the concepts used for expressing the transnational power relations within feminist and gender theory still routinely ignore the post-socialist contexts either by, at best, equating them with Western Europe and its colonial past, or, at worst, ignoring them as a "non-region."[13]

It is therefore in this post-socialist, power-laden context of neoliberalization, NGO-ization and Europeanization, that the right-wing references to 'colonialism,' the overwhelming changes in gender policy, and the legitimization of those changes must be understood.

a. Institutional Framework and Feminist Actors

As part of the 2004 EU accession procedure, certain institutional mechanisms had to be established to secure gender equality and dialogue between government and civil society. After 2010, these institutions were dismantled, downsized, subsumed under other governmental bodies, or – as is the case in many other countries –

---

13   For a good overview on related literature, see Suchland 2011.

filled with non-feminist, conservative actors, albeit concerned with the status of women in society.

There is already some literature on the new forms of 'civil society' that emerged in relation to the circumstances created by the present government: These are partly made up of conservative NGOs, ignored or under-funded prior to 2010, and partly of newly established, loyal entities, in part founded and maintained by people or organizations associated directly with the government. Research on these organizations has only recently started to include inquiries into new organizations in the field of women's rights. What we can already see taking place includes a right-wing attempt to re-signify the concept of 'civil society,' as established in the 1990's as part of the ideology of neoliberal capitalism and governance, where NGOs are the 'good' actors (compared to the state) jumping in as service providers. However, the loyalties of these organizations to the government do not exclude their abilities to self-organize or exert agency, nor do they simply represent a conservative agenda. For example, several organizations pursue agendas hitherto confined to feminism, such as support for single mothers, work-life balance, or awareness-raising campaigns for fathers to take up more unpaid work at home.

While this parallel loyal and/or conservative NGO sector was established, the feminist projects and NGOs formerly dependent on the state lost their funding. This led to the disappearance of many organizations, but also to some rethinking about the available tools of resistance, including how far being organized as NGOs is compatible with a feminist movement in the current system.

In recent times, there have been two types of successful organizing. The first is what Andrea Krizsán and Raluca Popa identify as a window of opportunity in the momentary positive effects of a strongly gendered opposition (2018: 107). This emerged when a blatantly misogynistic speech of a Fidesz MP[14] in the Parliament provoked public outrage (including from conservatives), which then led to the passing of legislation introducing domestic violence (as 'intimate partner violence') into the Penal Code from July 2013 onwards.

The second has been the emergence of single-issue women's movements, which have successfully organized women throughout the country. The mothers of disabled children, for instance, built a movement and fought a five-year struggle that succeeded in pressuring the government to considerably increase state support for parents who take up full-time domestic care responsibilities for disabled children. Some feminists criticized their agenda as cementing the gendered division of care for disabled children, suggesting that financial rewards keep women out of the labor market and fail to acknowledge the state's lack of responsibility for investing in institutional care. Others emphasized the practical interests of the children and

---

14 This MP suggested that if women had more children, they would be more respected in the family, and would thus experience fewer episodes of domestic violence.

their caregivers, who are primarily women – and who thus become less dependent on their male partners, or become less poor – and pointed to the gradual character of their struggles, as their movement continues to work and press for more substantial changes.

These single-issue movements have proven to be good tools for mobilizing people with a personal interest, but they have also helped to set achievable goals in difficult circumstances. However, it was and remains a challenge for these movements to broaden their constituencies and form coalitions in an era when the government actively tries to pit social groups against each other, to discourage cooperation of such organizations with stigmatized groups and demonized organizations, and to keep social concerns away from oppositional parties.

b.   Gender Policy = Family Policy = Demographic Policy = Fertility Policy

The new Constitution (also known as the Basic Law of Hungary), which was adopted in 2011, includes a provision that protects the fundamental right to life from the moment of conception. At the time, this provoked public outcry from human rights NGOs and opposition circles, which anticipated the arrival of legal restrictions on the country's long-standing, liberal abortion regulations.[15] The new Constitution also states that marriage is only possible between a man and a woman, thereby making any future possibility of transforming the legal recognition of gay and lesbian relationships from registered partnerships to marriages more difficult.

In February 2019, Orbán announced a seven-point family policy package to start in July 2019, which again led to an international outcry from the West. However, this response failed to appreciate the policy's progressive and emancipatory aspects, thereby falling into Orbán's trap (Orenstein 2019). The seven points are: (1) preferential loans for newly-wed couples planning to have children; (2) the extension of preferential loans under the former family home purchase scheme (CSOK) (see Szikra 2018); (3) mortgage subsidies; (4) definitive exemptions from personal

---

15 This has not yet happened. Some argue that it will never happen given that, according to the polls, over 80% of the population continues to support the current regulation (whereby the foetus can be aborted until the 12th week of pregnancy), and also given that, according to all studies in the field, the overwhelming majority of abortions (the numbers of which are in steady decline since 1990) are initiated by lower-class women with lower levels of education, who are disproportionately Roma. Others argue that newly-established constraints (e.g. obligatory counselling for women seeking to abort), non-compliances to EU recommendations (e.g. the government decided not to allow abortion pills so as to not make abortion too easy; morning-after-pills must be prescribed by a gynaecologist, and are thus not available over-the-counter) and regular public pro-life speeches forebode that the liberal law is subject to substantial changes in the future.

income tax payments for women who have had and raised at least four children; (5) a subsidy program for families raising at least three children so that they can purchase a car seating at least seven people; (6) the government creation of 21,000 crèche places over three years; and (7) the possibility for grandparents to look after young children instead of their parents, and to be eligible for earnings-related child-care benefits (GYED).

Gender policies of the Hungarian government are in essence reduced to family policies, thereby excluding issues not directly connected to the family and which might obligate rethinking the state-market relationship. Family policy, in turn, is narrowed to demographic policy, thereby excluding issues that are not related to demography – e.g. the education system for existing children, the issue of child poverty, the legal situation of gay and lesbian couples, or care for the elderly. The latter is obviously also an issue of demography as the ageing of the Hungarian population is of utmost importance, and there has been a constant flow of alarming reports about their grave states of health, and the consequent growing pressures placed on the system of care for the ageing in the country. However, care for the elderly has been omitted because demographic policy is understood solely as fertility policy: It aims to boost the child-bearing capacities of women, meaning, in practice, upper or middle class, non-Roma women. In his speech announcing the new family policy package[16], PM Orbán clarified that they want to support families who "live for their children" rather than "off their children." In the Hungarian context, it is clear that this is an anti-Roma remark, as Roma people are often accused in public discourse of having children for the sake of state support. The class dimensions and ethnic exclusions are the most striking elements of the generous family policy scheme, which is based on financial incentives. In addition to these aspects, men are left fully unaddressed, as if childbearing were an issue exclusive to women. Labor market policies are also left untouched.

While there is no reason to doubt the sincerity of the government's efforts to boost fertility among the preferred classes, the government is constrained in its capacity to maneuver by a workforce shortage and pressures by (multinational) companies to respond with more flexibility for employers. The biggest problem of employees with children is the inability to combine paid work with care duties (Gregor/Kováts 2019). Nonetheless, from January 2019 onwards, a new amendment to the Labor Code makes it possible for employers to order up to 400 supplementary hours per year in overtime (to be paid within three years). These generous family policies, based on financial incentives for couples with employment status, can thus hardly fulfill the aspirations of the government in the field of fertility: working conditions, as the biggest burden of caregivers, is still not being addressed.

---

16 For a brief summary of family policy measures implemented in practice from 2010 to 2017, see Szikra 2018.

However, this limited focus of the government, when it comes to issues of gender, cannot be reduced to the self-comforting narrative of a "conservative backlash." Prior to 2010, leftist-liberal governments were not champions of gender equality either, which poses a serious credibility problem for the opposition, whenever it criticizes the policy's exclusionary class and ethnic dimensions.

At the same time, the current policy package presents, paradoxically, a certain opportunity of emancipation for large groups of women. This is not because Hungarian women are possessed by a false consciousness, but rather because it addresses what Maxine Molyneux calls 'practical gender interests' (1985) - i.e. interests that arise within the constraints of a given gender order (though without questioning the order itself). Indeed, this phenomenon can partially explain the popularity of the Right among women. This is an issue that has been addressed in papers co-authored with Weronika Grzebalska and Anikó Gregor respectively, in which we argue that treating care responsibilities as burdens to labor market participation (and GDP production) does not sound like an emancipatory promise in a context where most people (men and women alike) experience paid work as exploitation and slavery (Gregor/Kováts 2019; Grzebalska/Kováts 2018), and where the main concern of women is not how to escape home duties, but rather how to escape the workplace to be able to be with loved ones, while making a decent living from one job (not two or three), in which a primary objective would be an 8- rather than a 12-hour workday.

Obviously, a proclaimed emphasis on motherhood does not address the root causes of the contradictory relations between capital and care (Fraser 2016), which are exacerbated by labor conditions, especially on the semi-periphery; as described above, the government hasn't taken up conflicts with employers to alleviate the tensions between paid and unpaid work. However, enjoying a finally recognized motherhood entails a certain dignity that demands understanding rather than condescension.

Despite a deeply conservative rhetoric centered on motherhood, the government policy provides certain practical support, as we have seen, which calls for some differentiation between ideology and policy. As described by Dorottya Szikra (2019), with regards to Hungarian family policies, there is a certain inconsistency between the two. Although these policies foreground the primary care role of women (also by not speaking at all about men), they open serious policy incentives for women's paid labor, too[17] Accusations that Fidesz is 'sending women back to the kitchen' are therefore clearly misplaced, and criticizing the rhetorical emphasis on motherhood misses the point. Also, while their policy can be rightly criticized, it is

---

17 These include, for example, that benefits are dependent on employment status. Aside from its class-based exclusions, this policy means that women's paid labor is taken for granted. See points 4., 6. and 7.

very often conflated with anti-democratic developments in progressive discourse – e.g. the family policy is cited as proof of Hungary 'sliding back to the 1930s.' In the interest of developing effective solutions, these two issues should be separated, so as to avoid the risk of discrediting critique from the start.

Recognizing care as a societal value and as indispensable for the reproduction of society is long overdue. As described by much scholarly literature in core countries where welfare states are shrinking, such tasks are increasingly outsourced to lower class or migrant women from the Eastern peripheries or from outside of the EU. This is also why Western European countries score better than their Eastern or Southern peripheral counterparts in terms of gender equality (for instance, with regards to the labor market participation of women). Therefore, one cannot claim that certain peripheral societies are 'lagging behind,' when in reality the better scores of the West are contingent on inequalities between women of different classes and countries with different positions in the economic world order.

What has also been overlooked by the ferocious critiques of the current family policy plan is that it presents a positive vision. Even if it may very well fail to bring about the much-desired baby boom of the middle classes, it represents a new rhetoric that is a contrast to the fear-mongering security narratives of previous years.

While political communication surrounding this package sustains the dichotomy of those who look to solve Europe's demographic crisis by migration versus those who employ "family-friendly policies," nevertheless it sends a positive message that is centered around a certain popular image of the family by communicating that "we are building a country where it is good to have children."

From this perspective, fact-based criticisms about class and ethnic exclusions of this vision can seem anti-family, petty-minded, and negative. Although I am not arguing in support of the government position, I believe that we cannot just point to its deficiencies and delusions; instead, a broader counter-vision is needed.

c. Gender as a Fear-Mongering Mobilizing Tool[18]

As described above, it has become a defining feature of the regime to orchestrate hate campaigns on the public dime. The concept of 'gender' became an enemy image as late as 2017.[19] Andrea Pető and I predicted in a paper, that was finalized in the Autumn of 2016, that organized opposition to the perceived threat of 'gender

---

18 This subchapter is the edited version of one of the subchapters of this article: Kováts, Eszter (2019): Limits of the Human Rights Vocabulary in Addressing Inequalities – Dilemmas of Justice in the Age of Culture Wars in Hungary. Intersections, 2019/2. 60-80. https://intersections.tk.mta.hu/index.php/intersections/issue/view/19

19 This does not mean that there has been no anti-"gender ideology" discourse, but that it has remained quite low-key and sporadic. For a chronology, see Félix 2015 and Kováts/Pető 2017.

ideology' would be organized by the government and its corollary organizations and media in Hungary if it sees an interest in creating a new enemy (Kováts/Pető 2017). And in the end, our predictions came to life.

Contrary to most countries, where grassroots and/or religious organizations have mobilized against so-called progressive bills that reference 'gender ideology,' in Hungary it is the government itself that maintains the perception of danger so that it can present itself as the protector of the country. Here, mobilization does not occur on the streets but rather through government-organized NGOs (so-called GONGOs, Varga 2016) and the use of their own media outlets, which constitute the largest segment of the Hungarian media landscape (Polyák/Urbán 2016). The two main campaigns of the government against what they call 'gender ideology,' which both date back to 2017, were forwarded in the context of a so-called war of independence against foreign influence. They focused on the ratification of the Istanbul Convention and the Gender Studies MA programs of the Budapest University ELTE and the Central European University.

In December 2016, Prime Minister Viktor Orbán announced that 2017 would be the year when Hungary would finally settle accounts with the interests and objectives represented by Hungarian-born billionaire philanthropist, György Soros. Launched soon thereafter, in February 2017, the campaign started with waves of posters and national consultations.[20] In this context, the Central European University, founded by Soros, was also targeted together with all liberal values, including LGBT issues. 'Gender ideology' fit into a string of issues used by the government to distinguish itself from the 'corrupt West.' The campaign against Soros, based on the alleged threat posed by the CEU, LGBT affairs, NGOs and the wider 'gender ideology,' created a new enemy that could be used as an incentive for continued mobilizations after the (temporary) attenuation of the migration crisis.

Eötvös Loránd University (ELTE)'s new Gender Studies MA program was targeted by government propaganda in February 2017. First, it was Youth Christian Democratic Alliance (IKSZ), the youth section of the KDNP – the smaller coalition partner, who wrote an open letter to the rector of the university against the Gender Studies program. They urged the rector to stop bowing to "pressure from the gender and gay lobby":

> "You, the management, have decided to offer a Master's course that is of absolutely no use to Hungarian society in a misguided topic that is *choked by political correctness* and disguised as science. We believe that Hungary cannot afford the same luxury as certain Scandinavian countries, where *the signs posted on bathroom doors* are among the most important points of public debate, and effort is made

---

20   and lead up to the Stop Soros Act, that pitched an attack against NGOs funded by organizations affiliated with George Soros, among others, and was enacted in May 2018 by the newly elected Parliament

to market as many neutral toys and school books as possible *to avoid influencing the belonging of boys and girls to their own sex*. It must be accepted that there are biological sexes, not social ones,[21] making even the designation of the course false and misleading."[22] (emphasis added)

All forms of government media then began to churn out propaganda materials against gender studies. In one of her first television interviews, hosted by the governmental ECHO TV, the first question posed to Ágnes Van-Til Kövér, the head of the gender studies program, was why they had launched a program that affects only 0.3% of Hungarian society, by which the reporter was obviously referring to the estimated percentage of transgender people in society.[23] The government-led resistance argued that the traditional family model was under threat, and referred to international phenomena related to transgender and queer activism as the supposed curriculum for gender studies, but also, more broadly, to such things as political correctness.

Initially, the fiery debate and propaganda were not followed by government action. The MA program was launched as scheduled with a dozen students in September 2017. However, the second wave of debates started in August 2018 after PM Orbán announced a cultural war and a desire to finally settle accounts with culture and academia in his yearly programmatic speech. With the terrain discursively prepared, the threat of "gender ideology" took root. In line with earlier arguments, it revolved around recalling the accreditation of the MA program but with higher political stakes. In mid-October it was announced that the program will be de-accredited; only those who started the program in 2017 and 2018 were permitted to finish it - until June 2019 and 2020 respectively.

The Council of Europe Convention on preventing and combating violence against women and domestic violence (i.e. the Istanbul Convention) was signed by the Hungarian Government in March 2014, but it has not since been ratified.[24] In response to the inquiries regularly lodged by women's rights organizations, the government followed a pattern of confirmation (stating that yes, they will ratify it) and adjournment, creating the impression that the issue was not treated as a priority or was not being followed up within governmental structures. Hence, linking the convention with 'gender ideology' enabled an ideological anchor for remaining passive – perhaps all the more so because it was easy to incorporate it into the new mobilization strategy of the government. While the government was

---

21 In the Hungarian language, there is no sex/gender distinction, it is expressed by an adjective indicating whether it refers to biological or social sex (i.e. gender).
22 pestisracok.hu/iksz-azelte-kiszolgalja-gender-es-meleglobbi-nyomulasat/.
23 www.youtube.com/watch?v=3auaFOl1N20.
24 For a brief history and analysis of framings and movement-opposition dynamics of the fight against domestic violence from 1990 to 2012 in Hungary, see Krizsán/Popa 2018.

correct in expecting that no mass protests would follow if it made a U-turn on the matter of ratification, this shift in discourse made it possible to present itself, once again, as the guardian of national sovereignty and the tireless warrior in the struggle against foreign influence by rejecting yet another international treaty that was allegedly incompatible with Hungarian values.

The main argument against the Istanbul Convention was that it uses the non-consensual and ambiguous term 'gender.' For instance, the Center for Fundamental Rights, a government agency disguised as independent,[25] published a resolution on the Istanbul Convention in May 2017, entitled "No to the Gender Convention,"[26] and recommended that the government should not submit the Convention to the Parliament because, so went the reasoning, despite its alleged goal to fight violence against women, its real purpose is to break down the traditional family model in every European country:

"Even though it is common sense that there are only two sexes in all creation, the Convention aims to go against this fact, do away with the notion of biological sexes and use the concept of gender instead for all legal purposes. People would stop being simply men and women and would belong to one of the infinite number of artificially created gender categories." (emphasis added)

This clearly distorts the gender definition of the Convention, which does not deny the biological reality of the two sexes (3.c.): "'gender' shall mean the socially constructed roles, behaviors, activities and attributes that a given society considers appropriate for women and men."

The ratification of the Convention was postponed and several government representatives stated that they would never support or ratify it. In the run-up to the Parliamentary elections in April 2018, the government media repeatedly warned that, if the opposition comes to power, they would ratify the "Gender Convention."

When these actors reject the concept of gender,[27] they regard the fight against gender stereotyping as a precursor to the advent of 'electable gender identities.' It

---

25   It has been identified as a government agency posing as an independent think tank or an NGO – a GONGO, government organized NGO, by definition (Varga 2016: 244-245). The Center is regularly called upon by the government-friendly media to comment on government measures as an 'independent specialist' to justify their actions.
26   alapjogokert.hu/wp-content/uploads/2017/05/Nem-a-genderegyezm%C3%A9nyre.pdf .
27   While the focus of this paper is on the Hungarian government and its corollaries, one must note that the government has several allies in Hungarian opposition circles when it comes to the issue of 'gender ideology.' One of the three opposition candidates running for Mayor of Budapest in the October 2019 municipal elections, the anti-feminist and self-identifying centrist media celebrity, Róbert Puzsér, for instance, regularly comments on the Istanbul Convention and on gender studies, both of which are alleged to be spreading non-binary gender identities and the hatred of men.

may thus seem that they are using new language for the old antifeminist aspirations of deriving all gender roles from claims to biological reality. It may also seem that this new language would materialize in the creation of a straw man without any real-world reference. However, as exemplified by the italicized parts of the above-quoted arguments opposing the Istanbul Convention and the first Hungarian gender studies MA program, the discourse makes references to debates and disputes going on in (mainly) Anglo-Saxon countries, primarily about political correctness and transgender and non-binary gender identities.

It is especially striking that no reference is made to women's rights at all. While not ratifying the Convention and not subscribing to its comprehensive framework to combat violence against women, the government nevertheless has implemented certain measures in line with the convention: for instance, it has established new crisis centers and shelters in recent years.

As is supported by the quotations above, this entire phenomenon can be interpreted as the reception process of activism that defines gender as identity, and in line with the government's objective to create the image of an enemy that can be used for mobilization and to justify its failures to ratify the Istanbul Convention. Naturally, the real political motives behind such communication operations cannot be inferred from written documents or public speeches. In any case, it can be safely established that the phenomenon the government attacks is not a fictive enemy that lacks real-life reference but builds upon manifestations of actual activism. In addition to the other hate-based campaign building on the migration crisis, the current events and trends of foreign activism are interpreted here so as to uphold a war-time narrative that serves to generate a feeling of being under constant threat. These are, at this stage, imported threats in the Hungarian context, a copy-paste alt-right: Very few Hungarian feminist and LGBT activists have publicly exhibited such views so far. Nevertheless, what they refer to exists, and it is slowly but surely being imported to an activist scene that presents these issues and their corresponding social justice language as universal (Bajusz/Feró 2018).

The arguments deployed against 'gender ideology' draw attention to the fact that the meaning of the structural concept of gender itself has also changed over the years in progressive activism. It used to denote "the fundamentally social quality of distinctions based on sex" (as Joan Scott puts it), the power structures in a given society between men and women, and the societal roles, possibilities, and constraints accrued to being born male or female. The shifted meaning of gender is apparent in much of the current trans and genderqueer scholarship and activism, where gender has become conceptually synonymous with gender identity: "a person's felt sense of identity" (Green 2006: 247). Gender, in this sense, means either identifying or not with being born male or female, having the privilege or not to have one's "sex assigned at birth" in line with one's "felt sense of gender identity," which has also resulted in the proliferation of an infinite number of unique, non-binary gender identities.²⁸ This second approach, however, has very little in common with the original critique of the hierarchical social structures between men and women, and the fact that the gendered oppression we observe today is not a response to our identities but to how society identifies us (and, say, gives lesser pay to a woman or exposes her to specific forms of violence – independent of her self-assigned 'gender identity').²⁹ This polysemy (Kováts 2018b) is very well illustrated by the Hungarian debate on the Istanbul Convention, where the governmental actors did misrepresent the definition of the Convention, but used a definition that exists in certain Western countries' activism. And for this applies, what Gudrun Axeli-Knapp describes as the un-reconciliability of certain feminist theories (2018). As these theories visibly inform feminist activism and politics, taking up this conflict becomes of political significance.

Having uncovered this connection, the most common interpretation – i.e. that we would face a new form of anti-human rights movement, antifeminism and homophobia – can no longer be sustained or must at least be completed. It must also be acknowledged that this phenomenon is not a kind of backlash against existing women's and LGBT rights; at most, it opposes a certain strand of feminism and LGBT activism – that receives plenty of critiques from feminist, liberal and Marxist circles too.

Conclusion

While most scholarship on the origins of 'gender ideology' discourse, identifies the Vatican, since the end of the 1990s, as a key actor in its formulation (cf. Kuhar/Paternotte 2017), Mary Anne Case's recent philological analysis on the views of Popes Benedict XVI and Francis establishes that "[t]rans rights claims were [...] thus a foundational component, not a recent addition, to the Vatican's sphere of concern around 'gender' and to the focusing of that concern on developments in secular law" (2019: 640). This might be the missing link between two explanations that seemed to contradict each other in the Hungarian case: one, the long-established Vatican origins of the anti-'gender ideology' discourse, and the other, references to current incidences of trans and genderqueer activism and concepts in the discourse. The case of Hungary suggests that we need an interpretational framework that extends

---

28   For a thorough analysis of how "gender-bending Tumblr users" and alt-right strengthened each other in an online culture war becoming offline in the US, see Angela Nagle's Kill All Normies (2017).
29   In several countries, heated debates continue between various strands of feminist activism concerning the use of this term. See two accounts of the debates from the both sides in Bettcher/Styker 2016, and Reilly-Cooper 2016.

beyond dichotomous understandings of the phenomenon, as if it were a fight between democrats and populists, progressives and conservatives, egalitarians and authoritarians, or essentialists and post-essentialists. Such binary understandings miss the point as to how parties that are seemingly opposed to each other come to act according to the same logics and interact to produce the same result of a culture war (Kováts 2018a). Instead, we need to understand "how we got here" and what sustains and legitimizes the system.

First, the Hungarian governing parties' use of the ready-made discourse against 'gender ideology' is best understood within the broader context of its complete restructuring of the Hungarian state: If we separate these issues, we over-emphasize their critique of a critical concept (gender) that would potentially debunk its misogynistic views – as suggested by gender scholars who analyze critiques of 'gender ideology' as distinct from socio-economic and geopolitical stakes and from political issues other than gender. Fidesz is not only gathering enemies for the sake of using them politically against minorities or other opponents; but it interprets the global order and proposes – admittedly ugly – answers to existing phenomena, such as the power imbalances within the European Union.

Second, we must not lose sight of the fact that our tools for analyzing oppression are not free floating, universal concepts. Emancipatory movements do not exist in a vacuum: Their claims and vocabularies are also products of politico-economic processes and geopolitical power structures, and are therefore also subject to critique. In the Hungarian case, it is specifically the post-socialist context that plays a crucial role, and we must be wary (on both sides of the former Iron Curtain) of equating progress with imitation of the core countries.

Third, concepts evolve. Addressing the oppression of certain groups based on sex, race and sexuality was crucial, and we cannot underestimate the significance of 1970s-80s Western activism. But these developments also came hand-in-hand with the fragmentation of identities of postmodernism, which was – as described by many authors –instrumental to the growing individualism inscribed in our economic system, and opened the door to various co-optations and changes of scale from structural to individual realms.

All too often activists treat repeated reference to wounded feelings as the sole argument with epistemic authority on issues of representation, culture or identity. In the context of emancipatory movements and their emphasis on offended feelings, Paula Villa speaks critically of what she calls positional fundamentalism (2017) – that is, equating individuals with their positions in social structures (their race, their sex, their sexual preference) and thereby making them personally responsible for the oppressive societal structures that they come to represent. She calls this politics surrogate (Politiksurrogat): the tendency to retreat into emotional reactions and feelings of self-righteousness instead of engaging in constructive argumentation. While I more than agree with her critique of this phenomenon, I suggest that perhaps a different term – individualized intersectionality – would be more apt. The issue is not that this type of politics merely totalizes the otherwise just request of reflection on positionality, and treats it as an all-encompassing approach beyond any critique; rather, it reformulates what should be a structural critique in individual terms ("check your privilege"), thereby addressing it on the wrong scale and choosing wrong methods to counter it.

The concept of gender is the best example of this as I have tried to demonstrate in the last sub-chapter. Instead of dismissing any criticism of intersectionality, privilege theory, and gender as right-wing and anti-emancipatory; and instead of giving in to the temptation to tabooizations with references to a 'common enemy,' the right-wing, we should, before it is too late, not shy away from conflict, and look critically into the evolution of these concepts and why they have become so vulnerable.

Bibliography

Bajusz, Orsolya/Dalma, Feró (2018): "Progressivist Gender-Based Activism as a Means of Social Antagonism in Hungary Through Two Case Studies." In: Sociologija 1. Belgrad, pp. 177-193.

Bettcher, Talia M./Styker, Susan (2016): "Introduction: Trans/Feminisms." In: Transgender Studies Quarterly 3 (1-2), pp. 5-14.

Bozóki, András/Hegedűs, Dániel (2018): "An Externally Constrained Hybrid Regime: Hungary in the European Union." In: Democratization 25 (7), pp. 1173-1189.

Case, Mary Anne (2019): "Trans Formations in the Vatican's War on 'Gender Ideology'." In: Signs: Journal of Women in Culture and Society 44 (3), pp. 639-663.

Enyedi, Zsolt (2016): "Paternalist Populism and Illiberal Elitism in Central Europe." In: Journal of Political Ideologies 21 (1), pp. 9-25.

Enyedi, Zsolt/Krekó, Péter (2018): "Orbán's Laboratory of Illiberalism." In: Journal of Democracy 29 (3), pp. 39-51.

Félix, Anikó (2015): "Hungary." In: Eszter Kováts/Maari Põim (eds.), Gender as Symbolic Glue. The Position and Role of Conservative and Far Right Parties in the Anti-Gender Mobilizations in Europe. Brussels/Budapest: Foundation for European Progressive Studies and Friedrich Ebert Stiftung, pp. 62-82.

Félix, Anikó (2018): "Country Case Study Hungary." In: Elisa Gutsche (ed.), Triumph of the Women? The Female Face of the Populist and Far Right in Europe. Berlin: Friedrich-Ebert-Stiftung, pp. 108-121, (library.fes.de/pdf-files/dialog/14636.pdf).

Fraser, Nancy (2016): "Contradiction of Capital and Care." In: New Left Review 100, (newleftreview.org/issues/II100/articles/nancy-fraser-contradictions-of-capital-and-care).

Gagyi, Ágnes (2016): "'Coloniality of Power' in East Central Europe: External Penetration as Internal Force in Post-Socialist Hungarian Politics." In: Journal of World-Systems Research 22 (2), pp. 349-372.

Ghodsee, Kristen (2004): "Feminism-by-Design: Emerging Capitalisms, Cultural Feminism, and Women's Nongovernmental Organizations in Post-socialist Eastern Europe." In: Signs: Journal of Women in Culture and Society 29 (3), pp. 727-753.

Graff, Agnieszka/Kapur, Ratna/Walters, Suzanna Danuta (2019): "Introduction: Gender and the Rise of the Global Right." In: Signs: Journal of Women in Culture and Society 44 (3), pp. 541-560.

Graff, Agnieszka/Korolczuk, Elżbieta (2018): "Gender as 'Ebola from Brussels': The Anticolonial Frame and the Rise of Illiberal Populism." In: Signs: Journal of Women in Culture and Society 43 (4), pp. 797-821.

Green, Eli R. (2006): Debating Trans Inclusion in the Feminist Movement: A Trans-Positive Analysis. In: Pattatucci Aragon, Angela (ed.), Challenging Lesbian Norms: Intersex, Transgender, Intersectional and Queer Perspectives. Philadelphia: Haworth Press. 231-248.

Gregor, Anikó & Kováts, Eszter (2019) Work – life: balance? Tensions between care and paid work in the lives of Hungarian women. in: socio.hu, Labour relations and employment policies in times of volatility: Special issue in English No. 7 (2019) Dezember 2019. 91-115. https://socio.hu/uploads/files/2019eng_labour/2019eng_gregor_kovats.pdf.

Gregor, Anikó/Kováts, Eszter (2019): "Work – Life: Balance? Tensions between Care and Paid Work in the Lives of Hungarian women." In: Social Science Review. Hungarian Academy of Sciences.

Grzebalska, Weronika/Pető, Andrea (2018): "The Gendered Modus Operandi of the Illiberal Transformation in Hungary and Poland." In: Women's Studies International Forum 68, pp. 164-172.

Grzebalska, Weronika/Kováts, Eszter/Pető, Andrea (2017): Gender as Symbolic Glue: How 'Gender' Became an Umbrella Term for the Rejection of the (Neo)liberal Order. Online: politicalcritique.org/long-read/2017/gender-as-symbolic-glue-how-gender-became-an-umbrella-term-for-the-rejection-of-the-neoliberal-order/.

Grzebalska, Weronika/Kováts, Eszter (2018): Beyond the Anti-Women Backlash: How We Can Understand Women's Support for the Right in Poland and Hungary. Online: www.ips-journal.eu/regions/europe/article/show/beyond-the-anti-women-backlash-3160/,.

Kiossev, Alexander (2010): "The Self-Colonizing Metaphor." In: Zbyněk Baladrán/Vít Havránek (eds.), Atlas of Transformation. Prague: Tranzit, (monumenttotransformation.org/atlas-of-transformation/html/s/self-colonization/the-self-colonizing-metaphor-alexander-kiossev.html,).

Kiss, Viktor (2018): "A Poszt-Hatvannyolcas Szituáció – És Ami Utána Következik." [The Post-68 Situation – And What Follows]. In: Kommentár 5-6, pp. 73-80.

Kováts, Eszter (2018a): "Conservative Counter-Movements? Overcoming Culturalizing Interpretations of Right-Wing Mobilizations Against 'Gender Ideology'." In: Femina Politica. Zeitschrift für Feministische Politikwissenschaft 1, pp. 75-88.

Kováts, Eszter (2018b): The Consequences of the Differing Meanings of Gender in Policy and Activism for Politics. Online: blogs.lse.ac.uk/gender/2018/11/26/the-consequences-of-the-differing-meanings-of-gender-in-policy-and-activism-for-politics/.

Kováts, Eszter/Pető, Andrea (2017): "Anti-Gender Discourse in Hungary: A Discourse without a Movement?" In: Roman Kuhar/David Paternotte (eds.): Anti-Gender Campaigns in Europe. Mobilizing against Equality. Rowman & Littlefield, pp. 117-131.

Knapp, Gudrun-Axeli (2018): "Mut zur Kontroverse! Feministische Kritik zwischen Antigenderismus und Akademischer Spezialisierung." In: Friederike Beier/Lisa Yashodara Haller/Lea Haneberg (eds.), Materializing Feminism. Positionierungen zu Ökonomie, Staat und Identität. ,pp. 19-38.

Körösényi, András/Patkós, Veronika (2017): "Liberal and Illiberal Populism. The Leadership of Berlusconi and Orbán." In: Corvinus Journal of Sociology and Social Policy 8, pp. 315-337.

Krastev, Ivan/Holmes, Stephen (2018): "Imitation and Its Discontents." In: Journal of Democracy 29 (3), pp. 117-128.

Krizsán, Andrea/Popa, Raluca Maria (2018): "Contesting Gender Equality in Domestic-Violence Policy Debates: Comparing Three Countries in Central and Eastern Europe." In: Mieke, Verloo (ed.), Varieties of Opposition to Gender Equality in Europe. New York: Routledge, pp. 98-116.

Kuhar, Roman/Paternotte, David (eds.) (2017): Anti-Gender Campaigns in Europe. Mobilizing against Equality. Lanham: Rowman & Littlefield.

Kuhar, Roman/Paternotte, David (2018): "Disentangling and Locating the 'Global Right': Anti-Gender Campaigns in Europe." In: Politics and Governance 6 (3), pp. 6-19.

Mészáros, György (2017): "Reconsidering the Identity Approach of the EU LGBT+ Architecture from a Feminist Perspective." In: Eszter Kováts (ed.), The Future of the European Union. Feminist Perspectives from East-Central Europe. Budapest: Friedrich Ebert Stiftung, pp. 46-56, (fesbp.hu/common/pdf/The_Future_of_the_EU.pdf).

Nagle, Angela (2017): Kill All Normies. Online Culture Wars from 4chan and Tumblr to Trump and the Alt-Right. Winchester/Washington: Zero Books.

Nyklová, Blanka/Fárová, Nina (2018): "Scenes in and Outside the Library: Continuity and Change in Contesting Feminist Knowledge on the Semi-Periphery." In: The Czech Academy of Sciences, pp. 194-209.

Orenstein, Mitchell A. (2019): What Europe's Populist Right Is Getting Right. Online: www.project-syndicate.org/commentary/viktor-orban-family-policies-western-criticism-by-mitchell-a-orenstein-2019-03.

Pető, Andrea (2018): "Eastern Europe: Gender Research, Knowledge Production and Insitutions." In: Handbuch Interdisziplinäre Geschlechterforschung, Geschlecht und Gesellschaft, pp. 1-11.

Polyák, Gábor/Urbán, Ágnes (2016): "Az Elhalkítás Eszközei. Politikai Beavatkozások A Médiapiac És A Nyilvánosság Működésébe." [Instruments of Silencing. Political Interferences into the Functioning of Media Market and the Public.] In: Médiakutató XVII (3-4), pp. 109-123.

Reilly-Cooper, Rebecca (2016): Gender Is Not a Spectrum. Online: aeon.co/essays/the-idea-that-gender-is-a-spectrum-is-a-new-gender-prison.

Scheele, Sebastian (2016): Von Antifeminismus zu 'Anti-Genderismus'? Eine Diskursive Verschiebung und ihre Hintergründe. Online: www.gwi-boell.de/sites/default/files/uploads/2016/08/scheele_diskursive_verschiebung_antifeminismus.pdf.

Suchland, Jennifer (2011): "Is Postsocialism Transnational?" In: Signs: Journal of Women in Culture and Society 36 (4), pp. 837-862.

Szikra, Dorottya (2018): Welfare for the Wealthy. The Social Policy of the Orbán-Regime, 2010-2017. Budapest: Friedrich-Ebert-Stiftung, (http://library.fes.de/pdf-files/bueros/budapest/14209.pdf).

Szikra, Dorottya (2019) Ideology or Pragmatism? Interpreting Social Policy Change under the System of National Cooperation. In: János Mátyás Kovács and Balázs Trencsényi (eds. 2019) Brave New Hungary. Mapping the "System of National Cooperation." Lexington Books, pp. 225-242.

Szűcs, Zoltán Gábor (2018): "Mi A Jelentősége Annak, Hogy Magyarországon Jelenleg Kompetitív Autoriter Rezsim Van?" [What is the Relevance of the Fact that in Hungary There Is Currently a Competitive Authoritarian Regime in Place?] In: Ellensúly 1 (2018), pp. 43-54.

Valkovičová, Veronika (2017): "'Regrettably, It Seems That Breaking One Border Causes Other to Tumble' – Nationalism and Homonegativity in the 2015 Slovak Referendum." In: Politique Européenne 55, pp. 87-115.

Varga, Áron (2016): "A GONGO-Jelenség És Kormányzati Civilek Magyarországon." [The GONGO-Phenomenon and Governmental Civil Organizations in Hungary] In: Attila Antal (ed.), A Civilek Hatalma. A Politikai Tér Visszafoglalása. Noran Kiadó, pp. 234-248.

Villa, Paula (2017): Eure Gefühle Sind Mir Schnuppe. Online: https://www.zeit.de/kultur/2017-02/milo-yiannopoulos-populismus-usa-donald-trump-breitbart-10nach8/komplettansicht.

Wimbauer, Christine/Motakef, Mona/Teschlade, Julia (2015): "Prekäre Selbstverständlichkeiten. Neun Prekarisierungstheoretische Thesen zu Diskursen gegen Gleichstellungspolitik und Geschlechterforschung." In: Sabine Hark/Paula Irene Villa (eds.), Anti-Genderismus. Sexualität und Geschlecht als Schauplätze Aktueller Politischer Auseinandersetzungen. Bielefeld: transcript, pp. 41–58.

Zimmermann, Susan (2007): "The Institutionalization of Women's and Gender Studies in Higher Education in Central and Eastern Europe and the Former Soviet Union: Asymmetric Politics and the Regional-Transnational Configuration." In: East Central Europe/L'Europe du Centre-Est 35 (1–2), pp. 131–60.

Man, Woman, Family. Gender and the Limited Modernization of Right-Wing Extremism in Austria

Stefanie Mayer, Edma Ajanović, Birgit Sauer

1. Why Gender? Setting the Context

The electoral success of the far-right in many democratic countries, and the establishment of authoritarian, illiberal forms of government, have been important issues for social scientists over the last two decades (Canovan 1999; Mudde 2010, 2004; Taggart 2000; Wodak et al. 2013). But only in recent years, as far-right actors shifted their attention to 'gender' – or rather, to the denunciation of the concept –, has the notion of 'gender' become salient in analyzing these developments. Although anti-feminism has always been a defining feature of right-wing extremism (Goetz 2014; Schiedel 2007), it has not necessarily been at the top of the far-right's political agenda. This changed in recent years when a specific anti-gender discourse that had first been developed by the Vatican, and then spread via Catholic publications (Paternotte 2015), gained momentum and showed potential for capturing broad public support. It also proved successful in fostering alliances between different political groups that included but were by no means limited to the far-right (Mayer/Sauer 2017). This 'anti-genderism' – as its proponents label their anti-feminist mobilizations – targets feminist achievements and policies promoting gender equality and the liberalization of sexual regimes (Hark/Villa 2015; Kuhar/Ajanović 2018; Kuhar/Paternotte 2017). 'Anti-genderism' portrays sex and gender as biologically determined, 'natural,' and therefore immutable and unquestionable. Such an understanding of sex and gender provides, in turn, the basis for the notion of 'natural' families, which an alleged 'genderism' aims to destroy by abolishing the sexes – i.e. by creating a 'genderless human,' In recent critical literature, this new attention to gender has been understood as part of an attempt to overcome the social-democratic liberal hegemony of the Fordist era of the 1960s and 1970s (Sauer 2017).

In this article, we adopt a more modest approach, and aim to understand the role that 'gender' plays in the limited modernization processes that have taken place among the Austrian far-right in recent years. We use the term 'far-right' in a broad sense. For us, this encompasses what is usually labeled right-wing populism – in our case, most importantly, the *Austrian Freedom Party* (FPÖ) – and right-wing extremist actors and the so-called *New Right*, such as the self-proclaimed *Identitarian Movement* (IBÖ), but also fringe groups of the Christian conservative right, like *Agenda Europa*.

After the Second World War, the far-right in Austria had been characterized by its close relationship to National Socialism, especially its unfaltering adherence to German nationalism. This included an ethnicized ('völkisch') world-view that an Austrian nation – let alone an Austrian people – neither did nor should exist.[1] Over the decades following 1945, Austrian citizens increasingly accepted the idea of an Austrian nation (Reiterer 1988), and German nationalism started to become a political burden, limiting the reach and influence of the far-right in public discourse (Dobers/Mayer 2011).

Far-right actors applied two different modernization strategies to overcome this burden. The first strategy can be most clearly exemplified by the *FPÖ*, which publicly replaced German nationalism in the early 1990s by an aggressive 'Austrian patriotism.' Still, this pro-Austrian appearance did not significantly alter the party's ideological core; its current program, for example, still states that Austrians are part of the "German ethnic-/folk-community, language community and cultural community"[2] (*FPÖ* 2011: 5). While prioritizing Austrian 'nationalism,' the *FPÖ* remains silent about the ideological and foundational ideas of the nation.

The second strategy is most clearly exemplified by identitarian groups (Bruns et al. 2014). In accordance with the ideological modernization of the so-called 'New Right,' these actors have shifted their political focus from constructing hierarchies (of races, ethnic groups) to the construction of *differences* – naturalized and taken to be eternal. Moreover, identitarian groups downplay the political importance of the nation as a foundational political concept in favor of 'ethno-cultural groups' (Ajanović et al. 2015). Combining 'ethnos,' in the sense of biological descent, and 'culture' allows for shifting the intended meaning between these two poles. 'Culture' becomes a quasi-natural state deeply intertwined with biological ancestry, while it is simultaneously constructed in reference to local or regional specifics that appeal directly to common sense. This flexibility circumvents the question of the national.

We argue that in order to understand processes of strategic modernization within the far-right, the notions of right-wing extremism and right-wing populism should be defined as analytical tools that direct our attention to different levels of analysis, rather than as descriptive terms denoting different groups, different ideological positions or varying degrees of extremism. Thus, the concepts of right-wing extremism and right-wing populism are not mutually exclusive. Quite the contrary,

---

1   For example, in 1988, *Freedom Party* leader Jörg Haider famously spoke of the Austrian nation as an "ideological monstrosity" ('Missgeburt').
2   German original: "deutsche Volks-, Sprach- und Kulturgemeinschaft" (translated by authors)

we argue that many right-wing extremist groups have turned to right-wing populist strategies in recent years. In our empirical analysis of gendered, ethnicized and racialized constructions of 'We, the people,' in Austrian far-right discourses, we use both concepts to underscore the intersections of strategic and ideological elements of far-right politics. Moreover, our analysis of gendered arguments elaborates on changes and continuities, or, as we argue, on a limited modernization of the far-right's construction of 'We, the people.'

Our argument proceeds as follows: First, we introduce the terms right-wing extremism and right-wing populism and suggest a framework that treats these concepts as complementary analytical lenses rather than as mutually exclusive phenomena. Second, we employ this framework in our analysis of far-right discourses in Austria, unearthing the gendered constructions that facilitate the limited modernization of the Austrian far-right. The article concludes with an analysis of the strategic use of gender in constructing 'We, the people' as an ethnicized and racialized 'völkisch' entity.[3]

2. Conceptual Framework: Right-Wing Extremism and Right-Wing Populism as Two Analytical Lenses

Definitions of the terms right-wing extremism and right-wing populism vary largely. Right-wing populism has been criticized for de-politicizing far-right politics and undervaluing the analysis of extremist ideologies (Forschungsgruppe Ideologien und Politiken der Ungleichheit 2014). However, this criticism defines extremism and populism as mutually exclusive and understands right-wing populism as 'less extreme' in its views and ideological presumptions. In effect, it defines the two terms as referring to different phenomena with actors belonging either to the category of right-wing extremism or to the category of right-wing populism. We suggest a different perspective on the relationship between the two – an analytical understanding that treats these terms as conceptual tools pertaining to different levels of analysis.

---

3   This research was part of two EU-funded projects (RAGE, JUST/2012/FRAC/AG/2861, and e-EAV, JUST/2011/DAP/AG/3195, both 2013/2014) and a European project on 'anti-genderism' that started in 2015 and was funded by the City of Vienna and the German Friedrich-Ebert-Stiftung. The main focus of all three projects was on the analysis of texts that were published by relevant actors in the fields of right-wing extremism or right-wing populism and anti-feminism, which we analyzed using a critical frame analysis (van der Haar/Verloo 2016; Verloo/Lombardo 2007: 35). For the purpose of this paper, we selected material by far-right actors, such as the *FPÖ*, its functionaries and affiliated organizations, like its youth organization (*Ring Freiheitlicher Jugend, RFJ*) and the *Identitarian Movement Austria (IBÖ)*.

In our view, right-wing extremism must be understood as an ideology, a "right-wing extremist syndrome" – i.e. a variable bundle of ideological elements (Holzer 1994) –, which aims at naturalizing, legitimizing and normalizing inequality (Schiedel 2007). This ideology of inequality feeds into three axes; first gender and sexuality through anti-feminism and (hetero-)sexism (Goetz 2014), second ethnicity or race through anti-Semitism and racism, and third class as social Darwinism. Its ideological core is built on the idea of a 'natural people' (*Volk*), understood as a cohesive, biologically-defined entity. This also holds true for the most prominent endeavor to renew right-wing extremist ideologies after 1945, the so-called 'New Right' or 'Nouvelle Droite.' While today's New Right displaced the notion of 'the people' with the notion of 'ethno-cultural groups' the naturalization of culture serves to define an ethnically homogeneous in-group (Balibar 1991; Schiedel 2007). This idea of a biologically determined, homogeneous group is necessarily opposed to diversity, pluralism and (internal) conflict (Ajanović et al. 2015). Moreover, this idea of 'the people' as a homogeneous entity renders democracy an empty husk, and thus explains the anti-democratic thrust of right-wing extremism.

By introducing 'right-wing extremism' as an analytical concept, we draw attention to the ideologies of far-right parties, movements and groups. Furthermore, this analytical perspective allows us to depict which elements of the 'right-wing extremist syndrome' are articulated in different discourses, and how they vary between actors and over time.

However, this perspective lacks an understanding of how these articulations are actually realized in discourse. To understand the current success of far-right politics, we grasp right-wing populism as a specific construction of politics and the political field (Reinfeldt 2000). Right-wing populism is thus not based on an elaborate ideology (cf. Mudde 2004: 543; Taggart 2000), neither is it a mere form of communication or political style (even if it seems to be linked to specific discursive strategies, see e.g. Reisigl 2002, 2012). Instead, it is a specific political mobilizing strategy. Right-wing populism constructs the political field as antagonistic on the one hand, and as identitarian on the other. First, it builds on a double antagonism that opposes the populist 'We'-group against the elites, the EU or mainstream media, and second against Others (i.e. 'not us'). Currently, ethnicized and racialized Others are the main target of these discursive constructions, but processes of Othering might as well pertain to gender differences, sexual diversity or social status. The two enemy-groups – elites and Others – are discursively linked, and the interpellation of one antagonism always articulates the other 'enemy.' Second, right-wing populism's addressees – i.e. 'the people,' 'the real Austrians,' 'our families' – are directly linked to the 'We'-group that is grounded in an identity of the right-wing populist leader or group and their addressees (Reinfeldt 2000). One of the *FPÖ*'s election slogans precisely captures this: "They are against him, because he is for you," which was originally used by Jörg Haider in 1994, and then re-used by

Heinz-Christian Strache in 2008 (Richardson/Wodak 2009: 263). This construction entails an apparent contradiction to basic assumptions of democracies: As right-wing populism organizes politics in the form of either identity (of the populist leader and 'the people') or antagonisms (between 'us' and 'out-groups'), it negates ideas of diversity and conflict while at the same time promoting natural inequality.

While we define right-wing extremism as denoting an ideology and right-wing populism as a specific construction of the political field, we claim that the two concepts converge in their construction of 'the people.' Right-wing populism as an analytical perspective draws our attention to the way, in which far-right discourses construct the political field as a choice between 'friends' and 'enemies.' It thereby forges a connection between populist leaders and their addressees which is based on identification and emotional attachment and is therefore highly effective in gathering public attention for far-right movements and electoral support for far-right parties. Right-wing extremism directs the focus towards the ideological background of far-right actors and their definition of 'the people-' It allows us to analyze if, and to what extent, ethnicized and racialized definitions of 'the people' prevail. The relationship between these two elements of far-right politics needs empirical analysis.

3. Constructing 'the People,' Constructing 'the Family.' Far-Right Gender Discourses

In this section, we analyze far-right gender discourses using right-wing extremism and right-wing populism as conceptual tools. We draw on examples from the *FPÖ* and organizations directly affiliated with the party, and from the so-called *Identitarian Movement Austria (IBÖ)*. Our previous research on European and Austrian far-right movements (Kuhar/Ajanović 2018; Mayer/Sauer 2017, Mayer et al. 2016, 2014) has demonstrated that the Austrian far-right discourse on gender has two strands: The first strand includes the naturalization of gender difference, of hierarchical gender relations and of heterosexuality. The most obvious articulation of this far-right gender ideology is the rejection of so-called 'gender theory,' or 'genderism' – i.e. of feminist and queer-feminist idea that the two-gender-system is a social construct and not a natural biological 'fact' (Kuhar/Paternotte 2017). This heteronormative anti-gender discourse bears influence on the far-right's construction of 'the people' as it indicates what 'our' men, women and families ought to look like, how they ought to behave, and which (sexual and gender) relationships are deemed acceptable.

The second strand consists of anti-migration arguments and anti-Muslim racism, including the projection of unequal, patriarchal gender relations, of homophobia and of (sexualized) violence against women onto (Muslim) immigrants and refugees. This gendering of racism is most obvious in the demarcation between 'us,' 'the people' and Others. We will analyze both strands before turning to the ways in which these discourses are interlinked. We will present these two discursive strands by discussing them through the lenses of, firstly, right-wing populism and, secondly, right-wing extremism.

1. Heteronormative Imaginaries

In recent years, a discourse denouncing 'genderism' or 'gender theory' has spread among a diverse set of actors across Europe (including not only the far-right, but also conservative, Christian and single-issue groups, like Men's Rights advocates) (Kuhar/Paternotte 2017). In the Austrian public, a former *FPÖ* representative, Barbara Rosenkranz, introduced this anti-gender discourse: Her 2008 book denounces gender mainstreaming as a strategy for creating a "genderless human" (Rosenkranz 2008). Even though many of the arguments we present in the following are shared by a broader coalition of actors, including, for instance, parts of the Catholic Church, we will focus our analysis on the *FPÖ* and the *IBÖ*.

The shared far-right narrative might be summed up as follows: 'gender ideology' – a vague notion that includes policies of gender equality, sexual education, gender-neutral language and public reference to homosexuality – is mainly spread by elites, and aims at abolishing the two distinct sexes, and hence at destroying the complementarity of men and women. Thus, this 'genderism' threatens the very existence of 'healthy' (i.e. heterosexual, patriarchal) families (Lang 2015). The bleak picture is further enhanced by frequent references to the alleged 'totalitarian' power of 'gender ideology' and its authoritarian oppression of any form of critique. The most explicit anti-LGBTIQ stances are found in relation to parenthood, adoption and child-care, towards persons that (visibly) violate the gender binary or towards sex-education and gender-sensitive care at schools and kindergartens (Hark/Villa 2015; Kuhar/Paternotte 2017).

The pejorative notion of 'genderism' is also raised against feminist demands. While far-right actors avoid open opposition to gender equality, they nevertheless condemn current 'feminism,' which they construct as a militant ideology shared only by a small elitist minority (Mayer et al. 2014). One example is the following quote from a resolution proposal in the parliamentary committee on gender equality by *FPÖ* representatives titled "Stop the 'gender craze'!"[4] In her statement, one *FPÖ* representative generously quoted the well-known German anti-feminist Birgit Kelle:

---

4   German original: "Stopp dem ‚Genderwahn'!" (translated by authors)

"The biggest loser in this game is the normal heterosexual woman – i.e. the majority of women. [...] The mother, who still raises her children herself. The woman with two kids working part-time, who will hardly get any pension. The single mother, who is struggling and will end in poverty just like the married woman with four children. The vast majority of women do not benefit from all the fuss which is allegedly intended to emancipate women through gender mainstreaming." (Schimanek 2016)

The argumentative figure positions the "vast majority" of women – or more to the point: mothers – against the "particular interests" of "a minimal percentage of militant language feminists" (ibid.), who appear to be the only ones gaining from policies promoting gender equality. In contrast to the decrepitude of gender and sexual equality, the far-right constructs a seemingly self-evident, *natural* state of sexual and gender relations between *natural* men and women, who form *natural* families, engaging in the *natural* biological as well as cultural reproduction of 'the people.' In these discourses, references to *nature* invisibilize the (power-)relations at stake in equality policies (Ajanović et al. 2015: 212; Ajanović/Mayer 2017: 199).

Viewed through the lens of right-wing populist political strategies, these discourses construct an antagonistic relationship between their addressees and an aloof and uncaring elite that has lost touch with common sense and the *naturally-given normality* of social relations. This antagonism is complemented by the construction of Others: (visible) LGBTIQ people, who are positioned in opposition to *natural* families; and feminists, who are opposed to *normal* women with regards to their political aims and values. Against these constructions, 'the people' emerges as a heterosexual entity defined by clearly distinct gender roles. Heterosexual (non-feminist) women are discursively included into this group in their function as mothers and caregivers. This gendering of 'the people' constructs a binary gender difference as foundational to the 'We-group,' which is homogenized with regards to many other possible differences (e.g. class) (Mayer et al. 2014).

If analyzed through the lens of right-wing extremism, the discourse of 'genderism' strengthens *nature* as a seemingly self-evident foundation for social inequality along the lines of gender and sexuality. This, as we will show, also plays into right-wing extremist pro-nativist population policies. However, this line of reasoning must be complemented by yet another dichotomy, which we can analyze with regards to the "ethnicization of sexism" (Jäger 1999) – i.e. the gendering of racism.

2. Gendered Racism

Migration-related constructions of 'us' and 'them' emerge in all aspects of far-right rhetoric and policies that mobilize right-wing populist strategies. These constructions are part of social policies, including education and security. Simultaneously, the normalization of this antagonism between 'our people' and 'foreigners' in political and public discourse is one important condition for the success of the far right movement (Zuser 1996). This vicious circle is being further fueled by gendered arguments apt for "moral panics" (Hall 1985: 116) around migration.

One discursive strategy in this gendered demonization is the construction of 'non-natives' as threats to 'native women.' For example, the youth organization of the FPÖ, the RFJ, depicted young male migrants as a danger to native girls:

> "Public parks must be made safe again by monitoring those clan-line violent foreigners who have made it their territory. The sexual assault of native girls by foreigners must not be trivialized, but rather openly attacked." (*Ring Freiheitlicher Jugend*, n.d.)

This image of the aggressive young male migrant depends on the co-construction of a 'native girl' as the helpless victim deprived of agency and in need of a savior to fight on her behalf. Even though 'native men' are not mentioned explicitly in the paragraph, the above quote interpolates images of masculinity. A patriarchal gender order – i.e. men as protectors of women – becomes legitimized through gendered images of ethnicized and racialized Others. These constructions are often accompanied by attacks on elites who are allegedly to blame for migration (Pelinka 2013: 8).

Nearly all far-right led discussions, and the broader public debate on (sexualized) violence against women, follow this simple framework of 'foreign' perpetrators attacking 'native' women. These arguments gained even more salience in the aftermath of the 2015/2016 attacks in Cologne on New Year's Eve, which the far-right perceived to demonstrate the failure of liberal migration policies (Dietze 2016; Hark/Villa 2015).

This externalization, ethnicization and racialization of violence against women is a cornerstone of more abstract forms of Othering that manifest the irreconcilability of 'our' values and 'their' (non-) values, whereby 'they' are most frequently marked as Islamic:

> "Every active religious community in Austria must accept that in Austria, women and men have equal rights. [...] Forced marriages, forced genital cutting and the oppression of and violence against women are not covered by religious freedom [...] The right of women to self-determination must be accepted by all of the cultural groups that reside here." (*FPÖ Bildungsinstitut* 2013: 50–51)

These statements appear to contradict the movement's previously described heteronormative discourse. In contrast to the equation of women with motherhood, 'self-determination' emerges here as a desired frame of possibility. However, the discursive effects of the quote are not so much about gender equality or women's right to self-determination but rather about the construction of 'us' and 'them' through the "ethnicization of sexism" (Jäger 1999). At the same time, this framing renders feminism and struggles for equality things of the past.

Viewed through the lens of right-wing populist strategies, the gendering of racism exemplifies the strategic use of "intersectionality from above" (Sauer 2013). Sexism, gender inequality and homophobia are projected onto Others, while 'We' are constructed as an enlightened people that has already secured gender equality. This also promotes the rejection of additional domestic and European policies aimed at enhancing gender equality, which are viewed as already having been successfully embedded into 'our culture.' By evoking traditional images of virile masculinity against the construction of antagonistic, threatening Others, these discursive strategies mobilize notions of 'native' men in addition to 'native' women.

This discourse on violent immigrant masculinity, when viewed from the perspective of right-wing extremist ideology, aligns with both a gendered order of 'the people' and the right-wing extremist conviction that underpinning all politics is an endless struggle between two fundamentally different 'peoples.' As Julie Mostov (1999) has argued, women's bodies are not only symbols of the fecundity of the nation and vessels for its reproduction, but they are also markers of a territory that must be protected by 'real' native men. This alleged need to protect comes to legitimize the exclusion of ethnicized and racialized Others. Within right-wing extremism, naturalized understandings of culture and religion work to justify the exclusion of constructed Others. This example again demonstrates that what 'New right' ideas on 'ethno-culture' provide, is far from a break with right-wing extremist ideology, but rather the ideological underpinnings for this call for an ethnically pure 'We-group.'

The construction of a heteronormative, patriarchal gender order of the 'We'-group, which is distinct from an ethnicized and racialized Other, is based on two different strands of far-right political discourse that on the surface appear to be contradictory: first, the heteronormativity most clearly expressed in the anti-feminist denunciation of 'genderism,' and second, the gendering of racism that calls upon a patriarchal gender order even as it rhetorically affirms gender equality. We now turn to another concern of the far right that shows how the two are intertwined.

3. Nativist Population Policies

According to the far right, the demographic decline of the native European population is one of the worst threats to 'the people,' which leads to the positioning of the heterosexual (*natural*) family in stark opposition to ethnicized and racialized Others (see e.g. *Identitäre Bewegung Österreichs* n.d.). The *Identitarian Movement Austria (IBÖ)* evokes fears of an "Islamisation" that will be "our ruin." This pattern of anti-Muslim racism is accompanied by accusations that parts of the native population are responsible for falling birth rates and "ethno-cultural suicide." These people, the *IBÖ* argues, have lost their identity and fall prey to a "disease of the self and the common we" (ibid.).[5] Vaguely defined population groups are thus also constructed as Others, including women who fail to perpetuate the ethno-cultural 'We' by refusing their *natural* role as mothers. Targeting the elite, the text also blames a "ruling ideology" of "total egalitarianism" and a "manic anti-fascism," which both lead to "total openness" and "negate our right to determine our own future" (ibid.).

The discourse of demographic decline is an antagonistic populist thread connecting migrants, feminists and ruling elites – i.e. variously defined Others that either threaten 'us' from the outside, or destroy 'us' from the inside. Taken together, the 'We'-group, 'the people,' is under threat. This topos, in turn, legitimizes aggressive and exclusionary policies. The assertion of a 'demographic decline,' a seemingly technical assessment, emerges as a central tool in the construction of existential threats and corresponding fears, and thus also of an antagonistic political context that consolidates and produces a notion of 'the people.'

This discourse of demographic decline appears as a modernized version of biological purity – i.e. of the belief in an ethnically pure ancestry defined by blood. Although the terms 'race' and 'nation' have been carefully omitted in most instances, rhetoric combining a gendered social order, biological reproduction and ethnicity transfers core beliefs of an ethnicized ('völkisch') world-view of 'the people' into today's political discourse.

These examples of gendered arguments of the far right demonstrate a need to account for elements of right-wing extremist ideologies and their populist articulations so as to understand their (limited) modernization. Rather than asking whether a group or party is right-wing extremist *or* right-wing populist, we mapped out the interplay of ideological elements and political strategies in the far-right movement's use of 'gender.'

4. Conclusion: 'The people' as a Gendered, Ethnicized and Racialized Entity

Our analytical focus on gender in the far right discourse has revealed two functions of images of 'the family' as a discursive node in far-right constructions of 'We, the people': as the embodiment of a naturalized patriarchal gender order, and as a site

---

5   German original: "All die Verheerungen und Entfremdungen der heutigen Zeit sind Symptome eines Identitätsverlustes und einer Krankheit am eigenen Ich und am gemeinsamen Wir." (translation by authors)

of the biological reproduction of the 'We-group'[6]. This image of the heterosexual and patriarchal as well as ethnically 'pure' family provides a point of convergence where demographic concerns intersect with gender, sexuality and national identity. Images of ('real'/'our') families link the macro-level of the constructed 'We'-group, 'the people,' to the micro-level of individual behaviors and responsibilities.

Ethnicization and racialization clearly remain dominant ways of constructing Others within the far-right discourse, but today's ethnos is based on the naturalization of culture rather than on biology. Claims of a "demographic decline" rely on the idea of ethnically 'pure' reproduction and naturalized gender hierarchies. The biological reproduction of 'the people' and of the *natural* family, both of which depend on a patriarchal gender order, are thus important elements of right-wing extremist ideology. LGBTIQ people and feminists who oppose the traditional gender order are also presented as threatening Others. Right-wing populist antagonistic constructions articulate these ideological elements by defining the 'the people' through an exclusionary logic.

To develop analytical tools that direct attention to different levels of study, we defined two perspectives on the far right: first, right-wing populism as a political strategy; and second, right-wing extremism as an ideology. Hence, the two concepts are not mutually exclusive. On the contrary, our analysis has demonstrated how these concepts are interlinked in far-right discourse. Our analysis of gendered arguments exposed how the strategic construction of politics as a field defined by antagonistic relations on the one hand, and relations of identity on the other, introduces core elements of right-wing extremist ideology in public discourse: above all, belief in 'the people' as an ethnically-defined ('völkisch') entity and the naturalization of inequality. This right-wing populist communicative strategy does not necessarily rely on openly nativist or racist language. We therefore conclude that right-wing populist communicative strategies importantly contribute to the limited modernization of right-wing extremism, thereby strengthening its public appeal rather than changing its content or ideological outlook. Gender discourses of the Austrian FPÖ and identitarian groups might appear contradictory but show underlying commonalities that provide fruitful empirical foci for understanding the interplay of the ideological elements and political strategies of the far-right.

---

6   For a metaphor-oriented approach on the connection between 'the family' and 'the people,' see Norocel 2013; for an analysis of the strategic use of anti-feminism by right-wing extremists, see Lang 2015.

Bibliography

Ajanović, Edma/Mayer, Stefanie (2017): "Mann, oh Mann … Wenn der Schutz 'unserer Frauen' die Antwort ist, was war nochmal die Frage?" In: Brigitte Bargetz/Eva Kreisky/Gundula Ludwig (eds.), Dauerkämpfe: Feministische Zeitdiagnosen und Strategien, Politik der Geschlechterverhältnisse. Frankfurt/New York: Campus Verlag, pp. 195–204.

Ajanović, Edma/Mayer, Stefanie/Sauer, Birgit (2015): "Natural Enemies: Articulations of Racism in Right-Wing Populism in Austria." In: Časopis Za Kritiko Znanosti, Domišljijo In Novo Antropologijo 260, pp. 203–214.

Ajanović, Edma/Mayer, Stefanie/Sauer, Birgit (2015): "Umkämpfte Räume. Antipluralismus in Rechtsextremen bzw. Rechtspopulistischen Diskursen in Österreich." In: Österreichische Zeitschrift für Politikwissenschaft 44, pp. 75–85, (doi.org/10.15203/ozp.448.vol44iss2, 3.3.2019).

Balibar, Etienne (1991): "Is there a 'Neo-Racism'?" In: Etienne Balibar/Immanuel Wallerstein (eds.), Race, Nation, Class. Ambigous Identities. London/New York: Verso, pp. 17–28.

Bruns, Julian/Glösel, Kathrin/Strobl, Natascha (2014): Die Identitären. Handbuch zur Jugendbewegung der Neuen Rechten in Europa. Münster: Unrast.

Canovan, Margaret (1999): "Trust the People! Populism and the Two Faces of Democracy." In: Political Studies 47, pp. 2–16, (doi.org/10.1111/1467-9248.00184, 12.3.2019).

Dietze, Gabriele (2016): "Das 'Ereignis Köln." In: Femina Politica – Zeitschrift für Feministische Politikwissenschaft 25, pp. 93–102, (doi.org/10.3224/feminapolitica.v25i1.23412, 19.8.2019).

Dobers, Johannes/Mayer, Stefanie (2011): "Geschichts- und Gedenkpolitik in Österreich." In: AK gegen den Kärntner Konsens (ed.), Friede, Freude, Deutscher Eintopf: Rechte Mythen, NS-Verharmlosung und Antifaschistischer Protest, Kritik & Utopie. Wien: Mandelbaum, pp. 25–57.

FPÖ (2011): Parteiprogramm der Freiheitlichen Partei Österreichs. Online: www.fpoe.at/fileadmin/user_upload/www.fpoe.at/dokumente/2015/2011_graz_parteiprogramm_web.pdf, 1.3.2019.

FPÖ Bildungsinstitut (2013): Handbuch Freiheitlicher Politik. Ein Leitfaden für Führungsfunktionäre und Mandatsträger der Freiheitlichen Partei Österreichs. Online: www.fpoe.at/fileadmin/user_upload/www.fpoe.at/dokumente/2015/Handbuch_freiheitlicher_Politik_WEB.pdf, 1.3.2019.

Forschungsgruppe Ideologien und Politiken der Ungleichheit (ed.) (2014): Rechtsextremismus, Bd. 1: Entwicklungen und Analysen. Wien: Mandelbaum.

Goetz, Judith (2014): "(Re-)Naturalisierung der Geschlechterordnung. Anmerkungen zur Geschlechtsblindheit der (Österreichischen) Rechtsextremismusforschung." In: Forschungsgruppe Ideologien und Politiken der Ungleichheit (ed.), Rechtsextremismus, Bd. 1: Entwicklungen und Analysen. Wien: Mandelbaum, pp. 40–68.

Hall, Stuart (1985): "Authoritarian Populism: A Reply to Jessop et al." In: New Left Review 151, pp. 115–124.

Hark, Sabine/Villa, Paula-Irene (eds.) (2015): Anti-Genderismus: Sexualität und Geschlecht als Schauplätze Aktueller Politischer Auseinandersetzungen. Bielefeld: transcript.

Holzer, Willibald I. (1994): "Rechtsextremismus – Konturen, Definitionsmerkmale und Erklärungsansätze." In: Dokumentationsarchiv des Österreichischen Widerstandes (ed.), Handbuch des Österreichischen Rechtsextremismus. Wien: Buchgemeinschaft Donauland, pp. 11–96.

Identitäre Bewegung Österreichs (n.d.): Idee & Tat. Online: www.iboesterreich.at/?page_id=344, 16.3.2019.

Jäger, Margarete (1999): Ethnisierung von Sexismus im Einwanderungsdiskurs. Analyse einer Diskursverschränkung. Online: www.diss-duisburg.de/Internetbibliothek/Artikel/Ethnisierung_von_Sexismus.htm.

Kuhar, Roman/Ajanović, Edma (2018): "Sexuality Online: The Constructions of Right-Wing Populists' 'Internal Others' on the Web." In: Mojca Pajnik/Birgit Sauer (eds.), Populism and the Web: Communicative Practices of Parties and Movements in Europe. Abingdon/New York: Routledge, pp. 141–156.

Kuhar, Roman/Paternotte, David (eds.) (2017): Anti-Gender Campaigns in Europe: Mobilizing Against Equality. London/New York: Rowman & Littlefield.

Lang, Juliane (2015): "Familie und Vaterland in der Krise. Der extrem Rechte Diskurs um Gender." In: Sabine Hark/Paula-Irene Villa (eds.), (Anti-)Genderismus. Bielefeld: transcript, pp. 167–182.

Mayer, Stefanie/Ajanović, Edma/Sauer, Birgit (2014): "Intersections and Inconsistencies. Framing Gender in Right-Wing Populist Discourses in Austria." In: NORA – Nordic Journal of Feminist and Gender Research 22, pp. 250–266, (doi.org/10.1080/08038740.2014.964309, 14.8.2019).

Mayer, Stefanie/Sauer, Birgit (2016): "Gendering 'the People.' Heteronormativity and 'Ethno-Masochism' in Populist Imaginery." In: Maria Ranieri (ed.): Populism, Media and Education: Challenging Discrimination in Contemporary Digital Societies. London/New York: Routledge, pp. 84–104.

Mayer, Stefanie/Sauer, Brigit (2017): "'Gender Ideology' in Austria: Coalitions around an Empty Signifier." In: Roman Kuhar/David Paternotte (eds.), Anti-Gender Campaigns in Europe: Mobilizing Against Equality. London/New York: Rowman & Littlefield, pp. 23–40.

Mostov, Julie (1999): "Women and the Radical Right. Ethnocracy and Body Politics." In: Sabrina P. Ramet (ed.), The Radical Right in Central and Eastern Europe since 1989, Post-Communist Cultural Studies, University Park: Pennsylvania State University Press, pp. 49–63.

Mudde, Cas (2010): "The Populist Radical Right: A Pathological Normalcy." In: West European Politics 33, pp. 1167–1186, (doi.org/10.1080/01402382.2010.508-901, 19.8.2019).

Mudde, Cas (2004): "The Populist Zeitgeist." In: Government and Opposition 39, pp. 542–563, (doi.org/10.1111/j.1477-7053.2004.00135.x, 14.8.2019).

Norocel, Ov Cristian (2013): Our People - A Tight-Knit Family under the Same Protective Roof (Dissertation). Helsinki: University of Helsinki.

Paternotte, David (2015): "Blessing the Crowds Catholic Mobilisations against Gender in Europe." In: Sabine Hark/Paula-Irene Villa (eds.), (Anti-)Genderismus. Bielefeld: transcript, pp. 129–148, (doi.org/10.14361/9783839431443-008, 14.8.2019).

Pelinka, Anton (2013): "Right-Wing Populism Concept and Typology." In: Ruth Wodak/Majid KhosraviNik/Brigitte Mral (eds.), Right-Wing Populism in Europe: Politics and Discourse. London: Bloomsbury Academic, pp. 3–22.

Reinfeldt, Sebastian (2000): Nicht-Wir und Die-Da. Studien zum Rechten Populismus. Wien: Braumüller.

Reisigl, Martin (2012): "Zur Kommunikativen Dimension des Rechtspopulismus." In: Sir Peter Ustinov Institut (ed.), Populismus. Herausforderung oder Gefahr für die Demokratie? Wien: New Academic Press, pp. 141–162.

Reisigl, Martin (2002): "Dem Volk aufs Maul schauen, nach dem Mund reden und Angst und Bange machen. Von Populistischen Anrufungen, Anbiederungen und Agitiationsweisen in der Sprache Österreichischer PolitikerInnen." In: Wolfgang Eismann (ed.), Rechtspopulismus. Wien: Czernin, pp. 149–198.

Reiterer, Albert F. (ed.) (1988): Nation und Nationalbewußtsein in Österreich. Wien: Verband d. Wiss. Ges. Österreichs.

Richardson, John E./Wodak, Ruth (2009): "Recontextualising Fascist Ideologies of the Past: Right-Wing Discourses on Employment and Nativism in Austria and the United Kingdom." In: Critical Discourse Studies 6, pp. 251–267.

Ring Freiheitlicher Jugend (n.d.): RFJ-Programm. Online: bgld.rfj.at/programm/#endlich_sicherheit, 14.3.2019.

Rosenkranz, Barbara (2008): MenschInnen: Gender Mainstreaming: Auf dem Weg zum geschlechtslosen Menschen. Graz: Ares.

Sauer, Birgit (2017): "Gesellschaftstheoretische Überlegungen zum Europäischen Rechtspopulismus. Zum Erklärungspotenzial der Kategorie Geschlecht." In: Politische Vierteljahresschrift 58, pp. 3–22, (doi.org/10.5771/0032-3470-2017-1-3, 10.3.2019).

Sauer, Birgit (2013): Intersectionality from Above – Framing Muslim Headscarves in European Policy Debates. Paper Presented at the ECPR General Conference, Bordeaux, September 2013.

Schiedel, Heribert (2007): Der Rechte Rand. Extremistische Gesinnungen in unserer Gesellschaft. Wien: Edition Steinbauer.

Schimanek, Carmen (2016): Entschließungsantrag der Abgeordneten Carmen Schimanek und weiterer Abgeordneter betreffend Stopp dem 'Genderwahn'! Online: www.parlament.gv.at/PAKT/VHG/XXV/A/A_01587/imfname_514872.pdf, 12.3.2019).

Taggart, Paul A. (2000): Populism. Concepts in the Social Sciences. Buckingham: Open Univ. Press.

Van der Haar, Marleen/Verloo, Mieke (2016): "Starting a Conversation about Critical Frame Analysis: Reflections on Dealing with Methodology in Feminist Research." In: Politics & Gender 12 (3), pp. 1–7, (doi.org/10.1017/S1743923X16000386, 2.3.2019).

Verloo, Mieke/Lombardo, Emanuela (2007): "Contested Gender Equality and Policy Variety in Europe: Introducing a Critical Frame Analysis Approach." In: Mieke Verloo (ed.), Multiple Meanings of Gender Equality: A Critical Frame Analysis of Gender Policies in Europe. Budapest/New York: CEU Press, pp. 21–51.

Wodak, Ruth/KhosraviNik, Maji/Mral, Brigitte (eds.) (2013): Right-Wing Populism in Europe. Politics and Discourse. London: Bloomsbury.

Zuser, Peter (1996): "Die Konstruktion der Ausländerfrage in Österreich. Eine Analyse des Öffentlichen Diskurses 1990." In: IHS Political Science Series 35, pp. 1–89.

Sexual Politics as a Tool to "Un-Demonize" Right-Wing Discourses in France

Cornelia Möser

Introduction

In 2012, a huge conservative movement that claimed to have mobilized up to one million French people against the government project of a so-called "marriage for everyone" invaded the public space, including cyber space, but also the streets of several French cities. In 2013, SOS Homophobie[1] alerted that homophobic aggressions had tripled that year. An alliance between far-right and neo-Nazi organizations on the one side, and, on the other, conservative Catholics and other religious groups, nationalist and conservative parties, and right-wing opponents of the socialist government, led to a political climate that allowed for far-right groups to temporarily control the public sphere and terrorize the social groups they consider to be their enemies.[2] *La Manif pour tous* (LMPT, "Demonstration for everyone") focus on sexual politics was central in their strategy to "un-demonize" – i.e. render mainstream – far-right politics in the larger French population. This chapter will analyze how and why sexual politics have been such a fruitful arena for conservative and far-right politics. It will also interrogate a certain "modernization" of the sexual politics of right-wing movements, which has made them compatible with some fractions of feminism in France. This parallel will be laid out in reference to 1990s' debates internal to French feminism that took nationalist colors by arguing culturally and politically against a translation of gender into French feminist research (cf. Möser 2013; Möser 2017).

Recent research on what has come to be termed "anti-gender" politics has emphasized the religious institutions and networks behind this new form of antifeminism (cf. Paternotte/Kuhar 2017). While these groups are certainly central actors and financers of reactionary antifeminist and homophobic politics throughout the

---

1   http://www.sos-homophobie.org/article/rapport-annuel-sur-l-homophobie-2013-les-homophobes-la-noce, 27.01.2020.
2   One of the results of this political climate is the murder of Clément Méric, a 19-year-old antifascist who was beaten to death in the center of Paris on June 5th 2013.

world, my research situates these religious actors within a larger antifeminist alliance. A close analysis of the components of these movements demonstrates the importance of the nationalist and far-right organizations and personalities that have been largely overlooked in previous research, and which are also instructive for developing strategies to counter "anti-gender" initiatives and movements.

La Manif pour tous against "Gender Ideology"

Already in 2012, LMPT – a federation of conservative, religious and far-right organizations unified against the government's marriage expansion project – named two major topics of contestation on their website: "protecting our children" and "combating gender theory"[3]. Upon closer look, one realizes that "combating gender theory" was also advocated to protect "our children," who, allegedly, would be threatened by it. Also, in their 2014 poster campaign (Figure 1), LMPT continued their emphasis on children and the heterosexual family:

Figure 1: LMPT Poster Campaign[4]

The cover of a 2013 manual (Figure 2) against what is called "gender ideology," a term now homogenized throughout international right-wing networks, also depicts children as threatened by this supposed ideology. A white, blond child in a white shirt leans, eyes-closed, against a chalkboard with the words "gender experimentation" written on it.

LMPT was founded in 2012 to protest the socialist government's "marriage for everyone" project. Until then, same sex unions were possible in France only under the civil solidarity pact, which had been installed in 1999 and to this day still

---

3   Quotes taken from *LMPT* website in 2013 that has been modified ever since.
4   Poster taken from lamanifpourtous.fr, 27.01.2020.
5   Cover of the manual that can be downloaded at lamanifpourtous.fr (19.12.2019)

Figure 2: LMPT Manual[5]

excludes the ability to adopt children and a number of the financial benefits afforded to married couples.[6] Even as it was being voted into law, the PACS had already been met with much conservative and homophobic protest. It had also been dividing feminists, some of whom had joined the "child protection" bloc and argued publicly against the PACS (for example Théry 1997). The LMPT network itself includes religious organizations, familialist conservative organizations, organizations of fathers and masculinists, and organizations claiming to defend adopted person's rights. There are also right-wing "feminist" organizations claiming to defend a woman's right to be feminine. While they mostly agree on equal pay for men and women (but not throughout the social classes), and on condemning violence against women, they also agree on defending what they call sexual alterity and family values. The LMPT network presents itself as follows:

> "LMPT is a social movement born in 2012 to defend sexual alterity in marriage, respect for natural filiation, and the child's superior interests. [...] Given that the aim of marriage is to found a family, marriage and adoption by two women or two

---

6   For the exact differences between marriage and PACS check: (19.12.2019)

men threatens the needs and rights of a child to have a father and a mother. [...] LMPT is pacifist. It vividly condemns all violent acts and all acts of homophobia. It calls for the respect of people and public goods."[7]

This last part must be considered in relation to the aforementioned increased aggression and violence of their movement. Femen activists have been violently assaulted in LMPT demonstrations, and attendees of the annual LGBT fair in the Marais neighborhood of Paris were also attacked.[8] Indeed, the homophobic violent attacks necessitate such a positioning.

Contrary to what one might expect given their remarkable media presence throughout the protests, LMPT was not at the origin of the movement. Far-right religious and neo-Nazi organizations were actually the ones to call for and attend the first demonstration against the government's project. The far-right Catholic group Civitas mobilized against the marriage for all as early as June 2012. Their demonstration on November 18th, 2012 was organized to protest "the denaturation of marriage,"[9] "Let them live" being one of their central slogans. The demonstration was attended by far-right and neo-Nazi groups like Action Française, the Renouveau Français, and Parti de la France, and by fundamentalist Christian anti-abortion groups including SOS Tout Petit.[10]

The joining of less extremist Catholic circles and larger conservative upper-class people, who expressed their general disapproval of a socialist government in protesting the law, marked a renewal in several regards. LMPT had distinguished itself from similar previous movements in terms of both its form and content. Whereas former far-right protests were rather conservative in their forms of expression, LMPT mobilized a modern poster campaign and a professional PR campaign with a corporate color code and logo but also street performances, stencils and even comedy elements with their character Frigide Barjot (Virginie Tellenne) and openly gay people speaking out against the marriage initiative in favor of "protecting heterosexual marriage and the family," Their actions took the form of hap-

---

7   www.lamanifpourtous.fr/qui-sommes-nous/notre-message/ (2.4.2019). Unless otherwise noted, all translations are from the author's. The French term for sexual alterity is "altérité sexuelle," and it designates a biological dualism of men and women.
8   This action including LMPT posters was actually organized by a group of young far-right men who called themselves Hommen in reference to the feminist activist group Femen, who demonstrate topless and write slogans on their chest, such as "no gender." On the demographic and social composition of the group and their paradoxical sexual politics cf. Tricou 2016.
9   www.civitas-institut.com/2012/11/07/denaturation-du-mariage-laissez-les-vivre-appelle-a-manifester-le-18-novembre/ , 27.01.2020. For a detailed analysis of Civitas' history cf. lahorde.samizdat.net/2017/02/14/civitas-des-origines-a-nos-jours/. 27.01.2020.
10 lahorde.samizdat.net/2017/02/14/civitas-des-origines-a-nos-jours/, 27.01.2020.

penings and even included a theatricality that paradoxically borrowed from camp and queer cultures.

But the renewal of right-wing extremism is not only a question of form; the content and strategies of argumentation have also changed. While the aim to protect the heterosexual family is in alignment with traditional right-wing politics, both the LMPT and the leading right-wing party[11] have significantly changed their arguments as to why one should protect it. They no longer present sexual difference as just God's wish, or as a required element of nation-building, or as a simple national value. Instead, they present themselves as feminists - a framing through which they re-signify the meaning of feminism, but also of gender. Their feminism amounts to equal pay for men and women, combating sexual violence against women, and fighting for the right to be a woman, with all of its supposed specificities, a feminism which always falls back on a supposed need to protect women.[12] Opposed to most types of feminism, the LMPT and other right-wing organizations have sculpted their own interpretation of gender ideology, which ends up being a neoliberal construct that threatens the protection of women and their families. In the section "Why is gender ideology dangerous" of their manual, point 4 suggests that "gender ideology" contributes to "social pauperization":

> "In a world struck by ultra-individualistic and mercantilist violence, breaking traditional family and social solidarities (giving, receiving, giving back) bears the risk of pushing considerable parts of our society into social indignity."[13]

While the anti-marriage campaign spoke much about gender but never mentioned feminism, this manual, which was published after the vote for marriage, links "gender ideology" to radical feminism – for them, this is an obscurantist strategy to deflect from the women's movement's impasses and supposed transsexual appropriation of the initially legitimate quest for equality.

An advertising campaign by the Christian fundamentalist anti-abortion organization En Marche pour la vie (Marching for life, Figure 3) built on this new line of argumentation by presenting a widely published advertisement stating: "'Congratulations' (You just lost your job)." It shows a woman shaking the hand of a grey-haired man. An explanation for this quite complex (if not illogical) argument goes like this: neoliberalism forces women to undergo abortions because if they choose to have children, they will lose their precarious jobs. The man in the picture is her

---

11 In 2012 and up to 2017, it was the Front national (FN), which was renamed Rassemblement national (RN) in 2017.
12 Cf. for example the website Womanattitude that is linked from the LMPT website as "partner organization": womanattitude.com, 27.01.2020.
13 http://www.lamanifpourtous.fr/wp-content/uploads/2016/07/LMPT-L-ideologie-du-genre.pdf, 19.12.2019.

boss, and he congratulates her for a pregnancy that, ultimately, provokes her being fired. In the life-marching mindset, this absolutely scandalous circumstance would best be fought by criminalizing abortion and not, for example, by fighting capitalist exploitation or unfair work legislation.

Figure 3: Advertising Campaign March for Life[14]

A similar change of strategy can be observed in a campaign poster of the extreme right Front national/Rassemblement national. It juxtaposes an arguably "liberated" nationalist woman with French flags on her cheeks and a red hat, evocative of the revolutionary bonnet, with a woman wearing a hijab. The poster slogan challenges the spectator to "Choose your suburb!" It implies that there is a French mod-

---

14   12.01.2017.

ern, liberating sexual culture for women, which is opposed to the sexually un-modern Muslim culture. This constructed opposition only serves to prove a supposed incompatibility of Muslims to French society. This politically motivated rhetoric is not interested in the complex and sometimes difficult negotiations and strategies that women, Muslim or otherwise, develop in dealing with patriarchal structures and sexist violence.

Figure 4: Poster Campaign FN/RN: Choose Your Suburb

Marine Le Pen herself promotes this pseudo-feminism, which has the unique purpose to present Muslims as sexually unmodern and, therefore, unfit to be part of French society. In 2010, Le Pen was quoted by the French Press Agency to have said: "[I]n certain neighborhoods you should rather not be a woman, a homosexual, a

Jew, not even French or white."[15] She has also been called courageous by the former number two of the FN, Florian Philippot, who was outed as gay by the magazine Closer in 2014 and who described her courage for refusing to put on a headscarf when visiting Lebanon in February 2017 during her presidential campaign as a "beautiful message of emancipation and freedom sent to women in France and in the world."[16]

The huge mobilization efforts of the LMPT have had a massive impact on French society even as the so-called "marriage for everyone" ultimately came to be adopted in 2013.[17] The refusal to exclude far-right and neo-Nazi groups from the demonstrations allowed for a reorganization of the far-right and a form of modernization that has made them more appealing to a larger percentage of the French population. Although Marine Le Pen was not at the forefront of the anti-marriage initiative, she used the protest for her presidential campaign in 2017, stating right after the marriage vote that she will repeal the law if elected president. Her strategic involvement with LMPT can thus be seen as part of what is called an "un-demonizing" strategy according to unofficial FN/RN terminology - i.e. a rhetorical strategy of the far-right to gain greater political influence. Bruno Mégret, a consultant of Marine Le Pen's father, Jean-Marie Le Pen, initially developed this strategy by recommending the adoption of a double language to win over larger parts of French society:

> "In order to seduce, avoid scaring and creating rejection. In our soft and fearful society, excessive statements cause distrust and rejection in larger parts of society. It is therefore essential when speaking publicly to avoid scandalous or vulgar speech. One can say the same thing with just as much vigor in a calm and widely accepted language. To take an example that is clearly just a caricature: instead of saying 'throw the bougnoules[18] into the sea,' let's say we need to 'organize the return of third-world immigrants to their homes.'" (Mégret quoted by Igounet 2016: 167)

These rhetorical changes would make it more difficult for the media and critics to "demonize" their racist expressions by calling them racist. Sexual politics have played an important role in this strategy to un-demonize the FN. For example,

---

15　Agence France Press, December 11, 2010. "J'entends de plus en plus de témoignages sur le fait que, dans certains quartiers, il ne fait pas bon être femme, ni homosexuel, ni juif, ni même français ou blanc."
16　www.lefigaro.fr/elections/presidentielles/2017/02/21/35003-20170221ARTFIG00119-marine-le-pen-refuse-de-porter-le-voile-a-beyrouth.php, 27.01.2020.
17　www.textes.justice.gouv.fr/art_pix/JUSC1312445C.pdf, 27.01.2020. The supposed marriage for everyone excludes eleven countries, including Poland, Algeria and Serbia.
18　Bougnoules is a racist slur directed against North African immigrants and their children in France.

sexual modernity discourses have allowed for presenting the party as a modern rather than backward party. Marine Le Pen figures as a role model of sexual emancipation in the above-mentioned quote, which makes her a person with whom one could identify; not only for women but also for homosexuals.[19] A unique mixture of calls to unite for sexual modernity as a French national culture and to reject immigrants who threaten "our" women – who, it is presumed, need protection – managed to serve the different fractions of the far-right, which are not in agreement about all of these points. While the religious fractions of the conservative right-wing put less emphasis on racist politics (sometimes even arguing for and providing humanitarian help for refugees), working-class voters seem to care less about the homophobia and sexism that are promoted by upper-class FN/RN members (Challier 2016).[20]

To summarize the above analyzed changes in right-wing sexual politics, it is important to note that the far-right ideology no longer refutes feminism en bloc. Instead, it differentiates between a legitimate feminism for equal pay and the protection of women on the one hand, and another feminism that has "gone too far" by questioning biological gender, criticizing the family, and engaging with sexual minorities and supposedly sexually pre-modern cultures, like the Islam. What clearly distinguishes these two versions of feminism are the biological difference between men and women, nationalism, familialism and racism. This observation will help to identify response strategies after examining the parallels with, and differences between, earlier internal feminist debates about "gender" and this recent re-signification of the term.

The Feminist Gender Debates in France[21]

Only in 2005 was Judith Butler's Gender Trouble translated to French. For over a decade, queer activists had been trying to have it translated (cf. Bourcier/Zoo 1998), but French publishing houses kept on rejecting it as untranslatable due to its American communitarianism, which was supposedly incompatible with French republican values, but also for its queer reading of French theory, which was not seen as properly scientific. It was only in evacuating its queer activist inscription and in

---

19   According to a poll by the research institute Cervipof, 32,45 % of married gay couples voted for the far-right Marine Le Pen during the first round of the 2017 presidential elections. Online: www.lemonde.fr/politique/article/2016/04/12/l-attraction-en-hausse-du-front-national-aupres-de-la-communaute-gay_4900269_823448.html, 27.01.2020.
20   Challier also observed in the article that homophobia, on the other hand, has become a unifying symbol for opponents to Marine Le Pen's fraction within the FN party.
21   For a more detailed analysis of the French feminist gender debates, see Möser 2017.

presenting it as a philosophical œuvre that Gender Trouble could finally be translated and presented through the prestigious and elitist Ecole Normale Supérieure.

Throughout the 1990s, a short-lived and almost unanimous feminist "debate" claimed that gender was linguistically and culturally untranslatable to French. Feminist researchers also stated that they already disposed of a variety of scientific concepts of their own production that would make a further concept completely superfluous (Fraisse/Horn 1993: 48). One of the most celebrated French feminist sociologists, Christine Delphy, had already criticized the US-American construction of French feminist theory (of which Gender Trouble clearly is part) as another example of US imperialism (Delphy 2001: 322). Delphy also stated that, long before Butler, she had already introduced gender in France in arguing that gender preceded sex, and that we cannot access a biological or material reality without filtering it through social and political categories (Delphy 2001: 243). While it is true that both Delphy and Butler share an anti-naturalistic approach, Delphy's claim that she was at the origin of gender fails to account for the fact that her and Butler's concepts stem from completely different if not opposing theoretical backgrounds. While Butler relied heavily on poststructuralist and deconstructivist theory, Delphy's Engelsian approach is inscribed in a humanistic philosophy from which Butler intentionally takes distance, especially in Gender Trouble.[22]

A real discussion of the epistemological implications of Gender Trouble never took place in France. While the 1990s were marked by a complete rejection of gender as described above - perceived as untranslatable from the point of view of any imaginable scientific discipline (cf. Hurtig et al. 1991) - the strategies for engaging with it formed more or less three camps. The most frequent strategy, which was largely a response to the funding politics of governmental and supranational organizations, replaces former research on men and women with the label gender (gender in xyz, gender and xyz) but continues the exact same research comparing men and women in diverse contexts. The second largest strategy - at least if measured in social impact - continues the 1990s republican feminists' rejection of gender.

In the 1990s, this branch of feminism warned against an import of the Anglo-Saxon sex wars (in their view a war between men and women),[23] which they argued would be incompatible with the loving and seducing relations between men and women in France (Badinter 2003: 225; Picq 1995: 333). They called upon a "French singularity," according to which seduction and romance are imagined to be part of

---

22 Later, she will call for a renewed form of universalism (cf. Butler et al. 2000: 179).
23 This misguided translation of sex wars as a war between men and women has an almost Freudian slip quality given that the French gender debates represent a sort of French version of the feminist sex wars, which were actually a 1980s debate within US feminism about the place of sexuality in feminist thought (cf. Vance 1984; Snitow et al. 1984).

the French national culture, which made the notion of gender not only untranslatable, but also a national threat. Elisabeth Badinter called out deconstructivist feminists for following the wrong path (Badinter 2003) in questioning biological sex instead of just claiming equality in difference. Today, these same scholars mobilize against research on race relations by warning that usage of the category "race" in studies of the structures and workings of racism today would mean subscribing to the existence of biological races.[24]

The third strategy, which is most popular in sociological feminist research, equates Delphy and Butler, and then proceeds to operate only with Delphy's understanding of gender (Bereni et al. 2008; Dorlin et al. 2007). To gain academic legitimacy, scholars convinced others and themselves that deconstructivism and materialism are identical because they both question a natural biological order. Yet in proceeding this way, they not only participate in the evacuation of epistemologies of difference from the French translation of gender (which concretely means evacuating all of its engagements with queer theory and critical race theory), they also perpetuate – through Delphy's conceptual framework – a feminism that puts gender as the central category of social organizing, relegating class and race as less-important, secondary issues.[25] The dramatic outcome of this strategy is a complete neglect of the queer and racial dimensions of gender, and an even more absolute rejection of social class in research on gender. While French sociology had started out as research on working class women (Kergoat 1982), the Delphinization or materialization of gender through the still prominent sex-class perspective (understanding women and men to be social classes, men exploiting women) has paradoxically marginalized research on social class structures and gender and inhibited an in-depth understanding of political economy in French feminist academic research.[26] A real debate about the difference between oppression/dominance and power has yet to take place, and not only in feminist research in France.

Leaving aside the more opportunistic strategy of re-labeling research comparing men and women as "gender" research, parallels between the other two strategies (republicanist and materialist) and the right-wing's rejection of "gender ideology" are flagrant. The republican strategy quite obviously mirrors the LMPT's argu-

---

24 Cf. www.lepoint.fr/politique/le-decolonialisme-une-strategie-hegemonique-l-appel-de-80-intellectuels-28-11-2018-2275104_20.php, 27.01.2020. (Decolonialism: a hegemonic strategy. A call of 80 intellectuals)
25 Eleonor Lépinard in a keynote presented at the conference "Théoriser en féministe" (Theorizing in a feminist way) at University Lyon 3 on April 25th 2018.
26 A conference on "Croiser le genre et la classe" (Crossing gender and class) revealed that the organizers as well as the vast majority of the paper presenters and audience members rejected the Marxist meaning of class but failed to present an alternate definition. Based on their use of the term (which was never defined) one could deduce that class was mostly considered to be a cultural phenomenon, a lifestyle or a hierarchical status.

mentation almost one-to-one (insisting on a biological difference, on the seductive sexual difference or alterity between men and women, on national specificity etc.), leading some former women's movement veterans to not only join LMPT conferences, but also to become one of their prominent sources (Agacinski 2012). But even the materialized gender strategy shows numerous proximities with the LMPT argumentation: a rejection of queer theory, a rejection of any analysis that views class relations and political economy as anything other than just cruel or mean behavior (as shown also by the LMPT), and, most importantly, a rejection of the deconstructivist epistemological approach. Even those few French feminist researchers who actually study the construction of a biological difference between men and women, such as Pricille Touraille, do so from the materialist feminist standpoint, explaining a difference in physical size by the fact that men eat more than women in patriarchal society, and thus they grow taller (Touraille 2008). Even the queer feminists who had initially pushed for a translation of gender and queer deconstructivism have today turned their backs on it (Bourcier 2017).

Conclusion

Comparing these feminist gender debates to the more recent right-wing and conservative attacks on gender studies, the similarities are striking. Even today, the majority of feminist researchers in France have still not taken up a deconstructivist approach to gender analyzes. The ongoing importance of either "equality in difference" approaches (republican feminism) or sex-class approaches (materialist feminism) – not to mention the majority of scholars who are simply comparing men and women under the umbrella of "gender studies" – has been shown to weaken the use of feminist research in protesting right-wing attacks. Indeed, as most of them are largely in agreement with the content of the right-wing attacks on gender studies, their reactions are marked by a highly problematic denial.

As part of the widely publicized 2013 opposition to the "ABC of Gender Equality" – a school teaching unit designed to respond to heterosexist forms of discrimination - right-wing initiatives led to outbursts of anti-Semitic violence on the streets of Paris. The day of rage, on which parents were encouraged to keep their children from school in protest of the teaching unit, had been organized by a coalition led by the former anti-racist activist, Farida Belghoul.[27] On the same day, a demonstration took place in Paris, in which people shouted, "Jews out of France." The anti-Semitism of that demonstration was sufficiently visible and dramatic that the

---

27 The day of rage had not been the first right-wing action of Belghoul. She had already participated in political actions and debates with right-wing celebrities such as M'bala M'bala Dieudonné and the convicted anti-Semite, Alain Soral.

president at the time, François Hollande, was compelled to react publicly and condemn it. In response to a series of similar attacks against "gender ideology," which included the censoring of theater plays, parents intervening in schools, but also direct attacks on gender studies research, some gender studies and feminist researchers from the University of Strasbourg drafted a petition in which they stated that gender theory does not exist, that gender studies investigates, rather than questions, differences between men and women, and that boys will not be transformed into girls (or vice versa).[28]

In light of the above analyzes of right-wing sexual politics, the limitations of such a petition seem obvious: denying the anti-naturalist stance of gender theories positions gender studies closer to, rather than further from, the far-right. Moreover, refusing to support the possibility of transition for transgender or transsexual children contributes to further stigmatizing an already highly marginalized community. In addition, distancing themselves from other sexual minorities and dissident sexual cultures, the authors also wrote: "No, there will be no sexual films projected in school." Gender is quite surprisingly reduced to be a number of prejudices and stereotypes. While gender researchers do not agree on the origins of gender or how to change it, the panorama of approaches to grasp it, which include a system of material exploitation and a symbolic order based on misogyny, excludes viewing gender as a prejudice that can be changed by simply enhancing access to information. The approach expressed in the aforementioned petition is less surprising when one accounts for the earlier rejection of gender studies by the majority of feminist researchers in France. Even the LMPT took note of this rejection, and then offered an alliance with these feminist researchers:

> "Butler and gender are contested, sometimes violently, by feminists who remain attached to serious inquiry and reflection, and by those who understand feminism to be about the defense of women (especially in places where they are actually exploited and violated), who are rendered obsolete by a theory claiming that the category 'women' corresponds to no real entity." (LMTP manual 2013)

The LMPT took up accusations that the notion of gender de-centers women as feminism's political subject, which it does. Some feminists who share this criticism have taken up the invitation and joined the LMPT, such as the above mentioned Sylviane Agacinski, who wrote in her book Women between sex and gender:

> "People are outraged today to see religious activists in the United States defending creationist dogmas against life science, but nobody is outraged by the fact that a theory on sexuality, reduced to [...] the question of pleasure and sexual orienta-

---

28   petitionpublique.fr/Default.aspx?pi=P2014N45876, 04.04.2019.

tion, is doing the same thing in their general suspicion of life sciences." (Agacinski 2012: 63-63 quoted in the LMPT manual)

Far-right and right-wing feminism are nothing new (cf. Blee 1991) and there have also been manifold alliances of women with different conservative and right-wing institutions: Some women have tried to challenge gender norms from inside different religious institutions, and others have tried to use nationalist ideology to fight gender oppression (Meyer 2014). The proximity of some feminists, like the Malthusian Margaret Sanger, with eugenic politics is well-known today, as are the conservative aspirations of Victorian feminists, who sought to save working class women from "white slavery" (Walkowitz 1980). While some feminists might actually be convinced of the cultural superiority of white bourgeois heterosexual social arrangements, others might try to strategize and sacrifice sexual and racial minorities and working class populations for the greater good of an aspired women's emancipation. Anxiety is the fertile ground upon which far-right politics are working, and on which their sexual politics grow terrifying, monstrous flowers. In her introduction to Powers of Desire, Ann Snitow recognized and documented this exact process already in 1984:

> "The New Right has responded to the anxiety provoked by the acceleration of change with a politics of sex that is at once homophobic, ageist, sexist and sexually repressive. It is attempting to reinstitute sexual constraints and gender divisions from which we have barely begun to break free. Our task is to imagine a sexual politics to counterpose that of the Right." (Snitow 1984: 12)

Confronted in the early 1980s with what Gayle Rubin, borrowing from Jeffrey Weeks, called a moral panic (Rubin 1984: 294) - a conservative backlash to feminist successes, which was also an antifeminist familialist and nationalist counter-revolution - some feminists insisted on criticizing these institutions (i.e. nation, religion and family), which led to a violent inner-feminist debate that had high personal costs for some (Rubin 2011; Nestle 1987: 144-150). At that point, feminist theory not only renegotiated the relationship between sexuality and gender, but also the relationship between sex and gender that eventually led to Judith Butler's Gender Trouble and the rupture it provoked in feminist research. Appropriated from its mostly psychological and psychiatric origins, feminists, especially deconstructivist feminists, importantly transformed and re-signified gender. They sought to challenge the naturalist foundations and assumptions of a social order producing men and women. Nowadays, as shown above, gender is being re-signified again, this time by a far-right campaign that barely hides its antifeminism, claiming instead to defend common sense so as to protect children, and sometimes even women. A call to protect children that comes from the same Christian churches that systematically enable sexual child abuse in their own institutions might seem surprising. But the arguments of other parts of the far-right, organized in political parties and NGOs, are equally hypocritical considering that today the most dangerous place for women and children remains the family.[29] The heterosexual family is a corporate project that unites religious and racist far-right organizations, like political parties and neo-Nazi groups and networks from the past until today.

For Rosalind Petchetsky, who has analyzed similar right-wing politics in the 1980s in the US, what distinguishes the New Right from classical conservatism is "that it is spoken on behalf of corporate bodies rather than individuals. It is, in other words, corporate privatism – in the service of business, church, private school, and patriarchal family – that is intended, not individual privacy. In this regard, the New Right's appeal to privatism is much closer to fascism than to classical libertarian doctrine and is thus perfectly compatible, in theory as well as practice, with a program of massive state control over individuals' private lives." (Petchesky 1981: 224)

The protection of privacy as promoted by religious and other fragments of the right is also hypocritical given that churches, neo-Nazi groups and other conservative organizations do nothing to combat domestic violence against women and children in families; on the contrary, they promoted this violent institution in the past (Petchesky 1981: 226) and present it as shown above. For future feminist analysis and practice, the comparison of right-wing "anti-gender" discourse with feminist anti-gender discourse reveals the importance of situating this discourse in its context, and adding to the critique of religion a critical analysis of the institution of the family, the nation, and naturalism, but also of racism.

Bibliography

Agacinski, Sylviane (2012): Femmes entre sexe et genre. Paris: Le Seuil.
Badinter, Elisabeth (2003): "The French Exception." In: Roger Célestin/Eliane Dal-Molin/Isabelle de Courtivron (eds.), Beyond French Feminisms. Debates on Women, Politics, and Culture in France, 1981-2001. New York: Palgrave Macmillan, pp. 225-238.
Badinter, Elisabeth (2003): Fausse Route. Paris: Odile Jacob.
Bereni, Laure/Chauvin, Sébastien/Jaunait, Alexandre/Revillard, Anne (eds.) (2008): Introduction aux Gender Studies. Manuel des Etudes sur le Genre, Ouvertures Politiques. Brussels: de Boeck.

---

29   For France, cf. the ongoing study Virage on violence against women: www.ined.fr/fr/publications/editions/document-travail/enquete-virage-premiers-resultats-violences-sexuelles/, 27.01.2020.

Blee, Kathleen (1991): Women of the Klan: Racism and Gender in the 1920s. Berkeley: University of California Press.

Bourcier, Marie-Hélène/Zoo, Le (eds.) (1998): Q comme Queer. Lille: Gay Kitsch Camp.

Bourcier, Sam (2017): Homo Inc.orporated. Le Triangle et la licorne qui pète. Paris: Cambourakis.

Butler, Judith/Laclau, Ernesto/Žižek, Slavoj (eds.) (2000): Contingency, Hegemony, Universality: Contemporary Dialogues on the Left. London: Verso.

Challier, Raphaël (2017): "Les Paradoxes de la dédiabolisation. La Fragmentation du Front National au prisme des rapports de genre et de classe des militants." In: Métropolitiques, April 2017, (www.metropolitiques.eu/Les-paradoxes-de-la.html, 27.01.2020).

Delphy, Christine (2001): L'ennemi principal 2: Penser le Genre. Paris: Éditions Syllepse.

Dorlin, Elsa/Trat, Josette/Bourret, Sandrine (eds.) (2007), Femmes, Genre, Féminisme, Les Cahiers de Critique communiste. Paris: Éditions Syllepse.

Fraisse, Geneviève/Horn, Eva (1993): "Gespräch mit Geneviève Fraisse." In: Neue Rundschau 104 (4), pp. 46-56.

Hurtig, Marie-Claude/Kail, Michèle/Rouch, Hélène (eds.) (1991): Sexe et genre. De la hiérarchie entre les sexes. Paris: Éditions du CNRS.

Igounet, Valérie (2016): Les Français d'abord: Slogans et viralité du discours Front National (1972-2017). Paris: Inculte.

Kergoat, Danièle (1982): Les ouvrières. Paris: Sycomore.

Kuhar, Roman/Paternotte, David (eds.) (2017): Anti-gender Campaigns in Europe Mobilizing Against Equality. London: Rowman & Littlefield.

Meyer, Jennifer (2014): "La genèse du racial-féminisme. Race, classe et genre autour de Pia Sophie Rogge-Börner." PhD in Histoire de la Pensée Politique at the École Normale Supérieure in Lyon and the Universität Erfurt Directed by Michel Senellart and Claudia Kraft.

Möser Cornelia (2013): Féminismes en traductions. Théories voyageuses et traductions culturelles. Paris: Éditions des Archives Contemporaines.

Möser, Cornelia (2017): "Travelling Gender in France and Germany. The Feminist Gender Debates as Cultural Translations." In: Emek Ergun/Olga Castro (eds.), Feminist Translation Studies: Local and Transnational Perspectives. London, Routledge, pp. 80-92.

Théry, Irène (1997): "Le Contrat d'union sociale en question." In: Esprit (October), pp. 159-187.

Nestle, Joan (1987): A Restricted Country. Ithaca/New York: Firebrand Books.

Petchesky, Rosalind Pollack (1981): "Antiabortion, Antifeminism, and the Rise of the New Right." In: Feminist Studies 7 (2), pp. 206-246.

Picq, Françoise (1995): "Introduction: Des mouvements féministes entre spécificité et universalité." In: Ephesia (ed.), La place des femmes, les enjeux de l'identité et de l'egalité au regard des sciences sociales, Recherches. Paris: La Découverte.

Rubin, Gayle (1984): "Thinking Sex." In: Carole S. Vance (ed.), Pleasure and Danger: Exploring Female Sexuality. Boston: Routledge & K. Paul, pp. 267-319.

Rubin, Gayle (2011): "Blood under the Bridge: Reflections on 'Thinking Sex.'" In: GLQ: A Journal of Lesbian and Gay Studies 17 (1), pp. 15-48.

Snitow, Ann Barr/Stansell, Christine/Thompson, Sharon (eds.) (1983): Powers of Desire: The Politics of Sexuality, New Feminist Library. New York: Monthly Review Press.

Tricou, Josselin (2016): "Entre masque et travestissement résistances des catholiques aux mutations de genre en France: le cas des Hommen." In: Estudos de Religião 30 (1), pp. 45-73.

Touraille, Pricille (2008): Hommes grands, femmes petites: Une evolution coûteuse. Les régimes de genre comme force sélective de l'adaptation biologique. Paris: Éditions de la Maison des Sciences de l'Homme.

Vance, Carole S. (ed.) (1984): Pleasure and Danger: Exploring Female Sexuality. Boston: Routledge & K. Paul.

Walkowitz, Judith (1980): Prostitution and Victorian Society. Cambridge: Cambridge UP.

Identitarian Gays and Threatening Queers, Or: How the Far Right Constructs New Chains of Equivalence[1]

Patrick Wielowiejski

When it comes to gender and sexuality, the political left today is associated with the fight for minority rights and anti-discrimination. At the same time, those who identify as lesbian, gay, bisexual or trans* are generally thought to lean to the left politically. This connection – whether real or imagined – is so strong that it is often perceived to be a contradiction, or a sign of downright self-hatred, when LGBT people identify with the right wing, especially with the far right. However, there is nothing inherent about being homosexual, bisexual, or trans* that makes LGBT people more prone to the left. In fact, the association (at least discursively) of sexual and gender minorities with the left is the result of decades of political struggle. In their seminal book, *Hegemony and Socialist Strategy*, Ernesto Laclau and Chantal Mouffe described it as crucial for the left to recognize that the workers' movement and what were then called the "new social movements," such as the civil rights movement or environmentalism, were fighting for a common cause and against a common political antagonist. They called this strategy of constructing a common cause and a common opponent the articulation of a "chain of equivalence" (Laclau/Mouffe 2001 [1985]: xviii). Laclau and Mouffe were acutely aware that the field of social identities was a field of floating signifiers, and that fixity was never a given but always the result of a political practice: There was no necessary connection between the new social movements and progressive socialist ideals. In order to become hegemonic, then, the left needed to actively articulate what they called a chain of equivalence between the various social movements.

In this article, I would like to argue that it is within the political right today where we can find political practices that can be interpreted as an attempt to articulate a new chain of equivalence. In particular, I am interested in how some far-right actors construct a common cause between sexual and gender minorities

---

1   Parts of this article were translated from an article published earlier in *Feministische Studien* (Wielowiejski 2018). I would like to thank Gabriele Dietze and Agnieszka Pasieka for their insightful comments.

on the one hand, and conservative nationalists on the other.[2] This connection is anything but self-evident: After all, for traditional nationalists, homosexuals are viewed as potentially disloyal because they are suspected to undermine the patriarchal order and the central project of reproducing the nation (Nagel 2003: 163-164). But against the backdrop of a society in which "gay-friendliness" counts as a marker of modernity and "homophobia" as a label of backwardness, the far right, too, needs to find ways to counter its image as homophobic. Notions like "contradiction" or "self-hatred," however, assume that certain political identities are fixed once and for all: that gay people *must necessarily* be left-wing or deluded. Or, for that matter, that the right wing must be homophobic or lying. By engaging with the ethnographic material I have gathered during two years of fieldwork in the right-wing populist German *Alternative für Deutschland* (*AfD*), I will show how right-wing actors try to construct themselves as "identitarians" who are gay-friendly and in opposition to a political enemy they call the "liberal globalist elites"; who appear to be gay-friendly on the surface, but who essentially work to strip people of their identities. Thus, homosexuality becomes acceptable only *as a stable, unitary, and clear-cut identity*. Everything that questions, mixes, or hybridizes notions of identity – be it a politics of open borders or a queering of sex and gender – remains problematic in the eyes of the far right. This far-right problematization of mixture and hybridity does not mean that heterogeneity is rejected per se. In these discourses, a certain degree of heterogeneity can be accepted as an element of modern societies. What *is* rejected is the liberal notion of equality; Others are tolerated as long as they remain Other.

In what follows, I will shed light on two different discursive strands. The first one deals with the claim that the far right is not against homosexuals, but rather against "/g/ender"[3] – that is, against the purported dissolution of sexual and gender identities. The second one argues that "Islamization" is a specific threat to homosexuals, and, therefore, that "protecting" German cultural identity from Islam is tantamount to protecting gays. In the conclusion, I will recapitulate my argument and discuss whether or not these new chains of equivalence can be successful.

---

2   This article develops its narrative mainly from ethnographic material, and refrains from a lengthy discussion of the theory used. For an analysis of such partial openings in the equivalential chain that engages more thoroughly with Laclau's work, cp. Kim 2017.

3   By defamiliarizing the spelling of the word, I wish to indicate that the term /g/ender, as is used in these circles, has developed a life of its own: It does not have much to do with the term *gender* anymore, as it is used in gender studies. I believe that /g/ender is not simply a wrong interpretation of the analytical term gender, but rather a re-articulation aimed at vilifying the political opponent and influencing the discourse. This conceptual difference becomes visible through the alternative spelling, but also audible: Most of my informants pronounce the word with /g/ as the initial sound (as opposed to /dʒ/), ostentatiously German. The slashes are borrowed from the way linguists write phonemes, that is, sounds that distinguish one word from another.

First Discursive Strand: Not against Homosexuals, but against /G/ender

It is December 2016 and I am in the house of a student fraternity that is known to be part of the radical right wing in Berlin's posh Southwest, attending a meeting for people interested in joining the *Junge Alternative*, which is the youth organization of the *AfD*. There are six young people from the *AfD* in the room, one of them a woman, and about ten potential new members, all of whom are men. It is my first time in the field. Until now, I had only been in touch with *AfD* politicians via email. Faded pictures of the previous generations of fraternity members adorn the walls, alongside a portrait of Frederick II (the Prussian king Germans still refer to as "The Old Fritz"), and a large poster of *Windhoek Bier* complete with the image of a colonial equestrian statue. Above the bar, the original street sign of *Reichssportfeldstraße* points into the room, the Reich's Sports Field Street that was renamed in 1997. In the background, music of the folk punk band *Dropkick Murphys* is playing. We are drinking beer, the only appropriate choice if you do not want to seem odd in the room. Igor[4] and Julia are talking about social justice as I join their conversation, a topic that seems to be important to them. Julia says that she considers the leftist party *Die Linke* unelectable given their attachment to "Multikulti." Igor adds that *Die Linke* is in favor of same-sex unions, which to him is a no-go. I act a little surprised: "But the *AfD* is not against same-sex unions, are they?" "Well, everyone should be able to live as they please," Julia answers. "It's not true that the *AfD* is a homophobic party, but what is important to us is that same-sex couples shouldn't be given special treatment, they shouldn't be privileged in any way, and marriage between a man and a woman should be our guiding principle." Noah, who works for an MP, joins in on the conversation: "There's actually quite a lot of gay men in leading positions in the party! The parliamentary secretary of the *AfD* group in Berlin's House of Representatives is openly gay. And he's totally cool. Also, one of the chairmen of the *Junge Alternative* is gay, Sven Tritschler." And Julia adds: "And Alice Weidel, who is a party executive, she's lesbian."

Conversations like this one are typical in the *AfD*. The argument is not openly homophobic, but rather heteronormative: Homosexuals are "okay" (as one informant of mine put it) as long as they do not demand equality. My interlocutor Johannes, in his late 20s and gay, told me about his doubts prior to joining the *AfD*. He had consulted the leader of his local *AfD* chapter and asked him, if they would have a problem with him being gay. "Not if you don't rub it in our faces," was the answer that Johannes found acceptable. What is more, some of my informants openly embrace the definition of homosexuality as "abnormal," arguing that being abnormal – that is, deviant, uncommon – does not mean bad. They agree that in order

---

4 To maintain anonymity, all names have been changed and some descriptions altered.

to ensure the reproduction of the nation, "normal," heterosexual families should be promoted, while the existence of homosexuality can be tolerated as long as it remains marginal.

We could argue about the exact definition of heteronormativity and homophobia, and object that homophobia is always based on heteronormativity. However, what I find striking here is the absence of the common topoi of homonegative discourse. What happened to the 'perverts,' the 'sick,' and the 'sinners'?

Consider a speech given by Björn Höcke, the leader of the *AfD* group in the state parliament of Thuringia and the most prominent figure of the *völkisch*, extreme right wing of the party. In this speech, given at a Christmas party of the party's youth organization, Höcke talks about an "old friend" of his, "a talented artist" who, Höcke says, is homosexual and has told him "that for homosexual people, sexuality is all that matters, it takes center stage." Sexuality, Höcke continues, is something wonderful and "doubtlessly forms part of the synthesis of man and woman." However, the polarity of man and woman is about more, namely, the "eternal principles" of life itself. Interestingly, Höcke then goes on to say that he wants to carry this "spirit" into the *AfD* and promises: "We will expel the mental illness called /g/ender mainstream from our schools and universities!" (Höcke 2014, from 00:41:14, my translation) What I find remarkable is the way in which Höcke simultaneously constructs and neglects a connection between homosexuality and /g/ender: On the one hand, homosexuality seems to have its legitimate place in society, not coincidentally in the arts. That is a common benevolent conservative stereotype of homosexuality: Homosexuals might not have children, but at least they make great art. But on the other hand, Höcke implicitly calls anyone "mentally ill" who claims that hetero and homo are equal (because this is what he means when he refers to "/g/ender mainstream": the claim of equality). So, the accusation of insanity remains the same, but it no longer refers to homosexuality per se. Rather, the new antagonist is called /g/ender. I am now going to illustrate what this idea of /g/ender means to the people in my field by presenting the case of Andreas.

Andreas is a gay cis man in his 40s, and he is a member of a West German state parliament. He was a member of the *CDU* for many years, but his views were often considered too conservative or too far to the right. When he first heard about a new anti-Euro party being founded by an economics professor back in 2013, he was immediately interested, and he then became one of the founding members of the *AfD*. When I met him for the first time, I felt both surprised by his openness and uncomfortable with his eccentricity, in one moment playing around with a cuddly toy that he carries around at all times, and in the next moment losing his temper over Angela Merkel's alleged plans to do away with the German people. Andreas has a strong desire to portray the *AfD* as gay-friendly to the outside world, but also to convince his fellow party members that one can be gay-friendly, while also fiercely opposing "/g/ender ideology." Sitting in his one-bedroom apartment one afternoon, when I was officially his intern in parliament as part of my fieldwork, we argued over an action plan that the state government had commissioned to tackle homophobia, transphobia, and interphobia. Andreas claimed that, in the *AfD*, it is undisputed that the legal situation of gays and lesbians, trans* and intersex people could be improved. I, in turn, objected that the *AfD* reacted quite adversely to the constitutional court's decision that the government introduces a third legal sex. Andreas then went on to explain (my translation):

> "The third sex is out of the question because there are only two sexes. Intersexuality and transsexuality, all of these things, are clearly not ideas of /g/ender, at least not for us. They are rather clear decisions for being a man or a woman. For transsexuals, it's even clearer, that's even a decision for being a man or a woman against their biological being. In other words, we're not mad about transsexuals, we're mad about /g/ender! These people [people who promote "/g/ender", PW] twist our words and completely misjudge transsexuals. We don't believe that transsexuality is /g/ender, just because they know, against their biological being, to be something different. It is precisely this knowledge to be a woman in a man's body or vice versa that proves that there are only two sexes, and the identity of transsexuals is so unambiguously clear that it doesn't make sense to conflate these things with /g/ender. And with gays and lesbians it's even more absurd: to love a man when you're a man is a double decision for manliness."

The word /g/ender here can be interpreted as a cipher for a range of things that Andreas opposes (cf. Grzebalska et al. 2017). Intersex and trans*, he explains, are not dismissed per se, because they are not "ideas of /g/ender." He describes the identity of trans* people as "unambiguously clear," and the same goes for gay men: "a double decision for manliness." Having an "unambiguously clear" identity is precisely the opposite of what /g/ender stands for, and it is also what makes trans* people and gay people acceptable for the far right. But of course, Andreas' notion of trans* is limited to the idea of a transition from one sex to the other, of the cliché of being "trapped in the wrong body," which is reinforced by the word "transsexual," a pathologizing term that most trans* people reject. So, according to Andreas, trans* and gay people, while deviating from the norm, affirm the gender binary even more clearly than does the norm itself. That is why he thinks that "these /g/ender people" misjudge homosexuality, trans*, and intersex, because they believe that these things "are /g/ender." As a gay man, he feels offended by this conflation of his own identity with /g/ender.

Again, /g/ender, as it is used here, does not mean gender. Andreas associates the word with ambiguity, uncertainty, with the idea that gender is a social construct, with gender fluidity and the deconstruction of binarisms, with a skepticism towards biological determinism and with ways of being beyond the gender binary.

It is therefore /g/ender, and not homosexuality or trans*, that threatens a stable and unambiguous binary sex-gender system.

Gender scholars such as Sabine Hark and Paula-Irene Villa (2015), or Roman Kuhar and David Paternotte (2017), have coined the term "anti-genderism" (or, as I prefer to spell it, anti-/g/enderism) to denote both the anti-feminist discourse I have just outlined, and the social movements associated with it. According to these movements, "/g/ender ideology" is a political strategy employed by a conspiratorial transnational liberal elite that aims to eradicate essential differences between men and women, a totalitarianism more dangerous than Marxism or fascism. The following quote from one of the most well-known anti-/g/enderist authors, Gabriele Kuby, contains many of the most common tropes of this discourse:

> "For the first time in history, power elites are claiming authority to change men's and women's sexual identity through political strategies and legal measures. They had previously lacked expertise in social engineering. However, today this is happening before our eyes on a global scale. The strategy's name: gender mainstreaming. The battle is being fought under the banner of equality of men and women, but that has proven to be a tactical transitional stage." (Kuby 2016: 42)

Of course, I am not trying to say that anti-/g/enderism is a gay-friendly endeavor. Rather, I want to argue that some anti-/g/enderist actors claim that the charge of homophobia is unfounded, and that it is what they call the "globalist Left" that paints a distorted picture of the reality of gay men and women, exceeds common-sense understandings of gay-friendliness, and eventually even harms homosexuals. In claiming that /g/ender aims at changing or even eradicating "men's and women's sexual identity," anti-/g/enderism tries to appeal to those gays and lesbians who do not subscribe to, or who might even feel threatened by, a radical queer politics that questions sex and gender binaries. The contours of a new chain of equivalence begin to emerge: conservative gays and lesbians sharing a cause with the anti-/g/enderist right.

Second Discursive Strand: Protecting Homosexuals from Islam

But it is not just gender and sexual identity that is under threat in the eyes of national conservatives. Most of the time, the notion of "identity" in far-right discourse refers to ethnicity.[5] The accusation of "social engineering," that is, of want-

---

5 The most visible example of this reference to identity is the so-called Identitarian Movement. One of their mottos in German, "Wir sind die Jugend ohne Migrationshintergrund" ("We are the youth without migration background,, cf. *IBD* Redaktion 2015), alludes to the term that is

ing to forcefully transform society into some kind of liberal or leftist utopia, is omnipresent in this discourse. During the electoral campaign of the *AfD* for the Bavarian elections in 2018, I heard a speaker at a campaign event say: "There have always been so-called social engineers who [...] wanted to create the 'new human being': first the racially pure, then the uniform socialist human being, and now they're trying to create the ethnicity-free human being." The charge is that these social engineers do so by opening up borders and introducing Islam in Western Europe.

Now, in the second discursive strand that I examine, the opening of borders and introducing Islam in Western Europe are framed as specific threats to homosexuals. *AfD* politicians, in their views, bravely declare a truth that liberals dare not say because it does not fit into their worldview: that the biggest threat for homosexuals today is the violence committed by homophobic migrants. In this way, homophobic violence is both addressed and silenced because it is only ever raised as a topic if the perpetrators are (perceived as) refugees, Muslims, and Arabs. Eliminating German national identity by opening borders, then, becomes tantamount to eliminating homosexuals.

A lot could be said about the rejection of both Muslims and Islam, which is seen as a "political ideology." The most common theme that one finds in this discursive strand is the incommensurability of Islam with the liberal values of the West. The embrace of liberal Western values in the name of imperial and exclusionary national politics has been discussed under terms such as homonationalism (Puar 2007, 2013), sexual nationalism (Mepschen et al. 2010), and femonationalism (Farris 2017). These phenomena are powerful narratives in which LGBT and women's rights are invoked in order to legitimize the so-called "war against terror" or the isolation of "Fortress Europe." Homonationalism and femonationalism are in no way exclusive to the far right; in fact, as concepts, they are meant to shed light on the current state of hegemonic Western liberalism. To the extent that the far right proposes a neo-nationalist alternative to this hegemony (cf. Blyth 2016), homonationalism and femonationalism could even be interpreted as being at odds with a far-right political agenda. After all, as I argued above, heteronormativity plays a crucial role in the *AfD*. However, I would argue that this agenda is composed of a host of divergent ideas and goals, and labels such as "liberalism" or "national conservatism" cannot fully grasp the paradoxical diversity of discourses and practices active in a party such as the *AfD*. In any case, homo- and femonationalism

> most commonly (and problematically) used in German discourse to name Germans of non-German descent (*Menschen mit Migrationshintergrund*, 'people with migration background'). In this article, I use the word *identitarian* in a wider sense, not restricted to the Identitarian Movement. My argument is based on the premise that the recourse to identity, this 'identitarianism,' is one of the central ideologemes of the contemporary far right.

can certainly be employed as political strategies: They function as vehicles into the political mainstream. As Gabriele Dietze has suggested, we are dealing with a "dynamical paradox" (Dietze 2018: 35) that might be *constitutive* of the current successes of right-wing populism, rather than contradictory.

Consider the following example from a debate in the *Landtag* of North Rhine-Westphalia. In this debate, the *Landtag* discusses the rehabilitation of homosexual men who were convicted pursuant to Section 175 of the German Criminal Code, that is, the law that made sex between men a punishable offence after the Second World War. The *AfD* parliamentarian Sven Tritschler, at the time head of the *Junge Alternative* and himself gay, argues in favor of rehabilitation, but he adds:

> "When this is done, you can now start caring for the lives of those homosexuals who are not dead yet, and who would like to continue living for a while. As a result of your completely misguided migration and integration policy, you are exposing these people to a danger that makes a conviction according to Section 175 appear harmless. / (Applause from the *AfD*) / That is to say, your tokenism [*Symbolpolitik*] does not help the gay couple that gets beaten to a pulp by a horde of refugees because the two don't want to adapt to the ideals of their mullah. And your tokenism does not help the homosexual pupil who gets bullied by his newcomer [*zugereisten*] classmates." (Landtag Nordrhein-Westfalen 2017: 71; my translation)

Being strict on immigration and asylum policy, Tritschler implies, *is* gay-friendly policy-making. Everything else is *Symbolpolitik*. This is a typical, hyperbolic motif of this discourse: Homophobia among (white, non-Muslim) Germans is over or plays a marginal role, the bigger problem is the "imported" homophobia that overshadows even the state repression of previous decades.

My interlocutor Johannes, whom I met for the first time at a three-day meeting of the *Alternative Homosexuals* in Upper Franconia, argued in a similar vein. The *Alternative Homosexuals* are a small group of mainly gay men (and individual lesbians and trans* women) who are members of the *AfD* or the *Junge Alternative*. I worked with them ethnographically for two years between 2017 and 2019. While most of them are committed to the national conservative far-right wing of the *AfD*, simply called "The Wing" ("Der Flügel"), Johannes calls himself a "liberal conservative." He is in his late 20s and studies public administration at a midsize university in the Southwest of Germany. It is his first time with the *Alternative Homosexuals*; he had met one of their members online on a gay dating website. However, he is not timid about calling out "nationalistic bullshit" in conversations or to denounce the others' "*völkisch* vocabulary." The others, in turn, ridicule Johannes as a "liberal." On the third day, he and I are sitting in the back seat of a car, talking. Johannes tells me that he is surprised and annoyed by the fact that the *Alternative Homosexuals* are proper far-right nationalists. For him, the *AfD* is not the best political solution, but a necessary corrective to the political system. As a "militant gay", as he calls himself, he considers the *AfD* to be the strongest weapon against a reactionary Islam that, in his view, threatens his liberal lifestyle. Once a year, he goes to the gay summer camp that is organized by the German Federation of Trade Unions. Naturally, he meets a lot of leftists there, and he is puzzled: Why do they not see that it is precisely their dear Islam that endangers the freedoms they have fought for themselves?

Identitarian Gays and Globalist /G/ender Ideology

Martin Lichtmesz and Caroline Sommerfeld, two authors who belong to the intellectual movement of the "Neue Rechte" ("New Right"), have an answer to Johannes' questions. Their book "Mit Linken leben" ("Living with leftists") was quite a success in far-right circles and stirred controversy at the Frankfurt book fair in 2017. It claims to offer an insight, from the perspective of a self-confident intellectual right, into what leftists think and how to live with them – presupposing that the culture of the left is hegemonic and that, if you are on the right, you have no choice but to live with them. Not surprisingly, it thereby constructs a sharp political distinction between those who are on the left and those who are on the right, and, in my view, it tells us much more about the right than about the left. Johannes' puzzlement can be paraphrased like this: Why do leftists want to let in all those refugees who threaten their very own leftist values? Lichtmesz and Sommerfeld claim that one of the greatest dividing lines between left and right today is being "globalist" or "identitarian":

> "Another often mentioned dividing line [between left and right] is the one between *globalism* and *nationalism*, patriotism, populism, separatism, sovereignism – or however you want to call the 'identitarian' counter-movements that are likely to gain traction in the coming decades. They are a consequence of the exaggerated globalist claim to power." (Lichtmesz/Sommerfeld 2017: 46; my translation)

According to this view, every political difference, every opinion if you will, falls neatly into one of these two antagonistic categories: either "identitarian" or "globalist." All existing political differences, the plurality of opinions, become absorbed by this antagonistic relationship: The right is discursively constructed as the anti-left, *tertium non datur*. In the words of Laclau and Mouffe, what Lichtmesz and Sommerfeld are trying to do is to articulate two chains of equivalence, two different logics that oppose each other. I want to suggest that these chains of equivalence might look like this: On the one hand, we have the "globalists," the liberal elites, the cosmopolitans who are against borders and nations, the social engineers who want to create a genderless, "ethnicity-free human being" without an own identity, the constructivists who believe that one can change one's gender like one changes clothes, the EU technocrats, but also the *"Gutmenschen,"* the politically hyper-correct do-gooders, most of them women who are very often just politically naïve. On the other hand, there are the "identitarians," the common people, the conservative patriots who defend borders and nations, ethnic identities and also the gender identity of men and women, the essentialists who defend the "common sense," the "true Europeans," the men who are brave enough to utter, against the hegemonic status quo, that migration and mixture are the root cause of society's problems.

To wrap up, where do homosexuality and gay-friendliness fit into this picture? As became clear in my interview with Andreas quoted above, homosexuals and binary trans* people can very well be accepted as respectable representatives of a static gender binary. As such, they fit into a far right that is fixated on identity. The appropriation of a gay-friendly discourse by national conservative actors is therefore not per se a contradiction. My thesis is that, in this discourse, the dividing line between 'healthy' and 'mentally ill,' between 'normal' and 'perverted,' does not run between hetero and homo, but rather between forms of life that affirm identity and those that are critical of identity. The more homosexuality is integrated into national conservative narratives, the more a new enemy image is constructed. This new enemy image includes queerness, feminism, non-binary trans*, drag queens and kings, and rainbow families, under the umbrella term /g/ender. And I believe that it is precisely for this reason that emancipatory movements should avoid reproducing this divide into 'conservative' homosexuality and 'progressive' queerness, but instead accept a wide spectrum of forms of life, no matter how binary or deconstructivist they are. Rejecting 'friend vs. enemy' antagonisms means rejecting the worldview of the far right. The embrace of complexity opens up a space for conflict in which the other's right to exist is not disputed, as difficult as this may often be. The undeniable differences between LGBT identity politics and queer critiques of identity should therefore be debated based on the democratic values they share, and as an alliance that cuts across the frontiers of identity.

Laclau's and Mouffe's theory of the political has helped me to connect some of the bits and pieces in my data. This theoretical lens is admittedly one that emphasizes antagonism and conflict; it is one way to look at the data. I do not want to generalize my findings and say: This is what "the *AfD*" is doing. I am also not saying that "the far right" is gay-friendly. Rather, my point is that some far-right actors, the ones I have come to know, construct a certain version of gay-friendliness, and a version of themselves as gay-friendly in opposition to "liberal elites."

To end on an optimistic note: establishing new "chains of equivalence" is hard work.[6] Stuart Hall in particular has emphasized the powerful ways in which history structures the ideological terrain (Hall 1986: 41). The idea of anti-heterosexism has

---

6   Thanks to John Clarke for raising this observation after I presented a paper at a conference in Göttingen on October 27, 2018.

been so consistently articulated by the left that it is difficult to conceive how it could be given a socially regressive, conservative meaning. Given that the gender and sexual politics of the right are all but unequivocal, it is at least doubtful that a chain of equivalence between conservative nationalists and sexual and gender minorities will take hold of the political imaginary anytime soon. But if we take democracy seriously, that is, if we take the political moment of the social seriously, we must also accept its radical openness. Or, to say it in the words of Laclau and Mouffe: "[W]e must understand in all their radical heterogeneity the range of possibilities which are opened in the terrain of democracy itself" (Laclau/Mouffe 2001 [1985]: 168).

Bibliography

Blyth, Mark (2016): Global Trumpism. Online: www.foreignaffairs.com/articles/2016-11-15/global-trumpism, 02.03.2017.
Dietze, Gabriele (2018): "Rechtspopulismus und Geschlecht: Paradox und Leitmotiv." In: Femina Politica 27 (1), pp. 34-46.
Farris, Sara R. (2017): In the Name of Women's Rights: The Rise of Femonationalism. Durham: Duke University Press.
Grzebalska, Weronika/Kováts, Eszter/Pető, Andrea (2017): Gender as Symbolic Glue: How 'Gender' became an Umbrella Term for the Rejection of the (Neo)Liberal Order. Online: politicalcritique.org/long-read/2017/gender-as-symbolic-glue-how-gender-became-an-umbrella-term-for-the-rejection-of-the-neoliberal-order, 06.04.2018.
Hall, Stuart (1986): "The Problem of Ideology – Marxism without Guarantees." In: Journal of Communication Inquiry 10 (2), pp. 28-44.
Hark, Sabine/Villa, Paula-Irene (2015): "'Eine Frage an und für unsere Zeit': Verstörende Gender Studies und symptomatische Missverständnisse." In: Sabine Hark/Paula-Irene Villa (eds.): Anti-Genderismus: Sexualität und Geschlecht als Schauplätze aktueller politischer Auseinandersetzungen. Bielefeld: transcript, pp. 15-39.
Höcke, Björn (2014): Björn Höcke spricht auf der Weihnachtsfeier 2014 der JA in Stuttgart. Online: www.youtube.com/watch?v=YhYCrQR-xBI, 20.05.2017
IBD Redaktion (2015): Wir sind die Jugend ohne Migrationshintergrund. Online: blog.identitaere-bewegung.de/wir-sind-die-jugend-ohne-migrationshintergrund/, 20.05.2017.
Kim, Seongcheol (2017): "The Populism of the Alternative for Germany (AfD): An Extended Essex School Perspective." In: Palgrave Communications 3 (5), pp. 1-11.

Kuby, Gabriele (2016): The Global Revolution: Destruction of Freedom in the Name of Freedom. Kettering: Angelico.

Kuhar, Roman/Paternotte, David (2017): Anti-Gender Campaigns in Europe: Mobilizing against Equality. London/New York: Rowman & Littlefield.

Laclau, Ernesto/Mouffe, Chantal (2001 [1985]): Hegemony and Socialist Strategy: Towards a Radical Democratic Politics. London/New York: Verso.

Landtag Nordrhein-Westfalen (2017): Plenarprotokoll 17/10. Online: www.landtag.nrw.de/portal/WWW/dokumentenarchiv/Dokument/MMP17-10.pdf, 24.10.2018.

Lichtmesz, Martin/Sommerfeld, Caroline (2017): Mit Linken leben. Schnellroda: Antaios.

Mepschen, Paul/Duyvendak, Jan Willem/Tonkens, Evelien H. (2010): "Sexual Politics, Orientalism and Multicultural Citizenship in the Netherlands." In: Sociology 44 (5), pp. 962-979.

Nagel, Joane (2003): Race, Ethnicity, and Sexuality: Intimate Intersections, Forbidden Frontiers. Oxford/New York: Oxford University Press.

Puar, Jasbir (2007): Terrorist Assemblages. Homonationalism in Queer Times. Durham/London: Duke University Press.

Puar, Jasbir (2013): "Rethinking Homonationalism." In: International Journal of Middle East Studies 45, pp. 336-339.

Wielowiejski, Patrick (2018): "Identitäre Schwule und bedrohliche Queers: Zum Verhältnis von Homonationalismus und Anti-/G/enderismus im Nationalkonservatismus." In: Feministische Studien 36 (2), pp. 347-356.

Why Are Women Attracted to Right-Wing Populism? Sexual Exceptionalism, Emancipation Fatigue, and New Maternalism

Gabriele Dietze

Preface

La Femme est l'Avenir de l'Homme (woman is the future of man, or, figuratively, women are the future of mankind) is the title of a French chanson by Jean Ferrat from 1976. There is a long tradition (in) believing that women are better people than men, or to put it differently, that women command a superior concept of ethics and morality (Gilligan 1977). The idea is that women feel uncomfortable with aggression and the exclusion of fellow human beings. This vague opinion can lead one to hope that it may ultimately be women who will stem the current wave of right-wing populism (RWP). There is some theory and data supporting this assumption, such as with regards to the famous gender gaps: In some European countries, significantly fewer women vote for right-wingers.[1] Feminists in particular are thought of as embodying the natural resistance that could deprive the populists of the ground on which they currently flourish. The following article will scrutinize this set of benevolent preconceptions. First, it will dig into concepts of emancipation and its paradoxes, and how they travel with female right-wing supporters (key term: *emancipation fatigue*). The second part deals with the linkage constructed between women and anti-Muslim sentiments (key term: *sexual exceptionalism*). And the third part will connect the RW populists' claim for traditional heteronormative family politics and ethno-national demographics (key term: *new maternalism*).

---

1   Exceptions are visible in France, where the gender gap is currently closing (see Mayer, 2015, 391-414). In Poland, 39,7 % votes by women for the populist party are significantly fewer than 88,5% of votes by men in the general election of 2014. In the US, 53% of White women have voted for Trump, which is quite an impressive figure (Jaffe, 2018: 18-26) but they are still topped by the 63% of White men among Trump-voters.

Emancipation Fatigue

It is commonly believed that women fear that RWP will revoke or reverse the hard won *emancipation* of women. Before discussing this argument, it seems useful to pursue the original meaning of the term 'emancipation,' which is made up of three words: 'e' – meaning from, 'manus' – meaning hand, and 'capere' – meaning to take. Manucipatio thus means to take someone in possession by laying a hand on the person's shoulder. E-manicipatio accordingly means to bestow someone with freedom (i.e. to take the hand away). In Roman law, emancipation refers to the action or process of setting children, especially sons, free from *patria podestas* (fatherly violence/power). The term was also used for the freeing or delivering of people from slavery. Figuratively speaking, emancipation meant setting free on a general level, delivering from intellectual, moral, or spiritual fetters (OED 2004: 155). So, the term 'emancipation' always carries a double meaning. It can be something awarded to somebody from a higher, mostly male, power, or something somebody has accomplished on his or her own. This kind of ambivalence towards emancipation can also be found among female supporters of RWP.

Although it is still true that a lesser number of women vote for European RWP parties (except in France), social surveys and attitude studies show that as many women as men share the resentments and convictions of right-wingers (Küpper/Heitmeyer 2005; Küpper 2018). Women are, however, less inclined to manifest this resentment at the ballot box because of their social environment, their family loyalty or their disinterest in institutionalized politics (Wippermann 2016). The picture gets even more interesting in the field of racism. One German long-term study about "group-focused enmity" (gruppenförmige Menschenfeindlichkeit) found that, when measuring for racism, sexism, anti-Semitism, and social Darwinism, women respondents show more racist inclination than men over a long period of observation. Men are more sexist than women but with a much less quantitative difference than might be suspected (Zick u.a. 2019). So seemingly the 'gender gap' does not prove lesser support RWP than men.

Women and family issues rank high on RW populist parties' platforms and constitute about one third of their programmatic content (Kemper 2014a). If you look at any European RWP party's platform, you find many points that favor traditional hetero-normative family models (Norocel 2010; Kemper 2014b; Spierings/Zaslove 2015). Most of the women who vote for RWP parties are aware of this and yet it does not seem to scare them off. The youth organization of the *AfD* (Alternative for Germany) started a YouTube campaign in 2014 in which young people displayed handmade posters with texts such as, "I am no feminist because a housewife is a profession" (Gerster 2014).

The *AfD* advertises traditional family imagery as an asset. An election poster shows a happy family with the text: "'Traditional?' We like it." Interesting is the subtitle on the poster: "Trau Dich, Deutschland!" (Go for it, or better 'Dare,' Germany) Conceptualizing traditional family images as a dare reverses common ideas about revolutionary turns: rather than liberation from the fetters of family-bonds, a return to nuclear family is sold as revolutionary thereby feeding into the idea of an alternative modernity.

Figure 1: AfD Wahlplakat Bundestagswahl 2017

I will now come back to the old meaning of emancipation as something awarded by a higher authority. This corresponds with the imagination of right-wingers that 'emancipation' is 'dictated' by elites and feminists. There is a grain of truth in this sentiment. Western feminists have to some extent been quite successful within a short period of time and have set up a kind of emancipation that is thought to be desirable for *all* women. Maxine Molyneux calls the achievements of classical Second Wave Feminism *strategic objectives*, and lists as its assets, "the abolition of the sexual division of labor, alleviation of the burden of domestic labor and childcare. The removal of institutional forms of discrimination, the attainment of political equality, the establishment of freedom of choice over childbearing, and the adoption of adequate measures against male violence over women" (Molyneux 1985: 233). Notwithstanding that Molyneux's article is more than 30 years old and was designed to analyze how little or no progress Nicaraguan women have made since the left-wing Sandinista Revolution, her title "Mobilization without Emancipation" could be applied to RWP women's politics. For an explanation of this development, the author advocates looking more thoroughly into class and poverty issues, where *practical gender interests*, such as feeding the kids and staying loyal to the revolution, predominate. For right-wing populist women there are other objectives at play; see below in the text. These practical gender interests do not necessarily challenge the patriarchal order, and 'strategic objectives' are sometimes even seen as threatening because they might remove forms of male protection without replacing them with alternatives (ibid.: 235).

If one looks into social positionings of women who back RWP, one finds a majority of supporters in the so-called 'mainstream milieus,' mostly represented by the lower middle and working classes (Wippermann 2016: 62-94). Obviously, the question of class plays an important role. If some of the strategic interests of radical feminism have ever made inroads in mainstream milieus, one can now see a kind of 'emancipation from the emancipation.' I would like to frame this mindset with the term *emancipation fatigue* (Emanzipationsverdrossenheit). The present-day cohort of working women in mainstream milieus – especially mothers with small children – did not personally experience the 70s and 80s rise of the *New Women's Movement*. They did not suffer individually from the depressing patriarchal gender regime of the post-war period and did not experience personally the conquest of reproductive freedom, divorce beyond the guilt principle, and access to higher education and employment. Subsequent generations encountered a pre-installed emancipation program and benefited from it accordingly so long as it catered to their interests and needs. However, the anti-patriarchal impetus of radical feminism has since gone out of fashion. Feminism became a swear word in many places, standing for humorlessness, fixation with victimhood and being unsexy.[2]

Birgit Kelle, a prominent German anti-feminist, erupted into an angry jeremiad about the felt imposition to 'emancipate':

> "I'm fed up with apologizing. Because feeling at least a little bad is a minimum for a housewife and mother in Germany. I am fed up with feeling bad about the fact that I have no problem with men in general, or with the husband in particular, who feeds the family; feeling bad about the fact that I am 'only' a housewife and mother instead of embarking on the higher orders of a career, even though I'm not trained to do so; feeling bad about the fact that I insist on raising the children myself rather than leaving them in a state-sponsored day-care facility; feeling bad for embarrassing the larger women's collective with my old-fashioned existence as a wife and mother" (Kelle 2013:10, author's translation).

Arlie Russell Hochschild received very similar answers from the female Tea Party supporters she interviewed for her study. One of her interviewees said that she was angry with the so-called 'femi-nazis' who wanted to force women to catch up with men. She continued, "[...] liberals think that Bible-believing Southerners are igno-

---

2 Angela McRobbie calls this phenomenon "double entanglement" - to simultaneously profit from feminist achievements and join the contemptuous discourse against feminism (McRobbie, 2009).

rant, backward, rednecks, losers. They think that we are racist, sexist, homophobic and maybe fat" (Hochschild 2016: 23).

The women uttering these sentiments want to be protected and financially cared for by their husbands. As housewives, they feel devalued and antagonized by requests 'to emancipate.' They want recognition of their position, which is ennobled in RWP rhetoric as 'choice.' RWP programs promise stress reduction from the efforts of equality-work and an opportunity to save face in light from a structure one can call *emancipation dispositiv* (Dietze 2018: 38). Emancipation comes here as a norm dictated by an elite, something to which one has to adapt if one wants to count as an acceptable and self-confident woman. Feminist rhetoric for emancipation is thus perceived as a sort of sermon imposing bad conscience onto fellow women and condescendingly identify them as 'White trash.' When Hillary Clinton called 2015 Trump voters a "basket of deplorables," the indignation with mainstream White feminism grew out of proportion.

The norm to 'emancipate' can be stressing in many ways. The feminist credo that a personal and independent income is a crucial precondition for emancipation places high demands on women. A new 2019 study by the German Institute for Economic Research (*DIW*) shows that, in families with children older than six, mothers do three times more household duties than fathers, and, in childless families, women do two times more reproductive work than their husbands (Samtleben 2019). For women who work full-time and have the primary responsibility for children, emancipation feels very exhausting. Every day is dominated by agenda-checking and mini-crises, such as sick kids. Moreover, working mothers often suffer career losses because employers do not promote employees who need extra-leave for family emergencies. German studies show that if women work part-time, a good share of their earnings is needed for childcare, and because of the high percentage of part-time work retirement benefits decrease accordingly. But especially lower middle-class and under-class women need to work to make ends meet. The German study *Was junge Frauen wollen* (What young women want), conducted with 18-40year-olds, found that respondents of this social strata often would prefer to stay at home, but are unable to do so, because they need the money (Wippermann 2016).

Furthermore, the emancipation dispositive leads to frictions in close relationships, meaning conflicts with husbands and life-companions regarding the gendered division of labor. The feminist critique of patriarchal even 'toxic' masculinity is thus felt as an undeserved castration and expulsion of the sexiness from the heterosexual relationship. Under the title *Die Feminismusfalle* (The Feminist Trap), a young woman associated with the right-wing extremist *Identitarians* (*Die Identitären*) wrote under the pseudonym Franziska: "It's great to be a woman and we should take advantage of the benefits that nature has given us." As a lover and mistress, women could also influence the world; Franziska then turned her message to men, instructing them: "Stop being washcloths. Not only is this insanely unalluring, it also ensures that crazy femi-nazi women declare your whole gender as brainless and perverse" (quoted in Sigl 2018:168, authors's translation).

However, as convincing as the statements from women sporting emancipation fatigue might sound, their concerns are generally not articulated in the public sphere. And if they are, they are met with some disbelief and amusement in liberal camps. The *AfD*, on the other hand, sensed a potential lying dormant in these existing but seldom expressed sentiments. Shortly before the 2019 European elections, a great many pro-*AfD* postings appeared on Twitter, allegedly written by women. The press became aware of this Twitter barrage and characterized the women posting the messages as "young, female, hyperactive."[3] According to a joint study by t-online and Netzpolitik.org,[4] these seemingly real women posted tens of thousands of tweets referring to and retweeting each other, thereby collecting 'real' likes and comments from 'real' *AfD* politicians during the process. One of them called herself "Beate," whose profile picture was obviously from a Russian site with beauty tips (as a search on the net shows). These clearly forged accounts of alleged young *AfD* female fellow travelers share a romantic iconography in the imagery surrounding their internet appearances. Mostly arranged in 'beautiful' nature, they let their femininity shine.

Numerous media outlets reported on the afore mentioned studies, documenting this unprecedented whirlwind of fake *AfD* Twitter messages. The American media scholar Trevor Davis of George Washington University warned on the German television channel *ZDF* about this attempt to influence possible female *AfD* voters: "We have not found anything similar in any other country in the world that we have studied. That should alarm the Germans."[5] But only two publications focused on the fact that this wave of propaganda was allegedly emanating from women[6] – neither of which raised the question as to why the *AfD* is suddenly supported by a propaganda initiative allegedly directed by women for women with bots, trolls, and fake accounts. In the following, I am going to offer some more reasons for the fixation of RWP on young women.

At this point, it can be stated that some European RWP parties try to conjure up the impression that young women are of paramount importance for the politics of their parties. The first section has described how they are turned into crown

---

3   www.tagesschau.de/faktenfinder/twitter-afd-101.html, 28.06.2019.
4   www.t-online.de/nachrichten/deutschland/id_85764202/wie-die-afd-auf-twitter-taeuscht-und-trickst-exklusive-recherche.html, 03.06.2019.
5   www.spiegel.de/politik/deutschland/afd-ist-auf-facebook-haushoch-ueberlegen-a-1264562.html, 01.09.2019.
6   Except the TV-News the magazine *Der Stern* covered the story: www.stern.de/politik/deutschland/afd-auf-twitter--so-soll-sich-die-partei-zu-mehr-reichweite-tricksen-8723140.html, 03.06.2019.

witnesses of an allegedly misguided emancipation. The second section will show how useful they are for constructing an alleged Muslim sexual threat.

Sexual Exceptionalism

The key term for this paragraph I call *Sexual Exceptionalism*. Borrowing from Jasbir Puar, who used the notion to convey US arrogance in forcing Muslim prisoners – alleged to be backwards on account of their religion – to perform homosexual acts (Puar 2011), I will further develop the notion to criticize sexual politics aiming to fight migration (Dietze 2019). When I speak of exceptionalism, I do not mean 'exception' in the sense of omission or exclusion, but rather 'exceptional' in the sense of extraordinary, the incomparably excellent. The coinage is inspired by the notion *American Exceptionalism*, the still common idea that the United States of America is one of the most outstanding societies in the world, and that it should thus be 'obliged' to impose its societal model onto others (Lipset 1997). Sexual Exceptionalism then describes a narrative of Western supremacy based on a belief that the Global North possesses the most *progressive, privileged*, and *superior* conceivable sexual orders. This narrative claim to be *progressive* because it corresponds to the spirit of the Enlightenment and represents an aspect of the Kantian elaboration of man evolving from his self-inflicted immaturity. This sexual order is perceived as *privileged* because only the Global North has the necessary cultural techniques to 'civilize' sexuality into an emancipatory tool. And, following this narrative, the sexual order of the Global North is *superior* because it proclaims the equality of men and women and, with sexual freedom, also promotes the emancipation of women and sexual minorities.

What does Sexual Exceptionalism have to do with RWP and the *AfD* in particular – especially since RWP parties have previously claimed to support traditional patriarchal families? Here we come to the *young women*, whose real and alleged allegiance the party wishes to wear as adornment. If you look at the party programs, they focus on three closely linked main topics: (1) gender issues (in support of heteronormative family values and opposed to early childhood sex education, homosexual marriage, and so-called 'gender ideology'), (2) immigration (opposed to refugees and other 'foreigners' in their 'native' land) and (3) anti-Muslim racism.

'Young women' provide the nodal point for linking these three dimensions of right-wing gendered discourse: Young women are presented as the most vulnerable victims of sexually perpetrating Muslim migrants, as the New Year's Eve events of Cologne 2015/16 allegedly have shown. Only the *AfD*, as is suggested by the party, confronts the 'truth' and names the sexual danger emanating from young unmarried Muslim men. This position is summarized by the banner "Rape-Fugees not welcome," under which the *AfD* quickly assembled an anti-refugee rebellious stance shortly after the assaults (Dietze 2016).

However, there is more to it than the physical protection of young women. This pattern also addresses the alleged protection of (sexual) freedom in particular. As mentioned before, right-wing populist gendered rhetoric is also about the superiority of Western/Christian 'culture' in contrast to Arabic/Muslim 'culture.' This notion is manifested, for example, in the presumed fact that the women of the West are emancipated. Political formations of the extreme right, such as the German *PEGIDA* (*Patriotischen Europäer gegen die Islamisierung des Abendlandes*/Patriotic Citizens against the Islamization of the Occident), boast of the sexual freedom enjoyed by German women. Point 12 of their 2014 program states: "PEGIDA is for sexual self-determination." Point 10 clarifies the context of this bold statement: "PEGIDA is for resisting a misogynistic, violent political ideology, but not against integrating Muslims already living in the country!"

Without being specific about this point, it is clear, that Western sexual self-determination is being opposed to the alleged oppression faced by Muslim women. However, one should not misunderstand these 'emancipatory' program points in a libertarian way. Point 16 shows a clear edge: "PEGIDA is against this insane gender mainstreaming, often called 'genderization,' the almost obsessive, politically-correct gender neutralization of our language!"[7] In short, PEGIDA does not support women's liberation on an institutional level with quotas or equality laws, or through a politic based on an anti-discriminatory language. Just the opposite, they convey women's emancipation as already completed and in no need of further institutional and legal support but threatened by Muslim sexual assault.

The text of the *AfD* poster asks in its headline: "Do you also see a woman cooking in a kitchen?" And the banner in blue and red answers: "This is politically incorrect." There is a certain irony in using an image of a strongly made-up and sexualized woman with a wide cleavage who – consulting a cookbook – is seemingly not an experienced cook. I am unconvinced, moreover, whether the little slogan in the white circle, "WE speak for you," appeals to ordinary women. It is thus highly probable that the advertisement does not target possible female voters but rather the liberal public, which is implicitly criticized by ridiculing political correctness.

In the Netherlands, this RWP pattern found official expression. At the occasion of the international women's day in 2003, the minister in charge of Women's affairs, De Geus, declared that women's emancipation was fully achieved for 'autochthonous' women in the Netherlands. Emancipation policies from then onwards, he further declared, only need to focus on 'allochthonous' women, meaning

---

7   N.N. (2014): 19 points program: "Was PEGIDA wirklich will." Online: www.focus.de/politik/deutschland/woechentliche-demonstrationen-pegida-ist-gegen-hassprediger-egal-welcher-religion-zugehoerig_id_4359088.html, 02.04.2019.

Figure 2: AfD-poster of the chapter North Rhine-Westphalia

Muslim women (quoted in Bracke 2011, 34). Sarah Bracke then concluded: "The Dutch state thus effectively positioned itself as a flagship of women's liberation, while using women's emancipation as a demarcation line to position ethnic minorities as not fully belonging the Dutch nation. Their belonging is in various respects made conditional on complying with standards of emancipation set by the state." (ibid.) In Germany, a current project of the *AfD* is to fight against gender-mainstreaming, equal opportunity agencies and gender studies in state and federal parliamentary interrogations with the intent of cutting or abolishing the budgets for those agencies and gender studies professorships.

It has by now become more obvious why young women are so central to RWP propaganda and why they are targeted as desired sympathizers. Young women represent figures for merging the central program items – immigration, anti-muslim racism and sexual politics. At first glance, this political program appears contradictory because it presents emancipatory sexual politics together with traditional programs in support of heteronormative family values. However, as the success of such strategies among female supporters demonstrates, working with paradoxes and "calculated ambivalences" (Reisigl 2016) is one of the selling strategies of RWP. Such "dynamic paradoxes" (Dietze 2018) provide RWP with touches of modernity, which are needed to convey the impression that the parties are promoting a system-crashing 'revolution' in favor of women's status.

The best way to illustrate how the RWPs play with contradictions is to note their tendency – at least for the North European RWPs – to enlist women as party leaders and spokespersons (Meret u.a. 2016): Marine Le Pen in France, Siv Jenssen in Norway, or currently Alice Weidel and Beatrix von Storch in Germany. Despite the large majority of men in the parliamentary factions and party organs, these women are in the limelight and perform a variety of functions: They provide a pretty face to radical and racist positions, they perform modernity by their very existence, and they often bring something extra to the political stage (nobility and the right-wing Catholic establishment in the case of Beatrix von Storch, for example, or economic competence in the case of Alice Weidel, who formerly held a high position at the investment bank, Goldman Sachs).

New Maternalism

Reproduction is a third reason why RWP gives young White women a central place in their propaganda. It must be noted that it was not the *AfD* that first connected the issue of women's emancipation with demographic policies: in 2002, a German red-green coalition between the Social Democrats and the Green Party brought together family policy and population management into a programmatic union that was based on a so-called 'demographic change' (demographische Wende). This new discourse was based on a belief that the increasing lifespan would burden future generations with high costs, and that it would thus be advisable and necessary to develop a family policy that, on the one hand, encourages women to have more children and, on the other, to enter the workforce to supplement social security funds. A new law was created guaranteeing day care and a state-subsidized care allowance (Betreuungsgeld) that enabled mothers and fathers, the latter seldom applied for the allowance, to dedicate themselves to care-work for the first year after the birth of their child. This allowance excluded parents receiving aid money from the state and was thus restricted to well-off parents. The implicit goal of such a "selective pro-natalism" (Schultz 2012: 2) was to encourage predominantly White female academics to have children.

Although this neoliberal demography project was selective in terms of class, it did not yet come with a decidedly racist and anti-immigrant core. Parallel to these measures, immigration programs for qualified experts were launched by the German government – strongly opposed by the Right with the slogan 'Kinder statt Inder' (children instead of people of Indian descent) – that were also intended to solve the demographic 'problem.' The right-wingers were thus able to enter in a discourse that had been pre-conditioned. However, RWP gave the discourse a racist tilt by polarizing so called mass immigration against German children. The poster says: "More Kids instead of mass-migration."

Figure 3: AfD election poster from the Kreisverband Magdeburg

But how will RWP parties encourage 'bio German' fertility? In this context, Katharina Hajek speaks of a program of *New Maternalism*, "which advocates for the presence and participation of women in the political sphere precisely because of their supposed ability to care. In the context of a national-conservative ideology, such a 'caring' through 'strong' femininity is propagated. This may be much more connected to many life experiences than you might think at first glance." (Hajek 2017: 5, author's translation). Consequently, Swedish analysts of RWP speak of female 'Care-Racism' (Sager/Mulinari 2018), which covers racism under the disguise of 'caring for one's own,' meaning militantly protecting the family from 'Others.'[8]

---

8   New Maternalism differs in several essential ways from the Mother Cross ideology of fascism, which awards mothers of many children with achievement medals. The observed New Maternalism does not push women out of the public. RWP seeks to outnumber the fertility of immigrants. It follows an exclusionary paradigm *within* the nation but is not expansive in the sense of delivering future soldiers to 'conquer' other nations. Remnants of this ancient fascist mother ideology could still be found in Jean Marie Le Pen, the father of today's party leader, who was quoted to have said, "We are suffering [...] with regard to women from the demagogy practiced by all [political] parties. It is not easy to say to a woman, 'To protect our

The self-description of a young woman, Heidi Benneckenstein (Benneckenstein 2019), provides insight into the psychological setting of New Maternalism. Benneckenstein grew up in a neo-Nazi family and followed the ideology up to her twenties before she decided to defect to the former enemy, political anti-fascism. Before she had a change of heart, she derogatively characterizes modern 'emancipated' women: "If you take their designer garb and 20,000 Euro kitchens away, they are completely void of any identity [...] while they present their own children like an expensive necklace." (ibid.: 120, author's translation) At the same time, Benneckenstein presented her own project of femininity: "I experienced women who wanted to realize themselves (sich selbst verwirklichen). For me, a real woman was just a mother who was willing to sit back for her children and her family and face a bigger and more important task." (ibid., author's translation)

In these quotes, elements of New Maternalism clearly shine through, motherhood does not necessarily impede political activism. A woman who imagines herself as the facilitator of a larger project of a new (retro-)modernity and can also succeed in the public sphere. The attractiveness of the former *AfD* spokeswoman, Frauke Petry, who was a party spokesperson until the 2016 general election and now has six children, was certainly in part due to her ability to communicate her motherhood with the public. During the Bundesparteitag of the *AfD* 2017, Petry emphasized her pregnancy with a tight tube dress, and election posters showed her tenderly photographed with a newborn on her arm under the slogan: "And what is your reason to fight for Germany?" The aura of motherhood even works beyond ostentatious acts. The RWP Hungarian Prime Minister, Viktor Orbán, explained his decision to elect the German *CDU* politician, Ursula von der Leyen, as President of the European Commission as follows: "We have a German family mother, the mother of seven children at the head of the commission." (N.N. 2019) In other words, being the mother of many children qualifies a woman to be a good politician.

Reformed neo-Nazi Heidi Benneckenstein remembered that she always believed that full-time motherhood should not only be recognized, but also rewarded: "The left-wingers insulted the 'care allowance' as 'Herdprämie' (premium for cooking) or 'Gluckengehalt' (clucking hen salary), but I liked the idea and thought *it was contemporary, indeed modern: a woman who is rewarded for staying home and raising their children*, why not?" (Benneckenstein 2019, 121, my italics, my translation). This 'modern' mother-utopia is now put into practice by the Polish government. In the current "500+" program, each family receives 120 Euros for every second

---

societies and our future, our individual and collective lives, women need to bear children, *to accept that these children will eventually serve and perhaps die to defend the freedom of their native soil*; there is need for an authoritative figure and we believe that the most qualified authority in a household is the man," quoted and translated in Marchand-Lagier, 2018, pp. 50-65.

and subsequent child. In the current 'Mother + program' the state guarantees a pension to every woman who has had at least four children, regardless of whether or not she practiced paid work in her life (Grzebalska/Zacharenko 2018: 84 + 85). Through such measures, *family mainstreaming* policies (Grzebalska/Pető 2018: 4) have replaced gender mainstreaming.

New Maternalism in RWP works only partially as vehicle for the re-traditionalization of the family. It is as well a program designed to promote ethno-nationalist population growth. The objective is to motivate citizens of autochthonous descent to reproduce on a larger scale. If one takes all three components together – emancipation fatigue, sexual exceptionalism, and new maternalism – it becomes obvious why young White women central focus of RWP programming. First, women who already have children feel that they are not only left alone with their burden but also with condescension of 'emancipated' women for their full-time motherhood, resulting in what I call *emancipation fatigue*. This affective pattern results in a new attractiveness of the nuclear family with a sole male breadwinner (which conveniently fits into the worldview of RWP). Second, the superiority narrative of *sexual exceptionalism* positions the progressive, 'free' White woman as a potential victim of backward Muslim men, and the avatars of sexual self-determination. The Muslim 'Others' must be rejected as the endangerment of 'our' freedom and, even better, deported. And third, *new maternalism* promotes ethno-national population growth and awards young White women of reproductive age with a recognition the emancipation dispositive does not deliver.

Concluding Remarks – Agency versus Allegory

The fact that women's bodies play a central role in ethno-nationalist narratives (as reproducers of the 'right' nation) makes politics based on women's and family issues into a central arena for RWP. Young White women have become a strategic hotspot in the RWP discourse because their central political threads focus on women and their bodies: bipolar gender-concepts, anti-Muslim racism, immigration hostility, and the reconstruction of a seemingly benevolent patriarchy. Many women draw affective gain from the rhetoric of being protected from Muslim aggressors and wanting to enjoy motherhood instead of becoming stressed managers of fragmented child-care options.

The presumed recognition of motherhood and care work in the household by most RWP political formations hits a problematic field, which feminists, focused on well-paid professions outside the house, very often fail to see. In this respect, the two Polish authors of the study *Triumph of Women. The Female Face of the Far and Populist Right in Europe* (Gutsche 2018) are partially right to conclude: "It is no longer feasible to ignore the empowering effects of participation in the right-wing project.

In fact, it can be argued that women support for right-wing projects can serve as an alternative model of empowerment and advancement for women who do not find the neoliberal feminist proposal appealing." (Grzebalska/Zacharenko 2018: 89).

However, the fact that the supposed mass support from young White women for RWP was puffed up with fake Twitter accounts in Germany indicates that the RWP model of motherly and caring femininity does not work – at least not yet – the way it is desired. Nonetheless there is a certain attraction for women, which might be gratified via different channels. Therefore, I propose a model of the female investment in RWP as a field of enjoyable tension between agency and allegory. I base the term "allegory" on analyzes from feminist art history: they start with the fact that in Western history, male-dominated achievements and fields of knowledge, such as justice, wisdom, revolution are symbolized by female allegories. Carved in stone, mostly, though not always, half-naked, they adorn parks, squares bridges and buildings. In the allegorical mode, women can represent great achievements of mankind in the shape of monuments, but they cannot take part in or create the mentioned cultural techniques, abilities, movements or nations (Warner 1985; von Falkenhausen 1992).

My thesis is thus that the reference to young White women in RWP is partly allegorical in nature, no longer as monuments, but now as beautifully photographed icons. The *AfD* Facebook support group, 'Frauen für die AfD' (women for *AfD*), assembles the portraits of 181 women on a poster, all but one of childbearing age. Pasted together in one image, they are reduced to their gender, but the poster also importantly allegorizes power. The title says: "We women for the AfD." And then smaller: "So that we and our children can live here safely and well again." Interesting is the 'again' within the slogan, which implies that 'foreigners' have destroyed a formerly safe environment.

***

In this chapter, I have unfolded elements of female discontent taken up by RWP, challenging individualized modes of emancipation promoted by well-off (neo-)liberal feminists (Rottenberg 2014) in three affective arenas, which I call *emancipation fatigue*, *sexual exceptionalism* and *New Maternalism*. In all these arenas, women are given a seemingly (retro-)revolutionary voice. Women supporting RWP ask for a new gender-order that at the same time unburdens, authorizes and cherishes their supposedly 'female' ways of living, caring and loving. The element of allegory comes into play when young White women are set up to embody RWP as the future of humanity. Invested with beauty, pride, and generative glory, their allegorical encroachment by the RWP provides satisfaction. Combining both elements in the language of empowerment simulates an alternative *new* modernity without the stress of the individualized neoliberal but *old* modernity.

Figure 4: Promotion poster of the women's support organization for the AfD

Wir Frauen für die AfD
Damit wir und unsere Kinder hier wieder gut und sicher leben können.

www.facebook.com/FrauenFuerDieAfD

Beyond its surface, however, the mentioned 'modernity' does not include a new feminization of politics that puts women's interests first. As Gayle Rubin expounded as early as 1975: Without challenging the sexual division of labor between men and women, which is the last thing RWP would ever demand, every 'reform' of the gender-order plays into the hands of the patriarchal order. What we do witness in RWP discourse is not a feminization of politics but a politicization of femininity. By conceding to alleged female concerns, right-wing populists take advantage of an imaginary motherly, female self-image in need of protection against foreign threats. Racism and ethno-national demographic politics follow close behind.

Feminist politics of resistance against right-wing populism must grapple with the fact, that a liberal emancipation program, which does not account for class, fails the needs and desires of a great many women leaning to the right. It facilitates the projection of hatred onto feminists as the ones who humiliate and condescend 'good women.' Instead of targeting right-leaning women as allegedly unwilling to 'emancipate,' the political objective should try to disentangle rightful claims in gendered neo-liberal economic regimes from racism, the idea of a benevolent patriarchy and ethno-nationalism. In the study *Ost-Migrantische-Analogien* (Foroutan et al. 2019), migration scholar Naika Foroutan determined that the social and psychological condition of Muslim migrants and East-Germans exhibits some significant parallels.[9] In this respect, intersectional coalition-building with immigrant women sharing similar class positions and plight would be helpful but, at the current historic moment, especially in the German East, hard to realize. It might also be a good time to return to certain goals of early radical feminism such as opposing the sexual division of labor (Rubin 1975) and demanding wages for household chores (Dalla Costa/James 1975). It is clear that the pro-women anti-feminist stance of the RWP (Lang 2018) will continue to gain more support, if contemporary feminism does not fully understand the reasons why it is being attacked and fails to develop compelling strategies to win over sisters from the other side of the aisle.

Bibliography

Benneckenstein, Heidi (2019): Ein Deutsches Mädchen. Mein Leben in einer Neonazi-Familie. Stuttgart: Cotta Tropen.
Bracke, Sarah (2011): "Subjects of Debate. Secular and Sexual Exceptionalism and Muslim Women in the Netherlands." In: Feminist Review 98 (1), pp. 28-46.
Dalla Costa, Mariarosa/James, Selma (1975): The Power of Women and the Subversion of the Community. Bristol: Falling Wall Press.
Dietze, Gabriele (2016): "Das 'Ereignis Köln'." In: Femina Politica 25 (1), pp. 93-102.
Dietze, Gabriele (2018): "Rechtspopulismus und Geschlecht. Paradox und Leitmotiv." In: Femina Politica 27 (1), pp. 34-47.
Dietze, Gabriele (2019): Sexueller Exzeptionalismus. Überlegenheitsnarrative in Immigrationsabwehr und Rechtspopulismus. Bielefeld: transcript.
Foroutan, Naika/Canan, Coşkun/Kalter, Frank et al. (2019): Ost-Migrantische Analogien I. Konkurrenz um Anerkennung. Berlin: DeZim Institut.
Gerster, Livia (2014): Für Hausfrauen gegen Vorstandschefinnen. Online: www.tagesspiegel.de/politik/afd-jugend-gegen-feminismus-fuer-hausfrauen-und-gegen-vorstandschefinnen/9634926.html, 15.07.2019.
Grzebalska, Weronika/Zacharenko, Elena (2018): "Country Case Study Poland." In: Elisa Gutsche (ed.), Triumph of Women. The Female Face of the Populist and Far Right in Europe. Berlin: Friedrich Ebert Stiftung, pp. 82-92.
Grzebalska, Weronika/Pető, Andrea (2018): "The Gendered Modus Operandi of the Illiberal Transformation in Hungary and Poland." In: Women's Studies International Forum 68, pp. 164-172.

---

9   "Both East Germans and Muslim migrants, according to the study, are afraid of descent, social inequality and political alienation. Both are also affected by 'social, cultural and identificative devaluation.' East Germans, for example, are accused as often as Muslims of seeing themselves as victims" (my translation). Online: www.faz.net/aktuell/feuilleton/debatten/eine-studie-zu-ostdeutschen-und-muslimischen-migranten-16126652.html, 01.10.2019.

Gutsche, Elisa (ed.) (2018): Triumph of Women. The Female Face of the Populist and Far Right in Europe. Berlin: Friedrich Ebert Stiftung.

Hajek, Katharina (2017): Die Reproduktionskrise Politisieren. zwischen Neoliberaler Humankapitalreproduktion und rechter Refamiliarisierung. Online: www.zeitschrift-luxemburg.de/die-reproduktionskrise-feministisch-politisieren-zwischen-neoliberaler-humankapitalproduktion-und-rechter-refamilialisierung/, 25.07.2019.

Hochschild, Arlie Russell (2016): Strangers in Their Own Land: Anger and Mourning on the American Right. New York: The New Press.

Jaffe, Sarah (2018): "Why Did a Majority of White Women Vote for Trump?" In: New Labor Forum 27 (1), pp. 18-26.

Kelle, Birgit (2013): Dann Mach doch die Bluse zu! Ein Aufschrei gegen den Gleichheitswahn. Asslar: Adeo Verlag.

Kemper, Andreas (2014a): Keimzelle der Nation? Familien- und Geschlechterpolitische Positionen der AfD - Eine Expertise. Berlin: Friedrich Ebert Stiftung.

Kemper, Andreas (2014b): Keimzelle der Nation–Teil 2. Wie Sich in Europa Parteien und Bewegungen gegen Toleranz, Vielfalt und eine Progressive Geschlechter- und Familienpolitik Radikalisieren. Berlin: Friedrich Ebert Stiftung.

Küpper, Beate (2018): "Das Thema Gender im Rechtspopulismus. Empirische Befunde zur Anschlussfähigkeit bei Frauen und Männern." In: Femina Politica 27 (1), pp. 61-75.

Küpper, Beate/Heitmeyer, Wilhelm (2005): "Feindselige Frauen. zwischen Angst, Zugehörigkeit und Durchsetzungsideologie." In: Wilhelm Heitmeyer (ed.): Deutsche Zustände 3. Berlin: Suhrkamp, pp. 108-127.

Lang, Juliane (2018): Feminismus von rechts. Neue Rechte Politiken zwischen Forderung nach Frauenrechten und Offenem Antifeminismus. Online: dekonstrukt.org/impulse-3-feminismus-von-rechts-erschienen, 10.03.2019.

Lipset, Seymour Martin (1997): American Exceptionalism. A Double-Edged Sword. New York: Norton & Company.

Marchand-Lagier, Christelle (2018): "Country Case Study France." In: Gutsche (2018): ibid., pp. 50-65.

Mayer, Nonna (2015): "The Closing of the Radical Right Gender Gap in France?" In: French Politics 13 (4), pp. 391-414.

McRobbie, Angela (2009): The Aftermath of Feminism. Gender, Culture and Social Change. London: Sage.

Meret, Susi/Siim, Birte/Pingaud, Etienne (2016): "Men's Parties with Women Leaders: A Comparative Study of the Right-Wing Populist Leaders Pia Kjærsgaard, Marine Le Pen and Siv Jensen." In: Gabriella Lazarides/Giovanna Campani (eds.), Understanding the Populist Shift. London: Taylor and Francis, pp. 122-149.

Molyneux, Maxine (1985): Mobilization Without Emancipation? Women's Interests, the State, and Revolution in Nicaragua. Ann Arbor: Michigan Library.

N.N. (2019): Sieg oder Schuss ins Knie. Orban und Co feiern von der Leyen. Online: www.zeit.de/news/2019-07/10/sieg-oder-schuss-ins-knie-orban-und-co-feiern-von-der-leyen, 27.07.2019.

Norocel, Ov Cristian (2010): Constructing Radical Right Populist Resistance: Metaphors of Heterosexist Masculinities and the Family Question in Sweden. In: Norma 5 (2), pp. 170-183.

OED (2004): Oxford English Dictionary. Oxford: Oxford University Press.

Puar, Jasbir (2011): "Abu Ghraib and U.S. Sexual Exceptionalism." In: Works and Days 29 pp. 115-142.

Reisigl, Martin (2016): Kalkulierte Ambivalenz in der Politischen Kommunikation: Politolinguistische und Argumentationstheoretische Betrachtungen. Conference Paper in AG Sprache und Politik, Graz 28th till March 1st, 2019.

Rottenberg, Catherine (2014): "The Rise of Neoliberal Feminism." In: Cultural Studies 28 (3), pp. 418-437.

Rubin, Gayle (1975): "The Traffic in Women. Notes on the 'Politial Economy' of Sex." In: Rayna R. Reiter (ed.), Toward an Anthropology of Women. New York: Monthly Review Press, pp. 157-210.

Sager, Maja/Mulinari, Diana (2018): "Safety for Whom? Exploring Femonationalism and Care-Racism in Sweden." In: Women's Studies International Forum 68, pp. 149-156.

Samtleben, Claire (2019): "Auch an erwerbsfreien Tagen erledigen Frauen einen Großteil der Hausarbeit und Kinderbetreuung." In: DIW-Wochenbericht 86 (10), pp. 139-144.

Schultz, Susanne (2012): Demographischer Sachzwang und Politisiertes Gebären. Online: www.zeitschrift-luxemburg.de/demografischer-sachzwang-und-politisiertes-gebaeren/, 25.07.2019.

Sigl, Johanna (2018): "Identitäre Zweigeschlechtlichkeit. Über Männliche Inszenierungen und Geschlechterkonstruktionen bei den Identitären." In: Andreas Speit (ed.), Das Netzwerk der Identitären. Berlin: Links Verlag, pp. 160-172.

Spierings, Niels/Zaslove, Andrej (2015): "Conclusion: Dividing the Populist Radical Right Between 'Liberal Nativism' and Traditional Conceptions of Gender." In: Patterns of Prejudice 49 (1-2), pp. 163-173.

von Falkenhausen, Susanne (1992): "Das Geschlecht der Allegorien. Tagung am Kulturwissenschaftlichen Institut des Wissenschaftszentrums Nordrhein-Westfalen, Essen, 5.8. 12.1991." In: Kritische Berichte – Zeitschrift für Kunst- und Kulturwissenschaften 20 (4), pp. 122-126.

Warner, Marina (1985): Monuments and Maidens. The Allegory of the Female Form. New York: Doubleday.

Wippermann, Carsten (2016): Was Junge Frauen wollen. Lebensrealitäten und Familien- und Gleichstellungerwartungen von Frauen zwischen 18 und 40 Jahren. Berlin: Friedrich Ebert Stiftung.

Zick, Andreas/Küpper, Beate/Berghan, Wilhelm (2019): Verlorene Mitte – Feindselige Zustände. Rechtsextreme Einstellungen in Deutschland 2018/19. Berlin: Dietz Verlag.

Populist Mobilizations in Re-Traditionalized Society: Anti-Gender Campaigning in Slovenia

Roman Kuhar, Mojca Pajnik

Introduction: Populism Deforming Democracy

Despite the intentions of the EU to "unite in diversity," EU member states have increasingly fostered an atmosphere of hostility towards minorities, and increasingly embrace particular policies and acts of exclusion. These trends have been both exploited and reinforced by far right and populist forces in the context of the so-called post-democratic and post-truth society. The results of the European elections (2014), voting expectations in 2019, and the electoral campaigns at national levels across Europe have been marked by the rise of political parties that increasingly play on nativist stereotypes by claiming that "our nation" is threatened by minorities (Mudde 2014) and so-called "gender ideology" (Pajnik et al. 2016; Kuhar/Paternotte 2017). This exclusionary populist political communication seems to have been consolidated as "pathological normalcy" across Europe and globally (Mudde 2004).

As we have previously shown (Pajnik et al. 2016; Pajnik/Sauer 2017), contemporary societies have been marked by the rise of a distinct type of "populist political communication" that distrusts the principles of diversity and equality, and has shown to "spill over" when the political messages resonate in the media, which then often often uncritically reproduces these messages (Pfetsch et al. 2014: 12). The impact of these trends is visible in public opinion, which is formed under the influence of political and media discourses. In re-creating "we" versus "the Other" antagonisms, these discourses reproduce and transmit sexism, racism, and xenophobia.

Populism, understood as anything ranging from an expression of ideology (Mudde 2004) to a political style (Moffitt/Tormey 2014), is a contested concept known for its solubility. In countries of the former Soviet Union and Central-Eastern Europe, populism once referred to peasants' reforms and rebellion against absolutist power. It was initially central to radical democracy as a "rule of the people" (Campani/Pajnik 2017). With regards to contemporary European contexts, however, a growing strand of literature grasps populism as a "thin-centered ideology" (Canovan 1982; Mudde 2004: 544) that is exemplified by political parties that view society as divided into two antagonistic groups: "the pure people" and "the corrupt elite." Hence, the core elements of populism are "people-centrism" and "anti-elitism" (Mudde 2004: 543), which are manifested in the idea that "real" politics, unlike the "corrupt elites," should express the will of "the people" – i.e. "the common man" and his "common sense." "The people," a contested concept, relies on a construction of "the Other" – i.e. on those excluded from the dominant construction of "the we." Inclusion in and exclusion from "the people" is naturalized in populist communication; something transcendent lies in "the people" so that it is believed to be *above* differences based on class, gender, ethnicity, sexuality, etc. Populist communication ignores these differences by creating a hegemonic discourse of "the people," allegedly homogenous, who should be protected from "the outsiders."

Several scholars have suggested that dismissing populism as simply undemocratic might work to strengthen the elites by turning them into socially condoned gate-keepers who assert control over what constitutes "the truth" (Müller 2016). Grasping populism as inclusionary and decoupled from nationalism, one recent study introduced the notion of "transnational populism" (Moffitt 2017), defined through its capacity to reclaim popular sovereignty and overcome the post-democratic condition (Gerbaudo/Screti 2017). In light of the rise of exclusionary populist parties and movements, and given recent election trends in Europe, we and others have problematized populism as a variation of ethno-nationalism that is often, though not necessarily, coupled with "anti-genderism" as a facilitator of the on-going process of democratic erosion (Pajnik et al. 2016; Campani/Pajnik 2017; Pajnik/Sauer 2017). Analyzing populist communications in Europe, we have further argued that what we are witnessing is not the metamorphosis of democracy but rather an "anamorphosis," fueled by populism, of a "deformed democracy" (Campani/Pajnik 2017: 181).

Populism is neither homogeneous nor coherent (Katsambekis/Stavrakakis 2013: 2). Separating "the people" from the corrupt elites, it is often coupled with other "thicker" ideologies (such as nationalism or nativism), and includes a political style or discourse characterized by polarization, simplification and falsification (Moffitt/Tormey 2014). Not an isolated feature of a particular part of the political field, populism can be found across the political spectrum. We have analyzed "populism in the normal" (Pajnik/Sauer 2017: 2), stressing that populism develops across party families, and populist discourses and practices are essential elements of mediatized party politics *en masse*.

Even if we are living in "a populist Zeitgeist," with populism becoming mainstream (Mudde 2004), there are differences between parties and extra-parliamentary actors with regards to how populism is being exhibited. If, at least generally, the aim of a left-wing political strategy is to strengthen the responsible popular-democratic pole that opts for respect of diversity (Stavrakakis 2014: 514), the "people" of extreme right populism is exclusionary along the lines of ethnic, racial, sexual, and gender divides, reflecting the abandonment of equality as one of the core principles of democracy. Indeed, recent research has shown that "left populism" is more concerned with developing communicative strategies that address socio-economic differences, while populism of the extreme right is largely mobilized by creating outcast groups that allegedly represent a threat to "the majority," constructed as "the pure people." Empirical findings show that right-wing populism is primarily exclusionary, focusing on ethnic identity in constructing "the people", and it operates closely with a particular collection of ideologies, such as nationalism and nativism. In contrast, leftist populism has been found to be more inclusive, lacking the nativist component and abiding by more egalitarian ideas (March 2017).

In this chapter, we adopt "the ideational approach" to populism (Mudde 2004; Hawkins/Rovira Kaltwasser 2017), not in contrast – as is most common – but rather *in dialogue* with acknowledging ideological expressions through discourse. Indeed, populist ideology manifests itself through discourse. In analyzing anti-gender campaigning in Slovenia, we tackle a particular manifestation of populism – i.e. by right-wing actors who exercise a form of populism that is tied to nationalism. This, however, is not to say that anti-gender campaigning can be reduced only to nationalism. Anti-gender networks are made up of very diverse actors, whose ideological backgrounds vary and are at times in opposition (cf. Kuhar/Paternotte 2017).

Brubaker (2017) defines "national populism" as the polarized opposition between us and them. Our focus in this chapter is on "ethno-national populism," an ideologically thin variation of populism that stretches to ethno-nationalist and nativist ideologies. It targets, among other issues, "proper" gender roles, which are largely considered biologically given, ahistorical and vital for the continuation of the nation (Pajnik et al. 2016). Ethno-nationalist populist communication that centers gender roles and a "pure", "genuine" or "primordial" majority in imaginings of the nation and its people relies on what Judith Butler describes as a "heterosexual matrix" (1990), thereby reproducing the common-sense essentialist conceptualizations of what is, and is not, natural and normal. As we will show, for the populist right, gender is most often understood as a natural and biological category: male and female genders are perceived to be naturally compatible and determined by biological differences between men and women. Although the populist extreme right in Europe varies in its specificities from country to country, and we should be cautious not to merge all of these developments into one unqualified backlash (Paternotte/Kuhar 2018), ideologies of gender and sexuality appear to be a *fil rouge* of these political parties and their crossovers with anti-gender campaigns: extreme right-wing activism is visibly mobilized against marriage equality, reproductive rights and abortion, sex education in schools, and other issues similarly related to gender equality and sexual citizenship (Kuhar/Paternotte 2017).

This chapter documents the emergence and the development of the anti-gender movement in Slovenia from its "grass-roots" beginnings in 2009 to its announced entrance into party politics in 2015.[1] As the movement is part of a broader transnational anti-gender movement (Kuhar/Paternotte 2017), in which "genderism" has replaced "feminism" in right-wing rhetoric (Korolczuk/Graff 2018: 799), the chapter examines its national specificities and, in particular, its connections to the Slovene Roman Catholic Church and right-wing political forces. Together, these analyzes work to detect the functioning of what we call "patterns of populism." Grasping populism as an ideology and a style, our analysis shows both how anti-gender campaigning expresses a) people-centrism, b) anti-elitism and c) Othering as key features of populism. In addition, we analyze how populist ideas are communicated – i.e. how they are constructed in the discourses of actors of anti-gender campaigns in Slovenia.

The first part of this chapter analyzes engagements of anti-gender activists around two referendums against marriage equality in Slovenia. Applying content analysis to publications from the anti-gender movement's website *24kul.si* between November 2013 and November 2015, we critically assess key events of the movement, and the discourses and strategies of anti-gender actors. In particular, we focus on texts from the website's special section (a tab) on "gender theory," which features news about anti-gender movements in Slovenia and abroad, everyday accounts of the allegedly horrifying consequences of "gender ideology," most frequently on children and their parents, explanatory texts (imitating scientific discourse) on what gender theory is, and some excerpts from public speeches of anti-gender actors in the parliament during referendum campaigns against marriage equality in Slovenia. Generally, in their attempts to prevent what they call "gender theory" from becoming "the official ideology of the state," we show that these texts are based on populist strategies of people-centrism and Othering.

We also analyze how populist discourses and the communicative strategies of anti-gender campaigners mobilize fear and have provoked what Cohen has called a "moral panic." Indeed, the trajectory of the movement's activities exemplify Cohen's five key stages in constructing a moral panic: 1) a group is defined as a threat to social norms or community interests, 2) the threat is then depicted in a simple and recognizable symbol or form in the public (especially by the media), 3) depictions of this symbol rouse public concern, 4) authorities and policy makers respond, and 5) a moral panic provokes social changes in the community. Lastly, we explore correlations between re-domestification trends in Slovenia and the shifting role of the Roman Catholic Church in promoting the "apocalyptic threat" of so-called "gender theory."

---

1   Some parts of this text have previously appeared elsewhere (Kuhar 2015, 2017), and are here contextualized anew from the lens of populism research.

1. Populism of the Anti-Gender Network: People-Centrism and Othering

The late nineties and the first decade of the new millennium were marked by noticeable advancements in LGBT rights and gender equality in many European countries. Although these initiatives have all been met with opposition, certain European countries have faced remarkably massive counter-mobilizations since 2010. Common to these mobilizations was the propagation of feelings of threat about on alleged hidden plan called "gender theory" or "gender ideology." Gender theory as a new buzzword gained significant public attention around 2012, particularly during the protests by the *Manif pour tous* against marriage equality in France. However, this was not a uniquely French phenomenon as protests using similar rhetoric and tactics had already occurred in Western-Southern Europe (particularly in Italy and Spain) and Eastern Europe (in Croatia, Poland, Slovenia, and Slovakia).

The 2012 demonstrations denounced "gender" as the ideological foundation linking their targets of protest – marriage equality, the reproductive rights of women, and sexual education in schools. "Gender" became a conspiracy theory allegedly conceived by radical feminists and LGBT activists to destroy the silent (or even silenced) majority, society's "natural families," "natural gender roles" and the world as we know it (Kováts/Põim 2015; Kuhar/Paternotte 2017). We argue that these protests were mobilized through a distinct imagining of "the people," thereby demonstrating how exclusionary "people-centrism" is a core feature of populist mobilizations (Mudde 2004).

1.1 Gender Theory and the Whole(y) Family

Gender theory became a household issue in Slovenia during the public debates on marriage equality. It emerged as a signifier for the perceived devastating consequences if same-sex partners were allowed to marry and adopt children. Most impacted were believed to be "innocent children," but also "our nation" and the "natural order of things."

A new Family Code, introduced by the left-wing government in 2009, ultimately triggered the emergence of an anti-gender movement. While the Family Code introduced several innovations, only two attracted the attention of anti-gender activists. First, was a new inclusive notion of the family as a union of at least two generations. In other words, a family would be understood as a union of adults and children defined by either biological or social parenting, regardless of the gender of the parents or guardians. The second innovation that became a bone of contestation for anti-gender activists was the introduction of marriage equality – i.e. equal legal footing for both same-sex and opposite-sex unions, including the right to adopt. Protests of the so-called "concerned citizens" that mobilized against the Family Code soon revealed links to the transnational anti-gender movement.

Despite these protests, the new Family Code (in a slightly modified version, see Kuhar/Mencin Čeplak 2016) was adopted in the Slovenian parliament in 2011, but was then rejected in a 2012 public referendum. According to the Slovenian legislature, a referendum must take place if requested by at least 40.000 voters. The referendum was initiated in close cooperation with the Roman Catholic Church and the *Civil Initiative for the Family and the Rights of Children* (Civilna iniciativa za družino in pravice otrok, *CIFRC*), a newly established anti-gender group of "concerned citizens." It was during this referendum campaign that the emerging anti-gender movement experienced a first jolt of *momentum*.

A few years later, in 2015, the Slovenian government adopted amendments to the *Marriage and Family Relations Act*, which again harmonized the rights of heterosexual and same-sex partnerships, thereby introducing marriage equality into Slovenian legislation. Yet again, as requested by over 80,000 voters, the legislation was then put to a public referendum in 2015 (Kuhar/Mencin Čeplak 2016). Enabled through signatures collected by anti-gender activists, the referendum provided the anti-gender movement with another opportunity to establish itself as a relevant political actor. With much support from the Roman Catholic Church, the same group of "concerned citizens" – this time re-named *Children are at Stake* (Za otroke gre, *CAAS*) – initiated another public referendum, a typically populist instrument used to overcome the power of "the elites" and to ensure respect for the will of "the people" (Mudde 2004: 559). The majority of the electorate voted against marriage equality, and the amendments to the *Marriage and Family Relations Act* were rejected. Once the results were made public, the leader of the anti-gender movement immediately announced its entrance into party politics.

Both initiatives targeted "concerned parents" and, in 2015, also grandparents, who represented a vast pool of voters thought to likely oppose marriage equality. Unlike *CIFRC*, which began to refer to gender theory only at the end of the 2012 public debates (on the Family Code), *CAAS*' references to it emerged at the beginning of campaign and are clearer and more determined. The co-leader of the campaign, Metka Zevnik, explained at the very beginning of the campaign that "gender theory is (just a) theory. Natural sciences do not acknowledge theories that have not been confirmed. However, it has been confirmed by thousands of generations that a child can arise only from a husband and a wife."[2] Similarly, the founding document of the *CAAS*, the "Declaration for the Rights of Children, Parents and Grandparents," stated, firstly, that they aim to prevent the discrimination of those who believe that "a natural female and male sex exist" – thereby revealing the Catholic roots of the

---

2   Debevec, Marjana. 2015. Ustanovljena koalicija "Za otroke gre" (The coalition "Children Are At Stake" established), radio.ognjisce.si/sl/163/slovenija/16400/, 14.04. 2019.

anti-gender movement (Case 2019) – and that, secondly, it is in the best interest of children "to have a mother and a father." Hence, relying on the image of "the whole(y) family" that Rooduijn and Pauwels (2011: 1273) have termed the "pro-toto" imaginary, people-centrism reveals itself here as a central pillar of populism. An additional goal of the *CAAS*, as listed in this document, is to insert a definition of matrimony into the Slovenian constitution as a union between "one wife and one husband."[3]

The anti-gender movement in Slovenia at first appeared to be a secular initiative of "concerned citizens." However, it quickly became evident that there has been close cooperation between anti-gender actors and the Church. In fact, it was ultimately determined that several anti-gender activists were also satellite organizations of the Church. The populist roots of what is now known as Slovenia's anti-gender movement can be traced back to 2002, when the Slovenian Roman Catholic Church issued a comprehensive plan of action, entitled "Choose Life." This more than 120-page final document of the "Plenary Assembly of the Church in Slovenia" opted for a "new evangelization" in the 21st century. In her critical analysis of the document, Jogan (2008) explained that "new evangelization" is in fact a continuation of the "re-catholization" of Slovenian society, which is based on the idea that the failures of socialism must be corrected and that public life should be re-aligned with the morality of the Church. Women were among its main targets. Their economic independence and increasing social equality, which have been fostered by the socialist establishment's "state feminism" and its continuations in EU gender mainstreaming policies, present fundamental problems to the Church as they are thought to counter the "natural role" of women.

Since the adoption of this document (and even before), the Roman Catholic Church in Slovenia has been faced with an increasingly secularized society. In addition, their public image has been compromised due to several financial and sexual scandals. The goals and values of the Church were promoted by what initially looked like a grass-roots movement of concerned citizens, but which was later unmasked as a satellite organization of the Church.

1.2 Anti-Gender Actors' Networking

The leading figure of *CAAS*, Metka Zevnik, has referenced her role as grandparent of six and mother of three to explain her political engagements. The leading spokesperson of the *CIFRC*, Aleš Primc, has a long history of campaigning against

---

3   24kul.si. 2015. "Za otroke gre!" Deklaracija za pravice otrok, staršev in starih staršev! ("Children Are At Stake!" A declaration for the rights of children, parents and grandparents!), 24kul.si/preberite-za-otroke-gre-deklaracija-za-pravice-otrok-starsev-in-sta-rih-star-sev, 14.04.2019.

women's rights: In 2001, he actively participated in a referendum campaign against the availability of in vitro fertilization for single women (Hrženjak 2001); although he failed to collect enough signatures for a referendum, he also opposed efforts to decriminalize prostitution (Pajnik 2003). Like Zevnik, Primc presents himself as a concerned parent. The same is true for Tomaž Merše, father of five and president of the *Family initiative* (Družinska pobuda); Vesna Vilčnik, a journalist who regularly bemoans that she was raised in a single-parent family, claims to know from her own experiences that a child needs a mother and a father. She is the president of *Plum* (Češplja – a derogatory term for a female sexual organ), whose goal is to raise awareness of "sexual energy and healthy sexuality." Primc, Zevnik, Merše and Vilčnik were the main actors in opposing marriage equality at both the 2012 and 2015 referendums. In both instances, they worked closely with the Roman Catholic Church, and especially with the Franciscan father, Tadej Strehovec, who is secretary general of the Slovenian Bishops' Conference, a teaching assistant of Moral Theology and Applied Ethics at the Faculty of Theology, and the Church's leading anti-gender agent (see picture 1). Propagating a professional secularized image rather than visually aligning himself with the Church, he rarely appeared in public wearing clerical clothing. This corresponded with his primarily secularized discourse in media and parliamentary discussions. As has been observed by Korolczuk (2014) in Poland, populist actors often deliberately rely on misinformation and emotional, hyperbolic language to mobilize support.

Strehovec, from the Roman Catholic Church, is also the director of *KUL.si* (literal translation: You are cool), the *Institute for Family and the Culture of Living*, which was established soon after the government publicly announced the new Family Code. The institute's website functioned as the official website of *CIFRC*, and later of *CAAS*[4], and has proven a powerful tool for promoting anti-genderism and mobilizing support. The domain *KUL.si* exemplifies how the internet in general, and specifically social media, is becoming an important platform for populist efforts to turn ordinary people against the liberal establishment. The online "filter-bubbles effect" easily strengthens people's sense of commitment to a populist cause (Gerbaudo 2018).

On their website, we can see that the main goal of the institute is to "promote fundamental values: human life, human rights, family, solidarity, democracy, freedom and active citizenship." Such a framing closely resonates vwith anti-gender initiatives globally, which tend to focus on protecting human rights, particularly those of children. Recent research on populism (Brubaker 2017: 1209-1211) suggests

---

4 Although Strehovec claims that the *Institute 24kul* is his private initiative and is not connected to the Roman Catholic Church, it is located at the same address as one of Ljubljana's parishes, and its website was initially hosted on the official server of the Slovenian Roman Catholic Church.

Figure 1: The anti-gender network in Slovenia, initiated and supported by the Roman Catholic Church but largely implemented by satellite organizations

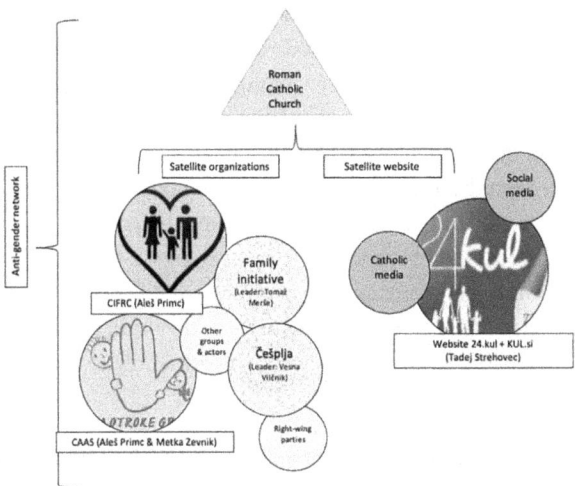

that populist leaders today are opposed to minority rights, while also framing their movement as supportive of democracy and human rights. The Institute's programmatic orientation mirrors this trend, thus further conveying populism as a thin-centered ideology that pragmatically stretches and bends in their appeals to "the people."

In public debates, gender theory was most commonly explained as a theory promoting the idea that one can freely choose and change one's own *"spol"* (i.e. gender), even "several times a day."[5] Faced with the common sense (i.e. essentialist) understanding of sex as a biological category, such a framing creates the desired populist effect: aversion. We can observe the reproduction of people-centrism mainly through references to children – i.e. claims that "our children" and their natural "gender roles," and, as a consequence, "what it means to be a man and a woman" in our society, are in danger. The focus on "our innocent children" is not specifically Slovene; such an approach is a strategy used in anti-gender campaigns all over Europe (Korolczuk 2014; Szelewa 2014; Kováts/Põim 2015; Kuhar/Paternotte 2017).

---

5 24kul.si. 2014. Zahtevajte, da poslanci ne ratificirajo kontroverzne Istambulske konvencije! (Demand that MPs do not ratify the controversial Istanbul Convention!), 24kul.si/zahtevajte-da-poslanci-ne-ratificirajo-kontroverzne-istambulske-konvencije, 14.04. 2019.

According to anti-gender activists, the enemies of children's well-being today are those who try to impose "gender theory" on "unsuspecting residents of Slovenia."[6] These are the features of what anti-genderists call "gender theory advocates," who are othered as an "out group" through venues like *24kul.si*, a website of the anti-gender movement in Slovenia, using typical populist claims, including that: (1) they are social elites and paid through the state budget; (2) they often use words such as human rights, equality, non-violence and tolerance; (3) they deny the existence of natural male and female genders and encourage people to change their genders; (4) they demand the right to same-sex marriage, artificial insemination for lesbians, and the adoption of children for same-sex couples; (5) they introduce gender theory into schools secretly, or against the will of parents, and encourage students to experiment with gender and sexual orientation; (6) they are often christianophobes who aim to change the cultural and religious meanings of gender, family and marriage; (7) they want to persecute anyone who dares to defend the right of a child to have a mother and a father; (8) in media outlets, they ridicule defenders of marriage; and (9) they threaten companies who support family organizations.

2. Fear and Panic: Populist Construction of the People vs the Elite

Reflecting wider European and global trends, the actions of anti-gender actors in Slovenia reproduce the same pattern of right-wing populist mobilizations by centering around the two core themes of populism: "people-centrism" and "Othering" (Mudde 2004; Brubaker 2017).

Protagonists of the anti-gender movement claim that "our children," and consequently "we" as a nation (the in-group), are endangered by homosexuals (the out-group) who will adopt "our children" and take over "our institutions" (i.e. the family and marriage). Stressing the virtues of "our people" and "our values" includes an inherent "Othering" – i.e. presenting the "homosexual elite," the rootless cosmopolitans who care for their own rights but are indifferent to struggles of the ethnic people, as the "source of evil." Such forms of mobilization correspond with the definitions of nationalist or ethno-nationalist populism that are built on the polarized opposition between people like "us" and "them", the outsiders who are believed to threaten our lives (Brubaker 2017: 1192).

We also found that the pairing of "people-centrism," "anti-elitism" and "Othering" in anti-gender mobilization relies on a sort of "common sense." Indeed, rather than trying to reform people or change their values, populist actors appeal to one's conscience (Mudde 2004). For populists, "common sense" is a form of politics that

---

6   24kul.si. 2016. Kako prepoznamo teorijo spola (How to recognize Gender Theory?), 24kul.si/kako-prepoznamo-teorijo-spola, 14.04. 2019.

addresses people's actual needs (Mudde 2004: 547). To address the fears of "the common man," the homosexual and leftist "elites" must thus be portrayed as corrupt, self-serving and indifferent to the real problems of the people. In the next section, we show how populism's core features, as presented above (people-centrism and Othering), function to activate fear and moral panic.

While the term "gender theory" did not exist at the start of the 2009 Family Code debates, the discursive structure it came to represent was already present: the *CIFRC*'s (and, in 2015, the *CAAS*'s) opposition to marriage equality centered around homosexuality as a threat to "our children," "our families" and "our nation." In short, it relied on a culture of fear. The anti-gender movement is based on the fundamental belief that marriage and gender equality are being imposed by elites onto hard-working and unsuspecting people (i.e. "us"). Precisely this belief provoked the use of the term "gender theory," which sounds as though it emerged from the ivory towers of universities and within the higher echelons of (trans)national political structures (i.e. elites). As such, its proponents are perceived to be detached from the "ordinary people" upon whom they nonetheless work to impose their ideology (cf. Pető 2015). Primc, for example, stated:

> As long as their (the proponents of marriage equality) scientific activists forge their own theories in which they may even ultimately start to believe, there is no problem. I have heard the occasional good joke about the absurdity of such "scientific sociological and psychological achievements." However, when they start to burden children in schools with this ideology, the joke is over. If children in puberty, when they begin to search for their own identity, are persuaded by activists in schools that there are no male and female genders, that they have to choose their own gender, that they should experiment with their sexual orientation, the consequences can be very painful, primarily for children, but also for whole families.[7]

Similar to other European anti-gender movements, anti-gender actors in Slovenia widely rely on images to appeal to the people. While they use the silhouette of a "normal family" as their visual trademark, they do not use the same pink and blue color palette as has been common to rallies against marriage equality in France (*Manif pour tous*), and later also in Croatia (*U ime obitelji*), Slovakia (*Aliancia za rodinu*) and elsewhere. Indeed, the Slovenian anti-gender movement emerged before the breakthrough of the French protests against *"mariage pour tous"* in 2012 and 2013, which might be why the family is colored yellow in Slovenia, quite similar to the

---

7   24kul.si. 2012. Politiki bodo razumeli sporočilo referendumua (Politicians will understand the message of the referendum), www.24kul.net/j/24kulsi-predstavitev/civilna-iniciativa/izjave-civilne-iniciative/117-ales-primc-politiki-bodo-razumeli-sporocilo-referenduma, 05.10.2013.

American (Mormon) campaign in California in favor of Proposition 8.[8] This color choice may have been arbitrary, but some of the materials – especially quasi-scientific interpretations of psychological and sociological studies on homosexuality and same-sex families – were used in both the American and Slovenian campaigns (Kuhar 2015). The Slovenian anti-gender movement retained the now recognizable yellow color in their latest campaign, "Children are at Stake," but they changed the silhouette into a boy and a girl, hidden behind a hand, meant to symbolize their efforts to stop gender theory and its devastating effects on children (see picture 1 above).

By juxtaposing the imagery of innocent children with stereotypically sexualized representations of allegedly hedonistic homosexuals and decorating this juxtaposition with several carefully selected results from different scientific studies on homosexuality, the movement effectively created a moral panic (Cohen 1972/2002; Kuhar 2015). Echoing claims that gender theory is targeting the innocence of children, the panic was fueled by insisting that homosexuals are imposing their excessive sexuality onto children, thereby prematurely ending their childhood. While the leading figures of the anti-gender movement never explicitly claimed that homosexuals would sexually abuse the children of the movement, this was their implicit message. It may have been even more effective because it was unspoken in that the implicit hints to (physical/verbal/symbolic) sexual abuse of the child triggered the "politically non-correct" (and, as such, unspeakable) imagery of unnatural and deviant homosexuals. In other words, the anti-gender populist discursive strategy lies precisely in the fact that their hints are always masked by the seemingly rational, supposedly scientific, arguments, which are strategically developed to evoke the emotions and power drawn from existing prejudices. In this way, anti-gender actors adopted a populist political style (Moffitt/Tormey 2014) of performative emotionalization by constructing distinct vocabularies of fear, urgency and severity (Fineman 2008).

In the zero-sum logic typical of populist discourse, the more homosexuality (and, by virtue, "gender ideology" as an empty signifier for anything, from gender studies to sexual education, to reproductive rights) is presented as normal, the more children, traditional families and the nation are threatened and under attack. It is therefore not surprising that the anti-gender movement started their referendum campaign by singing the Slovenian national anthem together with a group of like-minded people dressed in Slovenian national garb. [9] Appropriating

---

8   Proposition 8 was initiated by the opponents of same-sex marriage in California in 2008, with the Mormon church playing a leading role in its promotion. The proposition to ban same-sex marriage was initially confirmed, but later (in 2010) ruled unconstitutional by a federal court.
9   Srdič, Urša. 2011. V iniciativi pohiteli z zbiranjem podpisov. TV Slovenija, TV Dnevnik, 1. September 2011, www.rtvslo.si/slovenija/prvi-dan-zbranih-vec-kot-10-000-podpisov-za-referendum-o-druzinskem-zakoniku/265276, 20.01.2015.

the nationalistic sob songs about a "small Slovenian nation" facing a "demographic winter," they succeeded in constructing "the homosexual" as the Other *within* the nation, but also as the Other *against* the nation. Precisely this dual Othering was evoked when the CIFRC stressed that we need to protect our families and children if we want to survive "as a nation, society, culture and civilization."[10]

During both referendums, a coalition of primarily LGBTQ activists, feminists and some politicians emerged to oppose the increasingly successful and influential anti-gender movement. While they have succeeded in debunking certain anti-gender activists' claims, they were generally unsuccessful in providing an effective opposition to their populist rhetoric. Furthermore, the coalition fell apart immediately after the referendum when the members returned to their specific fields of interest and work. In many ways, this opposition to the anti-gender attack was far from what the anti-gender activists had imagined and portrayed: a strong and unified front, collectively fighting for gender equality and LGBT rights. In that sense, Case (2019: 659-660) is quite right in suggesting, "we should simultaneously both seek to emulate our opponents' newly unified front and, more profoundly, to be what they fear we are."

3. Strategies of Anti-Gender Mobilization

The anti-gender movement in Slovenia has applied different communication strategies using various channels to spread their populist messages, including online petitions, chain e-mails, round-table debates, public rallies and Family Day (as an antidote to Pride Parade), active participation at parliamentary readings of bills, and social media and the internet. These streams of communication have been further used to raise funds, sell merchandise and publish scandalous stories about the horrible effects of gender theory (mostly from the USA). They also used their website to collect signatures from persons opposing the Family Code. Although they had no formal legal impact, the hundreds of pages of signatures were put on display every time the leader of the campaign was given a chance to speak publicly. One thus sees similarities with Postill's (2018: 761-762) thesis that populist actors employ "hybrid media systems" ranging from telecommunication networks to public spaces, such as churches, to maximize the influence of their messages.

---

10 Magnetogram "Javna predstavitev mnenj o predlogu Družinskega zakonika", Odbor Državnega zbora Republike Slovenije za delo, družino, socialne zadeve in invalide (Magnetogram "Public Presentation of Opinions on the Proposal of the Family Code", Committee of the National Assembly of the Republic of Slovenia for Labour, Family, Social Affairs and Disabled people"), 12.10.2009.

In close collaboration with the Roman Catholic Church, anti-gender movement announcements are regularly transmitted during Sunday masses and are made available on the websites of local parishes across the country. Public lectures on gender theory are also organized in churches; Primc gave a speech at the annual Catholic pilgrimage to Brezje in 2011. As part of the movement's efforts to collect the necessitated 40.000 signatures to provoke a public referendum on marriage equality, priests were instructed to organize transport services (private cars or buses) to municipality offices for their flocks. Strehovec sent out a letter to all priests in Slovenia with instructions to invite people during the Sunday mass to sign in support of the referendum and to refer others to the *KUL.si* website for detailed information on how to submit their signatures as well.[11]

Inspired by the initiatives of other anti-gender movements, such as when the online platform CitizensGO and the European Dignity Watch sent thousands of e-mails with misinformation about the Estrela and Lunacek reports to European parliamentary representatives (see Hodžić/Bijelić 2014; Datta 2018), the *CIFRC* has also used chain emails to spread their messages among "unsuspecting citizens," and it has e-bombarded politicians, scientists and other public figures who spoke publicly in favor of the Family Code. Sending hundreds of identical e-mails per hour, this tactic at times led to mailboxes becoming total blocked. A typical e-mail featured a description of what they believe to be a homosexual lifestyle, an explanation about why "our children" are endangered, and a request to forward the e-mail to all of the recipient's personal contacts.

To provide empirical support for their claim that gender theory is imposed by elites spending "our money," anti-genderists also began collecting what is called "information of a public character." In practice, this means that they systematically gather financial reports from those LGBT and feminist non-governmental organizations in Slovenia that have received funding through the state budget. Public ministries and other governmental agencies are obligated to provide such information, which is considered "of a public character." This resulted in the drafting and posting of tendentious articles onto their website with inflated information about enormous amounts of money being spent by these organizations to promote gender theory, stimulate christianophobia and "perform social engineering on Slovenian citizens."[12] Such initiatives also put pressure on public agencies, which –

---

11   Ivelja, Ranka and Blaž Petkovič. 2015. Župniki – prevozniki do referenduma (Priests – drivers to the referendum), www.dnevnik.si/1042709779, 14.04.2019.
12   For example: The controversial Peace Institute, together with its satellite organizations, have already received over 8.700.000 Euro (Kontroverzni Mirovni inštitut s svojimi sateliti prejel že preko 8,700.000 EUR!, 24kul.si/kontroverzni-mirovni-institut-s-sateliti-prejel-ze-preko-8700000-eur, 14.04.2019).

similar to what happened with homosexual propaganda in public schools – began to self-censor and become increasingly reluctant to provide financial support for projects on gender and sexuality.

Lastly, it is important to note that the populist strategies and rhetoric, put to use by anti-gender activists during both referendum campaigns, worked, in part, because the opposing side did not adequately persist with counter-initiatives. It was believed that such outdated, traditionalist, homophobic and sexist claims would not resonate with the allegedly tolerant and progressive Slovenian society. However, the anti-gender activists targeted in particular "defeated groups" who believed that they have lost their positions of power because of the imposed tolerance, political correctness and alleged exaggerations of equality policies. They were told that they had lost their voice and their right to freedom of speech, which they would regain once the corrupt elites have been defeated and the natural order restored.

Conclusions

Anti-gender mobilizations across Europe and globally are made up of different initiatives that have seen numerous crossovers with other (populist) forces, including radical and alt-right projects. However, it is important that these phenomena are not conflated when countering and analyzing their practices. "Gender theory" is an empty signifier (Mayer/Sauer 2017) that can be filled with a variety of issues and even opposing positions.

In the Slovenian anti-gender movement, a great variety of actors have come to join forces as a direct result of the populist emptiness of "gender theory" or "gender ideology" – a void left to be filled by each group's unique issues of interest. Uniting these groups are the core mobilizing elements of populism, namely people-centrism, anti-elitism and Othering (Mudde 2004), and the sense of threat to the people (to the family, our children, the nation …) that these elements produce when taken together. While there are clear local specificities, similar populist rhetorical strategies, arguments, and discourses seem to be emerging everywhere, which are being transposed from national to international actors and back (Kuhar/Paternotte 2017).

In this chapter, we have analyzed anti-gender mobilizations in the Slovenian context. A focus on the actors of anti-gender networks and satellite institutions, and their populist use of media, exposed the centrality of people-centrism and Othering in populist mobilizations. We have grasped populism at the crossroads of ideology (the ideational approach) and discourse (populism as a style), arguing that the ideological underpinnings of the anti-gender movement demonstrate its ethno-nationalist populist ideology through discursive and communicative strategies. Our empirical findings suggest that right-wing populism, as part of anti-gender mobilizations, is primarily exclusionary, constructing "the people" in a narrow nativist frame, juxtaposing "the people" and liberal homosexual "elites," and then stressing the indifference of those elites to the common man's concerns. Further, we have shown how populist mobilizations of anti-gender actors can fuel fear and provoke a moral panic by centering the figure of the "innocent child," proclaiming "our children" as vulnerable targets and the most innocent victims of "the Others," which may be the most efficient way to ignite a moral panic.

Bibliography

Brubaker, Rogers (2017): "Between Nationalism and Civilizationalism: The European Populist Moment in Comparative Perspective." In: Ethnic and Racial Studies 40 (8), pp. 1191-1226.

Butler, Judith (1990): Gender Trouble: Feminism and the Subversion of Identity. New York, London: Routledge.

Campani, Giovanna/Pajnik, Mojca (2017): "Democracy, Post-democracy and the Populist Challenge." In: Gabriella Lazaridis/Giovanna Campani (eds.): Understanding the Populist Shift: Othering in a Europe in Crisis. London: Routledge, pp. 179-196.

Canovan, Margaret (1982): "Two Strategies for the Study of Populism." In: Political Studies 30 (4), pp. 544-552.

Cohen, Stanley (1972/2002): Folk Devils and Moral Panics: The Creation of the Mods and Rockers. London: Routledge.

Case, Mary Ann (2019): "Trans Formations in the Vatican's War on 'Gender Ideology'." In: Journal Articles 9669, pp. 639-664.

Datta, Neil (2018): Restoring the Natural Order. Brussels: European Parliamentary Forum.

Fineman, Stephen (ed.) (2008): The Emotional Organization: Passions and Power. London: Blackwell Publishing.

Gerbaudo, Paolo (2018): "Social Media and Populism: An Elective Affinity?" In: Media, Culture and Society 40 (5), pp. 745-753.

Gerbaudo, Paolo/Screti, Francesco (2017): "Reclaiming Popular Sovereignty: The Vision of the State in the Discourse of Podemos and the Movimento 5 Stelle." In: Javnost - The Public 24 (4), pp. 320-35.

Hawkins, Kirk A./Rovira Kaltwasser, Cristóbal (2017): "The Ideational Approach to Populism." In: Latin American Research Review 52 (4), pp. 513-528.

Hodžić, Amir/Bijelić, Nataša (2014): Neo-Conservative Threats to Sexual and Reproductive Health & Rights in the European Union. Zagreb: CESI.

Hrženjak, Majda (2001): "Legitimiziranje Neenakosti." In: Poročilo Skupine Za Spremljanje Nestrpnosti 1, pp. 104-113.

Jogan, Maca (2008): "Rekatolizacija Slovenske Družbe." In: Teorija in Praksa 1 (2), pp. 28-52.

Katsambekis, Giorgos/Stavrakakis, Yannis (2013): Populism, Anti-populism and European Democracy: A View from the South. Online: www.opendemocracy.net/can-europe-make-it/giorgos-katsambekis-yannis-stavrakakis/populism-anti-populism-and-european-democr, 10.10.2018.

Korolczuk, Elzbieta (2014): The War on Gender from a Transnational Perspective – Lessons for Feminists Strategizing. Berlin: Heinrich Böll Stiftung.

Korolczuk, Elzbieta/Graff, Agnieszka (2018): "Gender as 'Ebola from Brussels': The Anticolonial Frame and the Rise of Illiberal Populism." In: Signs: Journal of Women in Culture and Society 43 (4), pp. 797-821.

Kováts, Eszter/Põim, Maari (eds.) (2015): Gender as Symbolic Glue: The Position and Role of Conservative and Far Right Parties in the Anti-Gender Mobilization in Europe. Brussels: Foundation for European Progressive Studies and Friedrich Ebert Stiftung Budapest.

Kuhar, Roman (2015): "Konec Je Sveta, Kakršnega Poznamo: Populistične Strategije Nasprotnikov Družinskega Zakonika." Časopis Za Kritiko Znanosti 206, pp. 118-132.

Kuhar, Roman (2017): "Changing Gender Several Times A Day: The Anti-Gender Movement in Slovenia." In: Roman Kuhar/David Paternotte (eds.): Anti-gender Campaigns in Europe: Mobilizing against Equality. Lanham, New York: Rowman & Littlefield International, pp. 215-232.

Kuhar, Roman/Paternotte, David, (eds.) (2017): Anti-Gender Campaigns in Europe: Mobilizing against Equality. Lanham, New York: Rowman & Littlefield International.

Kuhar, Roman/Čeplak, Metka Mencin (2016): "Same-Sex Partnership Debate in Slovenia: Between Declarative Support and Lack of Political Will." In: Koen Slootmaeckers/Heleen Touquet/Peter Vermeersch (eds.): The EU Enlargement and Gay Politics: The Impact of Eastern Enlargement on Rights, Activism and Prejudice. London: Palgrave, pp. 147-172.

March, Luke (2017): "Left and Right Populism Compared: The British Case." In: The British Journal of Politics and International Relations 9 (2), pp. 282-303.

Mayer, Stefanie/Sauer, Birgit (2017): "'Gender Ideology' in Austria: Coalitions around an Empty Signifier." In: Roman Kuhar/David Paternotte (eds.): Anti-Gender Campaigns in Europe: Mobilizing against Equality. Lanham, New York: Rowman & Littlefield International, pp. 23-40.

Moffitt, Benjamin (2017): "Transnational Populism? Representative Claims, Media and the Difficulty of Constructing a Transnational 'People'." In: Javnost - The Public 24 (4), pp. 409-25.

Moffitt, Benjamin/Tormey, Simon (2014): "Rethinking Populism: Politics, Mediatisation and Political Style." In: Political Studies 62, pp. 381-397.
Mudde, Cass (2014): "The Far Right and the European Elections." In: Current History 113 (761), pp. 98-103.
Mudde, Cass (2004): "The Populist Zeitgeist." In: Government and Opposition 39, pp. 542-563.
Mudde, Cass/Kaltwasser, Rovira Cristóbal (2013): "Exclusionary vs. Inclusionary Populism: Comparing Contemporary Europe and Latin America." In: Government and Opposition 48 (2), pp. 147-74.
Müller, Jan-Werner (2016): What Is Populism? Philadelphia, Pennsylvania: University of Pennsylvania Press.
Pajnik, Mojca (2003): "Polarizacija Prostitucije: Biznis Ali Javna Morala." In: Medijska Preža 17 (18), pp. 7-8.
Pajnik. Mojca/Sauer, Birgit (eds.) (2017): Populism and the Web: Communicative Practices of Parties and Movements in Europe. London: Routledge.
Pajnik, Mojca/Kuhar, Roman/Šori, Itzok (2016): "Populism in Slovenian Context between Ethno-Nationalism and Re-Traditionalization." In: Gabriella Lazaridis/Giovanna Campani/Annie Benveniste (eds.): The Rise of the Far Right in Europe: Populist Shifts and 'Othering.' Basingstoke: Palgrave, pp. 137-160.
Paternotte, David/Kuhar, Roman (2018): "Disentangling and Locating the 'Global Right': Anti-Gender Campaigns in Europe." In: Politics and Governance 6 (3), pp. 6-19.
Petö, Andrea (2015): "'Anti-Gender' Mobilizational Discourse of Conservative and Far Right Parties as a Challenge for Progressive Politics." In: Ezter Kováts/Maari Põim (eds.): Gender as Symbolic Glue: The Position and Role of Conservative and Far Right Parties in the Anti-Gender Mobilization in Europe. Brussels: Foundation for European Progressive Studies and Friedrich Ebert Stiftung Budapest, pp. 126-131.
Pfetsch, Barbara/Silke, Daman/Bennett, Lance W. (2014): "The Critical Linkage between Online and Offline Media." In: Javnost - The Public 20 (3), pp. 9-22.
Postill, John (2018): "Populism and Social Media: A Global Perspective." In: Media, Culture and Society 40 (5), pp. 754-765.
Rooduijn, Matthijs/Pauwels, Teun (2011): "Measuring Populism, Comparing Two Methods of Content Analysis." In: West European Politics 34 (6), pp. 1272-1283.
Stavrakakis, Yannis (2014): "The Return of 'the People': Populism and Anti-Populism in the Shadow of the European Crisis." In: Constellations 21 (4), pp. 505-517.
Szelewa, Dorota (2014): "The Second Wave of Anti-Feminism? Post-Crisis Maternalist Policies and the Attack on the Concept of Gender in Poland." In: Gender, Rovne Prilezitosti, v yzkum Rocnik 2, pp. 33-46.

'You're Fired!' Retrotopian Desire and Right-Wing Class Politics

Simon Schleusener

Introduction

This essay will explore the way in which the populist right has utilized the realms of popular culture and the media in its struggle for hegemony.[1] Along these lines, I will focus on Donald Trump's former reality show, *The Apprentice*, drawing attention to the show's prefiguration of precisely the right-wing class politics that was in many ways constitutive of Trump's election as president – and which is still one of the key features of Trumpism today. In the course of the essay, I will also analyze certain facets of the online culture wars (cf. Nagle 2017), particularly examining right-wing efforts to pit feminists and working-class men against each other. Furthermore, I will draw on theorists such as Gilles Deleuze, Zygmunt Bauman, and Wendy Brown to investigate the retrotopian desires mobilized by right-wing populists in responding to the disaffections caused by neoliberalism and globalization. This retrotopian desire, I argue, is prominently articulated in the arena of gender, where it resonates with antifeminist impulses, the idealization of old-school masculinity, and calls for a return to 'traditional' gender norms. Moreover, it is deeply bound up with conservative efforts to overcode the concept of class by consistently presenting class matters as matters of culture and identity – a strategy that oftentimes involves gendered stereotypes and the performance of gender roles (such as Trump's rhetorical simulation of working-class masculinity).

Before turning to *The Apprentice*, I will like to start with two Trump-related paradoxes, at the intersection of which the show can be located. Naturally, after more than two years of Trump in office, nobody will in any way be surprised to discover that Trumpism entails contradictions and antinomies. I therefore do not claim to

---

1   The direction of my essay is inspired by a workshop I organized together with Simon Strick on "Rightwing POPulism: Remapping Popular Culture in the Age of Trump and the Alt-Right." The workshop took place in June 2019 at the 66th annual meeting of the GAAS in Hamburg. I want to thank Gabriele Dietze and Julia Roth for taking part in the workshop and for inviting me to contribute to this book.

'unmask' anything here. Rather, I will simply use these paradoxes as a starting point to come up with some suggestions as to how Trumpism functions – and as to how it has succeeded in coopting the domain of class politics, which has traditionally been identified with the left. With respect to this process, the essay is particularly concerned with two interdependent dimensions: its *ideological* conditions and its *affective* support.

Two Paradoxes

1) The first paradox I want to point out has to do with precisely this problem of 'class.' Here, an obvious question is why Trump, the golf-playing and blatantly corrupt billionaire from Queens, has been able to create a quite successful image of himself as the 'Champion of the Working Class,' as caring for 'the forgotten man and woman,' or as being determined to 'drain the swamp,' It is hardly worth mentioning that the discrepancies between such assessments and Trump's actual economic policies are all-too apparent. Indeed, as Naomi Klein writes: "Trump and his cabinet of former executives are remaking government at a startling pace to serve the interests of their own businesses, their former businesses, and their tax bracket as a whole." (Klein 2017: 21) Now, it certainly would be wrong to believe that working-class or low-income Americans are totally unaware of such contradictions. It would be equally mistaken, however, to qualify Trump's connection to working-class voters as nothing but a fantasy or myth. If we consider the 2016 exit polls (cf. Huang/Jacoby/Strickland/Lai 2016), for instance, the most striking developments, in comparison with 2012, took place among low-income groups, that is, among Americans who earn less than 30,000 USD annually. It is among these sections of the population that Republicans were most successful in gaining new voters, while Democrats lost around 10% of their share of the vote [cf. Fig. 1 and 2]. What these numbers demonstrate is not that the typical Trump supporter is working-class, but they confirm the general tendency that class difference and socioeconomic inequality increasingly become utilized by the populist right.[2]

2) The second paradox I seek to point out involves Trumpism's relationship with the media. It is of course one of Trump's signature traits to viciously attack liberal media outlets such as the New York Times or CNN, which he consistently labels as 'fake news.' I would argue, however, that Trump's attacks on the media are not only motivated by politics, but that in distancing himself from the mainstream media and its modus operandi, his own communication strategy is in turn presented as distinctly authentic, unfiltered, and immediate. Thus, his by now over 70 million

---

2   This seems to be not only an issue in the US, but, as the huge working-class support for Brexit in the UK demonstrates (cf. Harris 2016), it also is an issue in Europe.

Figure 1: Exit polls of the 2016 Presidential election (income).

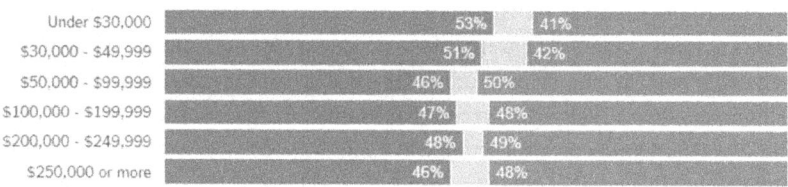

On the left are the percentage points for the Democratic candidate (Hillary Clinton), on the right for the Republican candidate (Donald Trump).

Figure 2: Exit polls of the 2012 Presidential election (income).

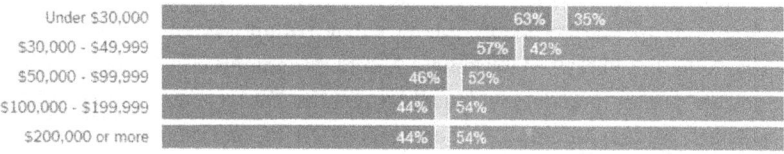

On the left are the percentage points for the Democratic candidate (Barack Obama), on the right for the Republican candidate (Mitt Romney).

Twitter followers are addressed in such a way as to get the impression of being directly connected with 'their' president. What is paradoxical about this situation is less that Trump's proclaimed authenticity is constantly undercut by the obvious 'fakeness' connected with his persona: from his fake hair to the Trump Organization's fake university or its fake charity foundation, etc. Rather, while Trump claims for himself a communication style that is direct and unmediated, there has in fact been no other candidate in the 2016 election whose success depended so much on 'the media' – and not least on precisely the mainstream media he continues to attack as 'the enemy of the people.'[3]

Neoliberal Resentment and the Society of Control

A case in point for how Trump's political career profited from an instrumentalization of the American media landscape is his former television show, *The Apprentice*.

---

[3] For more on Trump's relationship with the media, cf. Boczkowski/Papacharissi (eds.) 2018 and Koch/Nanz/Rogers (eds.) 2020.

This reality program (and several variations of the show, such as *The Celebrity Apprentice*[4]) centers around the business skills of various contestants and started in 2004 on NBC – ironically one of the networks that Trump now consistently attacks. As several authors have argued, there is a strong case to be made that without *The Apprentice*, Trump would have never become president. For not only had *The Apprentice* been vastly popular, supplying Trump with a publicity that exceeded that of almost all his competitors. It also is no secret that Trump's image as a successful businessman, on which much of his election campaign was focused, relied heavily on his depiction in *The Apprentice*, where he was portrayed as a larger-than-life alpha male and tycoon. Although Trump was considered a celebrity since the 1980s, he in fact went bankrupt several times and was at a low point in his career before the show initiated his comeback. As Patrick Keefe tells it, Trump's "business had foundered, and by 2003 he had become a garish figure of local interest – a punch line on Page Six. *The Apprentice* mythologized him anew, and on a much bigger scale, turning him into an icon of American success" (Keefe 2019).

According to Michael Moore, the fact that Trump was underestimated as a candidate by the liberal establishment had to do, among other things, with the Democrats' failure to understand just how popular *The Apprentice* was, particularly in so-called 'Middle America.' As Moore claimed in an interview with Amy Goodman:

> "Nobody thought it could happen, because – 'Are you kidding? He's such an idiot. He's crazy.' I said, 'That's why he's going to win. You don't understand. He's an incredible performance artist.' People love *The Apprentice*. I mean, people between the Hudson River and Interstate 5 love *The Apprentice*. They loved him on it, because here's what he did every week. Whoever the biggest jerk was on the show that week got to hear, 'You're fired.' And everybody works with that jerk. Wherever you work, there's that one jerk. And the cathartic feeling you got watching *The Apprentice*, of hearing somebody fire that jerk – people loved that show, and they loved Trump, and they loved hearing him say, 'You're fired.' But I couldn't get anybody to listen to this, because on the coasts, within the bubble [...] of the Democratic Party infrastructure, they don't watch *The Apprentice*." (Moore 2018)

This quote, I believe, is interesting for a number of different reasons. First off, Moore has of course warned for a long time that liberals and the Democratic Party have lost touch with so-called 'average Americans,' to the effect that someone like Trump is likely to win working-class votes if Democrats are unable to reestablish a

---

4 After Trump left *The Celebrity Apprentice* due to his presidential campaign in 2015, Arnold Schwarzenegger became the program's new host. Yet, after hosting a single season in early 2017 (under the title *The New Celebrity Apprentice*), Schwarzenegger announced that he would quit the show. Since then, the program has been discontinued.

'connection' to those who do not live in the coastal areas or in big cities. The popularity of *The Apprentice*, then, is a case in point for Moore, an example that underlines the ignorance of much of the Democratic establishment about the cultural tastes and preferences of working Americans.

There is another dimension of Moore's comment, however, namely his claim that working-class viewers of *The Apprentice* "loved Trump, and they loved hearing him say, 'You're fired.'" Of course, this ritual at the end of each episode – Trump's elimination of one of the contestants – was the show's signature routine and its most iconic cultural gesture.[5] Yet, it seems hardly self-evident that a working or lower-class audience, which has firsthand knowledge of precarious socioeconomic conditions, would identify with the show's host here: a billionaire who takes pleasure in firing people from their jobs.

To make sense of this phenomenon, it is necessary to contextualize the show within the recent history of American capitalism and, in particular, its 'neoliberalization' in the last couple of decades (cf. Harvey 2009). Neoliberal policies have not only led to a gradual dismantling of the welfare state and an "explosion" of inequality since the implementation of Reaganomics in the 1980s (cf. Piketty 2014: 294-298); they have also promoted new forms of subjectivity and social interaction based on notions such as 'human capital' (cf. Foucault 2008: 226-233), a generalized competitiveness, and an overall erosion of solidarity. In this context, one may attribute to *The Apprentice* a quote from Gilles Deleuze, who argued in his essay on 'Control Societies' that "If the most idiotic television game shows are so successful, it's because they express the corporate situation with great precision." (Deleuze 1992: 4). What *The Apprentice* expresses, then, is the intensification of competition and rivalry specific to the neoliberal mode of production. Along these lines, Katja Kanzler and Marina Scharlaj have argued that,

> "The show's rules are designed to fuel rivalry and conflict among contestants: They are assigned into teams which are not only set up to compete against each other; members of the less successful teams are also interviewed which team member is responsible for the poor performance, encouraging scenes of blaming and shaming that the show salaciously depicts. The chief dispenser of humiliation, however, is Trump himself, who heads the jury that decides on eliminations. These eliminations take place in a boardroom setting where the jury's discussions with the contestants [...] revolve around the 'strength' or 'weakness' of individual team members. Each episode culminates in an elimination, enacted by Trump with a sentence that became both the show's and his personal trademark: 'You're fired.'" (2017: 323)

---

5   Cf. Davis/Lukomnik/Pitt-Watson 2006: 205: "*The Apprentice* soon became a 'cultural phenomenon' among viewers in the key 18-49 age category. 'You're fired!' became such a catch phrase that Trump even tried to trademark it."

This overly competitive setting – epitomized not only by *The Apprentice*, but also by a host of other 'gamedoc' shows (*The Biggest Loser, Survivor*, etc.) – in many ways resonates with Deleuze's account of the neoliberal circumstances in so-called 'control societies.' Deleuze argues that what Foucault analyzed under the rubric of the 'disciplinary society' (cf. Foucault 1995) gradually gave way to a new type of regime in the second half of the 20th century. This new regime – namely the 'control society'[6] – both represents a "mutation of capitalism" (Deleuze 1992: 6) and a steady breakdown of "all the environments of enclosure – prison, hospital, factory, school, family" (4-5).[7] While the dismantling of these institutions has sporadically given rise to new freedoms, it simultaneously contributed to the emergence of new "mechanisms of control that are equal to the harshest of confinements." These new forms of control, however, no longer function as "*molds*" or "distinct castings," but rather constitute a continuous "*modulation*." As an example, Deleuze mentions the issue of wages:

> "the factory was a body that contained its internal forces at a level of equilibrium, the highest possible in terms of production, the lowest possible in terms of wages; but in a society of control, the corporation has replaced the factory [...]. Of course the factory was already familiar with the system of bonuses, but the corporation works more deeply to impose a modulation of each salary, in states of perpetual metastability that operate through challenges, contests, and highly comic group sessions." (4)

Hence, while the factory "constituted individuals as a single body to the double advantage of the boss who surveyed each element within the mass and the unions who mobilized a mass resistance," the corporation "constantly presents the brashest rivalry as a healthy form of emulation, an excellent motivational force that opposes individuals against one another and runs through each, dividing each within" (4-5).

Against this backdrop, the reactions of the viewers of *The Apprentice*'s (especially those with a woking-class background) that Michael Moore emphasized may become more understandable. In a context of enhanced rivalry, in which both class-based solidarity and the instruments to initiate a sustainable betterment of one's material conditions are lacking, the only thing left seems to be a sort of 'Schadenfreude' directed against those who, according Michael Moore, embody the 'jerks' (and competitors) at one's workplace – or perhaps in society at large.[8] Although

---

6   For a more extensive discussion of the transformation of 'disciplinary societies' into 'societies of control,' see Schleusener 2019.

7   In view of the massive rise in incarceration rates from the 1980s onward (particularly in the US and in Europe), this account is at least questionable with regard to the prison. Cf., for example, Wacquant 2009.

8   If this situation is reflective of the decline of the welfare state and the emergence of the neoliberal debt state (that is, the 'society of control'), it likewise signifies a crisis of the American

The Apprentice clearly displays an image of capitalism from the perspective of the entrepreneur or the top-management, working-class viewers are supplied with a 'compensation' as well, namely: "the cathartic feeling you got watching *The Apprentice*, of hearing somebody fire that jerk." Already in *The Apprentice*, then, Trump has in some sense succeeded in establishing a version of what Hannah Arendt termed the 'alliance between the mob and the elite' (cf. Arendt 1973: 326-340). In this respect, *The Apprentice* clearly anticipates Trump's presidency, whose way of governing in many ways resembles the authoritarian style of the show's host.[9]

Yet, if we view *The Apprentice* as a popcultural manifestation (and anticipation) of right-wing class politics, it is important to note that Trumpism both expresses the neoliberal conditions of contemporary capitalism and, simultaneously, presents a critique of them. This, I argue, is the case in *The Apprentice* as much as it is in today's White House. Obviously, the fact that Trump has been able to connect to working-class voters was to some extent based on actual interests and hopes triggered by his promises: to initiate a different, more protectionist trade policy, to bring American companies back to the US, to revitalize industries such as coal mining, and to counter illegal immigration, thereby diminishing competition and wage squeezing in low-income sectors. Such reactionary economic measures to deal with the disaffections caused by globalization and neoliberalism, however, are surely not the only reason for Trump's working-class support. Perhaps even more important are his straightforward language, his opposition to political correctness, his performance of 'traditional' masculinity (including the use of 'locker room talk,' etc.), and his particular affective and communicative style – a style that seems to suspend the tremendous class difference between Trump and the majority of his followers, even when he is bragging about his wealth and his luxurious lifestyle.

If Jim McGuigan has used the term 'cool capitalism' (cf. McGuigan 2009) to describe capitalism's cultural 'superstructure' in the era of neoliberalism – most visible today in Silicon Valley, with its seemingly flat hierarchies and its hybridization of counterculture and business culture –, then we may see Trump embody-

---

Dream, most notably since the 2008 financial meltdown. All this has certainly played in the hands of today's right-wing populism. As Trump declared in his presidential announcement speech: "Sadly, the American dream is dead. [...] But if I get elected president I will bring it back bigger and better and stronger than ever before, and we will make America great again." (cf. Trump 2015)

9 To be sure, the show's portrayal of strength, perseverance, and authority is decidedly gendered, with Trump acting as not only the successful businessman, but also as the typical 'alpha male.' In addition, gender roles are also relevant with respect to the show's contestants, who represent a colorful cross-section of American talent, being roughly divided into 'book smarts' and 'street smarts.' On the show's business-oriented take on cultural, racial, and gender difference, cf. McGuigan 2008. On its performance of gender identity (especially with regard to black femininity), cf. Blake-Beard/Roberts 2004.

ing a decidedly 'uncool capitalism.' In *The Apprentice*, along the lines of what Mark Fisher has termed 'capitalist realism' (cf. Fisher 2009), there seems to be no attempt at concealing the hierarchies and exclusion mechanisms of capitalist competition. Instead, the popularity of the show is precisely related to its depiction of old-school masculine authority ('You're fired!'), in connection with the viewers' malice for the show's losers, who are unable to meet the demands of the dog-eat-dog economy displayed on the screen.[10]

In another way, however, Trump's 'uncool capitalism' does in fact resonate with the 'new spirit of capitalism,' to quote Boltanski and Chiapello (2007) here. For Trump as well is eager to present himself as anti-elitist and anti-establishment: as a charismatic outsider who protects working Americans against careerists, Washington bureaucrats, and globalists. Again, popular culture plays an important role in this process. If the Rolling Stones song "You Can't Always Get What You Want" (1968) is ritually played at all of Trump's rallies, then there is a certain appropriation of the counterculture here as well: an affective charging of Trump's base with the cultural signs of protest, rebellion, and dissent. Yet, that Trump, of all people, seems to meet the sensibilities of the white working and lower class undoubtedly depends on a thorough process of 'culturalization,' in which class difference is consistently overwritten along the lines of race, culture, region, and identity (cf. Frank 2005; Michaels 2006). Hence, the compensation that Trump's working-class supporters can expect is not of a material but of a purely affective-symbolic nature. This, as well, can be heard in the soundtrack of Trump's electrifying rallies. "You Can't Always Get What You Want," in this regard, marks these events as not just protest-laden and countercultural, but also reminds their participants of what they can realistically hope for and expect – and what they cannot. Indeed, what they *cannot* hope for is any kind of economic redistribution that would substantially better their material situation, including healthcare, education, and social security. What they *can* expect, however, is a form of cultural-symbolic recognition, so far denied to them by both the liberal and conservative establishment.[11]

---

10   McGuigan himself seems to disagree with this take on *The Apprentice* (cf. McGuigan 2008). On Trump's 'uncool capitalism,' cf. also Schleusener 2020. For more on the notion of 'cool capitalism,' cf. Schleusener 2020: 58-60.

11   On the shift from 'redistribution' to 'recognition' in the neoliberal era, cf. Taylor 1992, Fraser 1995, and Michaels 2006.

Populist Affects and Retrotopian Desire

Trump's rallies are the site where this form of symbolic exchange is most obviously acted out, and it is done so in primarily affective terms. As Arlie Russel Hochschild has remarked about Trump's election campaign:

> "Trump is an 'emotions candidate.' More than any other presidential candidate in decades, Trump focuses on eliciting and praising emotional responses from his fans rather than on detailed policy prescriptions. His speeches – evoking dominance, bravado, clarity, national pride, and personal uplift – inspire an emotional transformation. [...] Not only does Trump evoke emotion, he makes an object of it, presenting it back to his fans as a sign of collective success." (Hochschild 2016: 225)

What Trump's rallies achieve, then, is an actual *affective transformation*. They operate like a giant therapeutic machinery transforming shame into pride, envy into mockery, and fear of socioeconomic decline into resentment against illegal immigrants. Trump's rallies are therefore much more than ordinary political campaign events. Rather, they are the sites of a concrete 'retrotopia' (cf. Bauman 2017): a retrotopia realized in the here and now, even if merely in the realm of affect. This is why specific policy proposals hardly matter to the crowd at Trump's rallies. What matters, rather, is what constitutes the foundation of Trump's affective economy: the impression that finally there is a politician who publicly says what formerly was deemed to be forbidden and unsayable.[12]

Analogous to the way in which Trump supporters resignified Hillary Clinton's 'deplorables' remark and turned it from an insult into a badge of honor (cf. Zak 2017), Trump's rallies transform his fans' "collective feeling of undeserved shame into pride-filled enjoyment of their shared contempt for the identity groups that political and media elites cast as 'victims'" (Pease 2019: 160)[13]. By undoing any feeling of shame for not being able to speak the 'politically correct' language prescribed by the establishment, Trump's theatrical transgression of the boundaries of polite speech and proper political discourse evokes an almost cathartic sense of community – a kind of "collective effervescence," as Hochschild explains with reference to Durkheim (Hochschild 2016: 225).

---

12   Cf. Pease 2019: 161: "What the norms of political correctness and state law have ruled unsayable in a public debate, Trump says with impunity."
13   Donald Pease refers to Hochschild's book *Strangers in Their Own Land* here, for which she conducted dozens of interviews with tea party activists and Trump supporters. While her predominantly white working and lower middle-class respondents strongly deny being racist or sexist, they frequently regard women, African Americans, and members of other minority groups as '*line cutters*' (cf. Hochschild 2016: 137-139) who receive undeserved help through affirmative action plans or similar federal programs.

But how can one account for the specifically 'retrotopian' dimension of this right-wing counterpublic – and for the 'politics of nostalgia' it is engaged in? According to Zygmunt Bauman, retrotopias are "visions located in the lost/stolen/abandoned but undead past, instead of [like their utopian forebears] being tied to the not-yet-unborn and so inexistent future" (Bauman 2017: 5).[14] Obviously, the retrotopian desire prevalent among Trump's base articulates itself not only in the wish to reinstate an ethnically charged form of nationalism or 'tribalism' (which Bauman analyzes in chapter 2 of his book, pp. 49-85). It is also, and especially, articulated with reference to gender relations, expressing a desire to return to more 'traditional' – that is, pre-feminist, androcentric, patriarchic, or heteronormative – forms of social organization.

As to the status of gender relations in the neoliberal era, most people on the left will probably agree with Wendy Brown that neoliberal policies have "intensified" gender subordination

> "through the shrinking, privatization, and/or dismantling of public infrastructure supporting families, children, and retirees. Such infrastructure includes, but is not limited to, affordable, quality early childhood and afterschool programs, summer camps, physical and mental health care, education, public transportation, neighborhood parks and recreation centers, public pensions, senior centers, and social security. When these public provisions are eliminated or privatized, the work and/or the cost of supplying them is returned to individuals, disproportionately to women. Put another way, 'responsibilization' in the context of privatizing public goods uniquely penalizes women to the extent that they remain disproportionately responsible for those who cannot be responsible for themselves." (Brown 2015: 105)

Trump's white working-class supporters certainly feel, and in many ways are the victims of, such 'shrinking' of the public infrastructure as well. Yet, their understanding of the situation is a fundamentally different one. Indeed, over the last few decades, class conflict in America's conservative 'heartland' has been systematically replaced by the so-called 'culture wars' (cf. Hunter 1991) – to the effect that economic insecurities are largely overshadowed by cultural anxieties, and 'the squeezing of the working class' is interpreted not as a result of the *neoliberal* economic policies outlined above, but of *liberal* (or feminist, socialist, multiculturalist, etc.) attacks on 'family values' and the 'American way of life.'[15] As Thomas Frank argued 15 years

---

14   Bauman's argument in many ways resonates with the analyzes of various Marxist critics who have diagnosed an "enfeeblement of Utopian desire" (Jameson 2007: 55) or "the slow cancellation of the future" (Fisher 2014: 2-29) in the neoliberal era. On the political and economic conditions of this "dystopian imagination" (Berardi 2011: 48), see also Schleusener 2017.

15   Cf. Frank 2005: 6: "In fact, backlash leaders systematically downplay the politics of economics. The movement's basic premise is that culture outweighs economics as a matter of public

ago in *What's the Matter with Kansas?*, the result of this operation is a seemingly upside-down political world, in which conservative Republicans receive working-class votes to dismantle the welfare state and lower taxes for the rich. Ironically, then, the populist backlash manifests itself as "a working-class movement that has done incalculable, historic harm to working-class people" (Frank 2005: 6).[16] Today's Trumpism, it can be argued, carries this logic to extremes.

But if conservative and right-wing accounts of American politics have largely superseded the economic dimension of 'class difference' (which is being redefined as 'cultural difference'), why should the left not reinsert materiality and the question of economic conditions into the debate when dealing with the current populist revolt (cf. Mouffe 2018)? Slavoj Žižek, for instance, has argued that the 'culture war' should be understood as a 'displaced class war' – a class war, that is, which eventually benefits the 'ruling class' since it enables "the lower classes [...] to articulate their fury without disturbing the economic status quo" (Žižek 2009: 33). There is, of course, a risk in making this argument. One might object, for instance, that such an understanding of the current populist moment would reinstate the traditional base/superstructure dualism by reviving a misplaced economism that may eventually downplay sexism, misogyny, racism, or xenophobia – rendering them as mere 'side contradictions' supposedly less important than the real antagonism between capital and labor. And even worse: Would such a reasoning not also return to an outmoded way of 'symptomatic reading,' disregarding the claims of contemporary theorists who advise us that cultural and literary analysis should operate 'close but not deep' (cf. Love 2009) and pay special attention to the 'surface' (rather than the 'depth') of our objects of investigation (cf. Best/Marcus 2010)?

Against such objections I will make the following two points: First, to analyze phenomena such as racism or sexism in their economic context does not justify but seeks to better understand them. In fact, the opposite way of approaching these issues – not trying to explain sexism or white supremacy but rendering them (quasi transcendent) explanations in themselves – appears to me as much more problematic, as it risks reifying, if not fetishizing, racist or sexist behavior. And second, if 'symptomatic reading' is understood (via Jameson) as the "the task of rewriting" a given text or utterance "in terms of a master code" (Best/Marcus 2010: 15), then to work out the economic dimension of populist discourse does not require – at least not with regard to Marcus and Best's understanding of the term – to be strictly

---

concern – that *Values Matter Most*, as one backlash title has it. On those grounds it rallies citizens who would have once been reliable partisans of the New Deal to the standard of conservatism."

16 For more on this 'great paradox,' see also the first part of Hochschild's *Strangers in Their Own Land* (2016: 1-82), which takes Frank's book as its starting point.

'symptomatic.'[17] Indeed, the economic is always already implicated in right-wing populist discourse, even if its more immediate reference seems to be gender or race. In other words, just as gender relations are deeply bound up with the specific (sexual) division of labor under a given mode of production, so can 'race relations' (from slavery to the current anti-immigration hysteria) not be strictly separated from their economic contexts. Therefore, to 'read' the retrotopian desires mobilized by right-wing populists as a response to neoliberalism and globalization does not require a 'rewriting' – and not even a particularly 'suspicious' hermeneutics (cf. Felski 2012). What is required is not a 'deep analysis' of populist discourse in order to uncover its 'latent meanings,' but, rather, to step back for a moment in order to get a clearer view of its particular socioeconomic constellation.

Nobodaddy Trump

One of the most notable outcomes of the neoliberal revolution of the late 1970s and 1980s is the way in which it altered and 'flexibilized' social relations. In this respect, neoliberalism seems to echo – and indeed realize – the famous words from *The Communist Manifesto* about the revolutionary role of the bourgeoisie:

> "Constant revolutionizing of production, uninterrupted disturbance of all social conditions, everlasting uncertainty and agitation distinguish the bourgeois epoch from all earlier ones. All fixed, fast-frozen relations, with their train of ancient and venerable prejudices and opinions, are swept away, all new-formed ones become antiquated before they can ossify. All that is solid melts into air, all that is holy is profaned." (Marx/Engels 2002: 223)

In the neoliberal era, it seems that this tendency – capitalism's propensity towards deterritorialization and 'creative destruction' (cf. Schumpeter 1954) – has even accelerated. Besides the obvious fact that neoliberal policies have introduced new forms of social insecurity through the politics of austerity (cf. Blyth 2013), privatization initiatives, and the disintegration of the welfare state, there are other factors as well. As, for instance, sociologists like Richard Sennett and Hartmut Rosa have demonstrated, neoliberal capitalism involves a significant *acceleration* of traditional temporal structures (cf. Rosa 2015) and a turn toward more and more *flexibility* in all aspects of social life (cf. Sennett 1999).[18] According to Sennett, what he terms

---

17   Of course, the reference is Jameson's *The political Unconscious* here. Cf. Jameson 2002: x: "Interpretation is here construed as an essentially allegorical act, which consists in rewriting a given text in terms of a particular interpretive master code."
18   Here, one could also think of the increasing erosion of the day/night distinction in what Jonathan Crary describes as today's 'round-the-clock' or '24/7' capitalism (cf. Crary 2014).

'the culture of the new capitalism' particularly corresponds with three cultural ideals: First, an orientation toward the "short term" rather than to long term planning and consistency; second, a willingness to focus and continually work on one's "potential abilities" rather than "learning to do just one thing really well"; and third, a willingness "to let go of the past" and "abandon past experience." (Sennett 2006: 4-5)

It is not difficult to see – especially with regard to Sennett's last point – how the retrotopian direction of the current populist moment is also a reaction against neoliberalism and the deterritorilization of traditional social assemblages. Naturally, neoliberal policies have not only given cause for critique from the left but also, albeit differently, from the populist right. Yet, while the current backlash certainly justifies speaking of a 'crisis of neoliberalism' (cf. Schleusener 2018), it would be mistaken to define it as effectively 'anti-capitalist.' Rather, the reactionary and retrotopian inclinations of the present seem to point towards what Deleuze and Guattari have described as capitalism's 'schizophrenic' axiomatic – that is, its "twofold movement" of *deterritorialization* and *reterritorialization*.[19] Despite capitalism's tendency to fluidify 'all fixed, fast-frozen relations,' it is therefore also the case that "Everything returns or recurs: States, nations, families." (Deleuze/Guattari 2007: 37)

Several years before the political rise of Trump and his signature campaign promise to build a wall at the Southern border ('and make Mexico pay for it'...), Wendy Brown analyzed how the retrotopian desire for walls needs to be understood in the context of the neoliberal erosion of nation-state sovereignty, which is increasingly outsourced to corporate actors and transnational forces (cf. Brown 2010). What Brown argues is that although the construction of nation-state walls has proven to be largely ineffective, "their often enormous costs and limited efficacy are irrelevant to the desire for them." For even if walls 'don't work,' they nevertheless fulfill an important psychological function. "They produce not the future of an illusion", Brown explicates with reference to Freud (1964), "but the illusion of a future aligned with an idealized past." (133)

Something similar can be said with respect to the relationship between right-wing populism and gender. If neoliberal policies have led to a an increased deterritorialization of social relations and – as Deleuze analyzed under the rubric of the 'control society' – a relative breakdown of institutions like the patriarchal family, then the retrotopian desire to return to 'traditional' gender roles can also be understood (in line with Žižek) as a displaced reaction against neoliberalism. In

---

19 "The more the capitalist machine deterritorializes, decoding and axiomatizing flows in order to extract surplus value from them, the more its ancillary apparatuses, such as government bureaucracies and the forces of law and order, do their utmost to reterritorialize." (Deleuze/Guattari 2007: 37)

other words, the backlash against the flexibilization of gender relations (the growing number of women at the workplace, the legalization of gay marriage, the more and more public manifestation of transgener identities, etc.) may at least partially be a response to neoliberal flexibilization in general. As in the case of walls, however, the anti-feminist backlash is hardly able to mitigate the actual (economic) insecurities and anxieties experienced by many working-class men. Yet, anti-feminist or heteronormative ideologies as well as the call for a strong male 'leader' to restore 'law and order' serve important psychological functions as they express the widespread retrotopian desire to regain 'sovereignty' – even if only in the realm of gender.[20]

Obviously, the election of Trump is in many ways bound up with this scenario as Trump not only appealed to the working class, but also presented himself as a strong-willed alpha male seeking to undo the 'weak' policies of his predecessor, President Obama. The rapper Kanye West – to return to the realm of popular culture here – probably best articulated the patriarchal imaginations projected onto Trump by many on the right. In October 2018, at a particularly awkward Oval Office meeting intended to boost Trump's popularity among African Americans, he said the following:

> "You know my dad and my mom separated so I didn't have a lot of male energy in my home. [...] [Hillary Clinton's] campaign 'I'm With Her' just didn't make me feel, as a guy that didn't get to see my dad all the time, like a guy that could play catch with his son. It was something about putting this MAGA hat on, it made me feel like Superman." (Izadi/Heil/Andrews 2018)

What these comments reveal is certainly not just the extent to which the arena of American politics is distinctly gendered. What is perhaps more significant here is the way in which Kanye's elevation of Trump, as the solution to his own being 'fatherless,' picks up on the right-wing talking point that the continuous problems many black neighborhoods in the US are faced with are not related to their economic poverty but to the cultural or social 'pathologies' that allegedly manifest themselves in phenomena such as single-parent families.[21] Once again, a class problem is turned into a problem of 'culture' here – a problem for which an idealized version of 'old-school masculinity' is deemed to constitute the solution in both the political and the private sphere.

---

20 Tellingly, the desire to undo the loss of sovereignty is expressed in the two most significant chants of Trump's 2016 election campaign: 'Build the Wall!' (related to the felt loss of national sovereignty) and 'Lock her up!' (directed against Hillary Clinton and entailing rather obvious misogynist connotations).

21 For one of the latest installments of the argument that not economic but cultural factors (a failing of 'social connections') are what drives certain places in America to 'collapse,' see Carney 2019.

Of course, there is a great irony in choosing Trump, of all people, as the embodiment of the strong and responsible 'father figure' America so desperately needs: Trump, that is, who is currently in his third marriage, who was caught on tape boasting about grabbing women 'by the pussy,' who declared that if Ivanka was not his daughter, he would be dating her, who paid hush money to a porn star during his election campaign, and who denied a sexual assault charge by claiming 'She is not my type.' Trump, it seems (and most Republicans are certainly aware of this), makes for the worst father figure imaginable. If anything – to loosely refer to William Blake's famous poem here – he is a 'Nobodaddy' (cf. Blake 1995: 154), a dad only in the pseudo-spiritual space of political fantasy. This discrepancy, however, is an instructive one, as it points towards the insurmountable gap that fundamentally distances the retrotopian impulse from its real-life, material conditions.[22] With reference to Wendy Brown's analysis of the desire for walls in the age of waning state-sovereignty, one could therefore claim that the election of Trump as well (at least from the perspective of working-class conservatives) was not just an 'error' but an 'illusion' – which makes remediation all the more difficult. For while an error could be corrected through reason and facts, an illusion – which, according to Freud, is always "powered by a wish" (Brown 2010: 132) – requires a much more elaborate procedure of undoing. Ultimately, then, it is not enough to point out right-wing populism's ideological inconsistencies and erroneous assumptions as long as its desiring-machines and affect structures are not tackled simultaneously.[23]

---

22 If Trump, then, is not a 'symbol' but a 'symptom' of our times (cf. Didi-Huberman 2001: 640), he is so precisely of their paradoxes and discrepancies: not just of the discrepancy between the neoliberal and social conservative (or, the deterritorializing and reterritorializing) directions of right-wing ideology and the current Republican Party; but also of the fundamental gap between today's retrotopian tendencies and the accelerating commodification of US society and the planet at large.

23 This does not mean, however, that the critique of ideology is completely useless. Different from approaches which imply that political struggles nowadays exclusively take place on the terrain of affect (cf. Massumi 2005), I argue that affect theory and ideology critique need to be combined rather than separated from each other. Indeed, the effectiveness of Trump's affect politics clearly depends on decades of economic disinformation, particularly in the working-class milieus I have drawn attention to. Evoking Kant's (1996: B 75) emblematic assertion in his *Critique of Pure Reason* ("Gedanken ohne Inhalt sind leer, Anschauungen ohne Begriffe sind blind.") one could therefore claim: "The study of affects, irrespective of their ideological conditions, is blind; ideology critique, without considering the crucial role of affects for political action, is empty." For an approach that goes in the direction just outlined, see Protevi 2016 and Peters/Protevi 2017.

Class/Gender

To conclude this essay, I would like to reflect once more on the relationship between gender and class by now analyzing one of a series of anti-feminist memes [cf. Fig. 3] that have been circulating on the internet since around the 'Gamergate' controversy in 2014 (cf. Nagle 2017). The meme – shared, among others, by James Damore on Twitter[24] – seeks to satirically undermine feminist discourse by rendering 'women issues' and 'working-class issues' (here characteristically coded as white and male) as antagonistic and incompatible. What the meme shows is two relatively well-dressed young women, perhaps university students, passing by (and seemingly looking down on) a laborer in work gear, cowering on the dirty ground over a manhole. On top of the image a line reads 'Stop oppressing Me' – answered by a 'Sorry' in much smaller letters on the bottom of the meme, next to the worker's face.

Figure 3: Stop Oppressing Me.

---

24 James Damore, a former engineer at Google, was fired from his job in 2017 after writing a memo that criticized the company's diversity policies as ideologically biased. While Damore denies being involved with right-wing politics and self-identifies as a 'classical liberal,' his case has been used by the alt-right as an example of a 'left-wing hegemony' in American society. The tweet he posted together with the meme on October 30, 2017 reads as follows: "One dimensional models of group 'oppression' are only useful for twisting reality to fit political agendas, not for understanding/improving."

What, then, does this meme *do*? Evidently, it turns the feminist critique of 'male privilege' against itself, demonstrating how college-educated feminists protesting 'gender oppression' are themselves highly privileged in comparison with other social groups – namely, white blue-collar workers who arguably possess less economic, cultural, and social capital.

Now, one way of responding to this meme from a left-wing perspective would be to contend that the image, as a representation of a segment of the social totality, is 'false.' For in its montage of words and image, and through its selective figuration of (underprivileged) men and (privileged) women, it supports a distorted narrative about the interlocking relations between gender, class, and identity. What is false, in other words, is that by framing a socioeconomic power relation in this particular fashion, it misses that constellation's actual dynamic. It misses, for instance, that women overall, in many countries and in many professions, still earn disproportionately less than men, just as underpaid hard physical labor is oftentimes executed not by whites (as the image has it) but by people of color. Obviously, the meme's aim is to provoke liberals and disrupt feminist ideas, but it does so by deliberately erasing their political context.

This response would certainly not be wrong. There is no question that the meme attempts to coopt class politics from the right, blatantly pitting working-class interests and feminist interests against each other. But does the meme, precisely by documenting this attempt in such obvious fashion, not also suggest a different response? Does it not highlight an actual problem? And would it not be fruitful, therefore, to engage with the meme not simply by dismantling its ideological message, but also in light of how this essay began, namely by pointing out the increasing working-class drift to the right? If right-wing online activists deem it strategically useful to attack feminists by confronting them with their 'class blindness,' then they certainly touch on (and exploit) a sore spot: one that involves feminism (cf. Fraser 2013; Rottenberg 2014) as much as it involves the more general history of critical discourse and the left since the early 1980s. Indeed, the gradual abandonment of the concept of class during the neoliberal era – even within the political left, as it shifted from focusing on 'redistribution' to prioritizing 'recognition' issues (cf. Fraser/Honneth 2003) – has been analyzed by authors as diverse as Adolph Reed, Walter Benn Michaels, Slavoj Žižek, Nancy Fraser, Thomas Frank, Jodi Dean, Mark Fisher, and Didier Eribon.[25]

---

25   Eribon, for instance, argues that while Marxism in the 1960s and 1970s had marginalized issues such as gender, race, or sexuality, the 'cultural left' reversed this hierarchy in the last few decades by largely "neglecting class oppression" (2013: 241). This neglect, he claims, has in many ways contributed to the working-class drift to the extreme right: "I am convinced that voting for the National Front must be interpreted, at least in part, as the final recourse of people of the working classes attempting to defend their collective identity, or to defend,

In this regard, memes as the one analyzed above should also be read as warning signs for the left to take class matters seriously and counteract, in Mark Fisher's words, the "*dis*-articulation of class from other categories" (Fisher 2018: 741). While issues such as economic inequality and poverty have certainly become much more central since the financial crisis of 2008, the current US left, despite all claims to 'intersectionality' (cf. Collins/Bilge 2016), continues to have problems building effective political coalitions that would include people like precisely the white blue-collar worker depicted on the meme in question.[26]

For a number of reasons, to reverse this process is surely a difficult task. It will likely not be enough to simply point out common 'economic interests,' fending off right-wing attempts (which are echoed by some on the left) to culturalize class difference. For what is also required is an 'affective' political strategy that counters neoliberal resentment and *Schadenfreude*, seeking to uncouple desire from the retrotopian impulse.

Bibliography

Arendt, Hannah (1973): The Origins of Totalitarianism. New York: Harvest/Harcourt Brace Jovanovich.
Bauman, Zygmunt (2017): Retrotopia. Cambridge/Malden: Polity Press.
Berardi, Franco (2011): After the Future. Oakland/Edinburgh: AK Press.
Best, Stephen/Marcus, Sharon (2009): "Surface Reading: An Introduction." In: Representations 108 (1), pp. 1-21.
Blake, William (1995): The Poems of William Blake. London: Senate.
Blake-Beard, Stacy/Morgan, Laura Roberts (2004): "Releasing the Double Bind of Visibility for Minorities in the Workplace." In: Center for Gender in Organizations (CGO). Simmons University, September 2004 (www.simmons.edu/sites/default/files/2019-03/CGO%20Comm%204.pdf, 08.09.2019).
Blyth, Mark (2013): Austerity: The History of a Dangerous Idea. New York: Oxford UP.

---

in any case, a dignity that was being trampled on – now even by those who had once been their representatives and defenders." (132)

26 As Asad Haider (2018) argues, 'intersectionality' in today's left activist usage oftentimes does not facilitate coalition-building but, on the contrary, tends to obstruct it: "Those whose identity is inscribed with the most intersecting lines can claim the status of most injured, and are therefore awarded, in the juridical framework to which politics is now reduced, both discursive and institutional protection. This protected status implies neither the political subjectivity that can come from organizing autonomously, nor the solidarity that is required for coalitions that can engage in successful political action." (35)

Boczkowski, Pablo J./Papacharissi, Zizi (eds.) (2018): Trump and the Media. Cambridge/London: MIT Press.
Boltanski, Luc/Chiapello, Ève (2007): The New Spirit of Capitalism. New York: Verso.
Brown, Wendy (2010): Walled States, Waning Sovereignty. New York: Zone Books.
Brown, Wendy (2015): Undoing the Demos: Neoliberalism's Stealth Revolution. New York: Zone Books.
Carney, Timothy P. (2019): Alienated America: Why Some Places Thrive While Others Collapse. New York: HarperCollins.
Collins, Patricia Hill/Bilge, Sirma (2016): Intersectionality (Key Concepts Series). Cambridge/Malden: Polity.
Crary, Jonathan (2014): 24/7: Late Capitalism and the Ends of Sleep. London/New York: Verso.
Davis, Stephen/Lukomnik, Jon/Pitt-Watson, David (2006): The New Capitalists: How Citizen Investors Are Reshaping the Corporate Agenda. Boston: Harvard Business School Press.
Deleuze, Gilles (1992): "Postscript on the Societies of Control." In: October 59, pp. 3-7.
Deleuze, Gilles/Guattari, Félix (2007): Anti-Oedipus. Capitalism and Schizophrenia. London/New York: Continuum.
Didi-Huberman, Georges (2001): "Dialektik des Monstrums: Aby Warburg and the Symptom Paradigm." In: Art History 24 (5), pp. 621-645.
Eribon, Didier (2013): Returning to Reims. Los Angeles: Semiotext(e).
Felski, Rita (2012): "Critique and the Hermeneutics of Suspicion." In: M/C Journal 15 (1), (journal.media-culture.org.au/index.php/mcjournal/article/viewArticle/431, 07.08.2019).
Fisher, Mark (2009): Capitalist Realism: Is There No Alternative? Winchester: Zero Books.
Fisher, Mark (2014): Ghosts of My Life: Writings on Depression, Hauntology and Lost Futures. Winchester/Washington: Zero Books.
Fisher, Mark (2018): "Exiting the Vampire Castle." In: K-Punk: The Collected and Unpublished Writings of Mark Fisher (2004-2016). London/New York: Repeater Books, pp. 737-745.
Foucault, Michel (1995): Discipline and Punish: The Birth of the Prison. New York: Vintage Books.
Foucault, Michel (2008): The Birth of Biopolitics. Lectures at the Collège de France (1978-1979). New York: Palgrave Macmillan.
Frank, Thomas (2005): What's the Matter with Kansas? How Conservatives Won the Heart of America. New York: Henry Holt.
Fraser, Nancy (1995): "From Redistribution to Recognition? Dilemmas of Justice in a 'Post-Socialist' Age." In: New Left Review 212, pp. 68-93.

Fraser, Nancy (2013): Fortunes of Feminism: From State-Managed Capitalism to Neoliberal Crisis. London/New York: Verso.

Fraser, Nancy/Honneth, Axel (2003): Redistribution or Recognition? A Political-Philosophical Exchange. London/New York: Verso.

Freud, Sigmund (1964): The Future of an Illusion. Garden City, New York: Doubleday.

Haider, Asad (2018): Mistaken Identity: Race and Class in the Age of Trump. London/New York: Verso.

Harris, John (2016): "If You've Got Money, You Vote In … If You Haven't Got Money, You Vote Out." In: The Guardian, June 24, 2016 (www.theguardian.com/politics/commentisfree/2016/jun/24/divided-britain-brexit-money-class-inequality-westminster, 07.08.2019).

Harvey, David (2009): A Brief History of Neoliberalism. New York: Oxford UP.

Hochschild, Arlie Russell (2016): Strangers in Their Own Land: Anger and Mourning on the American Right. New York/London: The New Press.

Huang, Jon/Jacoby, Samuel/Strickland, Michael/K.K. Lai, Rebecca (2016): "Election 2016: Exit Polls." In: The New York Times, November 8, 2016 (nytimes.com/interactive/2016/11/08/us/politics/election-exit-polls.html, 06.08.2019).

Hunter, James Davison (1991): Culture Wars: The Struggle to Define America. New York: BasicBooks.

Izadi, Elahe/Heil, Emily/Andrews, Travis (2018): "Read the Entirety of Kanye West's Uninterrupted Oval Office Monologue, Annotated." In: The Washington Post, October 11, 2018 (www.washingtonpost.com/arts-entertainment/2018/10/11/read-entirety-kanye-wests-uninterrupted-oval-office-monologue-annotated/?noredirect=on, 07.08.2019).

Jameson, Fredric (2002): The Political Unconscious. Narrative as a Socially Symbolic Act. London/New York: Routledge.

Jameson, Fredric (2007): Archaeologies of the Future. The Desire Called Utopia and Other Science Fictions. London/New York: Verso.

Kant, Immanuel (1996): Kritik der reinen Vernunft. Ed. Wilhelm Weischedel (2 Volumes). Frankfurt/M.: Suhrkamp.

Kanzler, Katja/Scharlaj, Marina (2017): "Between Glamorous Patriotism and Reality-TV Aesthetics: Political Communication, Popular Culture, and the Invective Turn in Trump's United States and Putin's Russia." In: Zeitschrift für Slawistik 62 (2), pp. 316–338.

Keefe, Patrick Radden (2019): "How Mark Burnett Resurrected Donald Trump as an Icon of American Success." In: The New Yorker, January 7, 2019 (www.newyorker.com/magazine/2019/01/07/how-mark-burnett-resurrected-donald-trump-as-an-icon-of-american-success, 07.08.2019).

Klein, Naomi (2017): No Is Not Enough: Defeating the New Shock Politics. London: Allen Lane.

Koch, Lars/Nanz, Tobias/Rogers, Christina (eds.) (2020): The Great Disruptor: Über Trump, die Medien und die Politik der Herabsetzung. Stuttgart: J.B. Metzler.

Love, Heather (2010): "Close but not Deep: Literary Ethics and the Descriptive Turn." In: New Literary History 41, pp. 371–391.

McGuigan, Jim (2008): "Apprentices to Cool Capitalism." In: Social Semiotics 18 (3), pp. 309-319.

McGuigan, Jim (2009): Cool Capitalism. London/New York: Pluto Press.

Marx, Karl/Engels, Friedrich (2002): The Communist Manifesto. With an Introduction and Notes by Gareth Stedman Jones. London: Penguin.

Massumi, Brian (2005): "Fear (The Spectrum Said)." In: Positions 13 (1), pp. 31-48.

Michaels, Walter Benn (2006): The Trouble with Diversity. How We Learned to Love Identity and Ignore Inequality. New York: Henry Holt.

Moore, Michael (2018): "Michael Moore: Democrats Made Fatal Mistake in Not Taking Trump More Seriously in 2016" (Interview with Amy Goodman). In: Democracy Now, September 21, 2018 (www.democracynow.org/2018/9/21/michael_moore_democrats_made_fatal_mistake, 16.07.2019).

Mouffe, Chantal (2018): For a Left Populism. New York/London: Verso.

Nagle, Angela (2017): Kill All Normies: Online Culture Wars from 4chan and Tumblr to Trump and the Alt-Right. Winchester/Washington: Zero Books.

Pease, Donald (2019): "Trump: Populist Usurper President." In: REAL: Yearbook of Research in English and American Literature 34 (Democratic Cultures and Populist Imaginaries). Tübingen: Narr Verlag, pp. 145-174.

Peters, Christian H./Protevi, John (2017): "Affective Ideology and Trump's Popularity." Online source: www.protevi.com/john/TrumpAffect.pdf, 07.08.2019, (Draft Paper, 28.09.2017).

Piketty, Thomas (2014): Capital in the Twenty-First Century. Cambridge/London: The Belknap Press of Harvard University Press.

Protevi, John (2016): "Stanley on Ideology." In: Theoria 31 (3), pp. 357-369.

Rosa, Hartmut (2015): Social Acceleration: A New Theory of Modernity. New York: Columbia UP.

Rottenberg, Catherine (2014): "The Rise of Neoliberal Feminism." In: Cultural Studies 28 (3), pp. 418-437.

Schleusener, Simon (2014): "Neoliberal Affects: The Cultural Logic of Cool Capitalism." In: REAL: Yearbook of Research in English and American Literature 30, pp. 307-326.

Schleusener, Simon (2017): "The Dialectics of Mobility: Capitalism and Apocalypse in Cormac McCarthy's *The Road*." In: European Journal of American Studies 12 (3) (Special Issue: Cormac McCarthy Between Worlds), pp. 1-14.

Schleusener, Simon (2018): "Political Disconnects: Donald Trump, the Cultural Left, and the Crisis of Neoliberalism." In: Coils of the Serpent: Journal for the Study of Contemporary Power 2, pp. 20-34.

Schleusener, Simon (2019): "The Surveillance Nexus: Digital Culture and the Society of Control." In: REAL: Yearbook of Research in English and American Literature 34 (Democratic Cultures and Populist Imaginaries). Tübingen: Narr Verlag, pp. 175-201.

Schleusener, Simon (2020): "Trump als Symptom: Populistische Schockpolitik und die Krise der Demokratie." In: Lars Koch, Tobias Nanz, Christina Rogers (eds.): The Great Disruptor: Über Trump, die Medien und die Politik der Herabsetzung. Stuttgart: J.B. Metzler, , pp. 47-70.

Schumpeter, Joseph (1954): Capitalism, Socialism, and Democracy. London: George Allen & Unwin.

Sennett, Richard (1999): The Corrosion of Character. The Personal Consequences of Work in the New Capitalism. New York/London: W.W. Norton.

Sennett, Richard (2006): The Culture of the New Capitalism. New Haven/London: Yale UP.

Taylor, Charles (1992): Multiculturalism and the Politics of Recognition. An Essay. Princeton, NJ: Princeton UP.

Trump, Donald (2015): "Full Text: Donald Trump Announces a Presidential Bid." In: The Washington Post, June 16, 2015 (www.washingtonpost.com/news/post-politics/wp/2015/06/16/full-text-donald-trump-announces-a-presidential-bid/?noredirect=on, 08.09.2019).

Wacquant, Loïc (2009): Punishing the Poor: The Neoliberal Government of Social Insecurity. Durham/London: Duke UP.

Zak, Dan (2017): "Embracing the Insult, Disarming the Enemy." In: The Washington Post, January 16, 2017, p. C1.

Žižek, Slavoj (2009): First as Tragedy, Then as Farce. London/New York: Verso.

The *Alternative Right*, Masculinities, and Ordinary Affect

Simon Strick

A foundational problem of the term 'Alternative Right' to describe the cultural cadre of right-wing populism is that the term's definitions have by and large originated from within the movement itself. The term 'Alternative Right' was popularized around 2008 by American white nationalist Richard Spencer[1] and his 'think tank,' the *National Policy Institute*, and initially meant to articulate an alternative to mainstream US-American conservatism. Spencer positioned his political vision as a 'race conscious' alternative to the 'colorblind' – or covertly racist – traditionalism of Republicans and libertarians. The Alt-Right was to stand for a conservative intellectual movement that explicitly advocates for what Spencer calls 'European American culture' and 'Western Civilization,' both euphemisms for racial whiteness. In the 10 years since the term was coined, it has grown and metastasized, not least because many right-wing actors have deployed it strategically. Antifeminist provocateur and former *Breitbart*-editor, Milo Yiannopoulous, inserted a counter-cultural appeal into Spencer's idea in his influential 2016 essay, "An Establishment Conservative's Guide to the Alt-Right" (Bokhari/Yiannopoulos 2016). He conjured a punkish attitude to the Alt-Right and its internet associates to distinguish the movement from 'Nazis' and old conservatives alike, calling it a "1968 from the right." In 2016, Donald Trump's former strategist, Steve Bannon, used the term to infuse the *Breitbart* news brand with notoriety and pop-appeal. In a 2017 video entitled *What is the Alt-Right?*, Canadian right-wing journalist Gavin McInnes (*Rebel Media*) used the term to invoke clear boundaries between white nationalists (like Spencer or Jared Taylor), 'western chauvinists' like himself (who allegedly do not care about race), and 'the real Nazis' (e.g. the KKK).[2]

Some scholars (Hawley 2017; Nagle 2017) have uncritically followed these strategic demarcations, simply reproducing between-group distinctions as dic-

---

1 Cf. Entry on Spencer at Southern Poverty Law Center. www.splcenter.org/fighting-hate/extremist-files/individual/richard-bertrand-spencer-0, 30.05.2019
2 Rebel Media, "Gavin McInnes: What is the Alt-Right?," Youtube.com, 7.4.2016. youtu.be/UQC-Z9izaCa4, 06.12.2019.

tated by Spencer, Yiannopoulous, McInnes, and others: ethnonationalists and white supremacists – i.e. people tied to 'hard' beliefs in racial separatism and racial identity are thought distinct from phenomena like the so-called 'Alt-Lite' (right-leaning without racial ideas), internet trolls, anti-feminists, and 'men's rights groups' (Coston/Kimmel 2012; Lin 2017). Related phenomena, like the rise of identitarian activists (Richard Spencer, Martin Sellner of *IBÖ*) and (ultra)conservative commentators and alternative media producers on YouTube (e.g. *Rebel Media, Laut Gedacht*), are thought to be discreet, separate groups from an alleged 'Alternative Right proper.' Populist parties and politicians, such as from the *UKIP* and *AfD*, are again portrayed as distinct from these internet-based groups.

Such fine distinctions are strategic demarcations that have emerged at various points from within what Adrienne Massanari describes as an "amorphous networked community" (2018: 4) that capitalizes on its own amorphousness. In this article, I propose the term 'Alternative Right' to denote precisely this shapeshifting, formless network as the core of the New Right's online manifestations. The term thus implies a discursive network rather than a coherent ideological movement. The fine distinctions articulated by this community – such as between 'Alt-Right' and 'Alt-Light,' or ethnonationalism and civic nationalism – serve, above all, to make right-wing politics seem more interesting, diverse, and relatable to a growing diversity of audiences. To insist on such distinctions in a political analysis of current right-wing agitation means to fail to understand that the Alternative Right focuses on connectivity and blurred alliances between disparate actors, rather than on far-right orthodoxy that maintains neat differentiations between 'levels' of radicalization. In the New Right's vying for public attention, the net gains received from internal quarrels and differences are larger than the losses scored from not being 'ideologically coherent.' Indeed, 'diversity of opinion' is again and again flaunted by these networks and used to mask ideological tenets and racist politics. I will turn to a short analysis of the demonstration *Day for Freedom* of 07.05.2018, described as the "most significant far-right gathering in London for years" (Right Response Team 2018), in order to illustrate the networked character of what I call the 'Alternative Right.' Their renewed focus on diversity and connectivity must be acknowledged if their relevance and function within right-wing populism is to be understood.

Day For Freedom and the Reassessment of the *Alternative Right*

On 7 March 2018, a diverse and international collection of personalities from the online and real-world branches of the English-speaking right convened at Whitehall, London. The event itself claimed to advocate for 'free speech,' alleged to be under attack in Western societies, and took as its primary concern the arrest of Tommy Robinson (née Stephen Yaxley-Lennon). Currently the most prominent anti-Islam propagandist in the UK, ex-hooligan Robinson had been arrested for filming outside a court building in which a trial against a so-called 'grooming gang' was taking place. The event had been heavily publicized in right-wing media, which resulted in the publication of an online petition to "Free Tommy Robinson" that attracted some 500.000 signatures and caused the German *AFD* to offer political asylum to the former member of the neo-Nazi organization *English Defense League*. On behalf of Robinson, a diverse assortment of right-wing celebrities spoke at Whitehall: Canadian white nationalist Lauren Southern (via Skype) and Gavin McInnes[3], both veterans of right-wing online journalism, talked next to Anne Marie Waters of *Pegida UK* and Milo Yiannopolous; *UKIP*-leader Gerard Batten appeared alongside *Count Dankula* (née Markus Meechan), a tattooed YouTube prankster who, weeks earlier, had been fined 800 GBP for violating the Communications Act.[4] Robinson himself, still months from beginning his sentence, served as MC at the event and gave tear-jerking closing remarks. A drag-queen act, singing pop songs to frequent howls from the crowd, performed between speakers. Counter-protesters numbered around 400 compared to an estimated 4000 to 6000 attendees.

The event was intended to exhibit a 'diversity of opinions' while at the same time bringing together different racist, nationalist, and 'white power' groups from various national backgrounds, traditions, and media genres. Planned as a reaction to the 'PR-disaster' of the openly neofascist *Unite the Right* rally in Charlottesville, Virginia 2017, *Day for Freedom* demonstrates that the landscape of right-wing extremism has profoundly evolved in recent years. Through real-world networking efforts, and especially the fast and lucrative dynamics of online activities, new synergies and strategies have emerged and led to unprecedented coalitions and constellations: Replacing torch-bearing Nazi marches, the *Alternative Right* in London presented itself as a motley group of video pranksters and YouTube journalists, politicians, ex-hooligans, gaming nerds, and empowered female nationalists, all speaking out for 'broader issues,' such as censorship. "I don't see many Nazi flags, a distinct lack of swastikas [...] I think I have been lied to," proclaimed speaker Carl Benjamin amusedly to the audience's cheers.

Day for Freedom thus showcased the common rhetoric and fraternal coming-together of disparate groupings. It signalled the reconstitution and rebranding of a network, energized by its own 'diversity' and common goals, to attract new audiences and form new connections. Obviously, the 'internal differences' in the right-

---

3   www.splcenter.org/fighting-hate/extremist-files/group/proud-boys, 06.12.2019.
4   The fine was for posting a video of a pug repeatedly raising its right paw as Meechan 'humorously' commands 'Zieg Heil' and 'Gas the Jews' in a deep Scottish accent. See: Eordogh (2018).

wing milieu (anti-feminists, EU-sceptics, islamophobes, neo-Nazis, ethnonationalists) follow from the fact that a diversity of political and cultural actors – from online journalism, 'Old Right' organizations, and right-wing political parties – came to argue a 'coherent movement' into existence. But at the same time, claims of 'diversity' function as a smokescreen to make shared racist and nationalist agendas appear more 'interesting and heterogeneous' to outsiders and orbiters. My redefinition of the term *Alternative Right* is meant to reflect how these very different groups and actors of the populist and far-right have entered into a complex network that seeks to synergize within the larger culture war that French ideologue Alain de Benoist has termed *metapolitics* (Casadio 2014). Internet trolls, right-wing podcasters, ethnonationalist influencers, identitarian organizers, and members of populist parties each have their place and position within this network, as do all other cultural figures who come to temporarily occupy positions within its relational web (Strick 2018b).

I propose that two shared characteristics define this new *Alternative Right*, or *Alternative Rechte* (The term is much needed in German and European discussions of right-wing extremism). The first is intuitive: As a *network*, all actors behave self-referentially and self-reflexively – i.e. they constantly define and orient themselves within the network to make its relations work. What differentiates the new from the old right is this interest in connectivity, visible in public networking events like *Day for Freedom*, countless online debates between actors (Lewis 2018), or collective calls for solidarity, such as the Hashtag *#FreeTommyRobinson*. Whereas the old right functioned as a gated community with inner circles, chief ideologues, and top-down hierarchies (Winkler 2001), this new *Alternative Right* constitutes an amorphous network that shifts and redefines itself to enter new relations and connections, using its own fractures and disagreements to generate public appeal.

This relates to the second characteristic: *Alternative* highlights not only a conviction to represent the 'true will of the people' against a 'hypocritical elite,' as Mudde's (2007) definition of populism suggests. The *Alternative Right* develops cohesion and energy by characterizing this elite or ruling system as radically oppressive, calling forth a discourse of self-defense. To clarify, what I term *Alternative Right* refers to a right-wing discourse that does not necessarily attack 'elites' or dehumanize immigrants in the name of racist/volkish intolerance and hate, but rather shifts its rhetoric to convince audiences that the EU, migrants, or gender studies are actively and maliciously *attacking and oppressing them*.

In that vein, the London demonstration also capitalized on a new 'diversity of masculinities' that is united, not in being 'militantly right-wing,' but rather in their performance of being 'harmless' and 'oppressed': Yiannopoulous presented a campy and comedic version of his 'gay provocateur' persona; Canadian Gavin McInnes, signaling his multi-cultural alliances by switching between a Scottish tartan bonnet and a MAGA hat, performed more as a comedian than an agitator; *Count Dankula* related how he was fined by the British government for making a 'funny' video featuring a dog giving a Nazi-salute; and Tommy Robinson, who, over the last decade, transformed from hooligan to suit-wearing street journalist, nearly cried while reflecting on his having been censored for 'speaking the truth.' The nameless drag-queen act only further reinforced their collective image as a gathering of innocuous and funny white masculinities.

That these actors gathered under the banner of 'defending free speech' – rather than to attack the EU, migration and migrants, or advocate for white ethno-states – indicates that the Alternative Right, at least on its surface, has mutated from a 'hate movement' to one rallying around self-defense and the empowerment of 'regular people.' Its actors adopt the optic of a subaltern and minoritarian movement resisting an omnipresent oppressor and understand themselves as defending against colonizing forces. This core message of the Alternative Right is expressed bluntly in a YouTube video entitled "It's ok to be white [explained]," which proclaimed "Mainstream = Anti-Christian Anti-Male Anti-White"[5] (Fig. 1). The transformation from islamophobia to 'Christians as victims,' or from 'anti-gender' to identifying as 'marginalized men,' is often cosmetic, but this strategic change is profoundly influential for a new rhetoric and discursive strategy that has emerged on the right in recent years. Instead of touting supremacy or denigrating others in the name of an increasingly indefensible normalcy, the Alternative Right wins credibility and attractiveness by occupying the – traditionally left-associated – discursive modes of ideology critique, satire, post- or anticolonial positioning, and identity politics. The term Alternative Right denotes a shift from a rhetoric of fear to what might be called a performance of anticolonial struggle.

This central feature of the *Alternative Right* entails a distinct radicalization in that its performativity is not (only) ideological, but *primarily affective*: Its actors have transformed the hate of others, fear of immigration, contempt for elites, and other such formerly defining qualities into feelings of victimhood, marginalization, and an affect of besiegement. The public performance of these affects, and the exploitation of their connectivity, is the chief work of the network and discourse I term the *Alternative Right*. In the following I will discuss three examples of actors to explicate some of the consequences of this radical *affective shift* on the right, and how gender and sexuality are the primary sources powering the production of *Alternative Right Affect*.[6]

---

5   The video has since been deleted but can be viewed in its entirety in a 'reaction video' uploaded by user *JB Gunner* TV (www.youtube.com/watch?v=JM3TP1jOCs0, 06.12.2019). On the 'It's Ok to be White' provocation, see also Strick (2018a).
6   On affect, see: Gould (2010) and Gammerl/Hutta/Scheer (2017).

Figure 1: Video "It's ok to be white [explained]", Screenshot

Sargon of Akkad and the Freedom to be Left Alone

One of the speakers at *Day For Freedom* was Carl Benjamin, a YouTube commentator from Swindon, better known by his channel-name *Sargon of Akkad*. He started his online career in the early 2010s uploading videos of himself playing videogames. Like many other so-called gamers, Benjamin became 'politicized' in 2014 during an event known as *Gamergate* (Massanari 2017), a "large-scale online coalition of anonymous trolls, right-wing pundits and social reactionaries who united to attack prominent women in the video game industry" (Donovan/Lewis/Friedberg 2018: 54). When a mild form of feminist analysis met the videogaming community – in the form of video essays by Canadian media critic Anita Sarkeesian entitled "Tropes vs Women in Videogames" about the unsurprisingly sexist representation of female figures in videogames – this coalition of gamers, trolls, and right-wingers fired off hate speech and death threats against recognizable women and minorities in the gaming subculture and the online sphere in general. The so-called *gamergaters* saw themselves as a 'secluded community' of geeks that had suddenly become invaded by the 'hostile force' of feminist analysis; they narrated the unfolding events as 'digital natives' heroically defending their terrain from evil, feminist colonizers enabled by corrupt journalists and the media industry.

The protagonists and coordination of these anti-feminist and misogynist attacks have been thoroughly researched,[7] and the *gamergate*-event has been identified as a vital precursor and catalyst for the current network of the *Alternative Right*

---

7   See previous footnote. A good summary can be found at rationalwiki.org/wiki/Gamergate, 06.12.2019.

(Lees 2016). American right-wing figures such as Milo Yiannopoulos or Mike Cernovich received their first publicity through *gamergate*, and its anti-feminist and misogynist core message translated easily into the anti-emancipatory politics of concurrently forming right-wing populists. In 2014, *Sargon of Akkad* also sided with the 'gamer activists' and began publishing extended opinion videos with titles such as "Reasons why people hate feminists" or "How feminism destroys videogames" with mostly sarcastic or vitriolic commentary. Benjamin has since gathered one million subscribers on his YouTube channels and earns several thousand pounds per month through online donations. Operating three channels with more or less daily activity, Benjamin is one of the most important and popular political influencers on YouTube. Like countless other channels on the platform, *Sargon of Akkad* provides an almost seamless filtering and commentary of mainstream news and politics. His channel, like many others in the 'Alternative Influence Network' (Lewis 2018), provides a *metamedial* style of reporting that refashions the news as leftist propaganda, commenting and decoding their alleged 'ideology' almost in real-time. This meta-approach relies on personal and intimate presentations of the commentator's reactions, thoughts, and affects while consuming the so-called mainstream media (MSM). The *Alternative Right* thus styles itself as a group of 'second order observers,' unmasking media bias and fraudulent liberal politics, and building a highly accessible paranoid view on mainstream culture in the process.

Using qualitative methods, Rebecca Lewis (2018) has shown how Benjamin's YouTube channels act as a major hub and connector among protagonists of the *Alternative Right*, organizing discussions and interviews between overlapping groups such as ethnonationalists and moderates, gamers and politicians, protagonists of the 'old right' (such as Jared Taylor) and populist figures, including Trump's former strategist, Steve Bannon. *Sargon*'s political work on YouTube is also a business model: The better he develops his brand of political commentary, and the more his connective efforts accumulate audiences, the more money he earns. YouTube's algorithm, which refers users viewing gaming content to his videos and, from there, to other right-wing opinion-makers, is a centerpiece to that model.

At Day for Freedom, Sargon of Akkad – the brand – performed mainly from the position of a 'concerned liberal' speaking out against oppression (Fig. 2). His sermon-like speech reveals the affective shift currently pursued by the Alternative Right, and the rhetoric this shift implies. Reading from a little black notebook, Benjamin performed a somewhat nerdish, calm, and harmless masculinity, a 'private persona' with which his online audiences are familiar through the countless online videos broadcasted from his home studio. His speech proclaimed:

> "They want your property. They want your identity. They want your immortal soul. And they have a moral compulsion pushing them on. Their consciences won't let them rest because their belief systems will not permit tolerance of the different.

Figure 2: Video "Sargon of Akkad – FULL SPEECH Day for Freedom", Screenshot

They are afraid of differences and their own ability to handle things that are different. [...] They are afraid of what comes next [...] but I can say something they can't say: I am not afraid."⁸

In Benjamin's phrasing, the *Alternative Right* is dissident, it stands for difference, and it seeks liberation from hostile and oppressive forces guided by their own ineptitudes. 'They,' in *Sargon*'s speech, are "the totalitarians," with which he identifies the mainstream media, political correctness, the EU, and Islam – all united by a pathological hatred of 'others' (aka himself). In Benjamin's view, large parts of the Western world are ruled by this totalitarian assembly, which will not tolerate difference in opinion out of a fundamental fear of diversity. Explicitly denouncing the feminist truism with the words, "[...] they are totalitarian because they want to erase the distinction between the public and the private [...]," Benjamin attacks a quasi-colonialist force invading his privacy. The 'personal' and the 'private' for him are the main battleground of the current culture war. His claim to freedom and resistance against oppression is precisely "the freedom to be left alone," as the opening line from his speech informs. "How much will you concede to these tyrants?," he asks the cheering audience.

The significance of this rhetorical reversal in *Sargon of Akkad*'s speech should not be underestimated. Indeed, a core political strategy of the *Alternative Right* is precisely this reversal of positions. Instead of conjuring stereotypes of islamophobia, anti-EU sentiment, or denouncing all things 'un-British,' the speech claims self-

---

8   Video Source: Bull Brand, "Sargon of Akkad - FULL SPEECH Day For Freedom #DayForFreedom", 20.05.2018. www.youtube.com/watch?v=Ky3HrZ_U-sY, 06.12.2019.

defense of private citizens against an oppressive, colonizing system invading their privacy and curtailing the freedom to speak and think. Identifying the enemy as a vague alliance between politicians, feminists, Muslims and the media, the *Alternative Right* embraces the resulting condition of 'crisis normal'[9]: "...every statement they make is in opposition to your natural rights. You must believe what they believe. You must act as they act and you must say what they say, and don't you forget it," Benjamin states. He claims the status of a 'colonized group,' and evokes a constant sense of being besieged and subjugated by hostile forces – constituted by a shapeshifting mixture of cultural, political, demographic, and fictitious actors. This conjuring of a hostile atmosphere and the resulting affect of besiegement is what *Alternative Right*-influencers on the internet produce, thus fleshing out the rigid binarisms that right-wing populism dispenses. In Benjamin's media productions, the fundamental populist opposition between 'the people' and 'the elites' is evoked as a rift tangible in videogames, media items, casual encounters, and private worlds. The primary point of Benjamin's 'postcolonial positioning' is thus not to argue for a 'volkish identity' in need of defense; rather, his basic intention is to conjure a pervasive state of embattlement that is palpable in the quotidian, the everyday, the intensely private. *Sargon* calls forth an "affective state" (Gould 2010: 34), a constantly palpable marginalization caused by terrifying totalitarians and invaders, preventing him and others from living in 'private' and forcing them to become 'dissidents.' "We just wanted to play videogames," *Sargon* jokes several weeks later at a protest against the EU's Article 13.

In this sense, the *Alternative Right* presents what Raymond Williams (2014) called a "structure of feeling," or an "affective community." It thrives on, in the words of Sara Ahmed, "feelings of structure" (2010: 216) – the sense of constantly edging against institutions, norms, and invisible regimes. Public debate over the reach of content policies on social media – such as by Facebook, YouTube, or Patreon – is a primary resource for producers like Benjamin to conjure such "feelings of structure," the ever-so-slight marginalization experienced by people like him.

Sargon of Akkad conjures such affect in thousands of hours of video commentary; he finds evidence for feminist colonization in the videogames he plays, the media he consumes, the conversations he has. That is the affect he produces, the feeling that his own private, normal, reasonable British masculinity is being constantly diminished, persecuted, and brainwashed by an evil conglomerate of feminists and liberals. After all, he just wanted to "play videogames" and share some "rational arguments backed up by evidence," as the description of his YouTube channel reads.

---

9   Martin Sellner, ideologue of the Austrian identitarians, termed this sense of quotidian embattlement "de facto Kriegsrecht"; similarly, the German identitarian movement's webpage compares its situation to that of Native American populations during the colonial period. See: www.identitaere-bewegung.de/category/faq/, 06.12.2019.

In that regard, *Sargon* projects populism's binarisms onto a nerd identity and casual consumptive habits, which evidence, no matter how minimally, the encroaching power of 'liberal totalitarians.' His move from "How feminism ruins videogames" to advocating for British nationalism and an end to migration into Britain therefore presents less a political radicalization, but rather the projection of a particular, intimate affect of 'besiegement' onto wider political scenarios.

The 'harmless nerd' image and personal branding did not prevent Benjamin from joining *UKIP* in 2018 and running as a candidate for the party in the 2019 European Elections. Discussions and analyses of right-wing populism in Europe and elsewhere should take note of figures like *Sargon of Akkad*/Carl Benjamin: They have not only *come into* right-wing politics from vastly different backgrounds and genres of social media and internet subcultures; they have also *contributed and pioneered* effective strategies, rhetorics, and the performance of affective tonalities that embed oppositional and populist politics into the everyday experiences of young audiences. In so doing, such internet influencers have transformed how the populist right presents itself, vies for public attention, agglomerates audiences, and acquires funding.

Roosh V and Neomasculinity

Another linkage between right-wing populism and the quotidian can be found in the politicization of sexuality, advanced in internet spaces comprising the so-called 'manosphere' (Ging 2017). Here, the racist theory of 'The Great Replacement' – centerpiece of the extreme right's paranoid worldview – is hooked up to casual and mundane sexual lifeworlds of male internet consumers looking for advice to achieve 'alpha-male status.' 'The Great Replacement' theory claims that the West is being (purposely) flooded with hypersexual ethnic men, infiltrating white societies and causing the 'repopulation' (in German, 'Umvolkung') of white countries with reproductively superior brown bodies. The theory, which rehashes eugenic claims of 'race suicide' from the early twentieth century,[10] came to recent global attention with the mass killing of 50 people in Christchurch, New Zealand, in March 2019: The perpetrator's manifesto featured the slogan prominently on its first page.

'The Great Replacement' features in the *Alternative Right* in many variations: argued through demographic projections that indicate ethnically white populations losing their 'absolute majority' in the coming decades; it figures as part of a global

---

10   This theory was expounded for example by prominent zoologist and eugenicist Madison Grant, in his bestseller *Passing of the Great Race* (1916).

Jewish conspiracy to minoritize white people and achieve 'white genocide'[11]; or as a result of the post-imperial, postcolonial, or post-fascist 'guilt complex' of European democratic societies, which is the result of internationally pervasive 'victim industries' that have undermined national and ethnic pride.[12] Especially this latter rebranding of racism as cultural critique, positing a sort of 'cultural death drive' in postwar European societies, has proven highly compatible with the *Alternative Right*'s views on gender and sexuality. Vital to 'The Great Replacement' is not only the migration of ethnic Others into allegedly white societies, but also the curtailing of white male sexuality by political feminism and political correctness, leading to the fundamental sexual disempowerment of men in the West.

Darius Valizadeh, also known by his online handle *Roosh V*, shall serve here as one protagonist of the online-based manosphere who has explicitly moved towards attuning the discourse of 'male sexuality' to these tropes of white racial paranoia. *Roosh*, who has Armenian and Iranian ancestors, long lived in the US and recently adopted the lifestyle of a nomadic traveler in Europe. Around 2005, *Roosh* emerged on various internet message boards as a so-called 'Pick-up Artist' (PUA) - i.e. a man giving advice to other men on how to 'pick up' women (Baker 2013). *Roosh* called his dating advice "GAME," a kind of self-help manual for heterosexual men seeking casual sex. After some success in the online community, he published a series of e-books titled *BANG*, which describe how he achieved – or "scored," in his terminology – sexual encounters with women in several countries. A series of misogynistic and utilitarian books followed: *BANG Estonia*, *BANG Serbia*, *BANG Poland*, *BANG Brazil*. These books are by-and-large manuals for adolescent male insecurity, which prescribe having sex and objectifying women as 'bait,' 'challenges,' or 'scores.' *Roosh*'s writing frames successful male sexuality as hard work and self-control: he elaborates how to correctly apply 'techniques' to 'conquer' and 'manipulate' women into sexual relations, and describes intercourse in technical terms, like 'insertion,' 'domination' and 'success.' Other writers have followed *Roosh*'s successful line of 'misogyny as business strategy': In the German market, for example, Orlando Owen occupies *Roosh V*'s slot, offering online seminars on how to improve masculine self-perception, pick-up tips, and so forth. In a video entitled "How Fascism oppresses your masculinity,"[13] Owen proclaims: "Political correctness is the

---

11 See e.g. the "Frequently asked questions" on the website *rightrealist.com*: rightrealist.com/#q18, 06.12.2019.

12 This latter theory is argued by British author Douglas Murray in his book *The Strange Death of Europe: Immigration, Identity, Islam* (2017), and is neatly summarized in an educational video Murray did for the far-right fake university *PragerU* entitled "The Suicide of Europe." See: PragerU, "The Suicide of Europe," YouTube.com, 14.05.2018. youtu.be/stR5nWkq3LU, 06.12.2019.

13 (www.youtube.com/watch?v=vDcZCwQxhCQ&frags=pl%2Cwn, video set to private, 06.12.2019)

definition of fascism" and "Feminism is the icing on the cake of fascism" – similar to *Sargon of Akkad*, these articulations of white men as victims of a hostile, totalitarian force (i.e. feminism) serve primarily to dispense an affect of besiegement that is to be felt intimately in one's sexual habits and corporeal states.

In 2010, *Roosh* launched the website *Return of Kings* (www.returnofkings.com), where he and other writers formulated the theories and worldviews underlying 'GAME' and 'BANG' under the term *neomasculinity*. The definition from the article "What is Neomasculinity/Game?" surmises the following cultural and sexual diagnostic:

> "Due to changes in mating behavior and pair bonding brought on by technology, shifting demographics, migration to cities from rural towns, universal suffrage, promotion of sexually promiscuous behaviors, and destruction of traditional sex roles, most men do not have the ability or knowledge to successfully reproduce with a modern woman on a comparable attractiveness and socioeconomic level. [...] 'Game' is a collection of socially-based tactics and reproducible behaviors that increase a man's sexual attractiveness to women and therefore his access to reproduction. [...] In modern Western societies, a man who doesn't at least subconsciously understand game concepts is unlikely to have sex at all." (Roosh 2016)

For *Roosh*'s presumably adolescent audiences, *neomasculinity* provides a convincingly technical and professional-sounding explanation for their insecurities in sexual and gendered behavior. Echoing the languages of sociobiology, and behavioral and evolutionary psychology, *Roosh* transforms simplistic and common-sensical observations – e.g. relations between men and women are difficult; sexual relations tend to follow market logics – into a cultural shift that has disempowered straight men, and 'requires' them to proactively self-improve within hierarchical models of so-called 'alpha' and 'beta' masculinities. While *Roosh*'s arguments do double duty to justify rape culture and anti-feminism, his core messaging relies in a deterministic and inescapable sense of straight men *not-being-okay*: Larger societal shifts have conspired to make them feel sexually awkward, unsuccessful, or unaccomplished, and this depressing feeling is tangible in very general, pervasive, and mundane terms. 'Not getting laid? No masculine confidence? It might be feminism,' the marketing slogan might read.

Posters on the like-minded Reddit Forum *r/theredpill*[14] excel at such dismal versions of 'doing masculinity,' and have assembled them in *The Red Pill Handbook, 2nd Edition* (2015),[15] an extensive collection of posts from the forum. Combining misogyny and male self-hate into a single formula, the handbook convinces young readers of their utter uselessness in the grand scheme of things sexual, social, and biological:

> "Men have always been the disposable sex. It's the biological truth of our species. The number of wombs in a tribe represented its most important resource: the capacity for reproduction. One very happy man could generate enough semen to impregnate the women of an entire tribe. So what about the other men? They have ZERO inherent reproductive value. What does that mean? Your life is inherently worthless. SOCIETY DOES NOT GIVE A SHIT ABOUT YOU. It sucks, but it's our biological tendency." (Red Pill Handbook 2015: 100)

The *Red Pill Handbook* and *Roosh*'s *neomasculinity* turn a very general and quotidian affect – insecurity, lack of confidence – into a shareable worldview and a political and personal program; *Roosh*'s countless YouTube-diaries constantly reinforce and validate this affect of 'just being a guy' who fights against the loss of his sexual *okayness* imposed upon him, and shares 'empowering' stories with his audience. The Alt-Right publication *Taki's Magazine* consequently called *Roosh*'s neomasculinity "a heroic grassroots information-sharing response to the sociological confusions that feminist tyranny generates" (Wyatt 2013).

The quotidian affect of finding it difficult to approach women is used by *Roosh* and his associates to legitimize anti-feminism and misogyny, and an identity politics of 'male victimhood' and 'masculine empowerment' in an adversarial society. Even beyond this, however, *neomasculinity* also seamlessly transforms into white nationalist discourse. In October 2017, *Roosh* published an article on his website entitled "Kill Whitey":

---

14   In reference to the first *Matrix* Movie (1999), 'taking the red pill' entails gaining consciousness of a society in which one is oppressed and exploited; becoming red-pilled means to free one's mind from the constraints of PC culture. The 'Red Pill' indexes a moment of awakening to the fact that one's way of life is under siege. The YouTube genre of 'Red-pill-moments' presents affective thresholds, personal and intimate scenarios of 'this is more than I can bear, and I see the structure that makes me feel so miserable. I have to speak my mind against it.' Red Pill moments, becoming prominent in post-2013 gamer commentary, build a community and an audience around a sense of 'identity' as members of an oppressed group (gamers, men, whites, etc.). Around 2004, performing this moment of awakening to see oneself forced into an ideological battle - a culture war - became a staple of the vlog-format, and helped many YouTubers to build their personal brands as internet celebrities and influencers. See also: Van Valkenburgh, Shawn P. "Digesting the Red Pill: Masculinity and Neoliberalism in the Manosphere." In: *Men and Masculinities* (2018).

15   See: www.reddit.com/r/AlreadyRed/comments/39cufk/the_red_pill_handbook/, 06.12.2019.

"I have come to believe that liberals have an explicit goal to crush men, primarily through the meme of feminism, but I now realize that that was only an intermediary step for a more comprehensive agenda: kill whitey. What I thought was a war against men is really a battle within a bigger war against white people. [...] By publishing masculine advice to a majority white audience, I was put in the cross hairs. But if I released GAME-guides in Urdu, Dari, or Pashto, I would get big financing and puff stories in the media about how I empower marginalized men of color whose ancestors were victims of white colonialism. The media attacked me for being 'pro-rape' [...] yet they can't seem to get around to reporting on the insane real-rape epidemic in Sweden and Germany. ... because I've helped red pill tens of thousands of white men on women, I get the public whip." (Roosh 2017)

The post is primarily a lament about Amazon's decision to drop his e-books from their online store, but nevertheless *Roosh*'s silly masculine sex advice easily blends into several discursive tropes popular with the *Alternative Right*: 'race suicide' facilitated through immigration of non-whites; the sexual and thus reproductive curtailing of white men; the feminist-liberal conspiracy to accelerate the 'Great Replacement' by culturally empowering non-white men and condoning their 'inherent rape-culture'; and the 'outlawing' of white men's heterosexuality. "Does your traditionalist family advice possibly help white women raise white children? You will be demonetized or banned from Silicon Valley's platforms," *Roosh* posits with a link to 'traditionalist' YouTuber *Wife With A Purpose*,[16] and then concludes: "History shows that wars and genocides happen after a period of dehumanizing a race or people. This is what's happening to whites as the kill whitey movement approaches its final stage." (ibid.)

In *Roosh*'s and much of the *Alternative Right*'s worldviews, the struggle for male sexual success is a struggle for white survival and the future of Western (white) civilization – which is under attack from within and without. The global conspiracy to 'kill whitey' is apparent in his every viewer's sexual insecurity and lack of masculine self-esteem. That white men feel insecure about how to approach women becomes evidence of the Great Replacement; and not getting laid is evidence of 'Umvolkung.' In response, the *Alternative Right* promises a sexual revolution for white men, and for white women as well, who "Secretly WANT Patriarchy," as like-minded vlogger *Blonde in the Belly of the Beast* contends.[17]

---

16   In the linked video, Ayla Stewart narrates how her 'traditionalist channel' was dropped from the funding website Patreon, which she sums up with the quote: "[...] traditional living and videos of a white family are 'hate speech' according to Patreon." Online: youtu.be/1gl9Y9Bno8Y, 06.12.2019.

17   Blonde in the Belly of the Beast, "Do Women Secretly WANT Patriarchy?", YouTube.com, 08.06.2018. youtu.be/KUL2pl1psSw, 08.06.2018. See also (Dietze 2019, 131-133)

'Kill Whitey' links up several racist talking points and network positions of the *Alternative Right*, and cushions them in an easily digestible 'red pill lesson' that dresses up to rationalize chauvinist-racist behaviors as 'white male empowerment.' However, the text's point is to hook up its readers' mundane lifeworlds to larger ideological, conspirational, and racist ideas: *Roosh*'s idea of 'getting the public whip' (being temporarily dropped by Amazon) and his global conspiracy against 'white people' links up with a cluster of feelings much more intimately known to *Roosh*'s online readership, lending them weight: sexual insecurity, the sense of being ostracized on a daily basis by political correctness, and losing their general *okay-ness* as white men: hence, one rallying cry of the *Alternative Right* proclaimed: "It's ok to be white." (see Strick 2018a)

What these minor points conjure is the tangibility of anti-male and anti-white bias in quotidian media consumption: Amazon's algorithms, the mere visibility of black men on social media, the very sense that white men are always already 'not okay/whipped' in the mediated public sphere – these are the millenial-targeted counterpoints to *Roosh*'s narration of sexual and racial disempowerment. Media behaviors in this sense are affectively linked to imagined sexual behaviors, and the confirmation of *Roosh*'s paranoid view on Western culture lies not only in how many women his readers can (fictively) 'score,' but also in the very landscapes of media consumption they navigate.

So, apart from the discursive short-circuiting of male sexuality with ethnonationalism, *Roosh*'s article demonstrates how important the specter of censorship and public outrage is to the *Alternative Right*. As media outlets and scholars denounce their speech acts and politics, the *Alternative Right* reaps constant validation for feeling entrenched, attacked, and outlawed from these same acts. Every move to 'de-platform' their videos or writings fortifies a sense of embattlement, providing them with yet another example of leftist censorship *and* sexual disempowerment. *Roosh* and many others in the *Alternative Right* relentlessly perform this lonely outrage over being publicly marginalized as sexual discrimination. They thus devise a 'libidinal economy' for one's presence in and consumption of media, where every tweet, every click, every 'MeToo'-Hashtag, and every story involving gender, sexuality, or race is exploitable to intensify the traffic of subaltern affect; to generate more feelings of *not-being-okay*.

In the online-sphere, 'white genocide,' antifeminism, media consumption and heteromasculine self-assurance thus become entangled to produce an affective atmosphere that is as much hysteric – triggered and intensified by countless quotidian occasions – as it is depressive: "[The war on men] is a defensive war. We have been attacked, shamed, and taxed by them and now there is not much of our blood left," as *Roosh* writes in his 2013 blog post "The War Against Men."

A considerable disadvantage of arguing the loss of white male potency and normalcy through a universalizing sociobiological framework of 'male disposability' (as the above-quoted *RedPill-Handbook* does) seems to be that it leaves hardly any plausible ways of empowerment to productively 'fight back': the sense of universal male victimhood is expounded to such a degree that 'liberatory' countermeasures become unlikely. Consequently, the online-based *MRA* and *MGTOW* movements, and their respective textualities, are deeply depressive, extoll mainly disillusionment-narratives of exiting society and/or sexual relations per se, and can frequently only resort to conjurings of homosocial societal models as a counterpoint to the alleged dominance of women. The *MGTOW*-movement, abbreviating the slogan 'Men going their own way,' consequently can imagine 'remasculinization' only through disengaging society and sexuality altogether: the final stage of *MGTOW* and its struggle against tyrannical feminism is the hermit living in the woods. Optimism, in such models, is a scarce commodity, and *Roosh*'s lonely YouTube-diaries (Fig. 3), broadcasted from so many empty and similar-looking rooms in Europe, give a bleak appeal to becoming a 'professional white nationalist bachelor.' The depressing affect prevents this particular sexualized fascism from developing its seductive powers.

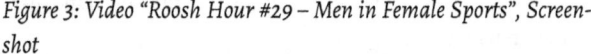

Figure 3: Video "Roosh Hour #29 – Men in Female Sports", Screenshot

The Golden One and White Optimism

Marcus Follin, better known as *The Golden One*, is a Swedish 'semi-fascist,' who also dispenses white masculine self-help on YouTube, but with a sustained focus on optimism. *The Golden One* is a developing online brand: As of January 2019, he has 85.000 YouTube subscribers and 20.000 followers on Instagram. A bodybuilder and martial arts fighter, he has diversified his business model to selling sportswear ('High Thumos Clothing *Legio Gloria*') and what he calls 'traditionalist nutritional supplements.' His YouTube channel is a mixture of videogames, dieting tips, work-out videos, opinion pieces – he calls those "the glorious teachings" – and regular challenges that his viewers can take up. Follin also travels Europe on far-right speaking engagements, or he works out with other muscular men in the US, Poland, Ukraine, or Thailand.

Two aspects about *The Golden One*'s performance and persona might further the discussion of the *Alternative Right* pertaining to masculinity and affect: 1) Follin pursues a 'campy aesthetic' or what might be called 'Nordic Kitsch'; and 2) he almost completely substitutes the tropes of right-wing paranoia for motivational and positive messaging. Both characteristics are crucial to further understand the affective and identitarian models that the online-based *Alternative Right* offers to audiences.

Kitsch presents a vital aspect of current populist and rightwing performances (Strick 2019). *Kitsch* as a term attends both to a) the populist efforts to reintroduce and revalidate archaic, nostalgic and obsolete forms of white heterosexuality, 'white culture,' and male dominance; and b) to the always metamedial processes and paradoxes at work when such archaisms are produced within postmodern digital media environments.[18] *The Golden One* embraces this *kitschy* or campy dissonance in his online-performance of 'heroic white masculinity.' As his Instagram channel reveals, Follin cherishes the performative silliness of embodying the viking-ideal of white superiority in 2018: his abundant muscle-posturings in the Swedish countryside, clad in Spartan armor, are pretentious and also somewhat humorous "fascist camp" (see: Cleto 1999; Halberstam 2011: 147-72); the accompanying mythology of 'white culture, history and heritage' comes straight from computer games that are mixed with quotes by Italian pro-fascist philosopher Julius Evola; he wears costumes that resemble the overblown proportions of Marvel comic superhero *Thor*; interviewing British neo-Nazi-veteran Marc Collett for his channel, the two talk at length about fantasy war-gaming rather than white supremacy; and his (rather witless) 'glorious teachings' are delivered in a daft Swedish pronunciation of antiquated English steeped in fantasy vocabulary: "I will issue an eedict, and say to all white man: stop being so terribly weeek."[19]

Instead of *Sargon*'s 'concerned nerd' or *Roosh*'s 'depressed nomadic masculinist,' Follin has adopted a fictionalized and campy self-branding: He is fully invested in the mediatized aspects of his viking-persona and proudly displays his audience's 'fan-art' on his Instagram (Fig. 4). This heightened fantasy-reality blend of

---

18   Media scholar Whitney Phillips discusses similar modes in their work, albeit under the normalizing term 'irony' (Phillips/Milner 2018).
19   The Golden One, "White Man. Stop Letting Your Woman Trample You Down." Youtube.com, 25.01.2018. youtu.be/dnE3mlQmeQE, last access 05.06.2019, since deleted.

Figure 4: Instagram Page, The Golden One@thegloriouslion, Screenshot

The Golden One – which internet communities call LARPing (live action role-playing) – can be understood within cultural traditions of fantastic 'hyperracial' imaginaries, such as Minstrel shows of black performers expressing what Tavia N'yongo calls "racial kitsch" (2002). Here, however, the exaggerated, ironic, and stereotypical performance is given to white, European masculinity, and exacerbated by the digital environments in which Follin commodifies his 'built' body and 'fantasy' identity: "And who am I? I'm the great angel," he says, flexing his muscles. The affective gain within the online communities Follin engages with is an irritatingly friendly and humorous persona. His performance links up with the fascist imaginary of a 'master race,' but articulates it within the slanted iconographies of fantasy texts such as *Warhammer* or *Lord of the Rings.*

Follin's *campiness* links to the second feature: *The Golden One*'s influencing is almost exclusively about optimism and personal improvement for 'members of the white race.' In his aforementioned opinion video on white male disenfranchisement through immigration, he does not preach regular right-wing topics, and there is no overt racism or hate speech: Follin comments on an image showing a white middle-aged couple in which the woman is embraced by a non-white man – a visual meme of the so-called 'cuckold'-trope. This reference to the 'Great Replacement' – white women exchanging white husbands for brown hypersexual men – is underhanded, and he makes his main argument not about racism, but about white masculine self-empowerment: He proposes workouts, physical culture, abstinence from pornography, and the rediscovery of 'white' heritage, honor, and confidence. Instead of hate speech or ideology, *The Golden One* remakes 'white pride' as motivational language: He asks his audience to overcome the negative thinking and depression induced by feminism and multiculturalism. His message is about positivity: "If you have a bad day, remember you're not this guy [the cuckolded husband]," and "treat yourself with dignity."

The comments' section to this YouTube-video highlights how the reframing of 'racial pride' as relationship advice produces a *shareable affect* between Follin and his audience. Referencing a revisionist film well-known among Holocaust-deniers (*Hitler: The Greatest Story Never Told*; Denis Wise 2013), Follin comments on his own emotional improvement through 'race consciousness': "I would never engage romantically in a fair maiden [sic] who hasn't even watched *The Greatest Story Never Told*. I am 100% serious. If she doesn't respect me enough to spend 6 hours attaining a higher level of Enlightenment I am definitely [sic] not going to invest time + emotions in her. It is important to respect yourself enough to set boundaries and expectations upon others."

His viewers easily identify with this view and concur with similar advice, and transpose Follin's commentary into different interpretations, from media wariness to conjurings of male strength to violent insurgence. User *MM* warns: "The media loves showing images like that to demoralize/emasculate white men. Don't let it get to you." User *Pax Americana* seconds: "Stop being weak. Strength is the core of being a man. No matter what normies tell you about (((toxic masculinity))). God I grow more militant by the day." User *Harley's Rule* applauds Follin: "Brilliant analysis... I cannot understand why ALL WHITE MEN cannot understand this also. We either fight or we die... it boils down to this. All governments must be for their people or they must be removed. Gather together, replace the governments, remove the primitive low IQ brown invaders by force."

In a different (since deleted) video, Follin explains his interpretation of *metapolitics* and the 'culture war from the right': for him, *metapolitics* means to promote notions of white positivity and white identity, and to oppose all forms of negativity, hatred, and 'degeneracy.'[20] He smiles as he proposes to give money to immigrants so that they leave Europe, "because that's what they came for and they will leave by the same token." *The Golden One* might come across like a fantasy-role-playing *Wehrsportgruppe*, but he isn't: He is not training for a violent riot, but to sell white supremacist ideology as optimism, humor, body positivity, and personal and spiritual lifestyle – a way to feel good about oneself amidst 'decadent mainstream culture.' His viewers hook onto this affect and radicalize the implicit far-

---

20 The Golden One, "Metapolitics of the Real Right. Humour is a True Friend," YouTube.com, 18.10.2015; youtu.be/Z_F5EV1zOuw, last access 02.06.2019, since deleted.

right messaging according to their own affective states. This does not prevent Follin from exploiting his audience with product placement or from joining the ranks of public agitators and networkers in the *Alternative Right*: The supremacist Viking has spoken at neo-Nazi meetings with many far-right leaders such as the former KKK grand-wizard David Duke, Dutch agitator Geert Wilders, and many others.

While the *Alternative Right* is, as I pointed out before, a highly operational and self-referential *network*, its primary habitation in the attention-market of the internet also results in a highly 'competitive' logistics shaping the field. *The Golden One* supplies the positive counterpoint to *Sargon of Akkad*'s quotidian state of besiegement and *Roosh*'s depressing sexual-racial determinism. Follin sells a proto-fascist sense of white male identitarian positivity, while others capitalize on acidic critiques of an alleged mainstream or dystopian messaging. These different performative registers of the *Alternative Right* match together to offer a holistic environment, and simple diagnosis-remedy-programs for young, millennial audiences. Competing with Follin's 'white-positive lifestyle advice' are numerous other channels – Roaming Millenial, Hunter Avallone, Rollo Tomassi – selling similar content. One hope might be that their versatile, audience-specific, and market-oriented commodifications of 'feeling alternative right' will at some point be stalled by their inherent neoliberal logistics: The 'attention economy' and self-cannibalizing habits of the online world might hopefully lead to right-wing popularity eating itself.

Conclusion

Populism, according to Ernesto Laclau, requires an investigation into "[...] how social agents 'totalize' the ensemble of their political experience" (4) – that is, how people learn to use populism's modes of fundamental opposition for orientation in their own political choices, in their always-complex lives, and for ways of navigating these complexities. Laclau's pertinent question, how people make use of simplistic ideological models like 'us vs. them' to navigate disparate experiences and contradictory circumstances (which are also produced by populist performances and politics themselves), points us to the work that contemporary social media do within populism's frameworks. Bharath Ganesh phrases the function of right-wing spaces on social media as such: "Digital hate culture goes beyond offense; it employs dangerous discursive and cultural practices on the Internet to radicalize the public sphere and build support for radical right populist parties" (2018: 32). The *Alternative Right* in this reading provides the groundwork of radicalization and funnels private citizen into populist support. As my article has tried to demonstrate, this sells the crucial cultural and pop-cultural work of this online network short and underestimates its relevance as well as its dangers. Reiterating merely that the

Alternative Right's intervention into the political field offers (re-) legitimizations of racism, sexism, nationalism, and imperialism – i.e. populism's agenda of 'hate and division' – is not too helpful for understanding the scripts and scenarios that I have discussed here. Rather, I argue that the *Alternative Right* provides copious *affective value* to populism and articulates very granular worldviews and points of friction to consumers of these texts.

The *Alternative Right* provides plausible and 'feelable' scenarios – circling around freedom of speech, sexuality, and gendered and racial identity – in which (mostly) white, male, and heterosexual individuals can convince themselves of their oppression in majority white and heteronormative societies. Far from just stoking and channeling anger, these online producers offer ways to feel simultaneously better and worse about oneself: They excel in devising scenes of victimization by nebulous oppressive forces, and at the same time point to ways to resist this alleged totalitarianism. Gender and sexuality are fundamental aspects of these affective worlds that the *Alternative Right* builds for its audiences, since both gender performance (masculinity) and sexual habits multiply the amount of pressure points to which a 'feeling of lost *okay-ness*' can attach itself. This is what the elected cadres of the New Right cannot deliver: convincing, granular, and intimate affective performances of a white masculinity 'under siege,' palpable in everyday sexual and gendered experience, tangible in quotidian things such as playing videogames, looking for sex, or working out. The *Alternative Right*, capitalizing on the strangely intimate and consumptive publics of social media, makes the 'Great Replacement' or 'leftist censorship' things that can be experienced daily, simply by watching the news, consuming media or checking how one feels.

A second aspect following from my discussion here is that research on populism and far-right networks therefore needs to recalibrate its attention and methodologies. While right-wing populism has been conceptualized as a phenomenon in international politics, the *Alternative Right* offers a decidedly *transnational* and *multigeneric* prospect. The amorphous network described in this article dispatches its nationalisms across borders and beyond national contexts, as the discussion of *Day For Freedom* has shown. Moreover, transnationally impacting actors like *Sargon of Akkad* and *Roosh V* indicate that extremism research needs to consider other backgrounds and trajectories than the continuities between 'classic' forms of right-wing radicalism (neo-Nazi movements, fraternities, radical parties): The *Alternative Right*'s protagonists originate in very disparate contexts, like gaming subculture, masculinity movements, sexist online cultures, or fantasy fandom. Their affective scripts and attunements – like the anticolonial feeling of 'gamers' organizing against feminist scholarship infringing on their subculture – have been vital imports to nationalist and populist movements of the present, and shape their constantly recalibrating communication, self-presentation, and agitation. That a 'gaming nerd' like *Sargon of Akkad* runs (unsuccessfully) for the UK Independence Party is an indicator, not of populism winning over the youth, but of the confluence of very disparate cultures and scenes agreeing on a shared 'affective stance.' Whether this stance produces adversarialism against feminism and political correctness, or against migration and non-white individuals, is almost beside the point for the heterogeneous targeted audiences – the diversity of backgrounds, politics, and performances only amplifies the plausibility of the shared affect. As a bonus, such online cultures – invested in radically disparate functions such as sexual advice, gaming, or physical culture – offer even more ways to disarticulate the racist and *volkish* core ideologies of the populist right. That *Roosh V* manages to argue a connection between Amazon's offered choice of books and the 'Great Replacement' might seem ridiculous, but also increases the points of friction in which populist agitation can engage.

To give a last example: In the recent European elections, the *Alternative für Deutschland* (as well as the British Right) heavily advocated and advertised against the so-called 'Article 13,' a legislative proposition that would mandate the filtering of online content for copyright violations before it is uploaded. This talking point was adopted from online media producers such as *Sargon of Akkad*, who fear that their livelihood – earning money on YouTube by commenting on mainstream media texts – would be endangered. Both actors – the *AfD* and the internet community – agreed on the affective scenario in which this measure to protect copyrighted texts should be framed: politically correct censorship, an attack on 'independent online media' and 'free speech,' and a discrete measure to silence the 'undesirable voices' of the right, enacted by a totalitarian left. The playbook for this rhetoric comes straight from the online worlds of *gamergate* and the *manosphere*, whose members have decried their alleged silencing and oppression by feminism, leftist politicians, and large corporations for years. Such fruitful and increasing coalitions between party populism and the countercultural performance of the online-based *Alternative Right* may be fluctuating, but their volatility often only increases the public attention they generate. Research on right-wing extremism and political populism needs to acknowledge these connections, borrowings, and mergers with the very amorphous and diverse network of the *Alternative Right* – which may operate online, but, nonetheless, shapes real-world perceptions, actions and feelings with ever-growing influence.

Bibliography

Ahmed, Sara (2010): The Promise of Happiness. Durham: Duke University Press.
Baker, Katie J.M. (2013): "Cockblocked by Redistribution: A Pick-Up Artist in Denmark." In: Dissent 60 (4), pp. 8-11.

Bokhari, Allum/Yiannopoulos, Milo (2016): An Establishment Conservative's Guide to the Alt-Right. Online: www.breitbart.com/tech/2016/03/29/an-establishment-conservatives-guide-to-the-alt-right/, 04.12.2018.

Casadio, Massimiliano Capra (2014): "The New Right and Metapolitics in France and Italy." In: Journal for the Study of Radicalism 8 (1), pp. 45-86.

Cleto, Fabio (ed.) (1999): Camp: Queer Aesthetics and the Performing Subject: A Reader. Ann Arbor: University of Michigan Press.

Coston, Bethany M./Kimmel, Michal (2012): "White Men as the New Victims: Reverse Discrimination Cases and the Men's Rights Movement." In: Nev. LJ 13, pp. 368-381.

Dietze, Gabriele (2019): Sexueller Exzeptionalismus. Überlegenheitsnarrative in Migrationsabwehr und Rechtspopulismus. Bielefeld: transcript.

Donovan, Joan/Lewis, Becca/Friedberg, Brian (2018): "Parallel Ports: Sociotechnical Change from the Alt-Right to Alt-Tech." In: Maik Fielitz/Nick Thurston (eds.): Post-Digital Cultures of the Far Right: Online Actions and Offline Consequences in Europe and the US. Bielefeld: transcript, pp. 49-63.

Eordogh, Fruzsina (2018): A Nuanced Take on Count Dankula's Nazi Pug. Online: www.forbes.com/sites/fruzsinaeordogh/2018/04/30/a-nuanced-take-on-count-dankulas-nazi-pug/#7ae3e4b165b3, 06.12.2019.

Gammerl, Benno/Hutta, Jan Simon/Scheer, Monique (2017): "Feeling Differently: Approaches and their Politics." In: Emotion, Space and Society 25 (1), pp. 87-94.

Ganesh, Bharath (2018): "The Ungovernability of Digital Hate Culture." In: Journal of International Affairs 71 (2), pp. 30-49.

Ging, Debbie (2017): "Alphas, Betas, and Incels: Theorizing the Masculinities of the Manosphere." In: Men and Masculinities, no pages.

Gould, Deborah (2010): "On Affect and Protest." In: Janet Staiger/Ann Cvetkovich/Ann Reynolds (eds.): Political Emotions. New York: Routledge, pp. 32-58.

Halberstam, Jack (2011): The Queer Art of Failure. Durham: Duke University Press.

Hawley, George (2017): Making Sense of the Alt-Right. New York: Columbia University Press.

Lees, Matt: "What Gamergate Should Have Taught Us about the 'Alt-Right'." In: The Guardian, 1 Dec 2016, (www.theguardian.com/technology/2016/dec/01/gamergate-alt-right-hate-trump, 06.12.2019).

Lewis, Rebecca (2018): The Alternative Influence Network Report. Online: datasociety.net/output/alternative-influence/, 06.12.2019.

Lin, Jie Liang (2017): "Antifeminism Online: MGTOW (Men Going Their Own Way)." In: Urte Undine Frömming/Steffen Köhn/Samantha Fox/Mike Terry (eds.): Digital Environments. Ethnographic Perspectives across Global Online and Offline Spaces. Bielefeld: transcript, pp. 77-96.

Massanari, Adrienne (2018): "Rethinking Research Ethics, Power, and the Risk of Visibility in the Era of the 'Alt-Right' Gaze." In: Social Media & Society (April-June 2018), pp. 1–9.

Massanari, Adrienne (2017): "#Gamergate and the Fappening: How Reddit's Algorithm, Governance, and Culture Support Toxic Technocultures." In: New Media & Society 19 (3), pp. 329-346.

Mudde, Cas (2007): Populist Radical Right Parties in Europe. Cambridge: Cambridge University Press.

Nagle, Angela (2017): Kill All Normies: Online Culture Wars from 4chan and Tumblr to Trump and the Alt-Right. New York: Zero Books.

Neiwert, David: Alt-America: The Rise of the Radical Right in the Age of Trump. New York: Verso Books.

Nyong'o, Tavia (2002): "Racial Kitsch and Black Performance." In: The Yale Journal of Criticism 15 (2), pp. 371-391.

Phillips, Whitney/Milner, Ryan M. (2018): The Ambivalent Internet: Mischief, Oddity, and Antagonism Online. New York: John Wiley & Sons.

Right Response Team (2018): 'Day for Freedom': A New Threat Emerges. Online: www.hopenothate.org.uk/2018/05/08/day-freedom-new-threat-emerges/, 06.12.2019.

Roosh V (2013): The War against Men. Online: www.rooshv.com/the-war-against-men, 06.12.2019.

Roosh V (2016): What Is Neomasculinity? Online: www.rooshv.com/what-is-neomasculinity, 06.12.2019.

Roosh V (2017): Kill Whitey. Online: www.rooshv.com/kill-whitey, 06.12.2019.

Strick, Simon (2018a): "Alt-Right-Affekte. Provokationen und Online-Taktiken." In: Zeitschrift für Medienwissenschaft 19, pp. 113-125.

Strick, Simon (2018b): "Der Google Nerd und das Rechte Netzwerk." In: Gender Blog, Zeitschrift für Medienwissenschaften, 3 Sep 2018, (www.zfmedienwissenschaft.de/online/blog/der-google-nerd-und-das-rechte-netzwerk, 06.12.2019).

Strick, Simon (2019): "Tired Trump, oder die Erschöpfung der Theorie." In: Lars Koch, Tobias Nanz, Christina Rogers (eds): The Great Disruptor. Über Trump, die Medien und die Politik der Herabsetzung. Berlin: Springer, pp. 15-33.

Williams, Raymond (2015): Keywords: A Vocabulary of Culture and Society. London: Oxford University Press.

Angry Women: Poland's *Black Protests* as 'Populist Feminism'

Agnieszka Graff

Between April 2016 and March 2018, Poland witnessed a mobilization of women of unprecedented scale: marches, rallies, pickets, public debates and social media campaigns responding to a proposed total ban on abortion rights. The protests peaked on 3 October 2016 with the Polish Women's Strike (henceforth "the Strike") under the hashtag #BlackMonday, which mobilized 150 thousand people in 200 cities and towns throughout the country. With moving visuals – pictures of a 'sea of umbrellas' in Warsaw's Castle Square, faces of countless angry women in black, and radical banners with memorable symbols – the so called *Black Protests* hit international media and became an important reference point a year later during the International Women's Strike of 8 March 2017 (Korolczuk et al. 2019: 9; Gunnarsson-Payne 2019: 168-179). The black clothes worn by participants were meant as a sign of mourning for women's reproductive rights, but there is an additional symbolic dimension worth pausing over: The *Black Protests* revived the spectacle of women wearing black during anti-Russian demonstrations in 1861 (see Graff 2019: 485; Kowalczyk 2017: 14).

Both the scale and the emotional intensity, of what would later be called a 'women's rebellion,' exceeded everyone's expectations, including those of the organizers. What also took many by surprise was the mobilization's immediate effect: The Strike led to the withdrawal of the contested legislation. Scholars who have since examined the mobilization as a social phenomenon agree that this was, in fact, the birth of feminism as a grassroots movement in Poland: intersectional, inclusive and internally-diverse (Korolczuk et al. 2019; Majewska 2016). Prior to 2016, feminism had been a politically marginal phenomenon, centered mainly around NGOs, university gender studies programs and the largely middle-class Women's Congress. With the Strike, feminism emerged as a grassroots movement, marked by a radical political rhetoric and a penchant for hijacking national symbols, capable of mobilizing tens of thousands of women at a few days' notice (Graff 2019: 485-6; 489-91). Throughout the mobilization, the leadership group, known as the Polish Women's Strike (*Ogólnopolski Strajk Kobiet, OSK*), maintained strong bonds with other actors in the wider struggle against right-wing populism (in particular, with the civic organization *KOD* – Committee for the Defense of Democracy), while insisting on its autonomy as a feminist movement. Carrying distinctive Black Protest signs – e.g. with Women's Strike symbols, Gals4Gals banners, hangers, a fuck-you-uterus and Fighting Polish Woman images – the women who participated were also known to engage in, and sometimes initiated, demonstrations for causes other than women's rights. However, activists were remarkably consistent in refuting the expectation that women's issues have to be put on the back burner, sacrificed to, or delayed by, the greater cause of "saving democracy."

This essay is based on participant observation, dozens of discussions with fellow activists and a thorough examination of existing scholarship on the Black Protest movement. My central argument is that the movement can be understood as 'populist feminism,' a feminist version of what Chantal Mouffe's (2018) 'left populism.' Protesters rejected the ethnonationalist and moralist frames of right-wing populism – i.e. the assumption that 'ordinary people' are conservative and must be defended against 'liberal elites.' At the same time, the movement reiterated the binarism of 'people vs. elites,' which is central to populist mobilizations. It positioned angry women (and the men who supported them) as 'the people' in a struggle against ultra-conservative 'elites.' The first section of this paper offers a chronology of key events along with some basic explanations about the legal and political context. Part two examines the transnational connections of both sides of the conflict – the institutional links to international anti-choice groups of those initiating the 2016 effort to ban abortion, and the international sources and resonances of the Strike. Part three develops the argument concerning 'populist feminism,' asking in particular about the reasons for the mobilization's success: the significance of participants' self-definition as 'ordinary women' (Ramme/Snochowska Gonzalez 2019), the 'connective action' logic of mobilization "based on the use of flexible, easily personalized action frames" (Korolczuk 2016: 108), and the use of highly emotional language (Korolczuk 2019). I follow Jenny Gunnarsson Payne (2019) in reading the *Black Protests* as a gendered version of 'left populism.' In part four, I examine selected works of feminist art produced during the protests, arguing that profound cultural change accompanied the women's rebellion – the *Black Protests* led to the articulation of 'angry women' as a new collective in the public sphere. Women's struggle for reproductive freedom was successfully enacted as a popular uprising, a struggle for democracy, and against the violence of right-wing populism.

The Black Protest Story[1]

In Poland, civil society actors can introduce a piece of legislation for parliamentary debate under the rubric of a 'popular initiative' or 'civic initiative.' The law requires that the submitting group registers and then gathers 100.000 signatures within three months. The *Black Protests'* story began with two groups of citizens striving to change existing abortion laws by means of this procedure. On 14 March 2016, the legislative initiative "Stop Abortion" was registered with the Polish Parliament. Aggressively lobbied for by the *Ordo Iuris Institute*, an ultra-conservative Catholic legal group with strong international connections, the proposed law sought to outlaw abortion in cases of serious fetal damage, and stipulated up to five years of prison for women undergoing abortions. Fetal damage is one of three conditions under which abortion is legal as per existing legislation, and it constitutes the legal grounds for the vast majority of legal abortions in Poland. The proposed legislation was thus rightly perceived as an effort that would result in an effective ban on abortion in the country. If passed, the law would have forced women to give birth, not only to disabled children, but also to infants bound to die soon after birth. In addition, there was well-founded reason to believe that doctors would stop offering prenatal testing in fear of pursuit for facilitating abortion, and that criminal investigations would follow involuntary miscarriages. These were extreme goals even by Polish standards. Prior to 2016, neither the ruling *Law and Justice Party* nor Poland's Bishops Conference had supported the idea of putting women in jail for abortion. Yet, in the final days of March, the Episcopate of the Catholic Church made an official statement supporting the initiative (Komunikat KEP 2016a), and Prime Minister Beata Szydło communicated her personal support for the proposed law (Szydło 2016). The threat of "Stop Abortion" becoming law was very real.

Counter-mobilizations began on 1 April 2016 with the appearance of the *Dziewuchy Dziewuchom* (Gals4Gals) group on Facebook. The profile gathered thousands of members within hours, and provoked the creation of dozens of local groups in the subsequent few days. On 3 April, the left-wing *Razem* (Together) party organized the first demonstrations under the slogan "No to the torture of women." Participants were armed with wire hangers – a symbol meant to remind of the horrors of back-alley abortions. A video showing women walking out of church services began to circulate on social media – they would leave ostentatiously while the Episcopate statement was being read in parishes throughout the country. This was followed by an action involving a shipment of coat hangers to the prime minister's office; three former first ladies also announced their opposition to the proposed law and instead came out in support of the existing one.

---

1   This section relies heavily on a detailed chronology from the book *Bunt kobiet* (Korolczuk et al. 2019: 6-19)

On April 13, a group of feminists registered the legislative initiative "Save the women," which would have legalized abortion and guaranteed access to sex education and contraception. This opened a new stage of the conflict: Two rival committees would now simultaneously collect signatures under their respective draft laws. "Stop Abortion" filed 400.000 signatures in July, and "Save the Women" filed 215.000 in August. The difference can be explained by the fact that anti-choice groups collected signatures in churches, with active support of (and often pressure from) parish priests. The reaction of the parliament to the two initiatives speaks volumes about the political power of the Church in Poland: On 23 September, the "Save the women" initiative was rejected without debate, while "Stop Abortion" was directed for further work in committees. The following day, Poland's most famous actress, Krystyna Janda, wrote a Facebook post reminding the public of the Islandic women's Strike of 1975 and calling for mobilization. Hashtags #czarnyprotest and #BlackProtest gave the entire mobilization its popular name. During the Wrocław rally, a speaker named Marta Lempart (associated with local structures of the pro-democracy movement, KOD) called for a nationwide women's strike on 3 October. Lempart, along with Natalia Pancewicz, set up the Facebook profile *Ogólnopolski Strajk Kobiet* (*OSK*; Polish Women's Strike), which would remain the center of the movement's national and international connective leadership. Moreover, this site became known as the movement's "helpdesk" – the go-to contact for media and the model for regional "Strike" groups.[2]

The 3 October Women's Strike – known as Black Monday – was undeniably the *Black Protests*' largest success and most memorable event. Its iconic status is in part owed to the beauty of the images that soon flooded social media: the sea of umbrellas shot from above, and thousands of women dressed in black, soaking wet and visibly thrilled (see Fig.1).

The umbrella would become one of the protests' most popular symbols and, like the black clothes worn by participants, it carried additional symbolic significance. One of the core myths of Polish women's history – contested by historians but well-established in the collective imagination – is that in November 1918 a group of suffragettes gathered in front of the villa of the Chief of State, Józef Piłsudski, and (reportedly) knocked on the windows with their umbrellas to remind him of the need to grant women voting rights in the new republic. Thanks to the rain, the symbol was now revived and would soon become omnipresent in the movement's iconography and discourse (as in the popular slogan "We will not fold our umbrellas"). The Warsaw rally assembled over 30.000 people, but Warsaw was only a small part of what happened that day. There were demonstrations in 150 cities and towns, some with over 10 thousand participants. Solidarity events took place in 49 cities in 29 countries in Europe and elsewhere (Gober/Struzik 2018: 137). For the first time

---

2   (see: http://strajkkobiet.eu/co-robimy; Gober/Struzik 2019: 133).

Figure 1: Women's Strike (Black Monday), afternoon of 3 October 2016, Warsaw, Castle Square. "Sea of umbrellas" image, shot from the tower of St. Ann's Church.

in Polish history, there were women's demonstrations in small towns, where being seen at a protest could have immediate consequences at work and at home. All around Poland, women failed to show up at work (often with their employers' consent, but sometimes with serious risk involved) and joined the innumerable rallies around the country instead. Thousands of others went to work wearing black.

A poll conducted a month after the Strike testified to the impressive resonance and popularity of the protests: 90% of the population knew about the Strike; 64% of women and 52% men declared their interest and support; 17% of women and 6% of the men said they had dressed in black on 3 October to show their support; 4% of women said they had participated in demonstrations in person (CBOS 2016). According to another poll, the year 2016 witnessed the highest level of participation in public protests in 28 years (Kowalska/Nawojski 2019: 53). Politically, too, the Strike was a success: The "Stop Abortion" law was withdrawn from parliamentary proceedings. It was the first time that the *PiS* (*Law and Justice*) government backed down under public pressure. The Church, too, would soon regret its support for the initiative.

Black Monday gave organizers and participants a heady sense of the movement's power. It was the starting point of numerous initiatives leading up to the next great mobilization – a response to the next anti-abortion legislative initiative, which came to be known as Black Friday (23 March 2018). In the interval between the two massive protests, much activity demonstrated the ongoing strategizing that was taking place on both sides of the political feud. The government introduced a legislation on a special financial provision for women who give birth to disabled babies, measures were introduced against emergency contraception, and there were direct repressive actions (including police raids) against women's NGOs. Meanwhile, women continued to organize: There were protests against the emergency contraception ban and marches on Women's Day (in solidarity with International Women's Strike) and on Mother's Day 2017. A network of doctors was established to advise women in crisis (*Lekarze Kobietom*, Doctors4Women). In July, Black Protest activists played a central role in street protests in defense of independent courts, and women dressed as handmaids (based on Margaret Atwood's classic novel) to protest against Donald Trump's visit to Poland.

On 3 August, the struggle picked up pace as the "Save the Women 2017" committee announced its intent to collect signatures for a liberal abortion law. By 23 October, the signatures counted almost at half a million. The anti-choice response was to also set up a new committee ("Zatrzymać Aborcję") and write a new law, one that dropped penalization and focused on banning abortion based on fetal damage. By November, they came up with 830.000 signatures. Starting in January of 2018, history appeared to have repeated itself: The Episcopate announced its full support for the new restrictive law, Parliament rejected the liberal law in a close vote and accepted the restrictive law for further proceedings, and a number of small protests led up to the big event: Black Friday of March 23. This time, the women's movement opted for a concentrated effort: Protesters from all around Poland descended on Warsaw employing a quasi-militaristic rhetoric. The main slogan was "Idziemy na Nowogrodzką" ["Marching to take Nowogrodzka street" – *Law and Justice* headquarters]. It was the largest gathering in defense of women's rights in Poland's history – the headcount varied from 50 to 90 thousand. Banners and speeches showed a new level of anger aimed specifically at the Catholic Church: "I decide about religion, not religion about me"; "My uterus is not your chapel"; "Freedom of choice, not terror"; "Fuck the curia." Some signs alluded to recent church pedophilia scandals: "Priest! I don't look up your dress"; "Go play with your own organs." Another favorite that appeared at this march and many others read: "I think, I feel, I decide" (see figure 2 below). As with Black Monday of the previous year, the protest's outcome was a temporary victory: In June, the Parliament held a debate on the abortion ban without the participation of the anti-choice movement's leader, Kaja Godek; the reactionary law was ultimately rejected. Nonetheless, it was clear to all that its proponents would renew their efforts. The slogan "We are not folding our umbrellas" was circulated widely on social media.

Figure 2: 23 March 2018 (Black Friday) in Warsaw. Large banner reads "Women's Strike." Hand-held sign: "I think, I feel, I decide."

Black Protests as Part of a Global Struggle

In retrospect, it is clear that Poland's 2016 "Stop Abortion" campaign was part of a wider, transnational effort. Global reactionary networks have been "globalizing family values" since the mid 1990s (Buss/Herman 2001); in recent years, they developed sophisticated strategies that Neil Datta (2018) describes in his report "Restoring the Natural Order." Since 2010, their focus was on demonizing "gender ideology" and building up a collaboration with right-wing populists throughout Europe. Poland's "Stop Abortion" was the logical next step. To these networks, Poland – a predominantly Catholic country ruled by right-wing populists – is a promising testing ground for radical solutions to what they perceive as "the culture of death."

While many pro-choice actors view the anti-abortion crusade as single-minded and homogenous, there are in fact significant internal differences and conflicts among ultra-conservatives. The *Ordo Iuris Institute*, a legal think tank that represents the most radical wing of the Polish pro-life movement, led the "Stop Abortion" campaign; the law they drafted, which included the penalization of women, was an extreme one. Both the Episcopate and the local anti-choice movement (i.e. the Polish Federation of Pro-Life Movements) ultimately joined this effort, although they viewed it as excessive and anti-humanitarian (see discussion in Korolczuk 2019: 135-136). The *Ordo Iuris Institute* likes to present itself as a local group, but is in fact a daughter organization of *TFP* (*Tradition, Family and Property*), a Catholic fundamentalist organization founded in Brazil. It collaborates closely with the *World Youth*

Alliance (set up at the UN in 1999) and with the *Catholic Family and Human Rights Institute, European Dignity Watch*, and the *British Society for the Protection of Unborn Children*, the world's oldest anti-choice organization, in existence since 1966. *Ordo Iuris* revealed that its budget for 2016 amounted to 3.3 Million PLN (almost a Million Euro) (Suchanow 2018).

After Black Monday and the resulting withdrawal of the "Stop Abortion" law, the Polish Bishops' Conference withdrew its support for "Stop Abortion," claiming that the Church had never supported laws that stipulate prison sentences for women undergoing abortions (KEP 2016b). At this point, transnational networks ceded ground, allowing local anti-choice groups to take over. The result of this shift was the 2017 effort in which the penalization clause was removed. Moreover, the initiative's name was changed ("Zatrzymaj Aborcję" instead of "Stop Aborcji" – the Polish verb 'zatrzymać' replaced the English 'stop'), and the campaign itself was re-focused on the "eugenic abortion" of babies with down syndrome. The committee behind the law included the Polish pro-life organization, the *Life and Family Foundation*, but not *Ordo Iuris*. International connections were de-emphasized. The public face of the new committee was Kaja Godek, a young woman with links to the nationalist right. The new effort appeared to draw heavily on American Christian fundamentalist strategies: dramatic images of aborted fetuses, the dissemination of information about the number of babies being "murdered" in Polish hospitals, and extensive use of the argument that abortion is a form of discrimination against people with disabilities.

The transnational context mattered on the feminist side of the struggle too. The *Black Protests* were an authentic grassroots movement with no external institutional funding, but with a keen awareness of the broader context of our struggle. Thanks to social media, the local groups that emerged built links with one another, sharing ideas and images (memes and symbols), and established lasting transnational connections. The Polish Women's Strike received online support from women all over the world who posted photos of themselves – singly and in groups – with solidarity signs. These images were disseminated in Poland as evidence that "we are not alone." Mobilization inside the country also led to the formation of a sizeable "transnational feminist diaspora," comprised of Polish women living abroad who organized solidarity protests wherever they happened to live. According to Greta Gober and Justyna Struzik, who have studied this phenomenon, the experience had a transformative effect on participants – guided by a sense of solidarity and responsibility for "sisters" at home, they built new connections to Poland and to each other, and emerged with a new definition of feminism (2018: 143).

While Black Monday was modeled on the 1975 Women's Strike in Iceland, the Polish Women's Strike, in turn, inspired the International Women's Strike. As early as 9 October 2016, the Facebook group Black Protest International (established by the Gals4Gals network) posted the following call for a global mobilization for women's sexual rights and autonomy:

> "Sisters and Brothers! An outrageous reminder of how much there is still to do about women's rights in the context of rape culture. We must reclaim our feeling and thinking bodies from the hands of those who usurp power over us. Trump is just one striking, globally visible example, but there is so much more violence occurring that goes uncovered by the news. It is hard to believe the ways in which rapes committed by powerful men, like Julian Assange, Dominique Strauss-Kahn and Roman Polanski, are publicly excused on the grounds of the high social and political positions and merits of the rapists. [...] Let us learn from this experience and not let our voices fade!" (cited in Gunnarsson-Payne 2019: 167-8)

Slogans and graphics originating in Poland enjoyed resonance around the globe, including the Women's March on Washington on 9 January 2017. Two weeks after Black Monday, on 19 October 2016, the #NiUnaMenos protest against femicide took place in Argentina in response to the murder of 16-year-old Lucía Pérez. Similar demonstrations were organized in Mexico, El Salvador and Chile, leading up to the #NiUnaMenos strike in Brazil (27 October 2017). As Gunnarsson-Payne documents, these mobilizations used slogans and images from *Black Protests*, resulting in a kind of "echo" effect. Of course, Polish feminists were themselves echoing international feminist voices, as in the following Facebook description of Black Protest International:

> "This page was created as a platform for international campaign of solidarity with Polish women #blackprotest. We want to signal the events in Poland to our sisters and brothers abroad. [...] Let us remember Audre Lordes words "Any power you don't use yourself is gonna be used against you. Let's remember Lorde's concept of 'joint survival' - the notion that each individual survival is interrelated with the survival of others, so is the wellbeing. Let's stand together and imagine the tools for the fight together!" (Black Protest International FB Profile)

Activists in Poland were both proud and somewhat surprised by the global resonance of our 'revolution.' Prior to 2016, the Polish women's movement had perceived itself as somewhat isolated in Europe, a "special case" viewed as hopeless by women from the West, due to the political power of the Catholic Church in the country. The leadership of the Polish Women's Strike took enormous pride in having initiated a broader movement; activists followed closely the unfolding feminist struggles in other countries, especially Ireland's struggle for legal abortion ("Repeal the 8th"). With the *Black Protests*, feminist identity in Poland rapidly transcended the narrow bounds of national identity. Participants of the upheaval viewed themselves as partaking in a worldwide women's revolution, a struggle against patriarchal forces that are global rather than local.

A 'Populist Feminism'?– the Extraordinary Power of "Ordinary Women"

The Black Protest phenomenon has by now been investigated by a number of scholars: sociologists, ethnographers, cultural studies scholars and political scientists. How did so many women manage to become mobilized at such short notice? Why was so much anger triggered by the "Stop Abortion" law? After all, legal abortion had been almost impossible to obtain in Poland since the passage of the so called "compromise law" of 1993. Depending on their theoretical toolkit, scholars have offered various answers to these questions, but all studies emphasize the protests' egalitarianism, emotional intensity, spontaneity and reliance on social media. The proposed law was perceived as cruel and inhuman rather than just restrictive, and the fact that it received support from the Episcopate was an important trigger. The abortion ban became a symbol for much broader issues and grievances.

Arguably, the most remarkable finding about the mobilization concerns the activists' own self-perception as "ordinary women." A study conducted by Jennifer Ramme and Claudia Snochowska-Gonzalez (2019), based on interviews with 95 Women's Strike coordinators from around the country, shows that Black Protest participants persistently used this phrase to describe themselves, in marked contrast with representatives of the Manifa movement (organizers of annual feminist protests taking place since 2000). The postulated "ordinariness" has several meanings. First, it signifies the diversity of protesters in terms of age, education, class and region; second, it distinguishes them from seasoned activists or people involved in politics (Ramme/Snochowska-Gonzalez 2019: 95, 99). "Ordinary women," it appears, are women from all walks of life who had been living only their private lives until the "Stop Abortion" enraged them and provoked them to join the protests.

Scholars emphasize the egalitarianism of the mobilization, its inclusiveness and spontaneous, uncontrolled growth. The leadership was collective and there were no "stars" of the movement, though some women (notably Marta Lempart) became well known throughout the country. Solidarity was felt and demonstrated with the most vulnerable and least privileged women: e.g. those who could not afford abortion abroad, rape victims, single mothers, mothers of children with disabilities. The feminist philosopher Ewa Majewska (2016) examined the movement in light of Vaclav Havels' concept of "power of the powerless" and Antonio Negri's "the common," claiming that the protests were not driven by a sense of heroism, but rather by participants' confidence in their weakness and vulnerability.

An important source of the movement's success may have been its ability to mobilize powerful emotions in response to an immediate danger. Korolczuk (2019) has noted that the *Black Protests* differed from earlier struggles for reproductive rights in that they abandoned both human rights discourse and the liberal talk of individual choice, autonomy and the right to privacy. Instead, activists used language and imagery that were highly emotional and often dramatic. One strategy was to bring public attention to specific examples of women's suffering and death caused by abortion bans in Salvador and Nicaragua (Korolczuk 2019: 138-9). Slogans, chants, internet memes, signs and banners, made spontaneously by individual women, tended to take the expressive first-person form: e.g. "I am here because I am furious"; "I am here for my daughter's sake." The phrase "torture of women" was often used to describe the essence of the proposed law. Many of the signs were provocative and confrontational: "Take your rosaries off my ovaries," or "We want doctors, not fanatics." The words "dignity," "suffering" and "cruelty" were used far more often than the emotionally neutral word "choice" (although the latter would also appear in slogans such as "My body – my choice").

Personal accounts, media interviews with activists, and stories circulated in social media – all of these materials testify to a powerful emotional experience lived by individuals and immediately shared with the newly established activist community. Hearing about the "Stop Abortion" proposal, people felt angry, confused, humiliated and scared for their own safety. Thanks to the urgency of these emotions, the movement spread quickly despite the lack of centralized top-down coordination. Korolczuk (2016) explained the phenomenon of the movement's rapid growth by employing the social movement theory concept of connective (as opposed to collective) action: "Of key importance for the 'scaling up' of protests was the fact that the mobilization followed the logic of connective action based on personalized engagement, in which communication became an important element of organizational structure" (94). Clearly, none of this would have happened were it not for the direct threat of the proposed law and the technical opportunity offered by social media. "The Black Protest's core idea was very simple: in order to join, one had to simply post a photo of her/him self wearing black with hashtag #blackprotest. The uncomplicated and gender-inclusive formula was easy to personalize. [...] This formula allowed participants to be in control of what they share with others [...]" (Korolczuk 2016: 102). Viewed as a mobilization of public emotions, the *Black Protests* were an expression of collective outrage, despair and righteous anger. These emotions were shared by thousands via the logic of "connective action." Those who joined did not necessarily view themselves as feminists, but they had a common threat and a common enemy: ultra-conservative Catholics supported by the populist right-wing government.

Gunnarsson-Paine (2019) draws a link between the egalitarianism of *Black Protests* and Chantal Mouffe's (2018) theory of left-populism. Rejecting theories of populism that describe it as a type of ideology, Mouffe follows Laclau in proposing a framework that defines populism as a particular articulation of conflict: one that defines 'us' as the people and the opposing force as an arrogant and corrupt elite. If right-wing populism builds the collective identity of the 'people' in exclusionary terms (as a collectivity based on common ethnicity), left populism does the opposite. In other words, it is a political strategy that:

> "[...] aims at federating the democratic demands into a collective will to construct a 'we,' a 'people' confronting a common adversary: the oligarchy. This requires the establishment of a chain of equivalence among the demands of the workers, the immigrants and the precarious middle class, as well as other democratic demands, such as those of the LGBT-community. The objective of such a chain is the creation of a new hegemony that will permit the radicalization of democracy." (Mouffe 2018: 24)

In opposing right-wing populists, who were (and still are) in power in Poland, the *Black Protests* persistently strove to re-frame the ongoing political conflict by claiming the identity of the 'people' for the women whose rights were in danger. Within the movement's left-populist framing, the right-wing forces – well-funded, well-connected, cruel and manipulative – were positioned as a corrupt elite. Ramme and Snochowska-Gonzalez reach a similar conclusion: They interpret the persistent use of the phrase 'ordinary women' within a broader framework of competing populisms. "Our study shows that the respondents from Polish Women's Strike are not afraid to represent 'womenfolk' or 'the female sovereign,' but that they propose a different understanding of these collectivities – pluralist and inclusive" (2019:114).

It appears that the movement's success is due to its ability to capture the logic of populism for a progressive political project. This was achieved through the idea of commonness among participants ('ordinary women'), the disavowal of earlier engagements (one did not need to claim a 'feminist' identity in order to join the revolution), and the employment of a powerful rhetorical and symbolic repertoire, one that mobilized collective affect ('dignity,' 'torture' and 'cruelty' rather than 'choice'). Abandoning the established liberal discursive frames for defending abortion rights, the Black Protest built its power based on emotions that were both personal and collective. In effect, a new collective subject was constituted in Poland's public sphere: angry women with a strong political identity.

Black Protest Culture

In this section, my aim is to take the idea of "populist feminism" beyond the sphere of politics and into the realm of what is broadly understood as culture. The Black Protest can be conceptualized as a tidal wave of cultural change, one that included, not only shifting attitudes towards women's reproductive rights, but also new trends in popular culture, media, visual art, film and theater. Since 2016, there has been a huge outpouring of feminist creativity marked by an aura of collective anger, solidarity and claims of 'ordinariness.' Unlike earlier feminist artworks, which often expressed a sense of isolation and loneliness, this new wave speaks confidently on behalf of a newly constituted collectivity, addressing a new feminist (or at least feminism-friendly) audience. Much of it occupies the border between art and activism; in fact, the term 'artivism' is sometimes used to recognize that the works of art are in fact contributions to the protests.

My first example is drawn from the realm of popular culture. On 21 October 2016, two weeks after Black Monday, the popular singer Natalia Przybysz posted a song about her abortion on YouTube. The piece, entitled "In My Dream" (Przybysz 2016), tells the story of a couple in love, their discovery that a pregnancy is underway and their decision to terminate it. The song does not make excuses – the lovers seem rather out of touch with reality – but speaks frankly about their fear, confusion, and vulnerability, as well as about the woman's alienation from her own body. It also recounts her travel abroad in pursuit of a legal abortion. The refrain refers to a campaign to penalize women: "And in the year of mercy, I will spend Christmas in prison." True to its title, the song is intimate and dreamy; what makes it political is the brief comment posted along with the video: "On the day of the Black Protest I felt the enormous power of women, the power of our common voice. I decided to make this song public in advance (it has been written for my next album). I believe very strongly that women have the right to decide about their own lives." That same week, Przybysz appeared on the cover of the popular women's weekly magazine Wysokie Obcasy (High Heels) dressed in black (an obvious sign of participation in Women's Strike), her face showing a mixture of pain and determination (see figure 3 below). High Heels is an insert inside the weekend edition of the liberal daily Gazeta Wyborcza, but the magazine is known for its independence, feminist leanings and tendency to break cultural taboos. This time a taboo was, indeed, broken: The issue featured a lengthy and deeply personal interview with the singer, in which she recounted the details of her abortion experience and explained her motivations for coming out: "We live in a reality where everyone pretends that abortion does not happen. In effect, every woman is left alone with her own abortion. I want to speak out about it all" (Reiter 2016). The song and the interview did open up a new space in public discourse, making it possible to discuss abortion without guilt and shame, as something that happens in many women's lives.

My second example is the feminist art show titled "Polish Women, Patriots, Rebels," which was exhibited in the fall of 2017 at the Arsenal Art Gallery in Poznań.[3] As curator Izabela Kowalczyk (2017) pointed out, the works presented there were all immersed in the ongoing cultural and political conflict, but they also resisted its binary logic. Most of the artists employed a strategy Kowalczyk referred to as

---

3 Documentation of the show can be found here: www.arsenal.art.pl/wystawy/polki-patriotki-rebeliantki/. See also: www.youtube.com/watch?v=-SAUuoVl1tg

Figure 3: Cover of Wysokie Obcasy magazine on 22 October 2016, featuring singer Natalia Przybysz in black (at the time an obvious sign of participation in Women's Strike). The title reads" "The medicine whose name is NO."

"ironic take-over." National symbolism is transformed and appropriated, and the resulting artwork speaks against the various exclusions (ethnic, racial, religious, gender-based) of nationalism (Kowalczyk 2017: 25). The idea for the show was born during the cultural section of the Women's Congress that year, which was headed by feminist art critic Agata Araszkiewicz. The resulting exhibition can be viewed as an example of 'artivism' – an intervention in the sphere of culture that undermines the conservative opposition between aesthetic value and political commitment. In a number of pieces, the muscular masculinity central to Polish nationalism is subjected to ironic scrutiny, its commercially manufactured attributes borrowed and transformed. One of my favorite examples of this strategy is the "Caviar Patriot" sculpture by Agata Zbylut.[4] A life-size ball gown meticulously constructed out of soccer fans' scarves (an important attribute of men partaking in the nationalism of recent years); the piece mocks the hyper-masculine appeal of fan culture, which has strong links with the nationalist far right. Another piece employing the 'take over' strategy is the "Self-portrait with borrowed man" by Liliana Piskorska, part of a series called "Methods of camouflage in contemporary Poland"[5]. The "Self-portrait" is a photograph of a heterosexual couple in bed, taken from above, the woman being the lesbian artist herself. Here, the 'take-over' concerns the use of a set of patriotic bedclothes: a duvet cover and pillowcases decorated with the national emblem and the slogan "I am a Pole so I have Polish responsibilities," a quote from Roman Dmowski, the main ideologue of the Polish nationalist right in the interwar period. The artist herself looks us into the beholder's eyes quizzically, while cuddling with her 'borrowed man,' who is well-built, tattooed and bald. The effect is comical: Who is this guy? Where do you rent such men and at what price? Does he come with the bedclothes? But it is also frightening: Is this sufficient 'camouflage' for a lesbian in contemporary Poland? What happens when her true identity is discovered? These works – and many others presented at the Poznań art show – partake in a strategy often employed during Black Protests: the appropriation of patriotic symbols as a sign of resisting nationalism (for extended discussion, see Graff 2019).

Finally, let us take a brief look at a theater group named Witches' Choir (*Chór Czarownic*) – in my assessment, one of the most powerful artistic initiatives linked to the Black Protests. Formed in Poznań in 2016 by the artist and activist Ewa Łowżył, the choir sought to restore to public memory the women who were killed for alleged "witchcraft" in 16th century Poland. The artists – all female, most of them never trained as singers – emerge into view from darkness and dressed in skin-colored negligees (see figure 4 below).[6]

The songs – angry, dramatic, and filled with pathos – link the present condition of women in Poland to the suffering of "witches." Though vulnerable and exposed, women in the group seem militant, steadfast, unapologetic, and unwilling to be shamed. As the image above makes evident, their faces express anger and determination. Each performance by the group (I have attended several) has attracted crowds and provoked intensely emotional responses: People leave their seats, sing along, shout, laugh and hug each other. Much like the Black Protests themselves, the group creates an atmosphere of extreme excitement, personal transgression and liberation. My personal favorite among the choir's songs is one that deals with the endless pressure exerted on women to serve others and to 'be nice': "I'm on fire,

---

4   It can be seen here: agatazbylut.art.pl/en/projekty/10
5   See the whole cycle here: lilianapiskorska.com/en/praca/methods-of-camouflage-in-contemporary-poland/
6   For an excerpt from their performance, see: www.youtube.com/watch?v=7yaG7cvypTg

Figure 4: Performance of the Witches' Choir. Note the skin-colored negligees, very little make-up, all body types, angry faces.

and still/ I'm on fire, and still/ The dinner to cook/ The children to raise/ Nails to bite/ Elbow-deep in laundry/ Make yourself a deity/ Potatoes and cabbage/ Non-fat yoghurt/ A pill for the headache/ The butter's finished/ Be nice, be nice..., be nice, be nice" (trans. K. Webster). But let there be no mistake: Complaining about the fate of women is not the core of the choir's message. If the singers are today's witches, then their performance can be read as an extended and deeply furious curse, an adamant refusal to be intimidated and subdued by patriarchy.

Like many of the artworks discussed above, the Witches' Choir partakes in emotions that drive the mobilization; it embraces and amplifies them, giving them the form of a ritual. Each performance ends with the rebellious protest song that was also repeatedly heard at the demonstrations:

"Your power/ Your faith/ My fault/ My punishment/ My world is in your hands/ You've had me over a barrel for a million years!/ Look me straight in the eyes/ I am your mother, sister/ I am your daughter, wife/ I stand with my head held high/ A million of us are standing now, none of us are afraid/ I stand, I shout, I stand, I shout..." (trans. K. Webster).

Viewed as a whole, the performance has a ritualistic quality – it appears to establish a feminine sacred sphere, an act of obvious sacrilege in a Catholic culture that persistently excludes women from the sacred. Right-wing commentators have accused the Choir of paganism, demonism, even of starting a cult.

The feminist art created in the Black Protest period shares some of its themes with earlier Polish feminist art, as well as with the international feminist art scene. Three features, however, set it apart from most predecessors: (1) it is more radical (i.e. angrier, more iconoclastic and confrontational); (2) it is more directly political (i.e. it not only comments upon but openly partakes in the political conflict), and (3) it is more egalitarian (i.e. it tends to speak in plain language, addressing a broader public, which is assumed to be like-minded). Like the Black Protest demonstrators, artists often use and transform national symbolism, but they also introduce themes from outside of Poland, building parallels between Polish nationalism and other nationalisms, thus self-reflexively positioning themselves in a transnational conflict between right-wing populism and women's rights.

Conclusions: Putting Things in Perspective

The Black Protests need to be placed within the broader context of evolving relations between the Church and the state in Poland. Only by doing so we can understand why the mobilization happened in 2016, and why with such force. During the two decades following 1989, the Catholic Church occupied a position of unchallenged privilege in Polish public life. The Church was perceived as the stabilizing force of post-1989 liberal democracy; without its support for Poland's EU accession in 2003, it was argued, we may never had joined the European Union. The price for this support was the so-called 'compromise' law on abortion introduced in 1993, which is, in fact, one of the strictest bans in Europe. In the decade following accession to the EU, this law was rarely critiqued in the mainstream media since the Church was still broadly believed to be an ally of democracy and pluralism, a respected institution capable of stopping the dark forces of extreme nationalism. Hence, the marginalization of feminism: Women's silence was viewed as a necessary price for the peaceful co-existence of political elites and the Catholic Church. Around 2013, this harmony was upset. The Church explicitly cut itself off from liberal democracy by lending its support to the anti-European populist right. Motivations for this move had a lot to do with women's rights and the rights of sexual minorities: the church-inspired, conservative anti-gender campaign, which peaked in Poland in 2013, and was explicitly anti-European (see: Korolczuk/Graff 2018). Moreover, the anti-gender rhetoric in Poland is strongly linked to anti-refugee sentiments: The idea is that Western countries are trying to weaken the Polish nation through the invasion of 'gender' so as to populate our territory with refugees. The anti-gender discourse situates Poland as a frontier where forces of evil (liberalism) and Christianity meet. In retrospect, it is clear that the anti-gender campaign contributed to the right's electoral victory of 2015, and solidified the ties between Catholic hierarchy and the nationalist right.

From the point of view of defeated liberal forces, these developments constituted a betrayal of democracy. One sign of this changing attitude is an article published in June 2018 in the influential liberal daily *Gazeta Wyborcza* about the Church hierarchy's alliance with forces set to destroy the democratic state (Wroński 2018). Once a long-time supporter of the view that the Church is a necessary ally of democracy, *Gazeta* is now ready to announce the end of this era. The Church's betrayal of democracy has had many aspects and stages, but it revealed itself most fully in 2016 when the Episcopate lent its support to the "Stop Abortion" law. My point is that the Black Protests were both about women's rights and about much more than women's rights: What made them possible was a massive re-alignment in Polish politics and the public sphere. But the movement was also part of this tectonic shift in political culture, as well as a historic breakthrough in women's history. It introduced angry women as a new political, collective subject into Polish political life. Since the fall of 2016, women's rights have remained at the center of public debate, and women's rights activism has been the most dynamic and effective wing of the anti-*PiS* opposition. Radical women as a new collective political subject have refused to give up on their women's-rights-centered agenda; they will not be shamed, silenced or marginalized, neither by their opponents (the populist right, Catholic clergy) nor by allies (the broader movement of anti-*PiS* resistance).

Throughout this paper, I have argued that the mobilization known as Black Protests can be viewed as 'populist feminism,' a feminist version of the 'left populism' theorized by Mouffe (2018). I am not the first to reach this conclusion; the research I cited in part three shows that the self-perception of Black Protest participants coheres around the idea that they are 'ordinary women' – a 'people' rebelling against an arrogant patriarchal 'elite.' The same conceptualization is at the center of the artistic productions described in the final section of the paper. The content, conventions and forms employed in these works suggest a 'left populist' framing. These are works that flaunt their simplicity, a 'naiveté' of their message; they often employ a collective speaker – a group of anonymous figures addressing either allies or the enemy, articulating anger or making appeals for solidarity. This feminism is not a sophisticated intellectual project involved in the deconstruction of patriarchal myths and dwelling on its own complicated identity. It is a popular or grassroots feminism, a populist feminism engaged in the collective expression of powerful emotions, the production of inclusive and unifying symbols, and undermining the ethnonationalist definition of "the people" enforced by right-wing populist forces.

Bibliography

Black Protest International FB Profile. Online: www.facebook.com/pg/Black-Protest-International-blackprotestinternational-1162858547117141/about/?ref=page_internal, 10.11.2019.

Buss, Doris E./Herman, Didi (2001): Globalizing Family Values: The Christian Right in International Politics. Minneapolis: University of Minnesota Press.

CBOS (2016): Polacy O Prawach Kobiet, 'Czarnych Protestach' I Prawie Aborcyjnym. Online: www.cbos.pl/SPISKOM.POL/2016/K_165_16.PDF, 10.11.2019 .

Gober, Greta/Struzik, Justyna (2018): "Feminist Transnational Diaspora in the Making. The Case of the #BlackProtest." In: Praktyka Teoretyczna 4 (30), pp. 129-150.

Graff, Agnieszka (2019): "Claiming the Shipyard, the Cowboy Hat and the Anchor for Women: Polish Feminism's Dialogue and Struggle with National Symbolism." In: East European Politics and Societies and Cultures 33 (2), pp. 472-496.

Gunnarsson Payne, Jenny (2019): "Kobiety Jako 'Lud.' Czarne Protesty Jako Sprzeciw Wobec Autorytarnego Populizmu W Perspektywie Międzynarodowej." In: Korolczuk et. al. pp. 155-184. English forthcoming in Baltic Worlds as: "Women as 'the People.' Reflections on the Black Protests as a Counter-Force to Authoritarian Populism from a Transnational Perspective."

Komunikat KEP (2016a): Komunikat Konferencji Episkopatu Polski 30 Kwietnia 2016. Online: episkopat.pl/komunikat-prezydium-kep-w-sprawie-pelnej-ochrony-zycia-czlowieka/, 10.11.2019.

Komunikat KEP (2016b) Komunikat z 374. Zebrania Plenarnego Konferencji Episkopatu Polski. 5 October 2016. Online: episkopat.pl/komunikat-z-374-zebrania-plenarnego-konferencji-episkopatu-polski/, 10.11.2019.

Korolczuk, Elżbieta (2016): "Explaining Mass Protests Against Abortion Ban in Poland: The Power of Connective Action." In: Zoon Politikon 7, pp. 91–113.

Korolczuk, Elżbieta/Graff, Agnieszka (2018): "Gender as 'Ebola from Brussels': The Anticolonial Frame and the Rise of Illiberal Populism." In: Signs: Journal of Women of Culture and Society 43 (4), pp. 797-821.

Korolczuk, Elżbieta/Kowalska, Beata/Ramme, Jennifer/Snochowska-Gonzalez (eds.) (2019): Bunt Kobiet. Czarne Protesty i Strajki Kobiet. Gdańsk: Europejskie Centrum Solidarności.

Kowalska, Beata/Nawojski, Radosław (2019): "Uwaga, Uwaga, Tu Obywatelki! Obywatelstwo Jako Praktyka W Czarnych Protestach I Strajkach Kobiet." In: Korolczuk et al.: Bunt Kobiet. Gdańsk: Europejskie Centrum Solidarności, pp. 43-81.

Kowalczyk, Izabela (2018): "Polki, Patriotki, Rebeliantki... Sztuka Feministyczna Dzisiaj." In: Izabela Kowalczyk (ed.): Polki, Patriotki, Rebeliantki. Poznań: Galeria Miejska Arsenał, pp. 10-50.

Majewska, Ewa (2016): Słaby Opór I Siła Bezsilnych. #Czarnyprotest W Polsce 2016. Online: www.praktykateoretyczna.pl/ewa-majewska-slaby-opor-i-sila-bezsilnych-czarnyprotest-kobiet-w-polsce-2016/, 10.11.2019 .

Mouffe, Chantal (2018): For a Left Populism. London: Verso.

OSK: Ogólnopolski Strajk Kobiet Website. Online: strajkkobiet.eu/co-robimy/, 10.11.2019..

Przybysz, Natalia (2016): Przez Sen. Online: www.youtube.com/watch?v=owZAKdfgOt4, 10.11.2019.

Ramme, Jennifer/Snochowska-Gonzalez, Claudia (2019): "Nie/Zwykłe Kobiety. Populizm Prawicy, Wola Ludu A Kobiecy Suweren." In: Korolczuk et al.: Bunt Kobiet. Gdańsk: Europejskie Centrum Solidarności, pp. 83-118.

Reiter, Paulina (2016): "Natalia Przybysz: Aborcja – Mój Protest Song" (Interview with Natalia Przybysz). In: Wysokie Obcasy, October 22, (www.wysokieobcasy.pl/akcje-specjalne/7,156847,20861449,natalia-przyszbysz-aborcja-moj-protest-song.html, 10.11.2019).

Suchanow, Klementyna (2018) "Organizacji Antyaborcyjnych Przybywa W Polsce I Na Świecie. Czy Coś Je Łączy?" In: Gazeta Wyborcza, March 24, (wyborcza.pl/magazyn/7,124059,23183138,organizacji-antyaborcyjnych-przybywa-w-polsce-i-na-swiecie.html, 10.11.2019).

Szydło, Beata (2016): "Beata Szydło Popiera Całkowity Zakaz Aborcji" (Interview with Prime Minister Beata Szydło, Polish Public Radio I), Sygnały Dnia, March 31, (www.polskieradio.pl/7/129/Artykul/1601259,Beata-Szydlo-popiera-calkowity-zakaz-aborcji, 10.11.2019).

Wroński, Paweł (2018): "Dokąd Zmierza Kościół, Który Zdradził III RP.," Gazeta Świąteczna, June 2, (wyborcza.pl/magazyn/7,124059,-23480424,-do-kadzmier-za-kosciol-kto-ry-zdra-dzil-iii-rp.html, 10.11.2019).

Intersectionality Strikes Back: Right-Wing Patterns of En-Gendering and Feminist Contestations in the Americas

Julia Roth

The Latina actress with the paradigmatic name America Ferrera was the first speaker at the Women's March in Washington D.C. in January 2017, paralleling Donald Trump's inauguration as president. Ferrera did not limit her talk to her own personal experiences when opening her powerful speech with a reference to her own experience as a female immigrant: "As a woman and as a proud first-generation American born to Honduran immigrants, it's been a heartbreaking time to be both a woman and an immigrant in this country. Our dignity, our character, our rights have all been under attack." (Ferrera 2017) Ferrera rather took her experience as a point of departure to claim the rights of all marginalized and oppressed groups. By thus constructing a powerful "we" in opposition to Trump's politics, Ferrera rhetorically denied the new president the authority to represent and define "America":

> "We are gathered here and across the country and around the world today to say, Mr. Trump, we refuse. We reject the demonization of our Muslim brothers and sisters. We condemn the systemic murder and incarceration of our Black brothers and sisters. We will not ask our LGBT families to go backwards. We will not go from being a nation of immigrants to a nation of ignorance. We won't build walls and we won't see the worst in each other." (Ibid.)

Taking a decidedly inclusive stance, Ferrera positioned herself as speaking for and with all the mentioned minorities. Anti-racist, intersectional feminist movements are in full swing in many places and struggle for new spaces in order to make their claims publicly heard. The hashtag #MeToo – which the protesters at these strikes turned into a collective "#WeToo" – documents the global system of sexualized violence against women in all its articulations, which the activists of the ¡Ni Una Menos! movement all over Latin America also contest vehemently. Moreover, and most importantly, the new feminist movements seem to represent one of the most powerful and visible forces of opposition to the worldwide radical right-wing

Figure 1: Actress America Ferrera at the Women's March in Washington, January 2017

surge. What the new feminist movements have in common is their strong opposition to the ways in which gender has become a central platform for right-wing mobilization, which can be observed in a number of right-wing patterns of engendering.[1]

This essay examines the current intersectional feminist movements' politics, strategies and visions, and how they position themselves in relation to prior movements and their feminist and anti-racist predecessors. In contrast to feminist practices online – which have undoubtedly become crucial spaces for feminist organizing for all above-mentioned groups (and more) – the current protests are uniting actual bodies in the streets. This article will examine the role of bringing bodies together on the streets to form an oppositional collective "we" that claims to pursue an "intersectional" politics. Intersectionality, a heretofore predominantly academic term, builds on approaches from Black feminism and Critical Race Studies as well as feminist activism in order to address the "interlocking axes of oppression," meaning axes of stratification and inequality which are always also and always already addressed in their simultaneous articulation such as race, class, sex-

---

[1]   Parts of the following findings stem from my long essay *Can Feminism Trump Populism? Right-Wing Trends and Intersectional Contestations in the Americas*. Trier: WVT/Bilingual Press, 2020.

uality, and gender.[2] Thus, the article will elaborate on the current expression and future outlooks of intersectional feminist practices as a contestation and a counterbalance to right-wing populist politics.

Feminist Contestations to the Right-Wing Populist Patterns of En-Gendering

As I have argued elsewhere (Roth 2020a and 2020b), right-wing populist narratives, discourses, and affective strategies work along (at least five) "Patterns of En-Gendering" (see table 1). These patterns serve different functions and purposes in varying contexts, including (White) re-masculinization and self-aggrandizement, but also performed modernization, opposition to immigration, a "discursive fence" (Costa 2019), and the imagination of a re-establishment of a (binary) order through the transfer of economic and political crises to the gender dimension (see the contributions by Sauer, Dietze, and Strick in this volume). The right-wing patterns of en-gendering further show how right-wing populist programs – in different ways and to different degrees in different locations – usually share agendas that are decidedly anti-immigration, anti-sexual diversity and anti-pluralization of lifestyles, and that promote a re-traditionalization paradigm. Following Sauer, gender is particularly useful for mobilizing a new common sense and a "new hegemonic compromise," since the reference to gender allows populists to relate the long-standing sexual binary that still marks peoples' habits despite being "shattered" to equality politics (Sauer 2017: 14, translation JR). As we have argued in the introcution to this volume, gender is central for the workings of the right-wing populist logic and serves the respective actors as an arena and an "affective bridge" (Dietze 2019) to catapult diverse politics into the public sphere.

---

2   For a genealogy of intersectional theorizing, see The Combahee River Collective 1981, Crenshaw and 2016, Brah/Phoenix 2004. For transnational contexts and the Americas, see Viveros Vigoya 2013, Roth 2013, 2018, 2019.

Table 1

Communicative Pattern	(En-)Gendering	Antagonistic Populist Logic
"Fake News" and/or "Affective Truths"	Gendering of Scandals Gendering of ("ethnic") Others	Emotional Appeal Simplicity of Argument Facts vs. (Gender) Ideology
"Normal" people vs. politically correct gender police	Appropriating Women's Politics and Femonationalist Alliances	(Re-)naturalization of Binary Roles, Heteronormative Order
"Genderism" as existential threat	(White) (Re-)Masculinization: Anti-Genderism, Anti-Affirmative Action	"Genderism" and Immigrants as Scapegoats for all Wrongs
Gender as "Ideological Colonization"	Radical Religious and Femoglobal Alliances	Reverse Anti-Colonialism (Self-Victimization) "Natural" Order vs. "Chaotic," Menacing Gender Diversity
Ethno-Sexism and Intersectionality from Above	Gendering of Social Inequalities Gendering of Fear	Sexual Exceptionalism Self-Aggrandizement (Superior vs. Inferior Sexual Regimes) Modernization + Retraditionalization

Source: (Roth 2020a and 2020b, cf. Ajanovic/Mayer/Sauer 2017; Diehl 2017, Dietze 2015, Mudde/Kaltwasser 2017, Sauer 2017)

Moreover, by rendering the gender orders of Others problematic, the "proper," Occidental superiority and "sexual exceptionalism" is confirmed (Dietze 2016). Imaginations of the "untamed masculinity" of "other" men are instrumentalized to outsource emancipatory issues within the nation's own borders and to justify the expulsion of the perceived aggressor. The borders and/or limits of citizenship and belonging are also negotiated through this division, and the simulated progressiveness serves to dissimulate the group's own emancipation deficits, to maintain the traditional binary and heterosexual/-normative gender order and to co-opt women and gays for anti-immigration propaganda. Through their sense of community and superiority and by externalizing the threat to both "gender ideology" and "external rapists," right-wing populists deflect attention from the effects of globalization and social inequalities. Women supporting right-wing populists

Figure 2: Inter-American Alliances: Jair Bolsonaro and Donald Trump united against 'gender ideology': Palácio do Planalto. Meeting of Jair Bolsonaro and Donald Trump – exchange of shirts. March, 2019

seemingly suffer from a sort of "emancipation fatigue" (see Dietze's contribution to this volume), disappointed by the pressure to "have it all," expressed by neoliberal versions and appropriations of feminist claims. These only seem to work for a few wealthy women academics who can afford to outsource their care work to poorer women instead of negotiating and profoundly challenging the persistently gendered division of labor.

If, as explained before, right-wing populists pursue a politics of "exclusive intersectionality" (Mokre/Siim 2013) or "intersectionality from above" (Sauer 2013) by denying the equality and rights of Others, they are provoking intersectional answers, since all minorities and emancipatory programs are attacked. When the first Women's March brought millions of protesters together in February 2017, Amanda Hess claimed in an article for the *New York Times*, titled "How A Fractious Women's Movement Came to Lead the Left," that "Feminism brought the opposition together," since "[i]n parts of the popular imagination, it wasn't just a loss for Clinton or the Democratic Party. It was a repudiation of feminism itself" (Hess 2017). After a long phase of feminisms based on identity politics and pop feminisms that "preached individual solutions to systemic problems," we currently observe a new emphasis on coalition building and solidarity, particularly enforced by feminists-of-color who emphasized the sad fact that 52 percent of White women had voted for Trump (Hess 2017). And it was feminism, or rather women's rights, that managed to unite all those opposed to the newly elected Trump administration (Hess 2017). The related intersectional feminisms are still mostly initiated and led by women of color and are based on a long legacy of fighting "interlocking axes of oppression," starting with the resistance of enslaved women and feminists of color such as Sojourner Truth. These protests seemingly provide the most visible, active, and effective platform for resistance to the right-wing trend in many places in the Americas, as the following most prominent exemplary cases show.

The Women's Marches

Initially an online forum, the Women's March was aimed at uniting resistant bodies together in the streets from the start. The idea for a women's march on Washington spread by viral Facebook posts put up after the 2016 election by Bob Bland, one of the current co-chairwomen, and Teresa Shook, a retired lawyer in Hawaii, who soon joined forces. Before any logistic arrangements had been made, tens of thousands of women committed on social media to travel to Washington. Some of the women who made the initial preparations realized that it would be a disaster if the march seemed to be entirely by and for White women. They thus brought African American Tamika Mallory and Chicana Latina Carmen Pérez, both affiliated with the NGO Gathering for Justice, on board. They, in turn, brought in Palestinian American Linda Sarsour. The original idea to name the demonstration "Million Women's March" was abandoned after harsh critique, since it copied the title of the "Million Women's March" of 1997 in Philadelphia, which had focused on bringing together Women of Color. As director of operations and national organizer Vanessa Wruble recounts (WMO: 37), the team decided to call the protest the "Women's March on Washington" instead, as an homage to the 1963 march for the civil and freedom rights of African Americans, which united civil rights, labor, and religious organizations and during which Martin Luther King held his famous "I had a Dream" speech. The organizing team put the first Women's March together in just ten weeks, with the aim of mobilizing as many people as possible to oppose the politics represented by Donald Trump under a common banner. Like most social movements, the March did not emerge from a concrete political program. However, by uniting the struggles against different axes of oppression, the Women's March protesters brought the politics of intersectionality back onto the streets and to its activist roots. The protest effected a long-overdue transfer from the academic ivory towers back to political practice.

The intersectionality theoretician Kimberlé Crenshaw considers the different issues united under the Women's March banner and represented by the Pussy Hats as "the embodiment of the intersectional sensibilities that a lot of us have been working on for a very long time" (Crenshaw cf. in Hess 2017). The Women's March co-chairwoman Bob Bland recounts that she did not know the concept when they started, but that now she often uses it to emphasize the growing diversity of the March. In this way, the concept became a useful tool for the March on Washington

Figure 3: Time Magazin Cover: Pussy Hat (February 6, 2017); Figure 4: "Intersectional Solidarity," 8 March Protest March Berlin, 2019

to unite the feminist mainstream, its popular arm, and its dissenting factions in only two months (Hess 2017). Visually, the strategic solidarity of the protesters was expressed by the pink "Pussy Hats" that many of them wore. The ocean of pink headgear adorned numerous media articles and even made it to the cover of *Time* magazine's February 6 issue.

But the times they are a-changing: in 2019, two years after the first march, numerous voices, including *New York Times* columnist Michelle Goldberg (NYT 2019), accused the organizers of the March of having failed at assuming power once they were put at the top of a mass movement and of having alienated many supporters. The 2019 Women's March was split over accusations of anti-Semitism against organizer Linda Sarsour and several others, resulting in two distinct marches in New York City. Goldberg considers the division of the March as the result of the uncoordinated organization, which is typical of social media, where content and political differences are often subsumed under simple slogans based on protesting "against" something, rather than finding common ground with the other participants. Cassady Fendlay, the former director of communications for the Women's March, draws a more positive conclusion after the first two years of the movement. Fendlay joined the 2017 March, and became the director of communications for the Women's March until 2018. She coordinated the process leading to the "Agenda," which was published in 2019, and she asserts: "If we are going to work together and keep on sharing strategies, we're going to work this out" (Fendlay 2018).

As Hess confirms, the 2017 Women's March was one of the largest mass protests in American history, uniting a broad range of groups alarmed by Trump's election under one roof. Given the initially spontaneous character of the March and the diversity of people participating in it, the question soon arose of how sustainable the movement could be. For Crenshaw, the "million-dollar question" was whether these feminisms could survive under the anti-Trump umbrella (Crenshaw cf. in Hess 2017). Fendlay admits that the international dialogue of the Women's March activists was at first limited to other Women's March chapters abroad and less concerned with dialogue with movements such as *NiUnaMenos* in Latin America that were already in full swing when the Women's March started.

#NiUnaMenos

Starting as a protest against femicides and violence against women in 2015, *NiUnaMenos/NiUnaMás* in Latin America has also grown into one of the largest protests and the most visible feminist movements. The movements' slogan "Ni una mujer menos, ni una muerte más" (not one woman less, not one more dead/death) also relates back to feminist predecessors, although from the more recent past: the phrase "Ni Una Muerta Más" (not one dead woman more) was coined in 1995 by the activist and author Susana Chávez to refer to the fight against the femicides in Mexico (#NiUnaMenos: 36). In 2011, Chávez herself was killed. By identifying rhetorically with "all (injured/killed) women," the slogans further embrace a politics of solidarity and of joining forces beyond identity politics, which we also see in the context of the Women's March. The assassination of Chiara Paez in 2016 was the starting point of the protests, which intensified after the murder of Lucía Pérez in 2017 and the suspicious disappearance of activist Santiago Maldonado. The symbol of this protest are the green *pañuelos* (bandanas and/or headscarves, handkerchiefs) that the protesters wear on their heads, around their necks, or tied to their backpacks. In Latin America, the *pañuelos* have a long tradition as a means of female/feminist protest, ever since mothers and grandmothers protested their children's "disappearance" under the military dictatorship on the Plaza de Mayo in Argentina wearing white bandanas. Like the pink "Pussy Hats" of the Women's Marches, the green *pañuelos* that have become the symbol of the *NiUnaMenos* protests unite the different bodies gathering together in protest visually and semiotically as a unified "political" body of resistance.

The Women's Strikes that began in 2017 in Latin America could build on the organizational structures and networks of the *NiUnaMenos* protest. Every town participated in the international strike. Simultaneously, as María Cecilia Canevari, gender studies researcher and NiUnaMenos organizer at the Universidad de Santiago de Estero in Argentina, claims, "there is a clear consciousness that we are

Figure 5: NiUnaMenos (Green Handkerchiefs)

joining a global movement" (Canevari 2019, translation JR). The strikes of March 8 were also significant for the consolidation and internationalization of the movement, and Canevari emphasizes the economic and structural dimension of the inequalities that this movement addresses and fights, since the Women's strike "led to a turn of the international Women's Workers' Day that was considered a day of celebration and now it has become clear that it is a commemoration of the struggles of women workers, the ones that died. But it has also made visible the unpaid feminine work that sustains the economy." (Canevari 2019, translation JR)

Like the Women's March organizers, the *NiUnaMenos* protesters soon formulated more concrete political aims in the form of Manifestos, of which #NiUnaMenos published 24 on their website between June 3, 2015, and March 24, 2019. These manifestos include claims such as *Trabajadoras somos todas* (We are all workers) (Manifiesto #18, May 1, 2018), *Las guerrillas son nuestras compañeras* (the guerrilleras are our colleagues/comrades) (Manifiesto #24, March 21, 2019), *El grito en común: ¡Vivas nos queremos!* (the collective cry: We want them alive!) (Manifiesto #3, May 21, 2016), *Ni Una Menos Por Aborto Inseguro* (Not one less due to insecure abortion) (Manifiesto #13, September 25, 2017), or *#DesendeudadasNosQueremos* (We want to be without debt) (Manifiesto #11, June 2, 2017) (all from: Resumen Latinoamericano 2019). All the claims made in the manifestos point to an intersectional politics of solidarity and multi-level struggle as well as a holistic and strongly systemic understanding of inequalities and violence as embedded in capitalist economic and colonial power structures and a collective feminist body.

While in the US context, the narrative of the recent feminist movements focused predominantly on uniting different minorities, *NiUnaMenos* puts a stronger emphasis on the importance of the economic dimension and expresses an open critique of capitalism and violence against women. In Brazil, the movements that emerged following the assassination of Afro-Brazilian, openly gay politician Marielle Franco and the election of right extremist Jair Bolsonaro in 2018 combine both perspectives and furthermore emphasize a strong anti-colonial critique.

Marielle Presente in Brazil

After openly gay, Afro-Brazilian politician Marielle Franco and her driver Anderson Gomes were shot with 13 bullets on the night of March 14, 2018 in Rio de Janeiro, broad protests under the motto "Marielle Presente!" (Marielle [is] present) immediately emerged. The protests were led by afro-descendant Brazilian women and queers and soon took place all over Brazil, and also internationally. Many considered Marielle Franco's assassination as political, and Marielle's portrait started to adorn walls, streets, and sidewalks in many places in form of posters, graffiti, and stencils. During the 2019 carnival in Rio, the *Estação Primeira de Mangueira*, one of the most successful samba schools in Brazil, featuring prominently in the live screening of the carnival, dedicated their performance to Marielle Franco. By claiming "Marielle's presence" and her political legacy alive as well as demanding her murder to be investigated; by putting her portrait on walls in public spaces as graffiti and on posters, the protesters resist a politics that marginalizes murders motivated by racist, sexist, as well as homo- and transphobic motives.[3] "We have begun to destroy the myth of equality," politician, activist, and former advisor of Marielle Franco, Mônica Francisco, emphasized in a talk in March 2019 in Berlin, since, due to their history, afro-descendant Brazilians "are resistant, rebellious bodies" (Francisco 2019). Francisco thus described Marielle Franco as someone who broke "with everything normative," since she represented everything formerly marginalized, and thus was seen as a "threat to order" by conservative and radical

---

[3] See the memorial site for Marielle Franco: www.mariellefranco.com.br, Dec. 16, 2019.

right forces (Francisco 2019, translation JR). Francisco sees Marielle's murder as symbolic, because she stood for "all who had no voice in parliament." From these new – and still very few – positions of visibility, afro-descendants now oppose the "colonialist, extractivist state that discards our bodies" (Francisco 2019, translation JR).

Figure 6: Marielle Presente, column in Rio de Janeiro (Photo: Matti Steinitz); Figure 7: Monica Francisco (left) in Berlin (Photo: Julia Roth, 2019)

In August 2017, Ludimilla Teixeira, a black anarchist born in Bahia, one of the poorest communities of Salvador, created the Facebook page "Women United Against Bolsonaro." So far, almost 4 million women have joined the page. A movement under the slogan and hashtag: #EleNão – #NotHim emerged out of this group, which soon spurred hundreds of thousands of protesters onto the streets of Brazil and around the world, becoming the largest protest organized by women in Brazil's history (see Bruh 2018). On Twitter, #EleNão had more than 193,000 mentions between September 16 and 18, 2018, according to researchers at FGV university. Additionally, there were 152,000 tweets with the hashtag #EleNunca (#Never-Him). The list of women posting against the far-right candidate includes prominent actresses, journalists, and TV presenters. "#EleNão is not just about politics. It is about morals," actress Deborah Secco tweeted to her 3,4 million followers (BBC 2019). Lately, indigenous women have also started protests against the brutal, racist politics of the Bolsonaro regime (BBC 2019).[4]

A video was posted on the Facebook page of the São Paulo-based activist group *Bancada Ativista* (Activist Fraction), which is dedicated to elect activists to legisla-

---

4   "Brazil's indigenous women protest against Bolsonaro policies," BBC, 13 August, 2019, www.bbc.com/news/world-latin-america-49329680, Dec. 16, 2019.

tive power. The video starts with "Marielle Franco presente! Anderson, presente!" chants by protesters on March 15, 2018, in São Paulo. Posters show slogans such as *Preta LGBTQ Marielle Presente* (Black LGBTQ Marielle Present), *Vidas negras e faveladas importam* (Black and Favela Lives Matter) carried by a young Black girl, or *Somos Todos Marielle* (We are all Marielle). An interviewee (Bianca) states "Marielle está presente en cada uma de nós" (Marielle is present in every one of us). Repeating their names and publicly showing their photos on posters, the *Black Lives Matter* movement and the *Say Her Name* movement in the US initiated a similar politics of rendering the systemically marginalized deaths of African Americans visible and the structures and actors enabling and committing these murders accountable. And so did and do the Argentinian mothers and grandmothers of the Plaza de Mayo. In 1955, Momie Till insisted on publicly showing her son's dead body in order to oppose the racist rape-lynching complex of which he had become a victim, an action which led to protesters carrying posters with Emmet Till's photograph during Civil Rights marches.

The predominantly afro-descendant female and queer protesters, who are joined by allies of all positions, also unite their precarious bodies in the streets and claim Marielle Franco's presence in everything she represented – a Black lesbian woman from the favela who had reached a high position in politics and fought for social justice. By simultaneously claiming to be Marielle Franco ("we are all Marielle"), the protesters form a collective body of resistance to the violent racist, sexist, misogynist, and homophobic political climate they face, thus practicing a politics of embodied intersectionality from below – politically, symbolically, and discursively.

***

All of the recent feminist protest started out as spontaneous and momentous events based on very diverse politics. With the International Women's Strike starting on March 8, 2016, the different movements have become more organized and more concrete and focused politically, raising hope for a more institutionalized and longer-lasting way of contestation. Moreover, the Strikes tie gender and racial claims back to the underlying economic and colonial structures of inequality.

On October 19, 2016, in Argentina, members of the movement NiUnaMenos and other feminist organizations, like the Spanish Internacional Feminista, called for an hour-long strike and various protests, after seven femicides had been committed in one week. The first International Women's Strike, also known as *Paro Internacional de Mujeres*, was on March 8, 2017, and took place in more than 50 countries around the world. Protests such as the International Day for the Elimination of Violence against Women on November 25, 2017, and the massive response to the call of the Women's March 2018 in the United States can be considered as precedents.

During the third ITUC World Women's Conference/Women's Organizing Assembly in October 2017, 200 female trade unionists from around the world gathered in Costa Rica; and trade union representatives from Argentina and Brazil asked the unions to take part in the second International Women's Strike call on March 8, 2017. As of 2019, the Strike has become a global movement coordinated across 50 countries.

The feminist movements involved called for a strike of workers, students, care workers, and consumers under slogans like #NosParamos, #WeStrike, and "What they call love is unpaid work." They demanded a society free from violence against women, free from aggression against and murder of women for the simple fact of being women, a society without precarious work, the gender pay gap, and sexual harassment at the workplace. Moreover, the Strikes addressed poverty, racial violence, persecution of immigrants, and cutbacks in social and health programs.

The call for a strike, published in *The Guardian* on February 6, 2017, by prominent activists and intellectuals underscores the scope of the Women's Strikes. Among the authors were Linda Martín Alcoff, Cinzia Arruzza, Tithi Bhattacharya, Nancy Fraser, Barbara Ransby, Keeanga-Yamahtta Taylor, Rasmea Yousef Odeh, and Angela Davis (Alcoff et al. 2018a), who explicitly mention the impact of other movements (particularly the Argentinian one) with regard to intersectional politics, addressing structural problems, and coalition building (see Alcoff et al. 2018a). According to US American activists, the focus on the structural dimensions of oppression and the urgency of the entanglements with global capitalism as well as the division of labor had already been a central task in parts of the Latin American feminist movements.

By promoting, defending, and, most of all, embodying diversity, the present feminist movements make visible and open up the possibility for alternative forms of the social and political in light of neoliberal precarization of labor and right-wing populist "responses." As they call attention to violence against female and other non-normative and non-White bodies as a structural phenomenon related to colonial and patriarchal legacies ingrained in capitalism, the Women's Strikes in particular scandalize the structural devaluation of care work and reproduction as well as socio-political power relations of discrimination, exclusion, and deportation. The strikes provide a transnational instrument open to a multitude of actors, not only to women, but also for precarious and migrant workers (see Lorey 2019a). Again, like in the preceding protest, the participants' physical assembling on the streets embodied a stand against the historic and continuous control, precariousness and disposability of female and differently gendered and racialized as well as poor and colonized bodies.

Collective Bodies of Resistance as Political Tools – and some Theoretical Reflections

The currently emerging feminist struggles are embedded in the radicalization of reactionary White heteronormative masculinity in many places and contexts, which currently seeks to oppose the pluralization of societies and life forms, as expressed in the mentioned right-wing populist patterns of en-gendering. In her book *Notes Toward a Performative Theory of Assembly* (2015), Judith Butler describes the current moment as "a biopolitical situation" in which diverse populations are increasingly affected by so-called "precarization." As she argues, this precarization becomes operative through the overall pulverization of the active remnants of social democracy. Simultaneously, ideologies of individual responsibility are promoted, according to which subjects are obliged to constantly maximize their market value in an entrepreneurial way and see this as the ultimate goal (15). In turn, pursuing the question of what function public assembly can serve in this context, what "opposing form of ethics" it embodies and expresses, she concludes that, amidst "an increasingly individualized sense of anxiety and failure," public assembly "embodies the insight that this social condition is both shared and unjust." For Butler, then, "assembly enacts a provisional and plural form of coexistence that constitutes a distinct ethical and social alternative to 'responsibilization'." (15-16)

Isabell Lorey (2019a) argues that illiberalism, understood as the negation of liberal-democratic achievements, as the maintenance of the liberal form of democracy with its logics of representation and exclusion, appears to have no alternative. She asserts that struggles for recognition – such as feminist struggles – are then considered as a "lively" part and parcel of liberal democracies and they are "tamed." Liberal democracies thus lock themselves in in the name of the protection of freedom for the few and move closer toward the politics they had deemed "illiberal." The current feminist movements, however, do not act within the confines of "liberal democracies." Instead, they question the very conditions of possibility of such notions, since, as Lorey argues, notions of "liberal democracy" are embedded in the "liberal-illiberal" paradigm that defines liberal and neoliberal discourses. Thus, they do not only attack presidents that stand for right-wing sexist politics, but also the structures that enabled them. The Latin American movements in particular also remind us of the long legacy of the coloniality of gender (Lugones 2008).

These movements evoke a new sense of intersectionality which re-connects the concept to the radical activist roots it emerged from after it had long been restricted to academic and theoretical debates. According to Butler, the "bodies in alliance" (2015: 28) making their protest and claims visible in the streets of Washington, Buenos Aires, Rio de Janeiro, Berlin, New York, Warsaw and in many other locations, point to the social modality of bodies and "link gender and sexual minorities with precarious populations more generally" (28). By performing a political unity

Figure 8: The Future is Intersectional Women's Strike Berlin 2019

Figure 9: Women's Strike Berlin 2019

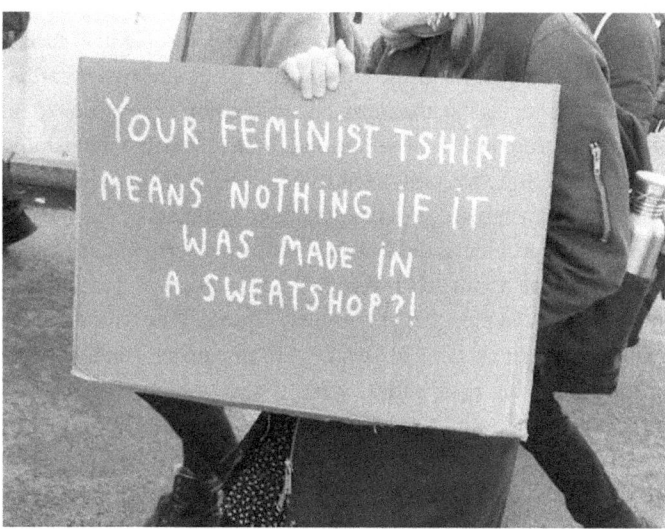

based on manifold positions and experiences – as expressed by the emblematic Pink Pussy Hats of the Women's Marches, the green bandanas of the *NiUnaMenos* movement, or the graffiti of and identification with Marielle Franco in Brazil – the protesters also make visible and audible the "conditions of interdependency" (45; 50) of all human interaction and sociability, as well as a politics of intersectionality restored into practice.

By building a strategic imagined (counter-)community, as formulated by America Ferrera in her speech at the 2017 Women's March in Washington, current intersectional transnational and transversal feminists raise hope for an effective counter-discourse to the current rise and revival of White supremacist and racist, sexist, and homo- and transphobic right-wing populism internationally. The feminist movements practice what I (following Mirza 2013) have coined as "embodied intersectionality" (Roth 2020a and 2020b) to confront and stop the right-wing trend by making their presences a "claim" (Butler 2015). Moreover, the current movements seek to problematize and overcome (some) feminism's/s' complicity with neoliberal logics, which are sometimes also co-opted by populist forces (see Dietze's contribution to this volume). The long legacy of anti-racist feminist struggles, in the Americas in particular, offers the current movements a rich repertoire of experiences and resistance strategies to counter the right-wing populist and extremist trend.[5] By their very presence and claims, they call into question the "repressive dogma that has cast so many genders and sexual lives into the shadows, without recognition and deprived of any sense of futurity" (Butler 2019: n.p.). They are therefore hated and feared by their right-wing and conservative opponents, as are their body politics and related notions of reproductive rights. Thus, despite these movements' impressive outreach, it may be too early to speak of the success of the new feminisms. It is questionable how successful the movements can be in the face of the current climate of alternative truths and realities, in which strategies like the complete defamation of constructed "enemies" or of self-victimization and "reverse anti-colonialism" create new paradigms, for which the language and tools still need to be invented. Sadly, the current trend points more towards a further polarization of our societies.

In the current movements, the dialogue between diverse histories and notions of the political brings about what Verónica Gago calls the "precipitate subject" (sujeto imprevisto; Gago 2018: 22) of feminism. Through the "corporal embeddedness" (arraigo corporal) this subject evokes the (for many: colonial) wound as a condition for dislocating the political scene (Gago 2018: 22-23). The creation of the communal body of feminist resistance enables people to think and imagine a new poetics and new figures of connectivity and dialogue between "Norths and Souths" (conectividad entre nortes y sures, Draper: 65). Butler also speaks about

---

5   Brah and Phoenix 2004, Hearn 2011, Zapata Galindo 2011 and Viveros Vigoya 2012 remind us that Black feminists and anti-slavery movements had already claimed the recognition of their racist discrimination by the 18th and 19th centuries and "probably before then" (Hearn 2011: 90).

the importance of "embodied" forms of resistance. Feminists of Color and post- and decolonial feminists like Alanna Lockward – who curated the series BE.BoP – Black Europe Body politics" foregrounding performative form of decolonial aesthtetics (Lockward 2013) – or Grada Kilomba – "the body as political tool" (Kilomba 2019) – have long emphasized a notion of the body similar to Butler's, particularly emphasizing its potential for using the "knowledges of the body" to attack the "colonial anti-capitalist unconscious" and politically "become one body" (Rolnik in Bardet: 110, translation JR). Persons racialized as Black in the context of colonization and enslavement have historically been denied the same status of a body as Whites, and have been reduced to the status of "pure flesh," as Hortense Spillers has shown. If right-wing populism tries to re-relate and subsume ("autochthonous") women's bodies to the nation and exclude, control, and govern non-White etc. bodies, as becomes visible in the prominence of the struggle over reproductive rights in the right-wing complex (see Fixmer Oraíz 2019), the intersectional feminist movements claim their bodies and their right over their bodies and subsume and are/embody the body/bodies of resistance. The feminist movements remind us of the long history of oppression of colonized women, silencing and restricting the female to the domestic, as well as by imagining the female body as territory (Federici). According to Butler (2015), the very presence of these bodies in public proclaims the fact that they are not disposable, "they are exercising a plural and performative right to appear, one that asserts and instates the body in the middle of the political field" (11). Acting in concert, then, "can be an embodied form of calling into question the inchoate and powerful dimensions of reigning notions of the political" (9).

Bibliography

Abi-Hassan, Sahar (2017): "Populism and Gender." In: Cristóbal Rovira Kaltwasser/Paul Taggart/Paulina Ochoa Espejo/Pierre Ostiguy (eds.): The Oxford Handbook on Populism. Oxford: Oxford University Press, pp. 2-22.

Ajanovic, Edma/Mayer, Stefanie/Sauer, Birgit (2018): "Constructing 'the People': An Intersectional Analysis of Right-Wing Concepts of Democracy and Citizenship in Austria." In: Journal of Language and Politics 17 (5), pp. 636–654.

Bardet, Marie (2018). "¿Cómo hacernos un cuerpo?." Entrevista con Rolnik, Suely. In: Verónica Gago/Raquel Gutiérrez Aguilar/Susana Draper/Mariana Menéndez Montanelli/Suely Rolnik: 8M: Constelación Feminista. ¿Cuál Es Tu Huelga? ¿Cuál Es Tu Lucha? Buenos Aires: Tinta Limón.

BBC (2019): Brazil's Indigenous Women Protest Against Bolsonaro Policies. Online: www.bbc.com/news/world-latin-america-49329680, 11.10.2019.

Brah, Avtar (2013): "Pensando en y a través de la Interseccionalidad." In: Martha Zapata Galindo/Sabina García Peter/Jennifer Chan de Avila (eds.): Interseccionalidad en Debate. Actas del Congreso Internacional "Indicadores Interseccionales y Medidas de Inclusión Social en Instituciones de Educación Superior," MISEAL, pp.14–20.

Brah, Avtar/Phoenix, Anne (2004): "Ain't I a Woman? Revisiting Intersectionality." In: Journal of International Women's Studies 5 (3), pp. 75-86.

Brum, Eliane (2018): "How a Homophobic, Misogynist, Racist 'Thing' Could Be Brazil's Next President." In: The Guardian, October 6 (online edition, 11.10.2019).

Butler, Judith (2018): Wenn die Geste zum Ereignis Wird. Wien: Turia + Kant.

Butler, Judith (2015): Notes Toward a Performative Theory of Assembly. Cambridge: Harvard University Press.

Butler, Judith (2019): "The Backlash Against 'Gender Ideology' Must Stop." In: The New Statesman America, January 21 (Online edition, accessed De. 16, 2019).

Canevari, María Cecilia (2019): E-mail to Author, April 27.

Case, Mary Ann (2019): "Trans Formations in the Vatican's War on 'Gender Ideology'." In: Signs: Journal of Women in Culture and Society 44 (3), pp. 639-664.

Costa, Sérgio (2019): Personal Talk. (Unpublished Manuscript).

Combahee River Collective (1981): "A Black Feminist Statement." In: Cherrie Moraga/Gloria Anzaldúa (eds.): This Bridge Called My Back: Writings by Radical Women of Color. New York: Kitchen Table, Women of Color Press, pp. 210-218.

Crenshaw, Kimberly (2016): TED Talk 'The Urgency of Intersectionality' on the Double Invisibilization of the Female African American Victims. Online: www.youtube.com/watch?v=akOe5-UsQ2o, accessed De. 16, 2019.

Diehl, Paula (2017): "Why Do Right-Wing Populists Find So Much Appeal in Mass Media?" In: The Dahrendorf Forum (www.dahrendorf-forum.eu/why-do-right-wing-populists-find-so-much-appeal-in-mass-media/, accessed De. 16, 2019).

Dietze, Gabriele (2018): "Rechtspopulismus und Geschlecht. Paradox und Leitmotif." In: Femina Politica 27, pp. 34-46.

Dietze, Gabriele (2016): "Das Ereignis Köln." In: Femina Politica 1, pp. 93-102.

Dietze, Gabriele (2016b): "Ethnosexismus: Sex-Mob-Narrative um die Kölner Silvesternacht." In: Movements. Journal for Critical Migration and Border Regime Studies 2 (1), pp. 177-185.

Dietze, Gabriele (2015): "Anti-Genderismus Intersektional Lesen." In: Zeitschrift für Medienwissenschaft 13 (2), pp. 125–127.

Dietze, Gabriele (2013): Weiße Frauen in Bewegung. Genealogien und Konkurrenzen von Race- und Genderpolitiken. Bielefeld: transcript.

Draper, Susana (2018): "Strike as Process: Building the Poetics of a New Feminism." In: The South Atlantic Quarterly 117 (3), pp. 682-691.

DuBois, Ellen Carol (2010): "Internationalizing Married Women's Nationality: The Hague Campaign of 1930." In: Karen Offen (ed.): Globalizing Feminisms, 1789-1945. London: Routledge, pp. 204-216.

Federici, Silvia (2004): *Caliban and the Witch: Women, the Body and Primitive Accumulation*. Brooklyn, NY: Autonomedia.

Fendlay, Cassady (2018): Informal Talk Organized by the Rosa-Luxemburg Foundation in Berlin. Notes by the Author and Conversation with Cassady Fendlay and the Author on the Same Day, March 9.

Fendlay, Cassady (2018): Interview by Rosa Luxemburg Foundation. Berlin, March 13.

Fixer Oraíz, Natalie (2019): Homeland Maternity. US Security Culture and the New Reproductive Regime. Champaign: University of Illinois Press.

Francisco, Mônica (2019): "Marielles Vermächtnis: Herausforderungen für den Schwarzen und Intersektionalen Feminismus in Brasilien." Paper Presented at a Conference of Rosa-Luxemburg Foundation. Berlin, March 24.

Gago, Verónica/Gutiérrez Aguilar, Raquel/Draper, Susana/Menéndez Montanelli, Mariana/Rolnik, Suely (2018): 8M: "Constelación Feminista. ¿Cuál Es Tu Huelga? ¿Cuál Es Tu Lucha?," Buenos Aires: Tinta Limón.

Goldberg, Michelle (2019): "The Heartbreak of the 2019 Women's March." In: New York Times, January 18 (Online edition, accessed De. 16, 2019).

Hark, Sabine/Villa, Paula-Irene (2015): Anti-Genderismus. Sexualität und Geschlecht als Schauplätze Aktueller Politischer Auseinandersetzungen. Bielefeld: transcript.

Hark, Sabine/Villa, Paula-Irene (2017): Unterscheiden und Herrschen. Ein Essay zu den Ambivalenten Verflechtungen von Rassismus, Sexismus und Feminismus in der Gegenwart. Bielefeld: transcript.

Hearn, Jeff (2011): "Neglected Intersectionalities in Studying Men: Age(ing), Virtuality, Transnationality." In: Helma Lutz/Maria Teresa Herrera Vivar/Linda Supik (eds.): Framing Intersectionality: Debates on a Multi-Facetted Concept in Gender Studies. Farnham, England/Burlington, USA: Ashgate, pp. 89-104.

Hess, Amanda (2017): "How a Fractious Women's Movement Came to Lead the Left." In: New York Times, February 7 (Online edition, accessed De. 16, 2019).

Kilomba, Grada (2019): "The Body as Political Tool." Exhibition and Talk with Paul Goodwin, Kadist, (https://kadist.org/program/the-body-as-a-political-tool/, accessed De. 16, 2019).

Lockward, Alanna (2013): "Black Europe Body Politics: Towards an Afropean Decolonial Aesthetics." In: Social Text ,July 15, 2013. https://socialtextjournal.org/periscope_article/black-europe-body-politics-towards-an-afropean-decolonial-aesthetics/

Lorey, Isabell (2019a): "'Nicht eine Weniger': Die Große Feministische Streikwelle gegen Il/liberale Politiken." In: *Springerin* 2/2019, pp.36-39.

Lorey, Isabell (2019b): 8M – The Great Feminist Strike. Introduction. Online: transversal.at/blog/8m-the-great-feminist-strike, accessed De. 16, 2019.

Lugones, María (2008): "The Coloniality of Gender." In: Worlds and Knowledges Otherwise 2, pp. 1-17.

Mirza, Heidi (2013): "'A Second Skin': Embodied Intersectionality, Transnationalism and Narratives of Identity and Belonging Among Muslim Women in Britain." In: Women's Studies International Forum 36 (January-February), pp. 5-15.

Mokre, Monika/Siim, Birte (2013): "European Public Spheres and Intersectionality." In: Birte Siim et al. (eds.): Negotiating Gender and Diversity in an Emergent European Public Sphere. Palgrave Macmillan, pp. 22-40.

Mudde, Cass/Rovira Kaltwasser, Cristóbal (2017): Populism: A Very Short Introduction. New York: Oxford University Press.

#¡Ni Una Menos! (eds.) (2018): Vivas Nos Queremos. Buenos Aires: Milena Caserola.

Resumen Latinoamericano (2019): Argentina. Resumen Gremial y Social. Llamamiento al Paro Feminista 8M 2019/Crece la Desigualdad en la Ciudad y Aumenta la Indigencia entre los Menores de 15 años/Panorama Político-Sindical: Inflación y Despidos en Ascenso (Más Información). Online: www.resumenlatinoamericano.org/2019/03/03/argentina-resumen-gremial-y-social-llamamiento-al-paro-feminista-8m-2019-crece-la-desigualdad-en-la-ciudad-y-aumenta-la-indigencia-entre-los-menores-de-15-anos-panorama-politico-sindical-inflacio/, accessed De. 16, 2019.

Roth, Julia (2020a): Can Feminism Trump Populism? Right-Wing Trends and Intersectional Contestations in the Americas. Trier WVT/Bilingual Press (in print).

Roth, Julia (2020b): ¿Puede el Feminismo Vencer al Populismo? Tendencias de Derecha y Disputas Interseccionales en las Américas. Bielefeld: Kipu Verlag.

Roth, Julia (2019): "Globale Achsen der Ungleichheit. Intersektionalität und/als Interdependente Ungleichheiten." In: Karin Fischer/Margarete Grandner (eds.): Globale Ungleichheit. Reihe Globalisierung Entwicklung Politik. Wien: Mandelbaum Verlag, pp. 172-186.

Roth, Julia (2018): "Feminism Otherwise: Intersectionality beyond Occidentalism." In: InterDisciplines 2, pp. 97-122.

Roth, Julia (2013): "Entangled Inequalities as Intersectionalities: Towards an Epistemic Sensibilization." In: DesiguALdades.net Working Paper Series 43. https://www.desigualdades.net/Working_Papers/Search-Working-Papers/working-paper-43-_entangled-inequalities-as-intersectionalities_/index.html, accessed Dec. 16, 2019.

Sauer, Birgit (2017): "Gesellschaftstheoretische Überlegungen zum Europäischen Rechtspopulismus. zum Erklärungspotenzial der Kategorie Geschlecht." In: Politische Vierteljahresschrift 58 (1), pp. 3-22.

Sauer, Birgit (2013): "Intersectionality from Above – Framing Muslim Headscarves in European Policy Debates." Paper Presented at the ECPR General Conference Sciences Po, Bordeaux, September 4-7.
Spillers, Hortense (2003): "Mama's Baby, Papa's Maybe: An American Grammar Book." *Black, White, and in Color: Essays on American Literature and Culture.* Chicago: University of Chicago Press, pp. 203–229. First published in *Diacritics*, Summer 1987.
The Women's March Organizers and Condé Nast (WMO) (2018): Together We Rise: The Women's March. Behind the Scenes at the Protest Heard around the World. New York: HarperCollins.
Zapata Galindo (2011): "El Paradigma de la Interseccionalidad en América Latina" Lecture Given at the Lateinamerikainstitut, Freie Universität Berlin, Notes Taken by the Author, November 17.
Viveros Vigoya (2012): "Movilidades y Desigualdades Espaciales y Sociales en el Contexto del Multiculturalismo Latinoamericano. Una Lectura en Clave de Género." In: Juliana Ströbele-Gregor/Dörte Wollrad (eds.): Espacios de Género. Adlaf Congreso Anual 2012. Buenos Aires: Nueva Sociedad; Fundación Friedrich Ebert; Adlaf, pp. 189-203.

Acknowledgements

The authors express their gratitude to the Center for Interdisciplinary Research (ZiF) in Bielefeld for hosting and financing the workshop "Right-Wing Populism and Gender" in which numerous of the authors of this book participated, and where the idea of this edited volume initially came up. We are also grateful to the Center for Interdisciplinary Center for Gender Research (IZG) at Bielefeld university for their support in planning the workshop and Bielefeld University – particularly the Prorektorat für Forschung und Forschungstransfer and the Dezernat FFT – for their support for a larger research project on the topic. Part of Gabriele Dietze's research was made possible through the support of the Volkswagen Foundation. Julia Roth's research was partly made possible due to the support of the BMBF research project "The Americas as Space of Entanglements" at the Center for InterAmerican Studies (CIAS) Bielefeld. Todd Sekuler and Edith Otero Quezada were of invaluable help in the process of finalizing the manuscript and Holly Patch for polishing the introduction last-minute. Last but not least, we would like to express our heartfelt thanks to Karin Werner from transcript for her confidence, her encouragement and her unconditional support for the project and to Gero Wierichs for the good and patient coordination of the publication process.

List of image sources

Image Sources Möser

Figure 1:
LMPT Poster Campaign, Poster taken from lamanifpourtous.fr, 27.01.2020.

Figure 2:
LMPT Manual, cover of the manual that can be downloaded at lamanifpourtous.fr.

Figure 3:
Advertising Campaign March for Life, Le Figaro, January 12, 2017.

Figure 4:
Poster Campaign FN/RN, regional elections 2015: Choose Your Suburb.

Image Sources Dietze

Figure 1:
AfD Plakat "'Traditionell?' Uns gefällt's."
   https://www.afd.de/bundestagswahl-2017-plakatmotive-faltblaetter/, 17.02.2019.

Figure 2:
AfD Plakat des Landesverbandes Nordrhein-Westfalen
   https://laemmerbiss.de/2017/08/07/afd-am-argumentativen-abgrund/, 01.10.2019.

Figure 3:
AfD Plakat des Kreisverbandes Magdeburg
   http://www.afd-md.de/mehr-kinder-statt-masseneinwanderung/, 01.10.2019.

Figure 4:
AfD Plakat "Wir Frauen für die AfD."
   https://www.facebook.com/FrauenFuerDieAfD/, 01.10.2019

Image Sources Schleusener

Figures 1-2:
"Election 2016: Exit Polls." Produced by Jon Huang, Samuel Jacoby, Michael Strickland and K.K. Rebecca Lai. The New York Times, November 8, 2016
   https://nytimes.com/interactive/2016/11/08/us/politics/election-exit-polls.html, 06.08., 2019.

Figure 3:
"Stop Oppressing Me." James Damore, Twitter Account (@JamesADamore), October 30, 2017
   https://twitter.com/JamesADamore/media, 06.08.2019.

Image Sources Graff

Figure 1:
Women's Strike (Black Monday), afternoon of 3 October 2016, Warsaw, Castle Square. "Sea of umbrellas" image, shot from the tower of St. Ann's Church. Photo: Agnieszka Graff

Figure 2:
23 March 2018 (Black Friday) in Warsaw. Large banner reads "Women's Strike." Hand-held sign: "I think, I feel, I decide." Photo: Agata Kubis.
   https://oko.press/macice-wstaja-kolan-inne-hasla-czarnego-piatku/.

Figure 3:
Cover of Wysokie Obcasy magazine of 22 October 2016, featuring singer Natalia Przybysz in black (at the time an obvious sign of participation in Women's Strike). The title reads" "The medicine whose name is NO."
   https://natemat.pl/blogi/michalgortat/192937,czarny-prostest-natalii-przybysz.

Figure 4:
Performance of the Witches' Choir. Note the skin-colored negligees, very little make-up, all body types, angry faces. Photo: Krzysztof Zatycki. Source: Witches' Choir Facebook profile.
   https://www.face-book.com/Chor-czaro-wnic/pho-tos/a.165460-20148-38235/16993-79427-027160/?-type=3&theater.

Image Sources Strick

Figure 1:
Video "It's ok to be white [explained]," Screenshot JB Gunner TV
https://www.youtube.com/watch?v=JM3TP1jOCso, Last Seen: March 2019. Video has since been set to private.

Figure 2:
Video "Sargon of Akkad – FULL SPEECH Day For Freedom," Screenshot Bull Brand, 20.05.2018
https://www.youtube.com/watch?v=Ky3HrZ_U-sY, 04.10.2019.

Figure 3:
Video "Roosh Hour #29 – Men In Female Sports," Screenshot Roosh V, 09.12.2018
https://www.youtube.com/watch?v=Gcq7CDSCGPs, 04.10.2019.

Figure 4:
Instagram Page, The Golden One@thegloriouslion, Screenshot
https://www.instagram.com/thegloriouslion/?hl=en
04.10.2019.

Image Sources Roth

Figure 1:
Actress America Ferrera at the Women's March in Washington, January 2017, Screenshot, Women's March on Washington: Full Rally, The New York Times, Youtube
https://www.youtube.com/watch?v=dDc9Ochrifw, accessed Dec. 16, 2019.

Figure 2:
Inter-American Alliances: Jair Bolsonaro and Donald Trump United Against 'Gender Ideology': Palácio do Planalto. Meeting of Jair Bolsonaro and Donald Trump – Exchange of Shirts. March, 2019. Wikimedia Commons.

Figures 3:
Time Magazin Cover: Pussy Hat (February 6, 2017); "Intersectional Solidarity;" 8 March Protest March Berlin, 2019 (Photo: Julia Roth)

Figure 4:
Ni Una Menos (Green Handkerchiefs), seen at Women's Strike Berlin, 2019 (Photo: Julia Roth 2019).

Figure 5:
Marielle Presente, Column in Rio de Janeiro (Photo: Matti Steinitz, 2019); Monica Francisco (left) in Berlin (Photo: Julia Roth, 2019).

Figure 6:
"The Future is Intersectional" (Women's Strike Berlin 2019, Photos: Julia Roth).

Figure 7:
Women's March Berlin, 2019 (Photo: Julia Roth).

Authors

Ajanović, Edma is currently working as post-doctoral researcher at Danube-University Krems, Austria. She finished her doctoral studies in political science at the University of Vienna. In her thesis she analyzed racism from an intersectional perspective in Austria. She is an associated member of the research platform "Mobile Cultures and Societies" at the University of Vienna and member of the research network "Queer politics." Research interests: Studies on racism and its intersections with gender, right-wing populism, anti-feminism and anti-genderism, neoliberalism and post-socialist transformations. Recent publication: "Constructing 'the People': An Intersectional Analysis of Right-Wing Concepts of Democracy and Citizenship in Austria." In: Journal of Language and Politics 17 (5): 636–54. 2018 (with Stefanie Mayer and Birgit Sauer).

Dietze, Gabriele (PD Dr.) conducts research from a cultural and media studies perspective on racism, sexism, migration and right-wing populism. She is a member of the Center for Transdisciplinary Gender Studies at Humboldt University Berlin (ZtG). She is, among other positions, currently Harris professor for gender studies at Dartmouth College (Hanover, NH) and was visiting fellow at the DuBois Institute at Harvard University (Cambridge, MA). Some of her recent publications include *Sexualpolitik. Verflechtungen von Race und Gender* (Campus 2017) and *Sexueller Exzeptionalismus. Überlegenheitsnarrative in Migrationsabwehr und Rechtspopulismus* (transcript 2019).

Graff, Agnieszka, associate professor at the American Studies Center, University of Warsaw. Author of five books of feminist essays, among them *Świat bez kobiet* (World without Women, 2001) and *Matka feministka* (Mother and Feminist, 2014); active in the Polish women's movement since the mid-nineties. Research interests: intersection of gender, sexuality and nation, forms of resistance to gender equality, transnational anti-gender movement, gender and right-wing populism. Recent publications: "Gender as 'Ebola from Brussels'...," co-written with Elżbieta Korolczuk, on anti-gender movements (*Signs*, vol. 43, 2018) and "'Claiming the Shipyard...' on the use of national symbols by Polish feminism." (East European Politics and Societies, vol. 33, 2019) Coeditor of the Spring 2019 special issue of *Signs: On Gender and the Rise of the Global Right*.

Kováts, Eszter is a PhD student at the Institute for Political Science, Faculty of Law, University ELTE, Budapest. She was working in the Hungarian Office of the German political foundation Friedrich-Ebert-Stiftung (FES) from 2009 to 2019, and from 2012 until the end of 2019 she was responsible for the Foundation's gender program for East-Central Europe. Research interests: political theory, political economy, demand side of far right politics, Central and Eastern Europe and West-East inequalities. Her most recent publications: "Limits of the Human Rights Vocabulary in Addressing Inequalities – Dilemmas of Justice in the Age of Culture Wars in Hungary" (Intersections. East European Journal of Society and Politics. Vol. 5. Nr 2. 60-80), and with Anikó Gregor: "Work – life: balance? Tensions between care and paid work in the lives of Hungarian women." (Social Science Review. Hungarian Academy of Sciences, 2019).

Kuhar, Roman is a professor of sociology of culture at the Faculty of Arts, University of Ljubljana, and teaches courses on gender, sexuality, popular culture and everyday life. He is currently the dean of the Faculty of Arts. His work has been published in numerous academic journals and several books, including *The Unbearable Comfort of Privacy* (with A. Švab) and *Beyond The Pink Curtain: Everyday Life of LGBT People in Eastern Europe* (co-edited with J. Takács). In 2018 he received the Excellency in Research Award from the Slovenian Research Agency for the book *Anti-Gender Campaigns in Europe: Mobilizing against Equality* (Rowman & Littlefield International, 2017), which he co-edited with D. Paternotte. He is also an associate editor at *Social Politics* (Oxford University Press) and vice president of the Slovenian Sociological Association.

Mayer, Stefanie, political scientist with a focus on critical gender research in the fields of right-wing extremism and right-wing populism as well as feminist politics and feminist theorizing. Lecturer at FH Campus Wien (University of Applied Science) in Vienna. In 2016, she finished her PhD at the University of Vienna with a dissertation on constructions of ethnicisation, racism and anti-racism in white feminist activism in Vienna, which was published in 2018 as *Politik der Differenzen* (Politics of Differences; Barbara Budrich). Research interests: Feminist – especially feminist-activist – theorizing and feminist-activist politics, right-wing extremism and right-wing populism and the intersections of racism, anti-feminism and homophobia in right-wing anti-gender campaigns. Recent publication: With Judith Goetz: Mit Gott und Natur gegen geschlechterpolitischen Wandel, in: FIPU (ed.): Rechtsextremismus III (Mandelbaum).

Möser, Cornelia, researcher in cultural and gender studies at the French National Center for Scientific Research (CNRS) working at the Center for Sociological and Political Research in Paris, France (Cresppa) in the working group Gender, Work and Mobilities. She is also an associated member of the Centre Marc Bloch in Berlin, Germany. Her current project analyzes sexuality as a concept in feminist and queer theory since the 1960s in France, Germany and the USA with focus on hopes and ideas of emancipation or liberation. Further research projects involve right-wing sexual politics in Europe and queer/feminist critique of the nation state. Recent publications: "Sex Wars and the Contemporary French Moral Panic: The Productivity and Pitfalls of Feminist Conflicts." (Meridians: feminism, race, transnationalism, vol. 16, no. 1, 2018, pp. 79–111) and forthcoming: Marion Tillous & Cornelia Möser (eds.). *Avec, sans ou contre. Critiques queer/féministes de l'État* (Paris/Éditions iXe).

Pajnik, Mojca is Associate Professor at the Faculty of Social Sciences, University of Ljubljana and senior research advisor at the Peace Institute in Ljubljana. Her research focuses on gender (in)equality, populism, racism, migration and citizenship. Her books include Prostitution and Human Trafficking: Gender, Labour and Migration Aspects (PI, 2008), *Contesting Integration, Engendering Migration: Theory and Practice* (co-edited with F. Anthias, Palgrave, 2014), *Populism and the Web: Communicative Practices of Parties and Movements in Europe* (co-edited with B. Sauer, Routledge, 2017), and *Gender and Media: Structures and Practices of Inequality* (co-edited with B. Luthar, FSS, 2019, in Slovenian). Currently she coordinates the research project POP-MED, Political and Media Populism: "Refugee crisis" in Slovenia and Austria, funded by the Slovenian Research Agency and the Austrian FWF Der Wissenschaftsfonds (2018-2021).

Roth, Julia, is professor for American studies with a focus on gender studies, board member of the Interdisciplinary Center for Gender Research (IZG) and the Center for InterAmerican Studies (CIAS) at Bielefeld University. Previously, she was doctoral member of the DFG graduate school "Gender as a Category of Knowledge" and postdoctoral fellow of the BMBF research networks "desiguALdades.net – Interdependent Inequalities in Latin America" at Freie University Berlin and "The Americas as Space of Entanglements" at Bielefeld University. Research interests: Feminist and gender studies, postcolonial approaches and decolonial thinking, intersectionality theorizing, gender, citizenship and global inequalities, afro-descendant feminisms, right-wing populism and gender. Alongside her academic work, she organizes cultural-politial events (e.g. polar Salons, bpb metro, BE.BoP – Black Europe Body Politics curated by Alanna Lockward). Recent publication: *Can Feminism Trump Populism? Right-Wing Trends and Intersectional Contestations in the Americas* (WVT/Bilingual Press 2020).

Sauer, Birgit, professor of political science with a focus on governance and gender at the University of Vienna. She is vice-dean of the Faculty of Social Sciences, speaker of the research group "Gender and Politics" at the department of political science, speaker of the research network "Gender and Transformation" at the Faculty of Social Sciences and vice-speaker of the university research network "Gender and Agency." She is faculty member of the Doctoral School "Mobility in Modern Societies" at the University of Vienna. Her research interests include gender and right-wing politics, comparative gender politics, emotion, affect and politics. Recent publications include "Constructing 'the People.' An intersectional Analysis of Right-Wing Concepts of Democracy and Citizenship in Austria," in: Journal of language and Politics, published online 13.9.2018, DOI 10.1075/jlp.18013.may, Vol 17, No. 5, 2018, 636-654 with Edma Ajanović and Stefanie Mayer.

Schmincke, Imke (Dr. phil.) is assistant professor in the area of gender studies at the Institute of Sociology, LMU Munich. She received her PhD from the University of Hamburg. Research interests: gender sociology, feminist and other critical theories, sociology of the body and sexuality, feminist movements. Recent publication: "Die Neue Frauenbewegung in den Medien," in: Dorer, Johanna/Geiger, Brigitte/Hipfl, Brigitte/Ratković, Viktorija (Hg.): Handbuch Medien und Geschlecht, Wiesbaden: Springer, 2019. Online first: https://link.springer.com/referenceworkentry/10.1007/978-3-658-20712-0_40-1

Schleusener, Simon is a postdoctoral researcher at the Freie Universität Berlin's Friedrich Schlegel Graduate School of Literary Studies, where he is engaged in the project "Das Philologische Laboratorium." Previously, he has taught at the University of Würzburg and at the John F. Kennedy Institute for North American Studies in Berlin. He is the author of *Kulturelle Komplexität: Gilles Deleuze und die Kulturtheorie der American Studies* (transcript, 2015) and has worked on topics like the neoliberal imagination, ecology and the new materialism, affect politics, and right-wing populism. Currently, he is pursuing a postdoctoral project on the cultural and affective dimensions of the new capitalism.

Spierings, Niels, associate professor in Sociology with a focus on political and gender sociology, at Radboud Social Cultural Research, Dept. of Sociology, Radboud University, Nijmegen, The Netherlands. He formerly held positions at the London School of Economics and Political Science and University of Essex. Research interests: voting behavior, Islam, populism, social media, gender, sexuality, intersectionality, migration, and their interrelatedness. Geographical interests: Europe and the Middle East. Edited a special issue on gender and the populist radical right in *Patterns of Prejudice* together with Andrej Zaslove. Published on populism, gender, sexuality, and social media in *West European Politics, Gender & Education, Patterns of Prejudice, Acta Politica* and *Information, Communication & Society*.

Strick, Simon is a scholar of American Studies and gender studies based in Berlin. He received his PhD from Humboldt University with a thesis on pain, sentimentalism and biopolitics; the book *American Dolorologies* was published by SUNY Press in 2014. He has held positions at Humboldt University, Paderborn University, JFK-Institute Berlin, ZfL Berlin and the University of Virginia. In 2018 he received a grant by the VW-Foundation for his research project Feeling (Alt)Right: Affective and Identity Politics of Online Extremism. Strick's specializations are in gender and critical race studies, popular culture, film, and cultural analysis. Currently, he is editing a special issue of the journal "Amerikastudien" on the subject of American eugenics, due later in 2020. Also, he is finishing the monograph *Rechte Gefühle: Affektpolitiken der transnationalen Online-Rechten*, which will be published by transcript in January 2020. Together with Susann Neuenfeldt and Werner Türk he founded the performance group PKRK, which is active in Berlin theaters since 2009.

Wielowiejski, Patrick, Ph.D. candidate at the Department of European Ethnology at Humboldt University Berlin, supervised by Prof. Beate Binder and Prof. Sabine Hark. Currently writing his dissertation, an ethnography of homosexuality in the contemporary German far right, particularly in the Alternative für Deutschland (AFD). Board member of the European Network for Queer Anthropology (ENQA). Holds an M.A. in cultural studies from Goldsmiths, University of London, and a B.A. in German linguistics and gender studies from Humboldt University Berlin. Research interests: political anthropology, anthropology of the far right, gender and queer studies, conjunctural analysis, homonationalism.

Kulturwissenschaft

Gabriele Dietze
Sexueller Exzeptionalismus
Überlegenheitsnarrative in Migrationsabwehr und Rechtspopulismus

2019, 222 S., kart., 32 SW-Abbildungen
19,99 € (DE), 978-3-8376-4708-2
E-Book: 17,99 € (DE), ISBN 978-3-8394-4708-6

Rainer Guldin, Gustavo Bernardo
Vilém Flusser (1920–1991)
Ein Leben in der Bodenlosigkeit. Biographie

2017, 424 S., kart., 39 SW-Abbildungen
34,99 € (DE), 978-3-8376-4064-9
E-Book: 34,99 € (DE), ISBN 978-3-8394-4064-3

Stephan Günzel
Raum
Eine kulturwissenschaftliche Einführung

2017, 158 S., kart., 30 SW-Abbildungen
14,99 € (DE), 978-3-8376-3972-8
E-Book: 12,99 € (DE), ISBN 978-3-8394-3972-2

**Leseproben, weitere Informationen und Bestellmöglichkeiten
finden Sie unter www.transcript-verlag.de**

Kulturwissenschaft

Katrin Götz-Votteler, Simone Hespers
Alternative Wirklichkeiten?
Wie Fake News und Verschwörungstheorien funktionieren und warum sie Aktualität haben

2019, 214 S., kart., Dispersionsbindung, 12 SW-Abbildungen
19,99 € (DE), 978-3-8376-4717-4
E-Book: 17,99 € (DE), ISBN 978-3-8394-4717-8
EPUB: 17,99 € (DE), ISBN 978-3-7328-4717-4

Thomas Hecken, Moritz Baßler, Elena Beregow, Robin Curtis, Heinz Drügh, Mascha Jacobs, Annekathrin Kohout, Nicolas Pethes, Miriam Zeh (Hg.)
POP
Kultur & Kritik (Jg. 8, 2/2019)

2019, 180 S., kart.
16,80 € (DE), 978-3-8376-4457-9
E-Book: 16,80 € (DE), ISBN 978-3-8394-4457-3

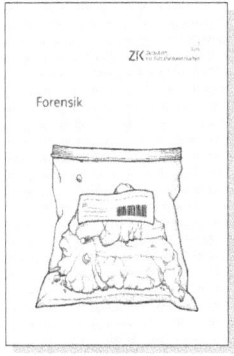

Zuzanna Dziuban, Kirsten Mahlke, Gudrun Rath (Hg.)
Forensik
Zeitschrift für Kulturwissenschaften, Heft 1/2019

2019, 128 S., kart., 20 Farbabbildungen
14,99 € (DE), 978-3-8376-4462-3
E-Book: 14,99 € (DE), ISBN 978-3-8394-4462-7

**Leseproben, weitere Informationen und Bestellmöglichkeiten
finden Sie unter www.transcript-verlag.de**

GPSR Authorized Representative: Easy Access System Europe, Mustamäe tee 50, 10621 Tallinn, Estonia, gpsr.requests@easproject.com